always up to date

The law changes, but Nolo is on top of it! We offer several ways to make sure you and your Nolo products are up to date:

 Nolo's Legal Updater
We'll send you an email whenever a new edition of this book is published! Sign up at **www.nolo.com/legalupdater**.

2 **Updates @ Nolo.com**
Check **www.nolo.com/update** to find recent changes in the law that affect the current edition of your book.

3 **Nolo Customer Service**
To make sure that this edition of the book is the most recent one, call us at **800-728-3555** and ask one of our friendly customer service representatives. Or find out at **www.nolo.com**.

NOLO

please note

We believe accurate, plain-English legal information should help you solve many of your own legal problems. But this text is not a substitute for personalized advice from a knowledgeable lawyer. If you want the help of a trained professional—and we'll always point out situations in which we think that's a good idea—consult an attorney licensed to practice in your state.

5th edition

Starting & Running a Successful Newsletter or Magazine

by Cheryl Woodard

Fifth Edition	NOVEMBER 2006
Editor	BARBARA KATE REPA
Book Design	SUSAN PUTNEY
Production	JESSICA STERLING
Proofreading	ROBERT WELLS
Index	BAYSIDE INDEXING SERVICE
Printing	CONSOLIDATED PRINTERS

Woodard, Cheryl.
    Starting & running a successful newsletter or magazine / by Cheryl Woodard. --
5th ed.
        p. cm.
    Includes bibliographical references and index.
    ISBN 1-4133-0523-7 (alk. paper)
    1. Periodicals--Publishing--United States. 2. Newsletters--Publishing--United
States. I. Title: Starting and running a successful newsletter or
magazine.
    Z480.P4W66 2006
    070.5'72--dc22

                                                                            2006048280

Quantity sales: For information on bulk purchases or corporate premium sales, please contact the Special
Sales department. For academic sales or textbook adoptions, ask for Academic Sales, 800-955-4775.
Nolo, 950 Parker St., Berkeley, CA, 94710.

Dedication

I dedicate this book to Katie, Leo, and Mick.

Acknowledgments

I've learned about publishing from many wonderful people.

Most recently, I've enjoyed serving on the board of directors of the Independent Press Association (IPA), an organization dedicated to empowering new and controversial publications. In particular, I've enjoyed working with Richard Landry, the IPA's executive director, and the IPA staff. My fellow IPA board members are also constantly inspiring and informing me.

I'm also grateful to all of the people I've met as consulting clients over the past decade. Clients continually surprise and delight me with their brilliant ideas and unquenchable energy. Some of them are listed on my website at www.publishingbiz.com.

And I extend a nod of appreciation to the folks who are working to educate and enlighten publishers through the Western Publishers Association, the Society of National Association Publications, and the Stanford Professional Publishing Courses. Each organization brings publishers together to share ideas and insights, making all of us stronger and better at what we do.

My editor on this edition has been Barbara Kate Repa, a woman who knows how to say "no" more gently than anybody I ever met. Thank you, Barbara.

And finally, forever, and for everything else, thanks to my husband Mick Wiggins, who is still the first person I want to talk to every single day.

Preface to the Fifth Edition

I receive emails every day from people who want me to help them sell a magazine idea to an established publishing company, much like an author sells a book idea to a book publisher. These folks hope to create the content of a magazine and then get a publisher to handle all the production and distribution details, splitting the revenues with the author much as a novelist would. Unfortunately, magazines and newsletters don't work like books. For one thing, a magazine idea by itself has very little value until somebody invests money to prove that readers and advertisers like the idea as much as you hope they will. And for another thing, periodicals normally take three or four years to become profitable, and many never do. Knowing the risks involved, experienced publishing companies rarely make deals with outsiders— unless of course you offer them something guaranteed to succeed like Oprah Winfrey did with *O* magazine and her 65 million daily TV viewers—and if you are Oprah, then you probably don't need to read this book.

Ordinary souls like us generally have to become the publisher to get a new magazine or newsletter off the ground. We have to find money, get talented people to help us, and launch the thing ourselves. Then, we might be able to sell our work to an established publishing company—but only after we have clear proof that the idea resonates with customers. Lots of people have come up with a good idea, invested a couple of years to prove that readers love it, and then either sold out completely to a big publishing company, or partnered with big investors to grow the business on their own. That's how we started *PC* Magazine in 1981, and you'll read other examples throughout this book,

The magazine world has changed dramatically since we started our four computer magazines back in the early 1980s. You may have read about ownership consolidation in the newspaper, TV, book, and radio industries—and periodicals have been through the same process. While there were hundreds of small companies owned by private families or investors 20 years ago, there are only a handful today. Those small companies used to provide start-up capital for entrepreneurial ventures in the past, and what's more important, there was plenty of room in the market for a small operator back then. Today, six companies own about 80% of the magazines you see on newsstands, and they have tremendous market power—over the shelf-space for magazines, their pricing, and even the postage rates.

Today's publishing entrepreneurs have adapted to that changing marketplace. People don't try to compete head-on with the mass-market titles such as Oprah's magazine, or *People*, or even *PC* magazine. Instead, entrepreneurs find opportunities the big players are not likely to exploit on their own—special interest titles, or quirky ones that appeal to a unique audience, or mission-driven publications that have social rather than commercial value. I've put many of those examples into this book, too, and also on my website. And you can find them yourself at bookstores or through some of the publishing associations listed in Chapter 14 of this book.

Another big change in publishing since the 1980s is, of course, the Internet. When we launched *PC* magazine in 1981, we didn't have a fax machine, let alone a website, and our staff didn't even have email accounts. Everything had to be accomplished face-to-face back then. But today, publishers routinely work with writers, designers, circulation experts, and other collaborators living far away. You can outsource nearly everything. We started *PC* magazine with about 40 employees in 1981, but publishers today can get by with five or six people on staff, some of them not even living in the same city, getting everything else from remote contractors.

The Internet also helps entrepreneurs reach their customers more efficiently than in the past. And the Internet is particularly suited for niche publishing. I've included many good examples showing how small-operator publishing companies have effectively used the Internet to economically reach a very loyal audience. You can see many other examples by combing the Web on your own.

Perhaps the biggest news in recent years has been the explosive growth of online ad spending. According to the Interactive Advertising Bureau, which measures online ad revenues, total spending increased 30% from 2004 to 2005, reaching $12.5 billion. Most of that money goes to the biggest websites: Google, Yahoo!, and MSN. But there are also some pie crumbs left over for smaller sites. Notably, all three major search engines have developed programs to place their ads onto other websites, allowing smaller publications to share in the estimated $5 billion spent on search ads in 2005.

And vendors are also helping smaller publishers capture some of the other growth categories, especially email ad sponsorships—up 260% last year, and commission-based "associates" programs—up nearly 400%. (See Chapter 11 for more on how smaller publishers can tap into these new dollars more readily than ever before.)

The publishing world is still evolving, and I encourage you to visit my website, www.publishingbiz.com, where I offer the latest information and trends. And please feel free to email me; I would love to hear your publishing adventures. My email address is Cheryl@publishingbiz.com.

—Cheryl Woodard, July 2006

Table of Contents

INDEX

Introduction

This book is a step-by-step guide to the business side of publishing. It will help you turn a wonderful newsletter or magazine idea into a viable publishing business.

Publishing looks easy from the outside. That's why so many inexperienced people launch newsletters, magazines, and e-zines every day. Many of them quickly give up when they discover that it's easy to start a publication, but very tough to keep one going, and harder still to earn any money.

Of course, people do make lots of money publishing newsletters and magazines, sometimes fortunes worth. I cofounded three magazines that turned out to be world-class moneymakers: *PC* magazine, *PC World*, and *Macworld*. All three were quickly profitable and all of them survive today.

But most new publications are not like *PC* magazine, *PC World*, or *Macworld*. All three of them enjoyed an almost magical combination of timing, luck, intelligence, and judicious advice from experienced people, and very few publications start out with the same advantages. Most new publications are started by independent people working alone or in small groups and often without the guidance of anyone with experience in publishing. And even experienced publishing people sometimes only understand one very narrow piece of the whole picture—for example, circulation, editing, or ad sales. It seems that the only way to learn everything you need to know about the publishing business is to try it.

To increase your chances of success, you should understand upfront that there are different ways to approach—and succeed at—publishing. One way is to raise significant start-up capital and launch a glossy national magazine. This may be the dream you have in mind—remember, though, that this is a high-end route, likely to cost $4 million or more, and there are plenty of other options. At the other end of the spectrum, you could keep your day job and create a magazine on a topic you care deeply about, and run the publication in your spare time. In the middle is the common strategy of starting a magazine and growing it into an independent publishing business. With this approach, you might keep the business and make a decent living from it, or sell the magazine to a bigger publishing company after a few years.

Look at examples of these different approaches.

- First, there is my own example, *PC* magazine, which we launched in 1981 with solid financial backing. About a year later we sold *PC* to a big publishing company in New York City. During that year on our own, we hired 45 people and created seven issues fat with paid advertising. We had about 70,000 paid subscribers and we were selling another 30,000 copies through computer stores by the end of that first year. We weren't making any profits before we sold the magazine, but it was clear that the business would eventually become very profitable (which it certainly did). The new owners laid off most of our people, shipped the whole operation to New York, and ran it completely without us for many years. Those of us who owned shares in *PC* magazine eventually collected a percentage of the profits, which was part of the buyout deal.

- Another publishing path can be equally successful, but in a different way. Many people start publications that achieve social, political, or cultural goals rather than commercial ones. My favorite example is *Glimpse*, a website and quarterly magazine started in 2001 by a group of students that promotes global awareness among young Americans. The founders said, "The need for understanding and communication across national, cultural, religious, racial, and ethnic lines has never been greater—and yet 85% of those 18 to 24 years of age cannot identify Afghanistan on a map. We believe that it is in the interests of our country and our world to ensure that everyone, young and old alike, can learn through the experiences of their peers and children who are living abroad. After all, what better way is there to improve international relations and encourage world peace than to foster new generations of global citizens who are constantly seeking to better understand the world they live in?"

Organized as a 501(c)(3) nonprofit, *Glimpse* solicits donations and grants to support a lively online community of young adults with a shared interest in traveling and living overseas, GlimpseAbroad.org, and an international news, travel and culture magazine, *Glimpse Quarterly*.

I have met hundreds of other people who publish arts newsletters, political newspapers, or Web publications devoted to their passionate interests—from health issues to social causes—who are also succeeding.

- *New Moon* is an example of a yet another publishing path: starting a magazine and growing it into a profitable publishing company over time by adding more and more products to the business. Two people started *New Moon*, a magazine for girls, with $10,000 of their own money back in 1992. Today, they have 12 full-time employees and a handful of spin-off business ventures, including educational tours for girls, a newsletter for parents, and consulting and speaking engagements for themselves. They make a comfortable living and thoroughly enjoy themselves—a successful life by any measure.

The point is that you can find many different ways to succeed at publishing, and this book can help you, no matter which path you choose. It addresses the concerns of all publishers, from the *PC* magazine to the *New Moon* variety, and everything in between.

Of course, it's expensive to train yourself on the job. Your mistakes can cost you much more than money: Sometimes you only have one chance to do something right before a competitor snatches away the opportunity or your funds run out. You can easily lose your business while learning how to manage subscriptions, sell advertising, and keep up a regular production schedule, plus all the other administrative details that challenge all small business owners.

This book won't guarantee your success, but it will save you the trouble of learning the hard way. I've added up all the mistakes I ever made, plus the ones my consulting clients have shared with me, and included them here so that you can avoid them all. I've also collected the good ideas I've learned from countless thoughtful publishing friends and advisors. That wisdom is in here, too.

Startups That Survived More Than a Decade

I looked back at the magazines started in 1993 to determine how they were funded and also which ones have succeeded. According to the standard record of magazine launches compiled by Professor Samir Husni (www.mrmagazine.com), there were 417 regular magazines launched in 1993. By my own count, 180 were financed and launched by entrepreneurs—including notables such as *Fast Company* and *Wired*. Established publishing companies launched the remaining 57% of the titles that year. I found 77 magazines still functioning ten years later, but only nine of them are the entrepreneurial ones. That means the average success rate is only 5% for entrepreneurs and 29% for established companies.

I don't think the established companies are smarter than the entrepreneurs. They just take fewer risks, favoring sure-fire launches that are clones or spin-offs from their other publications. In 1993, the big companies launched easy winners like *Nickelodeon Magazine* (tied to the TV network), *McCalls Needlework* and *McCalls Quilting*, *The Country Living Garden Guide* (from *Country Living* magazine), *The TLC Monthly* (from the Learning Channel cable TV network), *Sport Rider* (a motorcycle magazine from Petersen, the largest automotive magazine publisher at the time), and *Kids Discover* (from the makers of the magazine for adults, *Discover*). Some of these have survived and some have not.

The nine entrepreneurial survivors from the class of 1993 include: *Cowboys and Indians*, *Fast Company*, *Filipinas*, *Hero*, *New Moon*, *Shambhala Sun*, *Teen Voices*, *Wired*, and *Wizard*.

The book covers a lot of territory: selling subscriptions, ads, and spin-off products; raising start-up capital and managing your money; getting talented people to help you; fending off competitors; and finding a publishing home on the Internet. Some of the topics may have more meaning for you than others. For example, if you're planning to publish a free arts and entertainment weekly, check out Chapter 5 on ad sales. On the other hand, if you've got a newsletter in mind, skip the ad sales chapter and concentrate instead on subscribers (Chapters 3 and 4) and ancillary products (Chapter 6). E-zine publishers can skip ahead to the Internet chapter (Chapter 11) but should at least skim the other chapters, too: Most of the business advice applies in cyberspace as well as in the world of words-on-paper.

Like most things, there is a trick to publishing well: Take care of the day-to-day details, but keep your sights on the future. Every publisher confronts a thousand absorbing details every day, from the shape of a graphic image to the amount of cash left in the bank. All of them are important, but none of them will get you where you want to go if you don't have a vision for the future. Goals help you line up your day-to-day decisions into a path from one place to another. I've devoted a whole chapter to goals and strategic planning (Chapter 12) because they are so important to publishers.

A lot of smart people helped me learn the publishing business, and as I prepared this book I went back to some of them and asked, "What's the most important thing for new publishers to know when they're just getting started?" Amazingly, I got the same two comments from everybody:

Remember your readers. Everything good in your publishing business will flow from the bond you create with your readers. If you run into trouble, you can almost always find a solution by revisiting your basic connection with your audience. The first few chapters discuss in detail how to form and maintain that connection.

Always watch your money. You can't succeed as a publisher unless you fully understand how your business operates as a business. Study your finances as carefully as you study your audience and you'll have a good chance to be that one-in-a-hundred new publisher who strikes gold. This book offers many ways to raise and manage money, plus ways to manage your business as a whole efficiently and profitably.

In the end, you'll find that publishing success depends on striking the right balance between your dedication to your readers and your commitment to your personal business goals. If you give the readers too much, you may bankrupt yourself. But give them too little and off they'll go, taking your business dreams away with them. The right balance is very tough to find, and I wish you all the best luck in the world. Now keep reading, and see for yourself what a wonderful business this can be.

Top Three Publishing Questions

Year after year, these are the questions I see most often.

Q: *How much money does it take to start a magazine or newsletter?*

A: As I discuss in this introduction and throughout the book, there are many different approaches you can take in starting a magazine, so there are many different answers to this question. If you want to take the high-end approach, plan on spending at least $5 million to launch a glossy newsstand publication like *PC* magazine. If you want to start a more modest magazine—like *New Moon* described earlier—you would probably have to spend about $100,000. As for starting a magazine driven more by passion than a massive financial investment, I'm sure that the people who started *Glimpse* never spent more than their credit card limit to get their website and quarterly magazine off the ground. Many people launch Web-only publications for even less money.

Q: *Where do people get money for starting publications?*

A: It's very hard to get start-up publishing money from banks, venture capitalists, or private investors. A surprising number of people use credit cards, home equity loans, and savings. Others get loans from family, friends, and close personal associates. There is a whole chapter of the book devoted to this question. (Chapter 7.)

Q: *I have a great idea for a magazine or a newsletter. How do I get started?*

A: The fastest road to success is to read about the publishing business (with this book and the others that I recommend in Chapter 14), then find suitable models for the kind of publication you want to produce. Publications about a particular topic tend to operate pretty much by the same rules. Bridal magazines, for example, are all very much alike. They have roughly the same number of subscribers, the same group of advertisers, and similar numbers of employees. The same is true of publications for fishing enthusiasts, children, lawyers, or any other market that you want to name. If you study the publications already occupying your niche or in a similar market, then you can pretty well predict the size and scope of your publishing efforts.

I have also found that writing a business plan is immensely helpful in getting started, even if you aren't planning to raise money from outside investors or lenders. Writing a plan will help you consider all the options before you pick the wrong ones. With reasonable effort, you can write a business plan in about a month, and believe me, the process will save you weeks of missteps down the road. I offer suggestions for writing magazine business plans in Chapter 7. I also sell a magazine business plan kit at my website at www.publishingbiz.com.

Icons Used in This Book

 This icon alerts you to a practical tip or good idea.

 This is a caution to slow down and consider potential problems.

 This tells you where to go for more information. ●

Smart Publishing

Over the years, I've worked with and studied hundreds of successful publishers. Most make a good profit. Some, organized as nonprofit corporations, define success not in dollars and cents, but in their ability to affect public policy or educate people. And still others look at their publications as a way to increase profits in a separate business, often consulting. No matter how these publishers define success, all have had to do the same two things to create a thriving, successful publication: Create a great product and build a solid business operation.

First, creating a quality publication will help to establish a bond with the readers and advertisers in your market. This is the creative side of publishing, the art of it. Creative publishers consistently deliver informative products that meet the needs of their readers and advertisers, even as those needs grow and change over time. This may sound easy, but it isn't. Besides the obvious communication skills that are involved, it takes a healthy dose of imagination to come up with ideas for products that are both innovative and useful.

Second, having created a great publication, a publisher must build an efficient business operation to keep the publication afloat. From increased competition to a shrinking market to a surge in paper prices, publishers face critical business decisions every day. A publisher needs to make long-term goals and strategies to guide business operations. And at the day-to-day level, a publication must be run efficiently, which means its publisher must get the most from every dollar spent. These considerations make up the business side of publishing, which often presents the most difficult challenges to new publishers.

Any publisher will succeed who can make a good product that is responsive to the needs of people in a growing market, and who also can organize an efficient business operation. Unfortunately, very few people master both the creative and the business sides of the publishing puzzle, which explains why it takes a team to win at publishing.

Underlying both the creative and business skills needed to run a publication is the ability to work with people. Publishing is by nature a collaborative enterprise. Every publisher has to organize a group of helpers—vendors, employees, freelance contractors, editorial contributors, and the like—to produce a good product consistently. The great majority of successful publishers, even those with tiny niche publications, are skillful with people and know how to inspire them.

Fortunately, you don't need to be skilled at every key publishing task, so long as you know your own limitations and get help in areas where you are weak. Throughout this book, I will suggest many creative ways publishers have developed to make the most of their own skills, get the best from their resources, and ultimately achieve success in a challenging periodical publishing market.

Three Publishing Options

There are many different ways to organize a publishing business. Some magazines target mass audiences, while most newsletters speak to a small number of carefully selected readers. Some publications are funded by billion-dollar publishing empires and others by the sweat equity and moderate savings of a few people. And many of the biggest, most popular publications are published by nonprofit organizations, including *Sierra*, published by the Sierra Club, and *Modern Maturity*, among the world's most widely read magazines, published by the American Association of Retired People.

To illustrate the diverse options available, I've somewhat artificially broken down the universe of publishers into three general models: the solo operator, the lean-team organization, and the full-house publisher. The fact that in real life these categories often overlap won't detract much from this discussion, since the great majority of publishers can be placed in one of these three categories. You may find that one of these models closely matches your own circumstances.

Solo-Operator Publications

Newsletters, "alternative" publications, and e-zines probably make up the majority of the publications in this category. These publishers often rely on a strategy called outsourcing—concentrating their own efforts on the editorial vision or mission of the publication, and farming out all other tasks to independent contractors and vendors. Even with expert outsiders to help, though, a solo operator's success or failure usually depends almost entirely on the ability to find a good market niche, create a compelling publication, and manage business efficiently.

> **TIP**
>
> **Passion is an important contributing factor.** The desire to make a living is fine, but caring deeply about what you do and how you do it will be an important predictor of whether you'll succeed. The more you love your niche, the easier it will be for you to create a solid, long-term professional home for yourself.

You can start a solo-operator publishing business with very little money, which is surely one reason why thousands of these publications are founded every year. Commonly, the solo-operator publication is shrewdly used to enhance some other business—for example, a copyright lawyer publishing a newsletter for clients, or a massage therapist publishing a nutrition and fitness newsletter for regular customers. Publishers in these situations are sometimes content just to break even, or even to lose a few dollars, as long as it helps their underlying businesses thrive.

Lean-Team Publishing Businesses

A lean-team publisher's staff is typically small (three to ten people), and may include lots of part-time and freelance workers. Like the solo operator, a small team will usually send much of its production and distribution work to outsiders. One of the key roles of the team members, then, is to manage these outsiders.

Human intelligence and effectiveness (rather than money) are still the primary resources in small companies, but the owner is no longer the sole decision maker. In this model, success depends both on the abilities of the publisher and on the quality of people involved. Problems are easier to solve with more minds working on them, as long as dedicated, creative people are on board.

This model is particularly popular among magazines and newsletters sponsored by nonprofits or other organizations, whose object is to communicate well, but at a minimal publishing expense. Examples of lean-team publications are everywhere. For instance, one full-time editor plus six part-time people publish the magazine *Terrain*, the quarterly publication of Berkeley's Ecology Center. Each issue of *Terrain* contains about 40 pages, including hard-hitting articles about the environment and national news for the ecology movement. The total publishing budget for *Terrain* is under $500,000, and the magazine generates much of that money from ad sales. You can start a lean-team publishing company—and earn a comfortable living from it—for less than $200,000, assuming that you find a solid niche and serve it well.

The Bark magazine is another lean team publishing success story. It was started in 1997 as a newsletter for dog owners in Berkeley, California—and slowly expanded to a national magazine. The publishers kept their day jobs for many years, and volunteers helped them with key tasks, such as building a website and selling ads. They turned to the Independent Press Association (IPA) for help with newsstand distribution, which was limited at first to bookstores where the relatively high cover price of $4.95 was not a problem. Now, after a decade of slow, self-funded growth, *Bark* has moved beyond the IPA to a national distributor. The two founders are finally making a salary and have quit their day jobs, and some of the volunteers are also getting paid. Their business has expanded beyond the quarterly magazine to include a book, an annual sourcebook issue, and a lively webstore selling a line of goodies for dog lovers. The key to its survival, according to publisher Cameron Woo, is the slow pace of growth, which never went faster than he and his wife could handle with their own resources.

Full-House Publishers

Most monthly, special-interest consumer magazines like *Parenting* or *Soap Opera Update,* or newsletters like *The Kiplinger Letter,* employ a full complement of publishing professionals. For example, *The Kiplinger Letter* has over 350,000 subscribers and about 50 full-time employees. In a full-house magazine model, advertising often generates most of the revenues and nearly all of the profits. This means the publisher needs enough money and savvy to sustain two relationships—one with readers and one with advertisers. Although the editorial and marketing issues are usually similar to what solo and lean-team operators face, management issues are far more complex. Specifically, a full-house publisher must manage a fairly complex business operation, so will need help from professional publishing people from the beginning. While the potential profits are high, so is the risk of substantial losses, which means it's not a business for amateurs. At a minimum, you need good financial reporting and analysis just to stay on course.

In the full-house model, the biggest single key to success is leadership: Can you get a group of key helpers, often with conflicting personal interests, to work together efficiently toward a common set of objectives? One step toward this is to provide good benefits and rewards to an experienced staff. At least as important will be your ability to inspire their excellent work. And of course, funding is more critical in this model than the others because to get started with a full-house publishing operation, you typically need at least $500,000 to $1 million, probably more.

No matter what type or size of publication you have, to succeed, you must establish lasting bonds within your market and build an efficient operation to manage those relationships over time. This is always true, even though different publications deal with these issues in different ways.

Finding Your Place in the Publishing World

Most hopeful publishers ask the same question: "How much money will it take to get stated?" To understand why the answer is more complicated than it should be, consider the same question applied to some other product, like cars. Do you know how much it costs to produce a car? Say, a Toyota Camry? The answer depends on who you are. If you are Joe Smith, building a Camry by hand in your backyard, it might cost you hundreds of thousands of dollars to build just one car. But if you are the Toyota motor company, you can build a Camry for $15,000 or so.

Believe it or not, the publishing business is actually very much like the auto industry or any other manufacturing business in one crucial respect: Magazines and newsletters are cheaper to produce if you make a lot of them. And a few very big companies dominate the business, just like the auto industry.

The Dominance of Megapublishers

In the United States, a handful of companies control most of the resources in the magazine publishing industry: Just 15 companies own 78% of the largest U.S. magazines. In March 2006, the Publishers Information Bureau measured $2.1 billion in advertising revenues among U.S. magazines, and these same 15 publishing companies captured 79% of that money. Time, Inc., alone grabbed more than one third of all advertising revenue in 2005.

Major Magazines and Websites Listed by Parent Company

Conde Nast

Magazines: *Brides, GQ, Glamour, Gourmet, House & Garden, Lucky, The New Yorker, Vanity Fair, Vogue, Wired*

Websites: www.brides.com, www.style.com

Hearst

Magazines: *Cosmopolitan, Esquire, Good Housekeeping, Marie Claire, O—The Oprah Magazine, Seventeen, Smart Money*

Websites: www.ivillage.com, www.hire.com

Primedia

Magazines: *Gun Dog, Hot Rod, Motor Trend, Practical Horseman, Sail, Sew News, Shutterbug, Snowboarder, Soap Opera Digest, Surfer*

Websites: www.about.com, www.channelone.com

Rodale

Magazines: *Backpacker, Best Life, Bicycling, Men's Health, Mountain Bike, Organic Gardening, Prevention, Runner's World, Women's Health*

Websites: www.backpacker.com, www.bestlifeonline.com, www.bicycling .com, www.biggestloserclub.com, www.frenchwomendontgetfat. com, www.iyogalife.com, www.menshealth.com, www.mountainbike. com, www.organicgardening.com, www.prevention.com, www. rodalecustompublishing.com, www.rodalemusic.com, www.rodalestore. com, www.runnersworld.com, www.sugarsolutiononline.com, www. womenshealthmag.com

Time, Inc.

Magazines: *Entertainment Weekly, Fortune, InStyle, Money, Parenting, People, Real Simple, Southern Living, Sports Illustrated, Time*

Websites: www.aol.com, www.espn.com

Wenner Media

Magazines: *Men's Journal, Rolling Stone, Us Weekly*

Websites: www.mensjournal.com, www.rollingstone.com, www.usmagazine.com

Ziff Davis

Magazines: *Computer Gaming World, Expert Gamer, PC Magazine, Play Station*

Websites: www.baselinemag.com, www.channelinsider.com, www .cioinsight.com, www.desktoplinux.com, www.eseminarsalive.com, www.eweek.com, www.extremedap.com, www.extrememesh.com, www.extremenano.com, www.extremewimax.com, www.extremetech.com, www.extremeuwb.com, www.extremezigbee.com, www.linuxdevices.com, www.microsoft-watch.com, www.pcmag.com. www.pdfzone.com, www .publish.com, www.webbuyers guide.com, www.windowsfordevices.com

Each of these megapublishing companies owns several magazines and some own multiple websites. They wield tremendous power in the industry, even though their magazines represent less than 2% of the roughly 18,000 magazines currently published in this country. They lobby Congress for favorable postage rates. They pay rock-bottom prices for essential supplies like paper—some of them even own their own forests. They demand (and get) the best prices from printers, data processing companies, and other key publishing services. And they dominate all of the magazine distribution channels. Chances are better than 90% that any magazine you see in a grocery store checkout line belongs to one of these big companies. And you have almost no chance to get *your* magazine into a grocery store checkout pocket because the space is already sold out to these big players.

The table below shows the major magazines and an estimate of each one's share of advertising revenue and consumer magazine audience.

	The Largest Magazine Companies in the U.S.			
	Name of Company	# of Magazines	Share of 2005 Ad Dollars	Share of 2005 Consumer Audience
1	Time, Inc.	150	23.4%	16.3%
2	Reader's Digest	6	3.0%	8.2%
3	Primedia	85	4.3%	7.5%
4	Conde Nast	21	12.9%	6.7%
5	Hearst	16	8.8%	6.1%
6	Meredith	14	7.3%	5.8%
7	G&J USA	9	5.1%	5.1%
8	Hachette	17	6.4%	4.7%
9	National Geographic	4	1.2%	3.4%
10	Rodale	8	1.3%	2.2%
11	American Media	17	1.1%	1.5%
12	Ziff Davis	8	1.0%	1.4%
13	Newsweek	2	2.4%	1.2%
14	Wenner	3	1.9%	1.1%
15	American Express	6	1.1%	1.1%

Sources: Magazine Publishers of America Fact Sheets, Publishers Information Bureau, and Audit Bureau of Circulation

These big magazine companies earn most of their money from advertisers. For example, in addition to owning 150 magazines, Time, Inc., owns many businesses—including America Online, several local cable systems, movie and video companies, television networks such as CNN, HBO, WB, and others, and several book companies which together placed about 69 titles on the New York Times bestseller list in 2005. The corporation employs approximately 88,000 people worldwide. Its publishing operations of books and magazines generated $5.8 billion in 2005 revenues and earned $1 billion in profits. Advertisers contributed $2.8 billion just to the Time, Inc., magazines, which earned $1.6 billion revenue from readers. In other words, for the magazines, advertisers contributed about $1.2 billion more than readers.

This dependence on advertisers is actually increasing among the largest magazines because of the Internet. According to the Interactive Advertising Bureau (www.iab.net), 98% of the estimated $12.5 billion that will be spent by advertisers on websites in 2006 will go to the 50 largest ones, many of them owned by these same media companies.

Competing With the Big Guys

So how do smaller publishers compete with the behemoths? If you take time to look beyond the big, mainstream magazines, there are plenty of other publishing models you can follow with great success. There are over 18,865 U.S. print magazines listed in the 2006 *National Directory of Magazines*, and roughly 10,700 professionally produced print newsletters in another publishing directory. That's a total of almost 30,000 publications besides the 300 or so that are owned by big publishing companies. This does not include Web-only or electronic publications, which are not currently tracked with accuracy.

These "other" publishers—who are actually the majority of publishers by number if not by market clout and resources—share some common strategies that you should know about and consider when developing your own publishing plans.

- *Readers pay more.* Without the huge advertising subsidies enjoyed by big magazines, smaller publishers need to get more revenue from their readers. Readers of small, independent magazines often pay as much as $4 or $5 per copy with a subscription, and $7 or $8 per copy in a retail store. Newsletters typically earn 100% of their income from readers because they have no advertising—some charge readers as much as $25 or $40 per issue. And publishers develop all kinds of extra products or services they sell to readers, from books and how-to videos to T-shirts and coffee mugs.

- *Distribution is more targeted.* Smaller publishing companies cannot spend as much subscription marketing money as the big companies can. Instead, their retail distribution is carefully targeted: racks in sporting goods stores for surfing magazines, for example, or in sewing shops for crafts magazines. And smaller publishers often target their distribution geographically—*Brides in Atlanta*, for example, instead of just *Brides*.

- *Ad sales are targeted.* Again, without the huge circulation numbers that national advertisers demand, smaller publications focus on selling ad space to very targeted companies—surfboard and swimwear shops for *Surfer*, for example, not car makers or soft drink companies. Many smaller publications carry no ads at all. When they do have ads, the products are always closely linked to the subject of the magazine.

This book focuses on the publishing tactics and start-up resources that will be useful for backyard publishers, not the big companies. And it includes examples from alternative media, independent publishing companies, and niche magazines because these are the most realistic models for first-time publishers. Their low-budget strategies can be very effective, even if you aim to compete with the big players like Hearst, which spent about $20 million to launch Oprah's magazine, or Time, Inc., which spent about as much to launch *Martha Stewart Living*.

It's very hard, almost impossible, for backyard publishers like you and me to raise millions for a start-up publication. But there are other options. At the end of the day, the quickest way to understand how you are going to make money is to study how other publishers do it. If you're thinking about a magazine about mountain climbing, for example, then look at all the other mountain climbing magazines as well as other adventure sports magazines. And be sure to look at the companies with resources comparable to your own. Much of what you need to know is right there in the masthead or website. The rest is easy to see by looking through the pages. Let these small companies guide you. Take advantage of their experience and follow their leads.

Creating Relationships

From a reader's viewpoint, the relationship with a good periodical is a little like dining at a favorite restaurant: You know what to expect each time you visit. If the experience is a good one, you can repeat it often. Similarly, periodical publishers strive to establish a pleasant, comfortable relationship with readers based on familiarity. For example, the "Talk of the Town" section of *The New Yorker* magazine is always located in the same place and written in the same slightly irreverent tongue-in-cheek style readers have come to expect.

Having established a trusting relationship with readers, publishers can use that bond to build a healthy business by selling subscriptions and advertising space, or by creating new products that they can sell to their loyal customers. In other words, once the essential reader bond is firmly in place, many other profitable business opportunities become feasible for the publisher smart enough to efficiently exploit them.

Unfortunately, most new publications perish quickly because their publishers fail to master all the steps necessary to build a healthy and profitable reader relationship. Sometimes the expected audience doesn't exist in the first place. Sometimes it's there, but the publisher misunderstands its needs or wants. Surprisingly often, the publication itself is put together poorly. Occasionally, the publisher identifies a great audience and publishes a dynamite periodical to meet its needs, but the business is disorganized and inefficient. In short, establishing and profiting from a strong reader relationship is a trickier enterprise than most new publishers appreciate.

Building a solid relationship with readers is covered in detail in Chapter 2, but here is a summary of the three steps it takes: finding an audience, creating a product that meets its needs, and building a viable publishing business.

Finding the Right Audience

To find an audience, you have to understand what a group of potential readers want, figure out how to locate them at a reasonable cost, and determine how much they will pay for your publication. Depending on the scope and type of publication, carrying out these tasks can be quite different. Mass market publications, for example, must appeal to and locate lots of people—as many people as possible. By contrast, niche products need a much smaller number of customers, but must develop a very loyal following within their target group.

In all the world, there is a finite amount of money available for starting publications. In recent years, start-up capital has become more and more concentrated in fewer hands, both for magazines and for newsletters. Therefore, most publishers have to forgo the mass audiences of the past—because it simply costs too much to reach them—and focus instead on a more targeted and less expensive audience. Also, many niche customers spend more money per capita than the general reading population, so they have the potential to support a much more profitable publishing business. It's also true that most advertisers like to reach readers who match a targeted demographic profile (accountants, librarians, or swimmers, for example), so niche publishers can usually charge higher per-reader advertising rates than can their mass market counterparts. For example, *Architectural Digest* has a more affluent audience than *The National Enquirer,* so it can charge much more for ad space.

Having identified an audience you understand, and one that can support your business, you must next figure out how to reach it efficiently. Traditionally, magazines and newsletters find readers by using direct mail. Some also put copies onto newsstands or in other retail outlets. Almost all print publications also have websites to promote circulation. All of these circulation strategies are designed to locate good prospects at an affordable cost. (That process is discussed in detail in the next two chapters.)

Editors and Publishers Have Very Different Concerns

Although in a very small company, one person may be both editor and publisher, these two key roles are usually assigned to different people. Editors handle the readers and publishers handle the advertisers. Since advertising generates most of the profits for many publications, the publisher is also generally charged with managing cash and creating profits.

The editor's primary responsibility is to look out for the readers, by understanding what kind of information they want to have and finding ways to get it for them. No publication can survive without good editors. Recognizing this, they are sometimes called the "high priests" of publishing, or even the "Church."

The publisher's job is to look out for the business, set financial goals, and find ways to meet them. No publication can survive without somebody looking out for the bottom line. Because they handle the commercial problems and business operations, publishers are the "bourgeoisie" of publishing, or in the jargon of the business, the "State."

Traditional publishing companies try to keep Church and State separate. That is, they try to let editors concentrate on reader interests without the influence of commercial considerations. Often this is not possible, which means editors and publishers find themselves in conflict with one another. For example, while an editor worries about providing fresh, useful, and thorough information, a publisher worries about paying the printing bills and affording the rising cost of paper. Or it might mean that the publisher wants to see articles about areas particular key advertisers are excited about, while the editor is more interested in meeting reader needs and fanning their enthusiasms.

Another common conflict arises because advertisers and readers often have diverging interests. For example, when the automobile industry first introduced minivans, many publishers recognized a new advertising sales opportunity. But some editors saw the minivans as a topic for consumer safety articles because they were regulated by different standards than passenger cars: they weren't as structurally sound and lacked many safety features. While publishers were under pressure from automakers to gloss over the safety issue, editors knew consumers needed to hear about it. Fortunately, because of the editors who took a strong stand (including editors of such influential magazines as *Consumer Reports* and *Parenting*), the automakers eventually made minivans safer.

Creating a Good Product

All successful periodical publishers need to know what their audience wants to read, and how to package it appropriately and consistently so that readers will keep reading it, issue after issue. It almost goes without saying that if you want to make good publications, you also need to read them. I urge you to read closely the most popular periodicals in your niche, looking for the secrets to their popularity.

Knowing your direct competition is also essential when you're designing a new publication. The trick is usually to study your closest competitors carefully and then design around them. For example, offer features that your readers want, but that your competitors have ignored.

As you begin to design your product, you'll probably find yourself wishing you had endless resources to produce the publication of your dreams. No question, it's tough to create an appealing product that you can afford to produce on a regular basis, since the final package has to meet reader needs and your own bottom line at the same time. Success will require both a creative hand (usually the editor's) and a sound business mind (commonly the publisher's) working together.

Building a Viable Business

Short-lived relationships are rarely profitable. So even if a new publisher can find a good audience and create a product that grabs its attention, there is still a critical problem to solve: how to build a publishing business that will prosper well into the future. The trick is to build upon your initial successes until you have created solid, enduring relationships within your market.

In the very short term, most publications lose money, especially in their early years while they are working to find an audience and win its trust. Their initial losses can range from a few thousand to many millions of dollars, depending on the kind of publication.

Publishers start to make money only when they begin to transform their early connections in a market into lasting relationships by turning casual readers into regular customers, creating predictable relationships with advertisers, and developing new products that they can sell to their loyal customers. Although each of these activities is covered in detail later in this book, here's a brief introduction to what's normally involved.

Converting Casual Readers Into Regular Customers

Casual readers include people who buy your publication at a newsstand, buy a back issue from your website, or accept a free sample issue offer from your direct mail campaign. Sometimes casual readers get the publication free at trade shows and other venues. Whether or not readers pay for their copies, publishers rarely profit much from casual readers unless there is a rich pool of advertising money associated with the free distribution (like a local parenting magazine, for example), or the casual readers become regular paid subscribers. To make a profit on subscriptions alone, publishers "convert" as many casual readers as possible into full-fledged subscribers who will pay a full fare over an extended period. This is doubly true for publishers of newsletters, who depend almost exclusively on readers for income.

Establishing Relationships With Advertisers

Advertisers want to reach your readers. That is, once you've found an audience, you can usually find advertisers eager to reach the same people. Publishing a magazine or a newsletter is a bit like hosting a business conference. You set the agenda, create a congenial atmosphere, and invite all the most appropriate people. If your niche is broad or deep enough, advertisers who sell relevant products and services will want to address your readers.

In many situations, advertisers add to the publisher's relationship with readers—just as they are welcome participants at many conferences—since your readers will be actively shopping for products or services and may buy your periodical to see the ads.

In other situations, advertisers' presence is more challenging, and the publisher has to limit or control it to some degree. When the readers are young children or people with serious medical problems, publishers may try to restrict overly aggressive advertising by regulating it. For example, *Sesame Street Magazine*, which is written for preschoolers, excludes ads. But the magazine is bundled together with another one that is written for parents, and the parents' magazine is chock full of ads.

Occasionally, running ads in a publication would seriously compromise it or thwart its very purpose. *Consumer Reports* offers one example of an editorial mission that is incompatible with advertising.

It takes a lot of work to win the loyalty of most advertisers. And it can take three or four years to win advertiser support for a new magazine. Once they agree to use your publication, enduring advertiser support can be extremely profitable. (Chapter 5 will help you create long-term relationships with advertisers that will benefit your business and your readers, too.)

Developing New Products and Services

Once your readers are converted into loyal subscribers and advertisers are on board, you can increase your profits by selling ancillary products or services to the same customers. It's a similar idea to a popular lunch restaurant adding breakfast to its menu. Because new products and services grow out of the original publishing business, they will usually cost less to develop and promote, and therefore have a high potential to be profitable. Books, trade shows, and spin-off publications are common examples of ancillary products. Online databases, compact disks, and computer bulletin boards are newer versions of the same idea—delivering your publication's contents, in a familiar style but a newer form, to a closely overlapping audience. (Chapter 6 covers the many ways publishers make money from ancillary products.)

Surviving Through Efficiency

Obviously, your ultimate goal is to capture publishing revenues that match or exceed expenses. Unfortunately, revenues can be elusive, especially for a new publication in an unexplored market niche. Since it's tough to accurately predict how much money you'll bring in the door, it's absolutely crucial to control what you spend.

Producing and distributing a periodical, even a small newsletter, is not cheap. Printing alone is a major expense, especially if the production quality is high or if the periodical is published weekly or daily. Pre-press expenses like desktop publishing and design add to the production bill. And of course, writers, editors, and artists must be paid for their work even for online publications with no printing bills. Finally, marketing the publication to readers and advertisers can be very expensive.

No publisher starts out with unlimited resources, no matter how rich you are. And bear in mind that if you discover a profitable niche, fierce competition from other publishers is inevitable. The toughest challenge for any new publisher is to make the most of limited funds by using them where they will have the greatest impact. For example, however large your subscription marketing budget, you still need to find as many subscribers as you possibly can with each dollar that you spend. You don't want to waste any of that money chasing after the wrong kind of subscribers or trying promotion gimmicks that don't pan out. Waste of any kind is your Number One enemy.

There are three kinds of waste that plague publishers: wasted effort, wasted resources, and wasted opportunities. All three are very common among inexperienced publishers.

Wasted Effort

Wasted effort can mean misspending your energy pursuing the wrong advertisers or following poor strategies to sell subscriptions to readers. For example, if you publish a magazine about marijuana, such as *High Times*, it would be a waste of effort to try to reach subscribers using direct mail, since most readers will be trying to keep their interest in this subject private. Far better to reach them at appropriate stores or newsstands, where they can purchase your publication anonymously.

Sometimes a market is so new that its membership hasn't coalesced into a readily identifiable group. If your publication is ahead of its time, your chances of wasting time and money are great as you try to develop the market to the point where your publication can support itself. To succeed, you must adopt a strategy that minimizes this waste. For example, even though there had never been a successful magazine about the health concerns of men, *Men's Health* is a successful magazine today because Rodale adopted a strategy of starting slowly. It published only a few issues per year at first, holding back resources until the idea took hold with advertisers. Readers were quick to jump on board, but it took five years to convince advertisers. Waiting was a brilliant strategy. If Rodale's publishers had tried to launch a monthly magazine right from the start, they would have had great trouble selling enough ads to pay their publishing expenses, and might well have bled themselves dry.

To avoid waste, subscribers have to want what you are trying to give them. Publishers can easily talk themselves into the idea that an audience needs the information they want to provide. Often, however, this proves not to be true. For instance, an engaged couple might buy information that will help them make wedding plans. But once the wedding is over, their interest drops to zero. That's why bridal magazines have had to learn to buck industry wisdom and sell short subscriptions (six months or less). Trying to sell long-term subscriptions would be wasted effort.

Subscribers must not only value what you publish, they must also have the money to pay for it. For example, many new parents are information-hungry but short on cash. A significant percentage of seniors face the same predicament. That's why subscription prices for publications aimed at these groups are generally low, and it would be a waste of time to try to sell most people in these groups a pricey magazine. On the other hand, because businesses stand to profit from what they learn, business owners will generally be willing to invest in useful information. So, publications aimed at businesspeople can often charge hundreds of dollars for a yearly subscription. Here the key to success is offering compelling editorial content. It's a waste of time to try to get people to subscribe to a business-oriented newsletter unless it has a real edge.

Wasted Resources

Wasted resources simply means spending more money than you need to spend. For example, a children's mystery story magazine that carries no ads doesn't need to spend the big bucks involved in four-color printing on heavy, coated paper. The colorful printing and glossy paper are expenses the readers probably won't support in the form of a higher subscription price. Other common ways that publishers waste money include hiring more employees than necessary, investing cash in technologies that soon become obsolete, and paying too much for outside services, especially printing. Sometimes the biggest publishing companies are the worst at wasting resources—especially on new publications—because they have forgotten how to avoid spending a bundle on overhead. Thus, when a big company comes out with a flop, it often loses far more money than even the most inexperienced start-up publisher would lose.

Wasted Opportunities

You waste an opportunity when you let others exploit the niche you've found or, even worse, let them take it away from you. Sometimes this happens because you don't have enough money to keep up with competitors. Other times, it happens because your imagination gives out and you can't figure out how to match a competitor's creativity. It is almost sure to happen to anyone who does not understand that as soon as a market shows itself to be profitable, competitors are certain to appear.

EXAMPLE: Steve saw an opening in the mortgage market and created a newsletter about getting homeowners to refinance their loans—a subject that had never been covered before. Steve spent two years developing his newsletter called *Today's Refinancing Market*, and finally started making money. Just then, Frank and Ellen both launched competing newsletters.

Because Steve had defined the market for them, Frank and Ellen got going much more quickly than Steve had. Mortgage brokers were already receptive to their sales promotions because they were familiar with *Today's Refinancing Market*. The new competitors developed strategies based on Steve's weaknesses: Frank hired more editors and outspent Steve by nearly three to one. Ellen was more aggressive, doggedly chasing down the best stories, interviewing the most interesting people, and selling her publication for less than Frank or Steve. All of a sudden, Steve's readers had three good newsletters from which to choose.

Although Steve started with a lead, his newsletter failed because he ignored his competitors and didn't react appropriately to them. For example, he never added any value to his product to compete with Frank's beefier writing staff, and he never changed his pricing strategy to deal with Ellen's lower prices.

After Steve's newsletter folded, Frank and Ellen competed head-on for the lead in their market, and within a couple of years, Ellen secured first place because she was able to publish more efficiently than Frank and make a profit, even at a lower price. After taking the lead, Ellen was free to make creative decisions such as how much editorial material to put in each issue, what kind of information to provide, and how much to charge for subscriptions without bowing to outside pressures. As the number-two publication, Frank had to match Ellen's editorial quality at the same prices or drop out of the game.

Efficient publishers establish themselves quickly and without wasting effort or resources. They are always looking for ways to get the best possible results from the smallest possible investment. This often means getting more products from the same staff, or more profits from the same customers. Smart publishers work hard to put money in their piggy banks to increase their flexibility and to help deal with new rivals, unexpected opportunities, or unforeseen obstacles.

Most people develop efficiency and eliminate waste through trial and error. Sometimes you can save time by studying what other publishers have done, but often there really is no model for what you're trying to do.

Internet publishing (see Chapter 11) is a great example. Although you can't always escape wasting some of your time and resources while you're figuring out how to reach and serve your audience in a new market, you can always remember to make efficiency a primary goal.

The Publisher's Golden Rules

The job of a publisher is normally both demanding and intense, filled with seemingly endless details—and the occasional big decision—all vying for immediate attention. To keep from becoming overwhelmed, it helps to remind yourself of the basic, central tasks of any publishing business. Here are some tips to keep in mind as you consider, prepare for, and operate a publishing business.

Publish a Good Product

Your product is at the heart of your connection with readers. You can only succeed by making a product that your readers really want. It's better not to publish in the first place than to skimp in this area. Even if you identify a niche so golden that you initially succeed with a mediocre product, some competitor is almost sure to do a better overall job, possibly wiping out your business.

Good intentions are never enough. Your product has to be the best that you can make it. If others are already publishing in your market, study their products. If your publishing idea is unique, study good products in related fields. Look at what all successful publications do well and why their publications work for their readers. And once you do start publishing, communicate with your own readers to find out what they need and want. Again, providing valuable editorial (and in some cases advertising) content is the key to building and keeping reader loyalty. And gathering a loyal readership is the only way to make money.

Ready Made Scores a Bull's Eye

Ready Made proves the value of a good product targeting the right audience. Subtitled "Instructions for Everyday Life," *Ready Made* is the brainchild of two young women, Grace Hawthorne and Shoshona Berger. Their gutsy magazine shows what you can do with a good idea. Their magazine has been described as Martha Stewart for 20-year-olds, but that description undersells the creativity and power of their magazine, which features unique projects focusing on reuse, and eco-friendly, simple living that also happens to mesh with the limited budgets available to most first-time nest builders. The magazine recently ran a garden makeover contest, for example, asking readers to spend no more than $200 and use all existing features to renovate a 100-square-foot garden space. The winners included a rooftop garden in Brooklyn and a Los Angeles apartment patio. *The New York Times* featured the winners in its Style section.

   After only two years of running *Ready Made* on a shoestring, the founders were able to strike a copublishing deal with a larger company, mainly on the strength of their original editorial idea and its popularity among the target readers. The founders get to keep a 50% stake in the company, and the investor is providing funds to expand the magazine, raising distribution to more than 100,000 copies, increasing frequency from four to six times yearly, and hiring more staff. This is just about the best outcome an entrepreneur can hope to achieve.

Take Care of Your Customers

Publishing is a relationship carried out in an increasingly fickle world. In addition to putting out a good product, you must pay attention to and build good relationships with readers and advertisers in other ways. One key to doing this is to make sure your back-office services are good and efficient, even if you are a solo operator. This means you must process subscriptions quickly and mistake-free, and offer a full range of payment options. In today's world if you tell customers you don't take credit cards, you may lose them forever. And if you mess up their subscriptions, deliver time-dependent information too late to be useful, or print articles in an illegible typeface, you will immediately alienate them. Again, it comes down to seizing every opportunity to learn what your customers expect and making every reasonable effort to meet those expectations. For example, including a faxback or poll in your publication asking readers what types of editorial content or other services they like is money very well spent.

Don't Reinvent the Printing Press

Tens of thousands of other publishers are at this moment working hard to find the cheapest, most effective, and most profitable way to run a publishing business. Take advantage of all this research. Study what other publishers are doing or have done, and shamelessly borrow their best business ideas and innovations.

Many new services for publishers can help streamline the process, save money, and solve complicated publishing problems. For example, it is now relatively easy to sell ads on a small website through large networks that do almost all of the work for a small share of the income. (See Chapter 11 for more on this.)

> **TIP**
>
> **The less you know, the harder you should work.** This book includes many resources to help you learn the business quickly. You can also email me with simple questions, or check my website for FAQs from other readers. Always remind yourself "Somebody knows how to do this" whenever you run into a problem you don't know how to solve, and then go looking for that somebody.

Know Your Market

Publishing is intensely competitive. Almost as soon as a profitable new publication appears, imitators—sometimes dozens of them—will spring to life. You can best protect yourself by choosing a market you know, and then staying deeply involved with it. The fact is that your knowledge of your market will allow you to operate more efficiently and resonate more with your readers than competitors who know less than you do. Outsiders—even the ones with lots of publishing experience—will have more trouble identifying the best advertising prospects, for example, or finding loyal readers and engaging their attention.

Study the Results of Your Actions

You need to know how to watch and learn from what you're doing and respond appropriately. Are your efforts paying off or are you wasting lots of energy and resources? Do your decisions intermesh to allow you to carry out a sensible long-term plan or are you trying to move in too many directions at once? Chapter 12 discusses long-term strategies in general. Chapter 8 describes how to gather good financial and management information so you can be sure the sound and fury of your busy days adds up to a profitable publishing business.

Be Prepared for Change

One thing is sure: Your market will change. This change will come from many directions—for example, after the dot.com advertisers came and went, some magazines dropped from 2,700 ad pages per year to less than 700—and many others simply folded. As your business moves from start-up to maturity, you will be under constant pressure to adjust to new realities, such as managing a larger staff or dealing with outside investors. Since change is practically the only thing you can be sure of, you need to train yourself to look for it, cope with its effects on your business, and take advantage of the new opportunities it regularly presents. Chapter 12 covers long-range planning and other strategies for dealing with change.

Smart Publishers—Some Examples

Many of today's most prosperous publishing empires were started by one or two people with not much more than an idea that meant a lot to them. Some of those pioneering publishers lived on nothing but their own enthusiasm during the time it took for their idea to capture an audience. Similarly, as long as your publishing idea is a good one, your passion can help you survive and succeed. Not only will it help you attract readers, it will inspire other people to give you their support and best efforts. And if you're lucky, your true belief in what you are doing will help you squeeze that one brilliant idea out of your overtaxed brain that could make your business a big success.

Here are the stories of three passionate publishing entrepreneurs that should inspire you. There are plenty more great stories like these in the publishing industry. Reading about people who have made good lives in publishing can help you cope with the many start-up problems you're sure to face. At the very least, it's a help to know that many thousands of people have forged fulfilling careers for themselves publishing small magazines and newsletters. Most never build huge publishing empires, but a surprising number make money and have a good time.

The Kiplinger Letter

Willard M. Kiplinger launched one of the first modern newsletters, *The Kiplinger Letter,* in 1923. The weekly four-page bulletin, recently renamed *The Kiplinger Letter*, is still in print and also available online. It has been continuously published longer than any other newsletter in the United States. Written for businesspeople, it helps them to understand and predict the effect of government activity on their businesses. Kiplinger prided himself on the "insider" idea, and he is generally credited with inventing the style most of us associate with newsletters today—short, pointed items written in a plain-speaking, no-frills style by people with access to important information. Kiplinger's mission was to interpret the news, not just to report it, and he advised readers how to respond to and profit from events.

Today *The Kiplinger Letter* is the most widely circulated business-outlook letter in America. It costs $117 per year, which includes online access to a specialized website. His publishing company outlived Willard Kiplinger and grew far beyond the original newsletter. It currently publishes a number of successful newsletters, software, books, videos, and magazines, including *Kiplinger's Personal Finance Magazine.*

Reader's Digest

In February 1922, DeWitt and Lila Wallace, both children of ministers, founded *Reader's Digest.* They started out with about $5,000 of borrowed money in a basement office under a Greenwich Village bar, printing 5,000 copies of their first issue.

Their idea was simply to give people something decent to read. They reasoned that people generally lack the time to search out and absorb the most interesting material from the thousands of magazines and newsletters available to them. They determined to sift out the best articles and then condense them for easy reading. Their slogan was: "An article a day from leading magazines in condensed, permanent booklet form." The idea holds up, even today. Some think it is well suited for an electronic format, and *Reader's Digest* has developed a robust Web business. Look for its latest online offerings at www.rd.com.

The Wallaces were intent upon publishing according to their personal moral convictions. DeWitt explained: "Our overall emphasis has been a more or less conscious effort to find articles that promote a better America with a fuller life for all." Until 1955, the U.S. edition carried no advertising, and they still do not accept cigarette ads. DeWitt was once quoted as saying, "We do as we damn well please, and that's close to ideal."

In 1923, the Wallaces moved their offices 40 miles north of New York City to a friend's garage, which was both their living quarters and publishing office. Later, they expanded into a nearby pony shed, and eventually they built a home in the same neighborhood, editing the *Digest* from their study.

The Wallaces died without children many years ago, but even without heirs to carry on for them, their work survived. The Reader's Digest Association continues to employ more than 5,000 people today. And their little magazine now has over 10 million paid subscribers in the

U.S. It sells more than 500,000 copies of each issue on newsstands. The company went public in 1990, trading under the stock symbol RDA. Revenues in 2005 were $2.4 billion and pretax profits were $176 million.

The magazine accounts for only a fraction of the *Reader's Digest* company's overall revenues each year. The rest comes from a host of books, tapes, and other products. To keep up with a changing audience, *Reader's Digest* is launching special issues aimed at selected audiences, reaching out to younger readers, and developing new ancillary products. Some Wall Street analysts argue that the company has reached its limits and can't grow significantly in the future. Others argue just the opposite—that the basic publishing premise is still viable, even more so for today's readers than for their grandparents. Time will tell.

PC magazine

David Bunnell and I started *PC* magazine in his San Francisco dining room only two months after IBM announced its brand-new personal computer in 1981. We had financial backing from a New York software dealer who had put up about $150,000. With that money, David paid his own modest salary plus the salaries of a full-time editor, Jim Edlin, and a marketing director, me. I also owned a small equity stake in the magazine. In addition, David contracted a freelance art director, James McCaffrey, and a freelance production manager, Jackie Poitier, who was moonlighting from her day job at a California law magazine. Of the five of us, only David and Jackie had any previous magazine experience.

Even without any direct mail, subscriptions poured in because we were careful to place *PC* magazine wherever the IBM computer was being sold. Every IBM PC dealer in the country carried copies and sold them out quickly. In addition, whenever IBM took their PC to a trade show, *PC* magazine was there, too.

Our idea for the magazine was very simple: Since IBM wanted to sell computers to businesspeople who had never used them before, somebody would have to give IBM's customers impartial advice in plain English about how to use them. And, since the IBM PC was designed to let users pick their own add-on products (printers, monitors, modems, and the like) the makers of those products would need someplace to advertise them.

About a dozen magazines were launched at the same time as *PC* magazine, all designed to fill the same niche. Many of them looked like ham radio magazines, with dim black-and-white photographs of electronic equipment and articles you couldn't read without an engineering degree. We knew that we had to do something different, so from the start *PC* looked like a business magazine, with colorful images and elegantly designed articles printed on the best paper. The writing was very good, too, competitive with *Time, Fortune,* or *Business Week.*

Our other successful strategy was to stick close to IBM. Without giving up our editorial right to criticize their products, we befriended the engineers and marketing specialists in Boca Raton, Florida, who were behind the IBM PC. We were careful to collect feedback from our readers and advertisers, and to pass it along to IBM. Many times IBM listened to our suggestions about pricing and distribution and adapted its strategies. Our relationship with IBM helped us to match our growth strategies with theirs, and it gave our magazine a real edge against competitors.

Our troubles began less than six months after we published our first issue when David and I had a serious falling out with our financial backer. We wanted to beef up the staff because we feared that a competitor would wipe out the company if the magazine did not keep growing along with the explosively expanding PC market. The investor was scared, especially by the growth of our staff, which had already ballooned to 25 full-time and part-time people. He refused to put in any more cash, and his timidity forced us to operate very inefficiently. For example, we could not lease a fully functioning office without financial guarantees to the landlord, which our investor refused to provide. Without the means to house all of the employees under one roof, we had to find small and short-term spaces: a tax accountant's office that we could sublease for a few months, two converted apartments, and one converted retail space. Our phone system was a nightmare, we had no office equipment and employees often had to work at home because we couldn't give them a desk. We were telecommuting before anybody had personal computers or fax machines at home, so we had to hire a kid to run all over the city delivering mail and messages to our staff. We were young and having fun, but we also recognized that our chaotic organization was terribly wasteful and that ultimately it would kill the company.

We all began searching for a buyer. David and I wanted a new owner who had the resources to support our San Francisco group but who wouldn't overwhelm us. We began talking to several prospective buyers who matched our goals. Our original investor, on the other hand, had different goals. He wanted a buyer who would pay the highest possible price, with or without keeping me and David on board. Because he held a majority share in the company, the investor was able to cut a secret deal with Ziff-Davis, despite our express opposition. Ziff took over *PC* in November 1982 and moved the operation to New York City that Christmas.

Rather than negotiate with David and me and the other minority shareholders, Ziff took the position that our equity wasn't properly documented and claimed it had bought 100% of *PC*'s shares from the New York investor. We sued, and at the same time, started *PC World* with new financial backing from an established computer magazine publisher. Ziff sued David and me, attempting to prevent us from using *PC World* to compete with *PC* magazine. The litigation was very messy and it lasted for nearly five years. When it was all settled, we were finally paid for our work on *PC* and our shares in the start-up company. My small stake earned a modest fortune, but I paid hefty legal fees to collect it.

Once Ziff took over, it worked fiercely to protect *PC*s leadership position, hiring expert publishing people to work on it. Their sales and marketing aggressiveness during *PC* magazine's early years are legendary among publishers. Because of that ferocity, and a significant investment of money and expertise, Ziff kept *PC* in first place, even though many strong competitors tried valiantly to displace it.

Meanwhile, we secured a solid second-place position for *PC World* by aggressively growing our circulation from zero to 300,000 within two years. We spent several millions of dollars in the process. Still, *PC World* reached profitability by the end of its third year and spawned a dozen very profitable foreign editions and spin-off products. We went on to create *Macworld* (1984) and *Publish* (1986) magazines as well as founding the Macworld Expos with largely the same team of people. Each of our subsequent publishing products was profitable, and while we were not equity holders in any of them, David and I were both able to retire comfortably from *PC World* after a few years.

Ten years after he bought it, Bill Ziff sold *PC* magazine, along with several spin-off products he had developed, for over $1 billion. The magazine has since been sold yet again for over $1.5 billion. Wounded by competition on the Web—sometimes of its own making—and hurting from the recession, *PC* magazine is less profitable now, but still going strong. Paid circulation in 2004 hit 1.2 million and has settled at 700,000 in 2005.

Today, *PC* still follows the basic publishing formula we designed in 1981, providing impartial information about PC-related products. And the technical information in *PC* is still presented stylishly. In many ways, the magazine set a new standard for all computer publishers and helped to bring personal computers out of the hobby shops and into corporate environments.

Building the Reader Relationship

Maintaining a lasting relationship with an audience is a tricky job: Readers will lose interest if editors fail to consistently serve up a product with just the right mix of familiarity and freshness. Even publishers who understand this often can't build a publishing team that can get the job done, with the result that they don't earn enough money to stay in business. In short, although it seems easy to create a publication with staying power, it's actually very hard to do. But it can be done.

This chapter will help you figure out how you can bring together all of the necessary elements of a thriving and profitable relationship with your readers. First, it describes the qualities that make a good audience. Then it shows you how to define an editorial mission and create a publication that will appeal to your chosen audience. Finally, it discusses ways to keep your reader relationship healthy and profitable over time. If you get out your pen or your word processor, you can use this chapter to draft your own publishing plan, one that will help you identify potential opportunities and problems.

The Qualities of a Good Audience

Not all audiences are alike. Before you spend all your time and your life savings attempting to build a relationship with an audience, consider carefully which one to choose. You'll need to find an audience with the potential to support a periodical publication for as long as possible. The following list identifies some characteristics that generally indicate a good audience. As you read through the list, make notes about your own potential audience, especially whether or not your audience will be able to support your publication, and how you think you will find the readers and subscribers you need.

The Publisher's Road Is Bumpy

Although this chapter describes a straight path toward creating a good editorial product and winning support among readers, do not expect your own experience to go so smoothly. Your real-life experience is likely to be far more messy and chaotic. In the real world, tasks tumble into each other, and unexpected obstacles and opportunities present themselves, which, depending on how you deal with them, have the potential to forever change your future options. For example, in your publication's early days, you may use editors or marketers who aren't skilled enough to keep up with your publication as it evolves. If so, you may have to devise a way to push out of your business some of the very people who helped you get started. This is only one of many common—and often painful—situations that may influence your publication's growth. The point is that even the most successful publications tend to follow an irregular, often confusing, path. So don't lose heart if the business of being a publisher turns out to be significantly more chaotic than you imagined.

Active People

People who are very active in a given field are great audience candidates because you already know they're interested in that subject. If people go to conventions, buy products, join clubs, or even subscribe to other publications on a certain subject, they might well subscribe to your periodical on the same topic. It's true that you can sometimes find an audience made up of people who are more passive—when, for instance, many people hold jobs or lead lifestyles that suggest some level of interest in your subject—but active people are easier to find and more likely to buy your publication. For example, if you are considering a publication on childhood asthma, you might initially be inclined to target doctors' offices with your publication. However, a website about asthma is more likely to yield subscriptions than a mailing to every pediatrician in America. Many doctors won't be good candidates for your publication, since some doctors don't have much time to read, others already have another specialty, and, of course, some are retired. But people actively using the Internet to track down related information are prime prospects.

Publishers call a large, passive group a universe, since it includes everyone with any possibility of becoming a reader in the future. Many inexperienced publishers fail to realize that only a small percentage of people in any universe are sufficiently active at any given time to pay to receive a periodical on their subject area. That's why more experienced publishers try to identify the active people in a universe. Using the childhood asthma example, they would try to find the pediatricians who had asthmatic patients and who, by attending meetings, joining professional societies, visiting websites, or buying books, have demonstrated that they want more information on that subject. This might be only 5% of the entire universe of pediatricians.

Critical Mass

As you try to measure any potential audience, you'll be forced to make many guesses and assumptions. The best approach is to make a guestimate of best-case and worst-case numbers, and then ask yourself if you can survive happily under the worst-case scenario. Since the worst-case number is more likely to be the real one, it's by far the more critical of the two. For example, there are roughly 40,000 pediatricians in America. If you only expected at most to attract 5% of them, your publication about asthmatic children would have to be able to support itself with 2,000 readers, or less. That sounds like it could be enough to support a newsletter, especially if each reader would pay $150–$300 per year. But a more tough-minded—or worst-case—scenario would surely argue that many asthma specialists won't become subscribers, no matter how actively they are interested in the subject, because they'll be persuaded to read competing publications or won't have time to read any publications at all. With the likelihood of only 1,000 subscribers, you might have to abandon the newsletter idea.

On the other hand, if you could expand your universe (see "Think Big, Even When You Are Aiming at a Small Group," below), you might be able to salvage your newsletter idea by identifying other groups of highly interested people. What if you include nurse practitioners? They are often the primary care providers for asthmatic children. And what about allergists who also work with adults? Adding those groups would increase your universe by nearly 20,000 and would add 500 prospective subscribers (half of 5%). Leaving them out gives the false idea that the newsletter isn't viable. Including them might mean that your newsletter has a big enough potential audience to go forward.

Think Big, Even When You Are Aiming at a Small Group

It always pays to start out with the biggest audience you can imagine and then work your way down, through an elimination process, to the most likely candidates. If you work the other way, starting with only the most likely prospects, you're likely to overlook people with a genuine interest in your field, lose their support, and miss their valuable participation.

Define your universe like this: Think about everyone who might conceivably have an interest in your subject, and make a list. Then think about how your publication might address their needs. If there's a reasonable connection to a group, try to include them. For example, if your subject is soccer, consider everybody who might be even remotely interested, including coaches, players, the families of players, the makers of soccer equipment, associations that regulate the game, philanthropists who support amateur soccer teams, investors who own professional teams, sports doctors, sports newscasters, and print journalists.

Later, as you begin to make specific marketing and editorial decisions, you may decide to eliminate some people because you can't reach them efficiently, or because their interests don't match your editorial goals closely enough. For example, you may decide to focus your soccer newsletter on people who earn a living through the game, because they'll pay more for your information than amateur players, kids, and parents, and because you want to concentrate on commercial issues.

Besides knowing that a potentially profitable audience is "out there," it's obviously important that you and your circulation team can find them. Fortunately, people active in a field usually leave a trail that makes them relatively easy to find. Think about the trails you leave in your own life. Every time you send in a warranty card, visit a website, join a club, or put your name on somebody's mailing list, you leave footprints. People who compile electronic lists and sell them to publishers can sniff you out relatively quickly by searching through easily available computer databases. For example, they can learn you're a dues-paying member of the PTA, live in a middle-class neighborhood, and have subscribed to at least one parenting magazine in the past two years.

Unfortunately for you as a publisher, some people are active, but leave no trail. They don't send in warranty cards. They buy their magazines at the newsstand. And they go to PTA meetings but don't become registered members. Some people leave no trail quite deliberately, because their activities are embarrassing, illicit, or even illegal, or because they put a premium on their privacy. For example, psychotherapy is a sensitive, personal matter. For a newsletter on child abuse you might be able to find therapists who specialize in child abuse, but fail to locate patients who were abused as children or who have abused children themselves. When for any reason an audience refuses to come forward and identify itself, it can be very frustrating and expensive for a publisher who wants to reach it.

Facing such circumstances, persistent publishers have invented various techniques to locate an elusive audience. Sidewalk newspaper racks and newsstands are commonly used to locate people who can't be found in computer databases or on mailing lists. People who are new to a subject, or casually interested, will often pick up or buy a single issue of a strategically placed publication, giving a publisher a chance to convert them into a subscriber. Websites serve the same function, and most publications have websites these days. Another trick publishers have developed to reach a constantly changing or expanding audience is to put free copies in places where prospective readers congregate, like beauty salons or doctors' waiting rooms. For example, going to the obstetrician is often the first step a woman takes to identify herself as a prospective new parent, making this a good place for a publisher to make contact. The same is true when people wander into specialty retail stores like hobby shops or bicycle stores. Other publishers put promotional subscription offers into the packaging of products like bicycles, computers, or sporting equipment as a way to reach people who are just beginning to get involved in a new pastime.

Continuing Needs

A person who has a short-term problem to solve will probably buy a book or a computer program, not a periodical. That's why there are dozens of books about writing a résumé, but no magazines or newsletters on the subject. By contrast, periodicals work well with activities that span many years, like raising children, playing tennis, advancing a career, or retiring happily. Because profitable periodicals must establish a trusting, ongoing relationship with many readers, there's little future in publishing about subjects that can be covered in one sitting. So if you are considering a topic like recovering from the trauma of divorce or finding a new job, maybe you should publish a book instead of a newsletter or magazine.

> **TIP**
> **Pick an audience that is attractive to advertisers.** Advertisers generally want people with maximum purchasing power—homeowners instead of renters, for example. If you hope to sell ads in your magazine, then give your ad sales team a break and aim for the kind of readers your advertisers are trying to reach. (For more on this issue, see Chapter 5.)

Learning About Your Audience

There are many different ways to research your audience, and you should use every opportunity to learn as much as you can before you launch your publication. If you have no experience doing market research, you can benefit from the many books published on the subject. It's not as hard to study a market as you might think.

RESOURCES

You'll find some good tips and advice on this topic in a book called *The Market Research Toolbox*, by Edward F. McQuarrie (Sage Publications). The author suggests you begin simply by thinking of ways to find prospective readers and get useful feedback from them. The process has three parts: deciding what you want to know, creating a research plan, and analyzing what you learn.

Deciding What You Need to Know

Figure out what questions you want to ask and draft a reader response survey. Here are some questions publishers typically ask about a potential audience.

- **Participation**. How do people involve themselves in the activity? How often do they attend related conventions or shows? How long have they been involved? How much money do people spend on it? Do they belong to clubs?

- **Information Needs**. What are your audience's information needs? Are people looking for help advancing their careers? Buying or selling products? Finding out about new technologies? Traveling to pursue their activities? Meeting other people in their field? Are there influential people readers would like to meet or hear from?

- **Sources of Information**. What are people's current sources of information? What magazines, books, websites, or newsletters about your subject are people reading? What do people like (and dislike) about existing information sources? What topics should be covered, but aren't?

- **Demographics**. Most publishers also want to understand, in general, what kind of people are involved in the audience: Young people? Men? Women? Working people? Rich people? Retired people? Publishers look to see if there are groups who are underserved by existing publications.

Making Up a Research Plan

There are many ways to collect information and luckily, you'll find most of them are easy to afford. First, remember that other people may have already studied the same questions and published their results where you can easily find them. Check the library and the Internet for reports from trade associations, the government, educational institutions, and other publishers.

When your questions haven't been answered by someone else, you may need to conduct your own research. Again, the process doesn't have to be expensive or difficult. Many publishers create a simple questionnaire and mail it out to people, or hand it out at a trade show or fax it to a few key people in their industry.

RESOURCES

The book mentioned earlier, *The Market Research Toolbox*, by Edward F. McQuarrie (Sage Publications), describes several other low-cost ways to collect good information. You'll also find techniques for gathering good information in Chapter 12.

Applying What You Learn

Hopefully, the information that you collect will help you decide whether or not your publishing idea has a chance of succeeding. That is, can you find a good audience? Can you develop a unique product that is likely to capture its attention? Is it clear that you can hold that attention through the many months and years it will take you to build a profitable publishing business? Can you deal with the competitors who are already in your field or soon to come?

Remember to be realistic; now is the time to abandon your plans—before you've lost any money on them—if you discover that your ideas are flawed. And also remember this: If you have trouble finding any prospective readers or getting feedback, don't rule out the possibility that your audience is going to disappoint you, too. Maybe there aren't as many people in your audience as you had imagined. Or perhaps they are out there, but difficult to locate. Maybe you don't really understand your market like you thought you did. The earlier you realize your idea has some problems, the better chance you will have to fix them.

EXAMPLE: Tony Thomas decided to publish a magazine on model railroading. Tony was a retired computer programmer who had long been a model railroad collector. Tony was also the former president of a national model railroading association. He was a popular speaker at conventions, and he had a small following of people who liked to hear about model trains. Through his involvement in the hobby, Tony knew many people interested in model railroads, but he needed more detailed information to create a sound business plan for his magazine.

Tony already had a rough idea of what he wanted his magazine to be like. Working from this idea, he formulated questions about the audience that might be interested in such a publication. Here is the initial plan he wrote for his magazine, which he decided to call *Tracks*:

"*Tracks* will be a colorful monthly magazine written for current and future model railroading enthusiasts who want to expand their enjoyment of the hobby. Until now, the hobby has been largely limited to affluent men, who have the time, space, and money to build elaborate model railroad systems. These men enjoy reading about other people's models, new products, and hobbyist conventions. While *Tracks* will meet these basic interests it will go further. Feature articles will describe the colorful history of real trains and railroads, linking the trains to the communities that they served, so that readers can build historically accurate and interesting models. *Tracks* will include travel information so that readers can visit sites where train history has been preserved. *Tracks* will also cover new technologies, especially software programs that are being used to improve model system designs and operations. Finally, *Tracks* will help readers meet each other by featuring readers in the magazine and by offering online bulletin board services."

Given this plan for a magazine, Tony considered what specific information he needed to know about his audience. He came up with the following questions:

"Do they build models alone or with other people? Do model railroaders like to ride trains, visit train yards, or watch working trains? How many people are building models? Buying products? Attending local conventions? Traveling to see real trains in action? Do hobbyists want to meet other hobbyists? If a celebrity is also a railroader, would readers want to know about it and see his or her models? Are railroading enthusiasts using the Internet? Are the basic demographics of people in the hobby changing in any way?"

Tony developed a two-part research plan: First, he would use an upcoming railroading trade show to get a general feeling about *Tracks'* potential audience and to help him refine his specific questions. Later, he would mail out a questionnaire as a double-check of what he learned at the convention.

At the trade show, Tony walked through the entire exhibit hall studying the people, not the trains. In the middle of the day, he stationed himself at a lunch counter, watching people walk by and engaging a few in conversations about their information needs. In the evening, he chatted with people in the hotel lobby and at a couple of parties put on by equipment suppliers.

Watching people and talking to them, Tony noticed he hadn't given much thought to children. Not being a parent, Tony had rarely thought about his hobby in relation to children, but seeing so many of them at the show opened a whole new line of thinking for him. He realized that most of the kids didn't get to the show by themselves; an adult brought them. When he asked why, he learned that lots of parents—especially fathers and grandfathers—viewed time spent together with model trains as quality time with their children and used the hobby to help teach them good skills and habits. Excited by this information, Tony decided to ask more questions about how families got involved in the hobby.

For the mailed questionnaire, Tony rented lists of convention attendees, club members, and mail-order buyers from a mailing list broker. He picked 200 names at random and mailed them a home-made questionnaire containing 25 questions. He included a crisp new $1 bill to encourage responses. Tony soon received 97 responses.

The results confirmed some things he had already known about the audience, notably that the hobby appealed to many people much like himself: male, middle-aged, well-educated, and moderately affluent. But he also learned that the times were changing. More girls were involved, as were younger single men who liked to use personal computers to design models and run them. His research also indicated that the hobby was being passed on from one generation to the next. Many parents and grandparents simply wanted their kids to understand the romance of trains. Others saw the hobby as a good way to develop math, money management, engineering, and technical skills in young people.

Putting all this together, Tony saw that having their children design models and collect trains was much more important to many hobbyists than he had realized. Tony decided to modify his original editorial plans, including more material aimed at children. His readers would appreciate it, and he knew this was an angle covered by none of his competitors. The presence of children, especially the relatively new influx of girls, also encouraged Tony that this hobby would remain popular for many years, making it a good subject for the magazine publishing business that he planned to create.

Choosing an Editorial Mission

Even if you have found the best, most enthusiastic and loyal audience possible, you won't be able to build a profitable relationship with it unless you produce a quality product that appeals to its interests. To do this, always keep the reader's viewpoint uppermost in your mind. And don't just focus on the subject matter; be sure to also design your publication around the gender, age, and other lifestyle characteristics of your audience. For example, if your potential audience for a golf publication includes people who take golf holidays, then perhaps your publication can include a "Travel Planning" section that reviews golf resorts, tours, and travel services.

Experienced editors start developing their publication ideas by writing an editorial mission statement. Sometimes called a statement of purpose, the mission statement is simply a brief description of a publication's editorial focus. Mission statements are meant to be inspiring—editors create them both to help stay true to their own focus and vision as well as to communicate it to others. The statements are also used to motivate investors, employees, advertisers, and other supporters who need to know—in a nutshell—the fundamental purpose of the publication. Newsletter publishers sometimes include their mission statements in welcome letters to new subscribers. Or they periodically run the statements in their newsletters. Magazine publishers always include a mission statement in their media kits. (See Chapter 5 for more information on media kits.)

To give an idea of how several successful publications have stated their visions, read the following samples gathered from their publishers and from a reference directory for advertisers called *Consumer Magazine and Agrimedia Source*, published by the Standard Rate and Data Service. (See Chapter 14 for more on this useful resource.)

To provide some perspective, the summaries below include the date each publication was established, its current circulation, publication frequency, and the name and location of its publisher. Read these examples and then take a stab at writing your own.

The Bark was founded in 1997 by a couple living in Berkeley, California. Today, their bimonthly magazine has more than 50,000 paid subscribers and is sold at newsstands and bookstores.

The Bark is the voice of modern dog culture. It is both the acclaimed print magazine and an online forum, Bark Unleashed. *The Bark* brings readers a literate and entertaining approach to canine culture through essays, stories, poetry, reviews, interviews, and artwork. *The Bark* offers fresh viewpoints on emerging social and behavioral issues, ideas of health, recreation, and activism—while focusing on the relationship between humans and dogs.

Road & Track was established in 1947 and is published monthly by Hachette Filipacchi Magazines in Newport Beach, California. Average paid circulation per issue is 750,000.

Road & Track magazine is written for the automotive enthusiast and contains information about cars and driving blended with wide-ranging feature stories, entertainment, and racing coverage. *Road & Track's* road tests focus on enthusiast cars that are exciting to drive and well engineered, covering a gamut of imports and domestics from sports cars to sporting sedans that are a cut above the ordinary in terms of performance, handling, ergonomics, and design efficiency. In addition, *Road & Track* presents technical features on automotive subjects, nostalgic feature articles, humor and fiction, and analyses of industry trends, along with travel stories, book reviews, and coverage of international racing events.

Prevention was established in 1950 and is published monthly by Rodale Press in Emmaus, Pennsylvania. Average paid circulation per issue is over 3 million.

Prevention magazine is a source of practical consumer health information. Each month, *Prevention* provides actionable news, easy-to-follow advice, and motivating ideas on nutrition, fitness, weight loss, disease prevention, and alternative and psychological health to people looking to play a proactive roles in their own health and the health of their families and friends.

Trailer Life was founded in 1941 by an individual recreational vehicle (RV) enthusiast with funding from his family. It is currently published monthly by TL Enterprises in Ventura, California. Average paid circulation per issue is 280,000.

Trailer Life magazine is written specifically for people whose overall lifestyle is based on travel and recreation in their RV. Every issue includes product tests, travel articles, and other features ranging from cooking tips to vehicle maintenance.

The Kiplinger Tax Letter is published biweekly by The Kiplinger Washington Editors, Washington, DC. Subscriptions cost $59 per year and there are more than 65,000 paid subscribers.

The Kiplinger Tax Letter is written from the business and personal rather than the technical point of view for those who are not tax experts. Issues are devoted exclusively to domestic tax matters.

Now, stop reading and start writing your own mission statement. Try to describe the audience and what you will do for it in 200 words or less.

> ⚠ **WARNING**
>
> **If you have trouble stating your mission, maybe you don't have one.** When faced with defining a specific editorial purpose, some people have trouble finding the right words. If this happens to you, it can be an indication that you haven't refined your general publishing concept sufficiently to begin business. But it's always best to discover early on that your publication isn't sufficiently well thought-out—and think some more.

EXAMPLE: Heather was a psychologist approaching her middle age who was also the mother of three teenage daughters. Like Heather, many of her clients were mothers struggling against long odds to steer their children safely through their teen years. As she watched so many families struggle with problems like drugs, sex, and violence, she wondered if there was a way she could help. She developed an idea for a newsletter called *Parenting Teens* to help families through these difficult years.

However when she discussed her idea with some colleagues and tried to define an editorial mission, many problems came to light. For instance, she realized readers would want to hear from other parents, but families might not want to air their private problems in a newsletter. Heather also noticed that her own interest in the subject changed as her family matured, and she realized that potential readers might have the same experience: Once their own children were grown, they might lose interest in her publication. She could not count on readers sticking around long enough to sustain a newsletter.

In the end, Heather abandoned her newsletter idea because she could not make a long-term commitment to it herself and because she realized she couldn't expect readers to sustain their support for it either.

Evaluating Your Competition

If you've defined an important editorial mission and a sizable audience that's not too difficult to reach, chances are that several competing publications already exist in that niche. Healthy competitors can be a signal that a growing market exists and your publishing idea will succeed, so don't give up just because someone else is already publishing in your field. Especially if you plan to publish a newsletter, the existence of competitors may not be obvious, and you should actively look for them. The directories and references listed in Chapter 14 should help you find all of them. Don't leave anybody out. Even if there is no direct competitor, perhaps your subject is covered in the general-interest media or as a section in a publication that concentrates on a related subject.

To check whether your idea is good, you want to pay attention to potential competitors for three reasons.

1. If there aren't any competitors at all, your idea may be flawed, or too far ahead of its time. You may not want to be the first to jump into a new field, because it costs lots of money to explore new publishing territory. For example, you may have to teach your audience that it is in fact an audience. Advertisers, too, may have no experience in a brand-new market niche, and they'll need special persuading to support you. (See Chapter 5, Building Your Advertising Business, for specific advice about dealing with advertisers.) As a general rule, advertisers are more comfortable with a market that already has two or three publications in it or at least in a closely related field. Another problem with having absolutely no competitors is that you will inevitably make lots of costly mistakes. On the other hand, if there are a few established competitors, you can learn from their mistakes and borrow their best ideas.

2. You want to avoid being ambushed by competitors you don't know about or haven't seriously considered as rivals. Let's say your subject is traveling with children. Your first research indicates there are no other newsletters or magazines that specifically cover that subject. But what about other sources? Parenting publications run travel stories. Travel publications often cover family needs. Newspapers have travel sections that address family concerns. There are plenty of books, too. And of course, when you launch your newsletter, you may remind some of these other publishers how good this topic is. Consider how much each of them could hurt you simply by giving more space to the same subject.

3. From competitors, you can assess the business potential within your chosen niche. The publications in a specific niche tend to have similar profiles—same pricing, circulation size, advertisers, and so forth. Studying the others in your niche helps to predict what your publication can become.

> **TIP**
>
> **Big competitors aren't always frightening.** Don't necessarily be scared off if a big media empire seems to be testing the same waters as you. If its high profit goals aren't met quickly, it may withdraw. Your small size and low overhead may give you an advantage when a niche is very small and growing too slowly to be attractive to bigger publishers.

Starting immediately, train yourself to study all of your competitors and keep track of how they change. The best way to do this is to subscribe to each, renewing slowly so that you receive all of their billing letters and renewal notices as well as ancillary product announcements. If they sell advertising, you should also get their media kit. You can discover a lot from them about which ideas work and which don't. Think of them as market researchers who are testing your publishing ideas, at their own expense.

What You Want to Know About Every Competitor

Remarkably, some new publishers fail to carefully check out their competitors. Don't make this mistake. Be sure you can answer all the questions in the following categories:

- **The Publishers.** How much money or financial backing do they have? How much experience do they have? Have they done other publications? What are their overall business goals? Who are their key players? How many employees work on each publication?

- **Their Product.** How does the product further the publisher's mission? How is it distributed? How much does it cost? What's good about it? What's missing? What's bad about the publication?

- **Their Advertisers.** What advertisers use the publication? How much does it cost to advertise? How much does each advertiser spend in a year? How does the publisher sell to advertisers?

- **Their Readers.** What are their readers' occupations and income levels? Are they the same readers you're trying to attract, or different? In what ways are they similar or different? Besides this one competitor, what other media does the audience buy? How many readers are there?

All information you collect about competitors should be used to refine your own publishing plans. If you find that the field is already saturated, perhaps you can redefine your mission and carve out a different niche for yourself. But consider the possibility that your unique interests and abilities will result in your creating a unique publication competitors can't duplicate.

EXAMPLE: When Tony Thomas searched for competitors for his planned publication *Tracks*, he discovered four model railroading magazines and one newsletter. At first, several which had been founded many years ago by well-established publishing companies seemed formidable. But after studying all of them carefully, Tony decided that he could find a spot for *Tracks*, since no other publisher covered the family angle, or made a strong connection between computers and model railroad design and operation. Since Tony's research showed that these subjects were important to model railroad enthusiasts, he concluded that a model railroading publication that both addressed family issues and focused on using personal computers would be successful. And it might even draw new people into the hobby by updating it into a modern context.

Tony also concluded that his competitors were missing the boat in other ways, too. Perhaps taking their direction from the wealthy but aging enthusiasts of the past, the publishers took a conservative approach when reviewing new products and services. For example, their editors tended to concentrate on expensive products from a handful of manufacturers who used traditional materials like wood and metal, giving far less coverage to the products of several new companies who made excellent modeling parts from resins and plastics. Tony believed these companies were eager to expand their markets, and would welcome a new publisher not prejudiced against them.

Tony also came to believe that his fresh perspective would be good for the market as a whole because he might even help attract new, younger people to it. Competing publications might copy Tony's family and computer coverage, but as long as he stayed current with the hottest new trends, they would have a hard time duplicating his approach and style.

By studying the competitors, and reflecting on his own goals, Tony was able to find a place for his magazine among viable competitors. By covering subjects that his competitors overlooked and by contributing a fresh new voice to the model railroading hobby, Tony defined a promising niche for *Tracks*.

Designing Your Publication

Once you have identified a good audience, figured out your mission, and studied your competitors, you should be ready to design your publication. Your product itself will do a lot to make or break you, so naturally it should be the very best you can create. In the beginning, worried about a dozen other issues, you may not appreciate how much an excellent editorial product will pay off down the road. But it's crucial to your success. If people like your publication, everything else will go much more smoothly for you. Not only will more casual readers convert to subscribers, but subscribers will renew in greater numbers and competitors will find it harder to get ahead of you. And, if you have them, your advertisers will be more likely to support a publication they judge as being top-notch. In other words, if you get it right from the beginning, you'll have a better ride all the way down the road.

There are a million decisions you have to make about your product, including both creative questions such as the editorial tone and writing style, and business decisions like the pricing and frequency. It is often wise to get professional help putting together your first few issues and making these decisions because these early decisions about your publication are so important to its success.

Borrow as Many Good Ideas as You Can

As mentioned, other publications are a great source for ideas on how to design your own. Study many other publications (not just competitors) and pick out features you like about them. Notice how they put text and images together to support their editorial purposes. Study their "bones"—the structure of columns, news articles, feature stories, and departments. Also look at how their physical makeup and design help to match their mission.

Often, working with the right experts in your field can make all the difference between creating a so-so publication and one people are really excited to read. If you're going to hire employees—or outside expert helpers—the first one you should get is a good editor. (Chapters 9 and 10 describe how to find experienced people, both contractors and employees.) Whether you hire employees or freelance helpers, there are a number of concerns for which you might seek experienced help at the beginning.

Choosing a Look and Feel

Putting your publication together for the first time involves both creative and financial decisions. Unsurprisingly, these two considerations often conflict, especially when you don't have a big budget. A good-looking product can sometimes cost a fortune to produce, but it doesn't have to, meaning that it's always a mistake to conclude that you can't afford a good design. The tension between cost and design often comes down to deciding whether a certain design element is necessary. For instance, does your newsletter really need to include photographs of people, nearly doubling your production expenses? Perhaps you'll conclude that because yours is such a people-oriented mission, good-looking images of the people you're writing about are essential. On the other hand, you may decide to invest half as much in a design consultant who can show you how to use low-cost clip art to produce a terrific-looking newsletter without photos.

EXAMPLE: When we launched *PC* magazine, we struggled to strike a balance between saving money and publishing a good-looking product. At that time, IBM personal computers had black-and-white monitors, and there were no colorful games to play with them, so several publishers decided not to print in four colors because the expense seemed unnecessary. However, our publisher, David Bunnell, decided that high-quality, colorful editorial illustrations would be essential. He reasoned that in the competitive market surrounding IBM's new machine, advertisers would strive for any and all ways to create ads that would set themselves apart from their competitors.

To capture the biggest and most desirable advertisers, our magazine would need to provide the highest quality four-color reproduction.

But what about editorial content? David argued that black-and-white editorial material would too easily get overwhelmed by all of the colorful advertising we expected to sell. So we decided to use four-color photographs and illustrations in the articles—lots of them. We also chose a heavy, coated paper stock that would reproduce the colors well.

We quickly and happily realized that we'd made good decisions. Within a year, the initial field of about a dozen hopeful IBM PC publications dwindled down to three survivors—all of them looking much like *PC* magazine—full of colorful illustrations and stylishly designed articles printed on high-quality glossy paper.

Of course, our decision to spend money to produce *PC* magazine in color doesn't mean that every publication will benefit by spending lots of money in the same way. There are many real-life instances where publishers bankrupted themselves by spending too much for unnecessary design and production features. The point is that you will have to figure out what design elements will work best in your own situation.

Editing

As a rule, good editors create good publications. There is both an art and craft to editing. The art is knowing what will captivate readers; the craft is knowing how to accomplish it, issue after issue.

Even if you're a solo operator with an editorial background and you plan to do the editing yourself, it makes sense to find practiced periodical editors to give you a hand getting started. An experienced editor can show you how to put together the basic skeleton of a periodical publication—departments, feature stories, columns—and how to establish copy rules so that your contents are consistent from issue to issue. In addition, an experienced editor can teach you how to get good work from outside editorial contributors by giving clear assignments, setting realistic deadlines and sticking to them, and convincing writers to do their best work for a modest fee.

RESOURCES

An excellent editing book is *The Editor in Chief: A Practical Management Guide for Editors*, by Benton Rain Patterson (Iowa State Press), which offers a thoroughly useful overview of the process, especially for those new to the task. Another is *Editing by Design*, by Jan White (Allworth Press), which addresses both editorial issues and design. Editors might also appreciate these two books: *The Layers of Magazine Editing*, by Michael Robert Evans (Columbia University Press), and *Magazine Editing: How to Develop and Manage a Successful Publication*, by John Morrish (Routledge). You will find additional resources listed in Chapter 14.

Design

Printed copy should be easy to read. Charts and illustrations should complement and enhance the text. And the total package should support your basic editorial mission. Good design seems much easier to accomplish than it is. Unfortunately, we are bombarded with so much badly designed printed media nowadays, it's easy to forget what good design looks like. You can often learn to distinguish between good and bad design fairly quickly, but it takes a much longer time to learn how to consistently design well on deadline. It follows that talented and experienced designers can usually do a better job for you in less time and with better results than if you try to do it yourself.

Your job is to know your audience and to be sure any designer you work with is on the right wavelength. For instance, if your readers are over 45, the design should be easy for aging eyes to read—don't let the designer use tiny type faces you can't read without a magnifying glass, or run type over photographs or create a sort of hip (weird) look calculated to send teenagers into ecstasy. Because designers tend to be avant garde themselves, you'll often need to rein them in a little to get the design approach appropriate to your audience.

Production

Production is where art meets reality. The line you'll probably hear yourself uttering most often when conferring with your design consultant is, "Yes, it's beautiful, but how much does it cost?" You absolutely need to get the best possible production quality at the lowest possible cost. For example, use four-color printing if you must, but skip it if you can. And if you say "yes" to color, don't pay one more cent for it than is absolutely necessary. Unfortunately, an experienced production person who can help you make good decisions can be relatively expensive to hire, especially if you use a part-time consultant. But almost always, a good person will save you as much money as you pay him or her, and often more. A production person can help you choose paper stocks, production techniques, and printers to do the best job at the lowest cost. If you are going to sell advertising, any production manager or consultant you work with should be able to coach you about creating a design that will dovetail with your advertiser's needs.

EXAMPLE: Tony wanted *Tracks* to stand out from other model railroading periodicals. As a result, he (and his designer) initially selected an unusual larger trim size. But his production consultant persuaded Tony to change his mind and stick with a standard trim size when he explained that advertisers would balk at creating new original ads just to fit Tony's exotic size. In addition, the slightly bigger size would use more paper than normal, and the printer would charge extra for setting up and running an unusual size. Tony ultimately agreed that the possible gain in newsstand sales as a result of a more noticeable size were far outweighed by the extra production costs and advertiser headaches involved.

Making Business Decisions

In addition to defining what your publication will say and how it will look, you'll need to make some business-related decisions. Here are the main things you'll need to decide.

Frequency

Generally, your editorial mission dictates how often you will publish. News-rich subjects demand a high frequency; there are many events to cover, and readers will look elsewhere for information if you don't cover them in a timely manner. That's why many investment and political action newsletters are published on the Internet, faxed, or mailed often, sometimes even on a daily basis. Other subjects deserve more leisurely consideration: literary, hobby, and special-interest newsletters or magazines are generally monthly, bimonthly, or quarterly.

It is obviously much more expensive to publish more often: dailies cost more to produce than weeklies. Never choose a higher frequency than you absolutely need. Sometimes, to save money, publishers who have little competition start by publishing on a fairly relaxed schedule, working up to a higher frequency over time. For example, Martha Stewart launched her hugely successful magazine, *Martha Stewart Living,* by putting one test issue on the newsstands. It sold well, so she published a few more issues the next year, and even more the following year. Gearing up the frequency slowly like that allowed Stewart to perfect her publishing ideas before making the financial commitment to a monthly publishing schedule.

Distribution

For years, the vast majority of periodicals in this county have been distributed to individual subscribers via the U.S. Postal Service. Although innovations such as fax publications, computer bulletin boards, and online services are beginning to offer alternatives, U.S. mail is still the way nearly all of you will distribute your publications, too. Postal distribution generally involves renting or trading mailing lists, sending out promotional subscription offers, putting the respondents into a database, generating labels from your database, and mailing out issues.

If you want to consider using a different distribution method to reach part or possibly even all of your audience, you'll find many choices. Publishers often combine several different methods, such as the following:

- *Single copies.* These can be sold or handed out free at appropriate locations like newsstands, doctors' offices, coffee shops, trade shows, specialty retail stores, hotels, and even doorsteps or driveways. Publishers choose one of these options when their audience is transient, highly localized, or hard to find on mailing lists. Sometimes your editorial mission demands this kind of distribution, too. For example, if you want to reach all of the upscale tourists in New York City, putting your publication in hotel rooms may be the very best way to do it.

- *Product tie-ins.* Issues can be included with other people's products or services. For example, a baby care magazine might be distributed by diaper services. Or a sailing magazine might be handed out to members of yacht clubs. Publishers often choose this option when they want to capture people at a particular moment in their lives—such as having a baby or buying a yacht.

- *Internet.* Increasingly, publications are distributed on the Internet and through commercial online services. (See Chapter 11 on Internet publishing.) Even if you don't post the whole issue online, your publication will probably need a website to make contact with all the Web surfers out there.

- *Email.* Limited by convention to 300 words or less, email newsletters can include images and ads, as well as news and other reader-friendly information. In 2005, ads in email newsletters accounted for about 6% of all online ad spending.

- *RSS feeds.* Real-time Simple Syndication (RSS) is a technology that allows publishers to send Web articles or summaries of Web articles to subscribers who can follow a link back to the full text versions at a publisher's website. These Web "feeds" allow frequent readers to track updates on their favorite websites, sometimes through RSS aggregators, who collect the feeds from dozens of sites into a single broadcast. RSS aggregators are also sometimes called RSS Readers. You can find one popular example of an aggregator at www.rmail.com.

- *Fax.* Many newsletter publishers still fax issues to some or all of their subscribers. Fortunately, you can broadcast a fax newsletter to thousands of people at once via the Internet. Readers in time-sensitive fields will often pay a premium to get information this way.

Now take a break to think about how your publication might be distributed. Remember to concentrate on how best to meet your audience's needs, even if its needs are different from yours. For instance, sometimes the audience needs information quickly and would appreciate speedy distribution options, but you are not inclined or equipped to deliver publications that way.

EXAMPLE: Tony Thomas loved the Internet almost as much as he loved model trains. He was determined to publish *Tracks* online as well as on paper, and spent nearly $20,000 setting himself up to publish each issue online. Unfortunately he never got his money back. Many people in his audience of hobbyists used the Internet, but didn't take to viewing or downloading his publication this way, preferring the more aesthetic printed version. Tony also faced daunting problems collecting subscription money from online readers. He decided to simplify his website, trimming it down to a brochure format. His site invites visitors to order a sample copy of the print magazine, request advertising information, or buy a subscription.

EXAMPLE: Marsha Jones made the opposite mistake. She was computer literate, but nearly phobic about networks, especially the Internet. And she had never spent much time exploring any online communication services. Marsha preferred to distribute her newsletter for frequent business travelers called *Road Warriors* by U.S. mail, even though, in many ways, hers was a perfect product for online distribution. For one thing, her readers were active network users themselves, so electronic distribution would be very natural for them. And for another thing, *Road Warriors* was a workmanlike newsletter: little aesthetic value would be lost by viewing an electronic instead of paper version. In short, Marsha missed a big opportunity by not putting her newsletter online.

Price

Publishers' pricing strategies are generally based on their readers' ability and willingness to pay for information, and on the publication's competitive strengths. As discussed in more detail below, options range from selling information at a high price to a small but select audience, to selling it at a low price to a bigger audience, to giving it away and collecting money from advertisers. In addition to this overall pricing decision, most publishers set a whole range of prices for the same publication: a single-issue price, a subscription price that is discounted from the single-issue price, and introductory subscription offers that are discounted from the regular subscription price.

Here are some ranges for single-issue prices to look at as you consider your own pricing options. Notice that prices are based primarily on how much the readers need the information, what readers can afford to pay, and competition.

Top prices ($10 to $40 per issue). If an audience has an intense need to know something, can't find the same information anywhere else, and can use it to professional or financial benefit, then a relatively high single-issue price is justified. Daily business newsletters are in this category, charging between $1,000 and $7,000 for 250 issues per year. Weekly or biweekly specialized business publications also typically charge top prices. There are hundreds, if not thousands, of newsletters for professionals and businesspeople published six to ten times a year at an annual subscription price of $200 or $300. For example, *Cuba News* gets $36 per issue for a "nonpolitical, internationally oriented" newsletter about doing business in Cuba. *The Internet Lawyer* charges $149 for 12 issues per year, or $12.42 per issue, for information about using online technology in a law office.

If you decide to charge top prices, you must also make sure you can deliver first-class service. For instance, the most expensive professional newsletters always make several personalized contacts with subscribers throughout the year, not just to renew subscriptions, but also to inquire if the publication is meeting their needs. These subscribers expect a high level of personalized attention—no silly or inappropriate form letters—and they won't tolerate any mistakes: Don't spell their names wrong or make billing errors. Usually, these high-priced publications can be profitable with a relatively small number of subscribers.

Middle prices ($3 to $10 per issue). These prices are usually appropriate when readers are deeply interested in a subject, but a publication has many competitors. Often the audience is made up of relatively affluent consumers, willing to pay to gather excellent information about how to spend their money, improve their lives, or save time. For example, *DogGone* is a bimonthly 16-page newsletter that focuses on traveling with dogs—and sells for $25 per year, or $4 an issue. *The California Grapevine*, a newsletter that reviews wines for collectors and avid consumers, costs $36 per year or $6 per issue. And the *Green Money Journal* costs $12.50 for each 24-page issue covering investment opportunities in ethically or socially responsible businesses. Generally hobby, crafts, sports, and other special interest magazines charge between $3.50 and $5 per issue. Newsletters priced in this middle range can usually make money with a few thousand subscribers. Magazines in this range survive with relatively few subscribers because most of them also make money selling ads.

Low prices ($3 per issue or less). If a subject is of general interest, but there are many other sources for the same information—from television to paperback books to other periodicals—then prices usually need to be low. Examples include all of the general-interest and news magazines like *People, Ladies' Home Journal, Reader's Digest*, and *Newsweek*. There is so much competition for this type of publication that it must charge a low cover price. Since these publications have such mass appeal, however, they are attractive to advertisers. Magazines in this price range often generate nearly all of their profits from selling ads. Health newsletters and others written for the general public are often priced in this range, too. Their lower production costs make it possible for their publishers to make a profit, even with such low subscription prices. For example, The University of California at Berkeley *Wellness Letter* sells for $2 per issue, as does another one called *Consumer Reports on Health*. In another subject area, a monthly newsletter called *Cooking Contest Newsletter* sells for $25 per year—or $2.08 per issue.

Free. Publishers who have a high potential to earn advertising revenues sometimes give away their publications. Sometimes only qualified readers receive the free publications. This option is sometimes called "Non-Paid, Qualified" circulation. The readers generally have to match some criteria to earn their free subscription, such as having an influential job, earning a lot of money, or being extremely active in a market. For example, *Successful Dentist* is a biweekly, free newsletter from a Florida publisher who offers marketing consulting to dentists.

Other publications like local arts and entertainment weeklies simply circulate their publications free, making all their revenues from advertising and ancillary products. Personal advertisements, for example, have been widely used as a profitable ancillary product for this type of publication. (See Chapter 6 on additional related products.) And most Internet publishers are adopting this pricing model: They're giving information away to readers and looking to advertisers and others to foot the bill—with mixed success. (There is a lot more information about the Internet in Chapter 11.)

Look carefully at your competitors before you set your prices. Interestingly, you'll likely find that most of your competitors are in the same basic price range. Having worked with the same audience and editorial mission as yours, they probably already know how much their readers will pay. If you can justify being at the top of that range, then it's fine to take that position. But be cautious: Don't adopt the lead pricing position if your publication isn't obviously better than everyone else's. On the flip side, also be careful about staking out the lowest price. Readers rarely switch from one satisfactory publication to another simply to save a few dollars, and by charging less, you'll obviously have less income. One reason all of the publications in a field cost about the same may be that their publishers know they will gain little or nothing by raising or cutting prices.

Making a Test Issue

Once you've made a number of important business decisions (pricing, frequency, distribution) and you have a good idea about what your publication will look like, you're ready to see what your audience thinks of your plans.

Before you actually start publishing, you still have time to fix major problems. A common way to get reaction from the audience is to create a mock "dummy" issue with articles, columns, and illustrations—everything you expect to include in the regular magazine or newsletter—and show it to a sample group of prospective readers and advertisers.

Also, if they can afford to do it, many publishers hold focus groups to get feedback from readers. An impartial group of readers can almost always suggest improvements to your product.

If you are on a truly tight budget, you may not have the money to create an entire sample issue. A good fallback position is to show prospective readers and advertisers as much as you can, perhaps your editorial mission statement, a few sample articles, and a list of the topics you plan to cover in your first year. Find some willing and impartial people, show them what you've got, and then listen carefully for their reactions.

> **EXAMPLE:** Anne Cox, a travel agent, specialized in arranging cruises. For about ten years, she collected information from cruise companies that she organized in a database. Along the way, she developed relationships with many people in the industry. As a result, Anne frequently learned information about upcoming cruises long before anybody else. Using that edge, and the special reports she could pull from her database, Anne decided to launch a newsletter for other travel agents called *Cruises Update.*
>
> The newsletter business would use up all of Anne's retirement savings and if it failed, given her current age of 60, she would not have a second chance to recover that money, so she resolved to proceed very cautiously. For instance, she decided to spend about a year developing her publishing plans and gathering information before she would quit her agency job and begin working full-time on the newsletter.

When Anne sat down to design her newsletter, she immediately felt at a loss. So she studied other newsletters both in the travel field and in other industries. She copied some good ideas and made some critical business decisions by herself based on what she observed in other newsletters. For example, she was comfortable deciding how much to charge ($4 per issue) and how frequently to publish (12 times per year), but she struggled for days with a desktop publishing program and never came up with a design that would look as good as the other publications in her field. Knowing that her newsletter should look as good as possible, Anne decided to hire a professional designer. She found a good designer by calling the publishers of newsletters she liked and asking for referrals. She also asked an editor friend to help her develop her content ideas and polish up her writing style. Between them, the designer and the editor both helped Anne create a stunning first issue.

Wanting to hear what her audience would say about her newsletter, Anne created a questionnaire that she inserted into the middle of her first sample issue and then she took the shakedown issue to a travel industry convention and gave out nearly 800 copies to travel agents. She received 73 responses to her questionnaire during the next month. Her respondents made several useful suggestions about topics to cover and how to present some of her data more effectively. Most importantly, a significant number told her they'd like to have a one-page summary of cruises listed by destination. Many respondents also asked her about online and fax distribution.

Anne hadn't considered the destination-oriented summary, but immediately realized it was a great idea. And the feedback she received about online distribution was valuable because she had already considered it, but wasn't sure how much her audience would appreciate that service. The survey cost Anne almost nothing to do, and the results helped her identify two ways to significantly improve her newsletter's appeal.

Gearing Up Your Operations

So far you've been thinking about your audience and your product, two elements that are obviously crucial to a healthy reader relationship. Now, you need to create an organization that will bind them into a profit-making enterprise. At the simplest level, your business organization is made up of people and your relationships with them. Even a solo operator will depend on other people—probably dozens of them—to help get the work done. Since publishing businesses are so people-dependent, it's crucial to organize and manage them well.

As a prospective publisher, ask yourself: Can I work well with people? Can I attract good people, inspire them with my mission, and lead them through a complex and collaborative process? If not, then don't spend another dime until you get a good leader to help you. Many publications fail, even with everything else going for them, because their publishers didn't have the people skills necessary to get them organized properly. The employees of failing ventures often report that their publishers were inattentive, unfair, or uninspiring, and therefore drove away good workers or stifled the ones who stayed.

Assuming you believe you have the skills necessary to marshal an effective publishing team, start your organization-building by defining what your organization will need to accomplish. It should go without saying that it will be far easier to put together a successful publishing machine once you have outlined what the machine needs to do. Look at the essential tasks common to most periodical publishing operations, described below.

Renewing Your Readership

Every year, an average publication loses up to half of its paid subscribers. In the best circumstances, you will lose only 15% or 20% each year, and in the worst case, you'll lose much more. Some lose readers even more quickly: A newlywed couple will very likely switch from a bride to a home improvement or personal finance magazine, for example. The upshot is you will need an organized way to regularly attract new readers—that is, a marketing machine that can locate good prospects and sell new subscriptions. (Chapter 3 guides you through the process of building a complete subscription marketing plan, and Chapter 4 covers renewal promotions.)

Keeping Your Product Fresh

No matter what your subject, your publication needs an organized way to stay fresh all the time. Your editorial staff needs to keep investigating and innovating, or readers will lose interest. Maintaining contact with readers is the best way for editors and contributors to stay on top of what the audience wants. Be aware that keeping in touch with your audience takes valuable time. If you are the principal writer, then you need to be able to delegate some or all of the operational issues to others while you maintain this crucial link with your audience.

Giving Good Service

Even the tiniest newsletter with a few hundred paying customers must be able to answer subscribers' phone calls, faxes, email, and letters, if only to keep up with address changes and new subscription orders. Larger publications have many thousands of customers with the same demands. Whether you are tiny or huge, you must give good service if you expect to keep your subscribers.

Managing Money and Controlling Costs

When you decide to spend extra money on one aspect of your business, you must either have the money on hand or be sure your decision will quickly increase your revenues—enough to pay the inevitable bills. Controlling your finances is nearly impossible without some organized form of bookkeeping. Some publishers have developed complex accounting systems to track their revenues and expenses because they recognize how much easier it is to control their business when they have good accounting information. Other smaller operations may get by with simpler accounting methods. Even if you only hope to balance your checkbook and pay your taxes, you will need a good, easy-to-use financial system that will allow you to produce the documents and reports you and your accountant need. (Chapter 8 discusses financial reports and accounting systems.)

Managing Your Future

In addition to keeping track of what's going on in the marketplace, you will need a longer-term plan for your business. In a changing world, it helps to have a long-range perspective. How will you take advantage of new opportunities or weather hard times? (There is more discussion of strategies in Chapter 12.) Just make yourself a note right now, while you're still getting organized, that you will need time—and perhaps help from other people—to look after your long-term profitability and keep up with changes in your market.

Managing Your Relationships

Collaboration generally works well if you are very careful to completely communicate with everyone who works with you, from your employees to your vendors. (Chapter 10 deals more explicitly with tips about collaboration.) It's good simply to recognize that communicating with helpers takes time. You'll have to keep track of what you promised people, what they promised you, and the progress both of you are making to keep these promises. For example, if you tell workers that their freelance contributions might land them a full-time job, make sure that's a promise you can fulfill. There are legal considerations that can affect vendor and contractor relationships, too. And like all relationships, these will require personal time and attention or they will deteriorate.

Keeping Up With Technology

Print publishing is a manufacturing process that involves lots of technology, from telephone systems to personal computers to multimillion-dollar offset printing equipment. Online publishing is even more dependent on changing technologies. Every publisher has to assemble a different combination of equipment, either by buying it, or hiring vendors who already own it. Your phone system, for example, can be as simple as a residential telephone line and an answering machine. Or you can hire a service bureau that will handle your telecommunications needs with a complex multiline voice processing system. Using the appropriate and cost-effective technology for your business is an important business issue you'll have to face on an ongoing basis, since both your needs and the available technology will constantly change. This means you will almost routinely need to budget some time and effort for researching and updating your systems.

Think about how you are going to handle these essential business operations. Who will help you: Employees? Contractors? Vendors? What kind of organization will you create to be certain all core tasks are well done? Some people run their publishing businesses from home, while others run theirs from a "virtual office" that resides inside a group of networked computers spread far apart. Of course, people with the available funds may follow the more traditional approach of renting an office and hiring employees, but no matter how you organize your business, the essential job of keeping commitments to subscribers and advertisers must be done. Again, this means finding, organizing, and inspiring good people to help.

Publishers succeed by creating a whole web of relationships between themselves and dozens of other people. Even a really great editorial idea won't fly unless you are able to engage creative, capable people to help you bring it to life and keep it on course. (Chapters 9 and 10 will show you how other publishing operations recruit and organize larger teams of people.) From employees to vendors, the people that make up your publishing organization will be critical to your success.

> **EXAMPLE:** Anne Cox published her travel industry newsletter, *Cruises Update*, from a home office. It was a full-time occupation for her, but she had no employees. Still, she depended on many people to keep her "one-woman" newsletter business prosperous. The people on Anne's team included:
> - a desktop publishing designer who laid out each issue and designed her website
> - a freelance copy editor who edited each issue line-by-line
> - two freelance writers who occasionally contributed articles, interviews, and stories they collected from frequent cruisers
> - the printer, who printed, folded, and mailed the newsletters

- a subscription fulfillment bureau that handled the subscriber list, generated mailing labels, sent bills and renewal letters; it had four employees and Anne knew each of them well

- a subscription marketing consultant who helped her plan and manage direct mail campaigns (about two per year)

- two freelance promotional copywriters who created subscription promotion packages, billing solicitations, and renewal packages

- an accountant, who did some of Anne's bookkeeping in addition to preparing annual financial reports and tax returns

- the branch manager of her bank, whom Anne educated to understand the ebb and flow of *Cruises Update*'s cash and who increased her credit limit several times when he saw that her business was viable

- two other newsletter publishers who also became friends; they met with Anne regularly to swap publishing ideas

- her husband, who, in addition to giving her his unending emotional support, agreed to invest some of their savings in her business

- her niece, who was a technical whiz and got Anne's website up and kept it updated every month; she also helped Anne keep her computer, fax machines, modems, and copiers in working order

- her teenage children, who tried to resist interrupting Anne when she was working and to forgive her when she couldn't spend as much time with them as she did before she started the newsletter, and

- her parents, who loaned her the money to finance her first direct mail campaign and patiently waited 18 months until Anne repaid them.

Now imagine that you've taken all the steps toward establishing a healthy relationship with your readers. You've found an editorial mission that suits you and an audience that will buy it. You've created a great product that is well equipped to weather competitive pressures. And you've assembled your team members, provided them with the resources they need, and set them to work. There is only one problem left: You haven't received your first nickel of revenue, or hint of a profit. Right away, you need to start making money from your publication the old-fashioned way: by selling it. Subscription sales and profitability are the topics of the next two chapters. ●

Developing Your Circulation Strategy

The previous chapter described the qualities of a good audience. This chapter and the next will help you make a specific plan for finding readers and selling them your publication. To begin, consider four essential laws of circulation.

1. All readers leave you eventually. If you want your readership to grow or even just to remain constant, then you have to replace the readers who leave.

2. Some readers stay with you longer than others. An ideal reader has an ongoing information need that only you can fill. But in the real world, even within a narrowly defined market niche, there will be a wide disparity of interest levels among your readers, and, of course, each individual reader's interests will change over time.

3. The readers who stay with you are the most valuable. For one thing, you don't have to spend money to replace them. For another, they're probably the people who will buy your other information products. And finally, they're likely to buy products from your advertisers, which will make advertisers happy and more willing to support your publication.

4. It costs money to find readers. Some marketing techniques are less expensive than others, but none of them are free. You'll always need to find more readers—either to replace the ones who leave or to grow your total readership—so it pays to figure out how to do this cost-efficiently. It follows that the more you learn about which methods cost the least money and produce the biggest results, the happier (and wealthier) you will be.

Here is the main point: Finding readers efficiently is the key to a successful circulation strategy. There are two tricks to accomplishing this: First, target the best prospects. Second, use the most effective techniques to sign them up. Both depend on having good information and using it well.

Because circulation strategy can be complicated, it's a subject even many experienced publishing people do not fully understand. But developing a circulation strategy is really not that difficult, and it can mean the difference between a sizzling subscription business and a merely tepid one. Even if you ultimately turn over the circulation marketing job to a specialist or an employee, you should have at least a basic understanding of circulation strategies and methods. With this knowledge, you can clearly judge the performance of any experts you may hire.

This chapter explores the tricks of efficiently targeting and signing up the best subscribers in your niche. And the next chapter covers your circulation budget, plus the mechanics of renewals. If you make notes and take the time to do some research while you read these two chapters, you should be well on your way to designing your own circulation marketing plan. (To find out exactly what's required, see the complete circulation marketing plan at the end of the chapter.)

> **TIP**
> **Never neglect your renewal strategy.** Most of your subscription profits will come from renewals, which explains why most successful publishers spend at least as much effort on keeping readers as they do on getting new ones. Make sure you include an aggressive renewal promotions program in your overall circulation strategy.

One circulation director—let's call her Kathleen—describes her job as having to keep a leaking bucket filled with sand. Knowing her boss, the publisher, needs about 30,000 subscribers to make a profit, her job is to find subscribers who are both easy to sign up and slow to leave.

Building a successful circulation strategy often begins with the question: How many readers do you want to have in your bucket? Most publishers would quickly answer, "As many as possible!" Unfortunately, they would be wrong. Remember, since subscribers constantly leave, you have to spend money to maintain any circulation level. The faster readers leak out, the more you'll have to spend replacing them. No publisher can afford to sign up large numbers of fickle subscribers.

In practice, experienced publishers consider all of their publishing goals before they decide how many readers they want to have. They try to strike a balance between the money they spend selling subscriptions and single copies and the benefits they gain from having paying customers. Finding the right balance is actually a fairly complex issue. (See Chapter 4 for a full discussion.)

For a first draft of your circulation marketing plan, simply pick a subscriber number that seems to make sense; you can always change your goal later on if it proves to be too bold or too expensive. For clues as to what number to pick, consider the other publications in your niche. How many subscribers do they have? How many do you think you'll need to have if you want to compete with them effectively? How many do you think you'll need to attract advertisers?

New Orders, Conversions, and Renewals

The following terms describe the way a reader's relationship with a successful publication evolves.

- CASUAL READERS. These include people who pick up one issue at a friend's house or in a doctor's waiting room, and people who buy one or two newsstand copies. They have enough of an interest to read one or two issues, but not to buy a subscription.

- INTRODUCTORY SUBSCRIBERS. Introductory subscribers are people who say "yes" to a deeply discounted start-up subscription, but can't be counted as full-fledged subscribers because they aren't paying anything close to your full price. In circulation lingo, you have to "convert" introductory subscribers into regular subscribers by letting them try a few issues and then getting them to step up to your normal subscription rates.

- REGULAR SUBSCRIBERS. People who read all or most of your issues and pay the full price for their subscriptions are regular subscribers. These are generally your core customers, and to be successful you will have to convince a majority to renew.

- RENEWING SUBSCRIBERS. People who have already subscribed and agree to extend their subscriptions for another year or more are renewing subscribers. They are your elite readers, the heart of your publishing business, and most important, the source of most of your profits. A successful circulation strategy always involves moving lots of readers through the first three subscription stages until one happy day they can be called renewing subscribers.

Targeting the Best Subscribers

Now that you've thought about how many readers you want, look at whom you want to sell to first. Or, to go back to the leaking bucket metaphor, how will you fill your bucket with sand that is easy to find and unlikely to fall out? Not surprisingly, this means:

- identifying those people who are most likely to read your publication for the longest period of time
- finding them as quickly and efficiently as possible, and
- hanging onto them as long as you can.

People stop reading any publication primarily because it no longer meets their needs. Often, their needs were predictably temporary in the first place: They were planning a wedding, traveling for the first time to a new destination, or looking for a comfortable place to retire. Sometimes, even though they're still involved in the activity, they don't need as much information as they did at first. Once a new parent gains confidence or has a second baby, for instance, he or she may stop reading parenting magazines. There are many other obvious reasons why readers drop out: they die, change occupations, or move on to new sports, to name just a few.

Publishers commonly assume that their editorial quality is the main reason readers leave, but often this isn't true. Even the most brilliant editing cannot keep readers from dying, changing jobs, or falling in love with a new sport. In short, you can't hold onto everybody forever, no matter how good you are.

How fast you lose readers is determined by a number of factors, the most significant being the reason your subscribers needed your publication in the first place. Professionals with a monetary stake in a market tend to be longer-term readers than consumers. Thus, wedding planners have longer-lived information needs than couples organizing their own wedding. In fact, if you focus on bridal magazines for a moment, you can easily identify several other types of short- and long-term potential readers. A young girl who dreams about getting married someday might buy only one issue per year; while people actively planning their own weddings might buy six issues in a row and then never buy another; wedding dress designers, caterers, and other industry professionals will probably subscribe for many years or as long as they remain in the wedding business.

The Bull's-Eye

To cope with varying levels of reader interest and to target those who are likely to be the most loyal, circulation marketing professionals often use a bull's-eye analogy. Some marketers literally draw a target with three to six different circles at increasing distances from the center, each one signifying how much particular groups of people need the information in the publication. Then they fill in the target by naming the groups of readers who fit into each circle. As they develop their circulation marketing plans, they obviously start by trying to reach people at the center of the target, moving outward from the center as far as they have to go to put enough subscribers into their circulation buckets and to replace those that fall out.

People in the center of a publication's bull's-eye can be expected to read your publication for an indefinite period of time—perhaps their whole lives. Typically they either have an abiding interest in your topic, or the will and the means to profit significantly from the information you provide. As your core audience, and your most profitable subscribers, people in this group are not particularly price-sensitive, meaning they'll pay a relatively high subscription price to get your publication. They can also be expected to actively interact with you by writing letters to the editors, visiting your website, or attending your seminars and conferences. And best of all, if you know your market well, you should find it relatively easy to locate your core readers and to sell them your publication.

As you move out from the center, you are simultaneously moving along two spectrums—need for your information, and willingness or ability to pay for it. You are also moving into less profitable segments of your audience. People in the outer groups will read, and perhaps subscribe to your publication, but they will also quit reading and subscribing much more readily than your core audience. In addition, they may be harder for you to find in the first place. All this adds to your costs since your whole organization has to spend more energy finding, keeping, or replacing the people at the outer edges of the target.

The Rings of the Target

Audiences consistently fall into six categories, no matter what the publication's subject. Since these groups are probably active in your niche, too, this list should help organize your target.

1. Industry professionals. These are people who market products or services in your publication's niche. They include manufacturers, wholesale distributors, retail and mail order dealers, and convention organizers. All of them have continuing profit-driven interest in keeping current in a particular field.

2. Industry onlookers. These are government regulators, stock market investors, journalists, and educators. They belong in the center of your bull's-eye—even though they are not directly making products for your market—because they are so interested in knowing what's going on. Often there are not many people in the onlooker categories, but they can be influential and you should include them.

3. Professional consumers. These are people who buy the products of the industry or occupation you are writing about either for a business or in some other way that is related to their occupations. In the travel field, for example, this category includes corporate travel managers. These people are different from ordinary consumers because they either spend company money—sometimes lots of it—or their own tax-deductible funds, as would be the case of a lawyer who buys a CD-ROM containing updated state laws. Since many people in this group are responsible to an employer for how well they spend the company's money, they need good information and they tend to read nearly every publication related to their interests.

4. Avid consumers. These are hard-core enthusiasts who are spending lots of time and money in the field. Some are new to it, and some have been involved for a long time. All of them are eager to know how to spend their time and money to the best advantage. For example, an

Internet magazine would put people in this category who spend many hours online every day, go to computer conventions, and buy lots of new software and hardware products.

Some publishers distinguish among their avid consumers, dividing them according to some measure of activity: golfers who travel versus the ones who play near their homes, for example. Or to take another example, computer magazines often categorize households depending on how many computers they have, or how much they paid for them. One reason these distinctions are made is to help publishers concentrate on their most profitable prospects.

5. Casual consumers. These are people with a passing or a limited interest. Perhaps they're thinking about getting involved, but haven't. Or they used to be more involved, but have lost at least some of their interest for some reason. Typically, this means they are spending some money and time in the field, but not as much as the avid consumers. For example, a model railroading magazine would put someone in this category who owns a complete model but hasn't added anything to it for many years, doesn't visit hobby shops anymore, and isn't attending club meetings or conventions. Such a person might read the magazine once in a while, but his or her information needs are low.

6. Outsiders. These are people who might read an issue or two, but are unlikely to become subscribers. The main reason to include this category in your analysis is for future reference, to note markets that have the potential to intersect with yours. For instance, the model railroading publisher might put affluent parents and grandparents of younger children in the "other" category because he might try to engage their interest later.

Drawing Your Own Target

A good way to estimate the number of people in any field is to look at commercial mailing lists. One hallmark of a good audience is that you can reach it fairly easily. If your potential prospects are on commercial mailing lists, they are only a postage stamp away.

RESOURCES

In *Folio:* magazine's annual *Source Book*, you can find direct mail consultants and mailing list brokers who will help you find out what kinds of lists are available. You can also find circulation consultants at www. magazinelaunch.com. In addition there is a directory called *Direct Marketing List Source* published six times per year by the Standard Rate and Data Service (SRDS), 1700 Higgins Road, Des Plaines, IL 600118, 847-375-5000. A book called *Find it Fast: How to Uncover Expert Information on Any Subject Online or in Print,* by Robert Berkman (HarperCollins), can help you locate other information sources.

Also check online: Using a search engine to target "mailing lists" will produce thousands of sites. Any of them will help you research your audience.

WARNING

Pay attention to your research process. If you easily find the lists of prospects and other information you want to know, then you're probably sufficiently tuned in to your niche to consider launching a publication. But if you have trouble gathering specific information about your readers—how many of them there are, what they're doing, what they're reading, and so forth—then you may need to reconsider your publishing idea. At the very least, take the time to figure out what's wrong before proceeding.

Enough background. Now it's time for you to map out the circulation target for your publication. Start by making your universe of possible readers as large as you can. Then, determine the different levels of interest in your subject, and use those distinctions to create your different categories.

EXAMPLE: Anne Cox was considering publishing a newsletter about cruise vacations, *Cruises Update*. She did research at the library, online, and by contacting a few travel organizations by telephone to estimate the number of people involved in various aspects of the travel industry. Based on her research, she drew the following circulation target:

Target location	Category	Number in the universe
Bull's-Eye	Industry professionals:	
	Travel agents	50,000
	Cruise marketing executives	8,000
	Tour packagers	2,500
	Travel agency suppliers	1,000
First Ring	Professional consumers:	
	Individual tour leaders	20,000
Second Ring	Avid consumers (frequent cruisers)	90,000
Third Ring	(upscale travelers who are occasionally cruisers)	500,000
Outside Ring	Casual consumers (including upper-middle-income and retired people)	3,000,000

Choosing Efficient Marketing Channels

Once you have created your target, your next step is to line up specific ways to reach the people in or near your bull's-eye. Remember this: In publishing there is never one way to do anything—not only does each publication face a unique set of opportunities and obstacles, but also a variety of ways to cope with them. You will have to look at your own circumstances and make your own choices.

For example, even though lots of publications are launched via direct mail, other publishers cannot afford direct mail and they use completely different tactics. Some print a few issues and sell them on the newsstands, going forward only if response is strong. Others give away free samples to people at conventions and trade shows, relying on advertisers who wish to reach these groups to pay their publishing costs. And many publishers depend on Web promotions.

Consider as many options as possible before you decide which ones to use.

Here are a few tips:

- *Go where your best prospects are likely to be.* Just because you can find a mailing list doesn't mean you should ignore other opportunities to contact potential subscribers. For example, if you are publishing a newsletter for divorcing fathers, you might be better served by giving free samples to divorce attorneys.

- *Use whatever connections you can make and build from there.* For example, if you already belong to an association in your field, see if you can promote your publication to its other members.

- *Study what other publishers have done in similar circumstances.* That is, if yours is a professional newsletter, study how other professional newsletters are distributed.

- *Ask questions of everyone who could possibly help you.* This includes everyone even tangentially related to the publication, from printers and ad salespeople to competitors.

To help make a specific plan for getting the subscribers you need and keep as many of them as possible, consult the following list of marketing tactics publishers commonly use. Consider each method and then rank it according to its applicability to your audience and your marketing resources. For example, you might end up ranking direct mail near the bottom of your list, perhaps because it's too expensive or because there are not enough good mailing lists in your field. And do not stop with these suggestions, especially if yours is a highly specialized publication. You may well have better ideas of your own.

Direct Mail

Direct mail is ideal, even for publishers with limited funding, when your niche is relatively small and easy to identify, like chiropractors who also teach yoga, or people who manage small hotels in major cities.

Over the past 20 years, there have been huge improvements in the computer technology used for collecting and storing information about people. The information-gathering revolution has had an impact on every aspect of our lives from how we draw up our legislative districts to how much we pay for our automobile insurance. Direct mail relies on computer systems to compile vast amounts of highly specific information about individuals with the idea of predicting their spending habits. Naturally, direct mailers have also been beneficiaries of improving computer technology. Today, thanks to their wizardry, it really is possible to locate physicists who eat lots of bran cereal or chiropractors who read the Russian classics.

In addition to its powerful targeting capacity, direct mail is appealing to publishers because it works fast, especially for publishers with the cash and the expertise to do it well. Under ideal circumstances, you might even be able to do one big direct mail campaign that would sign up all the subscribers you need, and simultaneously recapture all of your marketing expenses.

The trouble is that circumstances are rarely so ideal. Many small publishers cannot afford to use direct mail. And even those who can are likely to make expensive mistakes. Getting professional help in planning and executing a campaign can help you avoid such mistakes, but can't guarantee success. (Chapter 9 discusses how to locate good consultants and freelance helpers.) But for now it's important to emphasize that direct mail is not a business for amateurs. For example, one publisher misprinted the response forms, sending all of her orders to the wrong place, and another ordered test quantities of a dozen different mailing lists and then forgot to code the order forms so that he could tell which orders came from which list. Professional helpers would have prevented both mistakes.

RESOURCES

Two excellent resources will teach you how direct mail works. One is *Hitting the Sweet Spot—The Art and Science of Direct Mail*, from the Independent Press Association (IPA). This technical report is based on the practical experiences of over 500 independent publishers using direct mail to sell subscriptions. The report is available at the IPA's website at www.indypress.org, where you'll also find other excellent technical reports. Another good publication on the subject is *Direct Mail for Dummies*, by Richard Goldsmith (IDG Books).

The Bad News About Direct Mail and Efficiency

This book, and this chapter in particular, emphasize the importance of efficiency, so this is a good moment to point out an anomaly: Even though publishers commonly use direct mail to find subscribers, it can be an expensive, inefficient way to go. Publishers who plan to make their money mostly from advertising may not care. I know one who lost as much as $60 recruiting every direct mail subscriber and then made it up and more selling ads.

Most publishers plan direct mail campaigns that break even—meaning they want revenues from new subscriptions to equal or exceed the out-of-pocket mailing expenses. But, even when direct mail campaigns accomplish this goal—and many don't—they are relatively wasteful activities. Not only does an enormous amount of effort go into copywriting, printing, posting, and delivering the letters (not to mention all of those trees), but the vast majority of recipients—typically 90% or more—toss them straight into the trash.

Even the small percentage of people who say "yes" to a direct mail letter probably won't stick with your publication for very long. Many will quit on you as soon as they see your first issue—it just wasn't what they expected to see, despite your wonderful brochures and descriptions. Others will subscribe for a short while, but won't renew. Before too long, you'll be revving up your postage meter again trying to replace the ones who said "yes" to last year's mailing but "no" to this year's renewal campaign.

Single-Copy Distribution

Many publishers use a circulation marketing strategy based on distributing free copies of their publications loaded with order cards. For example, they offer free sample issues at a website and then load up the issues with subscription promotions. This is a good tactic because it gives potential readers a chance to sample your product before they are asked to purchase a subscription. Done right, sampling campaigns can be cheaper than direct mail and produce subscribers who are more likely to become long-time subscribers.

Publishers are always inventing new ways to distribute single issues of their newsletters and magazines. Here are some of the tried-and-true favorites.

- *Newsstands.* Newsstands are located in grocery stores, bookstores, airport terminals, and other high-traffic locations. Magazines reach any particular newsstand through a complex system of national distributors working with local wholesalers and distributors. Space is very limited and competition very intense among the publishers who want to put their magazines at choice newsstands. Most publishers rely on consultants to help them develop an effective newsstand distribution system. (The Independent Press Association offers an excellent special report about newsstand sales at its site, www.indypress.org.)

- *Retail stores.* Many niches have their own retail outlets such as pet shops or cooking stores. Some of these outlets get their magazines from distributors, just like the newsstands, but some of them buy magazines directly from the publishers. You'll have to ask the retailers in your niche what works best for them and then start from there.

- *Trade shows and conferences.* Sometimes you can sell or give away magazines or newsletters at a trade show, or you can find someone else to distribute copies for you at conferences you don't attend. Ask the trade show managers in your niche to help you make the best use of the events they're organizing.

- *Centers of activity.* Any place your readers congregate is a reasonable place to distribute your publication, from a doctor's waiting room to a child care center to a coffee bar or barber shop.
- *Association memberships and other individuals.* Many newsletters send one or more free copies along with a sales pitch to members of professional associations, business owners, practicing professionals, and other key people in their niche.

The keys to successful subscription sales from single-copy distribution are first, to put the copies in the best possible locations, and second, to put lots of order cards in each copy. A typical consumer magazine that you buy on the newsstand will have three to six cards bound in (usually next to an ad that promotes subscriptions) and another couple of cards blown in—loosely inserted between the pages—by the printer.

Gifts

A gift promotion asks someone to buy your publication for another person. Some newsletter publishers insert a gift subscription order card in every issue. This has been a particularly successful tactic over the years for health and hobby publications. And publishers of business periodicals have also done well by convincing employers to give subscriptions to their employees for ongoing education and training.

Gift promotions usually run in the publication as a special, unique house ad or bind-in card. In addition, many publishers regularly mail gift promotions to all of their subscribers or include the gift idea with renewal promotions. While not suitable for every publication, gift promotions can be very effective.

For example, an upscale golfing newsletter called *Golf Odyssey* runs ads in *The New Yorker* magazine 12 times per year, promoting gift subscriptions with great success. The newsletter reviews golf resorts in places like Scotland, Hong Kong, and Hawaii, and it sells for $98 per year for 12 issues.

Tie-Ins

There are many ways to promote your publication by creating marketing links with related products or services. Giving a free subscription to members of an organization or society is often an effective tie-in. So is including a subscription card or a sample issue with merchandise—assuming the product really fits well with your publication.

Naturally, the product manufacturers will want you to return their favors in some way. They will want access to your subscription list, or discounted advertising space. Negotiate any trade that makes sense to you, but be careful to choose the right products with which to associate your publication, since the two products may become linked in the minds of their consumers. For example, if you bundle your exciting new lacrosse magazine with a brand of lacrosse stick that shatters easily, subscribers may not forgive you. It's far better to work with a top-quality manufacturer. Never bundle your publication with a product unless the association makes you proud.

Tie-ins can also be profitable when corporate sponsors want to associate themselves with your editorial approach. For example, a newsletter called *Education Today* features articles about how parents can help their children learn, reviews of educational software and books, news of innovative techniques in education, and other coverage of education-related issues. Within just three years of its launch in 1989, *Education Today* grew to a circulation of 70,000 by selling bulk subscriptions to large corporations active in education reform such as Merck, Bristol-Meyers Squibb, Polaroid, and IBM. Those corporations pay between $5 and $19.95 per year for each subscription depending on how many they buy. They distribute the copies free to the parents among their employees as a means of emphasizing the corporate involvement in education.

House Ads

Every publication should contain at least one prominent ad asking for new subscriptions and at least one subscription order card. Many new publishers often overlook this low-cost promotion opportunity, assuming that it's silly to advertise to people who already subscribe. They should think again. All publications—even obscure journals on linguistics—are regularly passed on to other interested people. Some publishers have as many as five or six "pass-along" readers. Often, order cards and subscription ads really do convince some of these second-hand readers to buy their own subscriptions.

Space Ads

These are ads that you run in other publications promoting yours. Because space is relatively cheap, many publishers trade ad space with other publishers in related fields. And, of course, most are willing to sell space to noncompeting publishers. Space ads can generate subscriptions directly, or they can produce leads that you will follow up later with a phone call or mailing. For example, you might decide to sell—or even give away—a particularly compelling special report or single issue of your periodical in a space ad, and then promote subscriptions to everyone who asks for the report. This is also a common tactic for generating qualified telemarketing leads.

Telemarketing

The telephone is an expensive method to use to sign up subscribers. Typically it only makes sense when your subscription prices are high enough to justify the cost involved, and when you have enough exceptionally well-qualified prospects to call. For example, a technical newsletter priced above $250 and aimed at a very selected group that is easy to locate (like public utility engineers) would be a good candidate for telemarketing sales. Publishers who use this approach rarely hire their own sales staff, but instead use a telemarketing service that hires, trains, and supervises salespeople and collects a commission on each sale. This can be the best way to go if you work with a top-notch telemarketing organization. Professionals in this field will write your sales pitch for you, using techniques that have worked well for other clients. But make sure to respect the new Do Not Call lists, since even one violation can cost you a bundle.

Radio and TV

Conventional wisdom among print publishers used to be that not enough people who watch TV or listen to the radio also read periodicals, at least not enough to justify the high cost of advertising on broadcast media. The result has been that many publishers have almost religiously avoided advertising on TV or radio. (There are some well-known exceptions, including *Reader's Digest* and others with a broad appeal and a huge audience.)

But cable television has done a great deal to change these traditional views. By offering specialized programming and cheaper rates, cable allows publishers the opportunity to narrowly cast their messages to interested people. For example, if you produce a food newsletter, advertising it on Food TV gives you a chance to pitch it to lots of people who are very concerned about cooking well.

Even if you can't afford to produce a commercial and buy air time, radio and TV can help you promote your subscriptions if you make your publication interesting enough to receive free coverage. For an example of how this can be done with huge success, consider the *Lundberg Letter*, a relatively obscure publication that, among other things, tracks the price of gasoline at the pump and is often quoted whenever prices rise or fall.

The key to getting media attention is to find points where your interests coincide with their needs—for example, by offering to appear as a guest in your role as publisher, or to have your contributors appear on relevant programs. Some people are born with the knack of creating interesting pegs on which news reporters or talk show hosts can hang a story. If you are not one of these, professional publicists can provide a lot of help. Find them in the *Folio: Source Book* at www.foliomag.com.

Books, Magazines, and Other Information Providers

Like broadcast or cable media, getting mentioned in books and other magazines puts information about your publication into the hands of your core audience. A good publicist—even one you hire as a part-time freelancer—can be a huge help in getting out the word about your publication to other publishers. The ideal is to start with your own list of media contacts and then add more, hopefully lots more.

This approach works because writers and editors like to let their readers know about valuable information sources. If you doubt this, consider how often newspapers, magazines, and books print sidebars or boxes listing sources for more information and how common it is for these lists to contain subscription information for specialty publications.

Perhaps the cheapest and easiest way to reach influential writers and publishers in your field is to give each a free subscription. And, of course, if you mention their publication favorably, you will want to call it to their attention. As with any other human endeavor, people will tend to support you if you have something nice to say about them.

General Publicity

Editors and publishers who are experts in a given field often find that publicity is their major source of business. If you can make yourself famous like Martha Stewart, or if you can become a respected analyst within your own field like Dr. Andrew Weil in the alternative health field, your notoriety will help sell subscriptions. Esther Dyson has been a public commentator in the technology business for more than 20 years. She speaks at conferences, gives quotes to reporters at *The New York Times* and *Wall Street Journal*, and consults with investment companies. Her newsletter, *Release 1.0*, was founded in 1983 and published out of her home office until about five years ago when she sold it to a professional newsletter company. Subscriptions cost $285 for a quarterly print newsletter, plus access to an online site that is updated daily. And there is also an annual conference that brings subscribers together for high-level discussions about the future of technology.

Internet Sales

These days, most magazines and newsletters maintain their own websites. Commonly, the site is used like a newsstand: to distribute single issues or samples to prospective subscribers. Many publishers post past issues and some portion of a current issue's content—one feature article, for example—for free at their site. Some publishers have also developed Web-only content (calculators, polls, and bookstores, for example). But if you look closely at most sites, you will see that their primary focus is to sell subscriptions. (See Chapter 11 for more on Internet publishing.) For example, *Vermont Life* is a glossy quarterly magazine published by Vermont's State Tourism Board. Its site at www.vtlife.com offers sample articles from the magazine, advertising information, and back issues— but its main purpose is to sell subscriptions to the print magazine.

Agents, Stamp Sheets, and Web Distributors

Publishers' Clearinghouse and American Family Publishers are the most well-known publishers' agents, but there are dozens of others that also send out magazine subscription offers, often linked to contests. The agent collects a commission, just like a telemarketing service, generally about 50% of the first sale—you get to keep the rest plus any renewal revenues. As you've probably noticed, agents do very little to promote the individual magazines they sell beyond listing them, often on a stamp sheet with individual magazines printed on each stamp. Subscribers order by affixing the stamps of their choice on an order card.

Amazon.com now sells magazine subscriptions, and in this way it behaves like any traditional subscription agent. Like other subscription agents online (see "Are Online Subscription Agents Right for You?" below), Amazon pays publishers quite a small share of the subscription money collected, about 20%. On the plus side, the publisher gets to handle renewals directly. Barnes & Noble also offers magazine subscriptions from its retail stores as well as at its online store. This is one of those new developments in publishing that changes rapidly, so you should rely on the Web for current leads and information.

Are Online Subscription Agents Right for You?

There are loads of agents online who will sell subscriptions to your magazine for a fee—often a hefty one. Online subscription agents typically pay you only about 20% of what they collect from subscribers, which is often a highly discounted rate to begin. For this reason, it usually only makes sense to use an online subscription agent if your magazine is well supported by advertising and is less dependent on subscription revenues.

When several publisher members of the Independent Press Association (www.indypress.org) were asked about their experiences, they had decidedly mixed reactions.

Jeremy Wieland, circulation director at the *Utne Reader* (www.utne.com), said this: "If you need subscribers to reach a circulation level large enough to support your advertising revenues, then Internet agencies are okay. They don't generate environmental waste, they're low maintenance (once you negotiate a deal with each agent), and it's easy money. But if less than 20% of your revenue comes from advertising, then forget about subscription agents.

Richard Tanana from *Caustic Truths* (www.caustictruths.com) has another perspective. "We find that Amazon works very well for us because we look at it from a marketing viewpoint. It is awesome advertising for us when people see our title at Amazon. Great exposure. And I believe that the extra online exposure increases our offline single-copy sales, too."

The bottom line is that an advertising-driven publication can make good use of online subscription agents. Here are some practical tips from IPA members who use them.

- **Control your own renewals.** Make sure the agent hands over enough information so that you can sell renewals directly to their customers. You can recover the up-front losses on agent subscriptions by selling the renewals at a regular price and cutting out the agent's commission.

- **Negotiate.** Most of the agents will negotiate. Jeremy Wieland said, "Most agencies will negotiate. I encourage everyone to check with other publishers and see what the market will bear."

- **Know your break-even costs.** If your publishing costs are low enough, then even getting 20% or less from agents can be a profitable deal.

New agents come and go frequently, so look around. Ask about the deals they offer to publishers. I found dozens of agents in a recent search engine visit, including Magazines.com, Discountmagazines.com, Magazines4cheap.com, and Magazinepricesearch.com.

Card Decks

These programs are similar to those run by direct mail agents except that instead of a sheet of stamps, the distributor sends out a deck of postcards, each advertising a periodical, book, or other product. Card deck distributors have mailing lists of people with common interests and a habit of buying things from card decks. As a client, you are asked to pay the production costs of your postcard, plus a commission on your sales. Card decks can be an effective source of subscribers when the distributor is good and their audience matches yours. It's also wise to investigate who the other advertisers in a card deck will be: Avoid associating with scam artists and disreputable businesses.

White Mail

This odd term refers to any subscription order a publisher receives that can't be traced to a specific promotion source or activity. The key to profiting from this phenomenon (in addition to cashing the checks, of course) is to find out as much as you can about why you are receiving the order and then to build that information into future promotions. For example, if you suddenly start receiving orders from Florida and Japan, you'll want to investigate if you can. Perhaps you'll learn that the Florida orders are the result of a local newspaper columnist who is a fan and has begun to quote you often, while those from Japan can be traced to an illicit reproduction of your material on the Internet. Observing these results, you may decide to cultivate the columnist and the Internet as future subscription resources.

Running Successful Promotions

Because experienced circulation people can save you lots of money and help you avoid mistakes, it is usually wise to get professional help when you sit down to design specific direct mail campaigns and other subscription promotions. However, you may not be able to afford all the experienced helpers you would optimally like to hire. So here are some tips about putting together your own ads, order cards, and other materials that you use to sell subscriptions. In addition, feel free to collect promotion materials from other publications and borrow from those you like best.

Keep Track of Every Promotion

Experienced circulation people know that even if their periodical is a big success, they'll still be putting sand into leaky buckets ten or 20 years from now. It follows that much of what they learn about how to attract new subscribers today is likely to be useful later. So they carefully monitor and file the results of every promotion with the idea of using them to continually fine-tune the subscription process. Specifically, each new order or renewal is linked to its source: an ad, direct mail letter, telephone solicitation, or whatever else made the sale. Over time this information is analyzed and reanalyzed to see which promotions had the greatest results. For instance, when it comes time to expand readership or launch a spin-off product, the information a circulation department has gathered about how to find the best customers allows it to immediately focus on the most effective marketing channels.

Stay Close to Your Mission

The more a promotion relates to your subject and supports your editorial mission, the better long-term subscribers you'll get from it. If you decide to create a promotion based on giving something to new subscribers, be sure it's closely related to your subject area. For example, *Organic Gardening* offers special reports on composting to new subscribers instead of a watch or a calculator. It has learned that if it gives away a high-tech gizmo, too many people will subscribe to get the gizmo, not the magazine.

Use the same reasoning if you develop a contest as part of a subscription offer, then choose a prize that relates to your subject. For example, a computer magazine should offer subscribers a chance to win a computer, not cash or a trip to Hawaii. Because they don't follow this simple rule, many publishers who participate in the famous American Family or Publishers' Clearinghouse promotions—which give away big bucks and glamorous cars—are disappointed to find that only about 15% or less of their gross orders turn into long-term subscribers.

Make Subscribing Simple

Make it as easy as you can for a reader to buy your publication. Lots of choices in terms of prizes, add-ons, or subscription offers can be so confusing that you'll receive fewer positive responses than if you gave away half as much, but kept your offer easy to understand. One tip: Picture your subscribers responding to your promotions. How will they fill out the card? Is there enough room to do it comfortably? Are all terms, conditions, and extras easy to understand? How will they pay: Will you bill them later or must they face the extra barrier of writing a personal check, printing a credit card number, or, even worse, having to requisition a check from an accounting department? Another tip: Look at the subscription promotions from a really experienced publishing company like *Reader's Digest* or *Time*. You'll notice how easy they make it to say "yes."

Test Everything

Practiced circulation marketing people use every chance they can get to test their ideas, looking for the ones that work best: Does $18.97 work substantially better than $19.00? Does a guarantee improve responses? If you offer longer-term subscriptions on the same order card as a one-year subscription, do you increase or decrease your total receipts?

Testing usually means splitting up your prospects and giving a different offer to each group to see which has the greatest appeal. Practiced circulation managers constantly test to try to come up with a new offer or a new sales pitch that will pull better than the promotion packages they currently use. In a sense, they're on a never-ending quest to increase efficiency and effectiveness.

> **TIP**
>
> **Deal with business subscribers carefully.** Many publications are addressed to business and professional audiences. If you study the habits of successful newsletters, like *The Kiplinger Letter* or *The Comptroller's Report* from the Institute of Management and Administration, you'll discover that they always write to subscribers at work, use a professional, understated tone, and emphasize the commercial benefits a reader can expect from subscribing. Like their newsletters, their promotions are to-the-point, factual, and informative because they understand that their readers are busy people who will buy a lot of information (if it is useful to them) who are also facing many competing demands for their attention. They avoid flashy brochures, contests, and other promotional gimmicks.

A Sample Marketing Plan

Now let's work through some of the strategies we have discussed with our fictional publisher Anne Cox and her newsletter *Cruises Update*. Of course, your circulation strategy will have to satisfy the unique demands that arise from your niche, your resources, and your competitive situation, but it is likely that at least some of the techniques discussed here will work for you.

Cruises Update

Anne Cox has already drawn out her circulation target for the newsletter she wants to publish, *Cruises Update*. (See the example in "Drawing Your Own Target," earlier in this chapter.) Now she needs to come up with ways to actually sell the newsletter to her targeted audience, particularly those in the bull's-eye. In the bull's-eye are industry professionals: travel agents, cruise marketing executives, tour packagers, and travel agency suppliers. Also important to her circulation plan are people in the first ring: professional and avid consumers. Her circulation marketing plan must focus on selling her newsletter to these core audience members.

Choosing Marketing Channels

As she looks over her circulation options, Anne rejects a few right away, especially those related to single-copy distribution. As is often true for newsletters, there aren't many good opportunities for single-issue distribution except for the annual travel agents' convention and some Web directories. Anne will use both. Anne also realizes that running ads in magazines for corporate travel managers and travel agents isn't likely to bring in enough subscribers to justify the cost. While the exposure couldn't hurt, Anne decides that as a primary marketing channel it would not be cost-effective.

After thinking about all of her other circulation-building options, Anne settles on a website as the most efficient way to sell subscriptions. She creates a modest site with many links to online travel sites. Most of these links are traded free, but sometimes Anne has to pay to get her link added to a major travel site. In addition to her website, Anne decides to conduct a small direct mail test, backed up by space advertising in industry journals and giving out sample copies at the travel agents' trade show. Sensibly, she will try to schedule her space advertisements and publicity campaigns so that they will increase the visibility of her newsletter before, during, and after her direct mail campaigns.

Having chosen her methods, Anne next makes a couple of other crucial choices: First, she hires a direct mail marketing professional to help her. And second, she includes a copy of the newsletter itself in her mailings, believing that it will sell itself to readers better than any descriptive brochure or literature could do.

With limited financial resources and no experience with direct mail or Web design, Anne realizes her choice of a circulation consultant will be a critical factor in helping determine if she succeeds or fails. Anne not only wants someone with plenty of direct mail experience, but a person who has handled campaigns for niche newsletters like hers, too. Her choice is a woman named Joanna, a direct marketing consultant with several other newsletter clients, whose name she originally found in *Folio:* magazine. (Chapters 9 and 10 offer suggestions about where to look for and how to check out consultants or employees who have the right background to help you.)

Anne asks Joanna to help plan all of her subscription marketing strategies. Specifically, it will be Joanna's job to develop schedules, contract copywriters and designers, manage the details of the mailings (through outside vendors such as direct mail houses), and help Anne to analyze the results. During the year they will work together, Anne agrees to pay Joanna $20,000. Anne also pays $5,000 to a designer named Michael who creates her website.

> **WARNING**
>
> **Your marketing choices have financial implications.** Obviously, you can't choose to launch your newsletter with a $100,000 direct mail campaign if you don't have that kind of money. So your budget will influence your marketing decisions. But which comes first, the budget or the marketing plan? For instance, if you think you can earn $250,000 from that $100,000 direct mail campaign, wouldn't you be smart to borrow the money and go for it? The answer is: Maybe. The trick is to be flexible: Keep your mind open. Be prepared to toss aside a cherished marketing plan if you can't make it work financially. Likewise, be prepared to stretch the budget a bit—maybe even borrow money—if a marketing test strikes gold.

Creating Promotional Materials

Anne and Joanna develop promotional material including, most importantly, the carefully crafted charter issues of *Cruises Update*, as well as direct mail materials, a modest website, conversion and renewal letters, and space ads. Together they research direct mail lists, as well as advertising and publicity opportunities. They decide on 24 mailing lists that seem to include just the kind of travel agents and buyers Anne is trying to reach. They develop a schedule for the mailings as well as for the space ads and single-copy distribution that will supplement the mail campaign.

They also develop a budget of expected revenues and expenses, obviously an important step in any promotional campaign. Budgeting is discussed in detail in the next chapter, but for now remember that you'll have to do both creative and financial planning whenever you plan promotions. You won't be able to launch any campaign if you don't have a way to finance it.

A Test Mailing and Supportive Publicity

Anne and Joanna decide to conduct a test mailing to find the best mailing lists among the 24 they had obtained. Some of these commercially sold lists have been compiled from government records, while others have been developed from lists of subscribers to travel industry publications, attendees at trade shows, and the members of trade associations. Later, based on the results of the test mailing, Anne will conduct a second mailing using the lists that worked best.

Anne and Joanna send out 100,000 letters for the test mailing, and launch a simultaneous publicity campaign of space ads in travel industry magazines. They collect 100,000 names by randomly selecting 5,000 names from each of the 24 lists, then eliminating the duplicates.

On Joanna's advice, Anne decides to test another variable in addition to testing lists: Package A will include a sample issue of *Cruises Update* plus an order form and a sales letter. Package B will have the same order form and sales letter, but it will include a descriptive brochure instead of the newsletter. Both will offer one free "trial" issue and 50% off the normal subscription price ($24 per year) for a one-year trial subscription. The same offer is used on Anne's website. In subsequent direct mail campaigns, Anne will use the package that performed the best in the test. Anne's order forms will be coded to identify every order from the test mailing according to the list it came from and the package the subscriber received.

To help keep track of the data they receive, publishers usually create a test "grid" that shows the code for every variable they are testing in their campaign. In addition to the variables just mentioned, Anne will separate the results of her first mailing from the second one she will do later on. Anne's codes and test grid look like this:

Mailing Lists	Package A (with Pub.)	Package B (with Broch.)
Business travel agents, list 1	Code: A00101	Code: B00101
Business travel agents, list 2	A00201	B00201
Airline marketing people	A00301	B00301
Corporate travel managers, list 1	A00401	B00401
Corporate travel managers, list 2	A00501	B00501
High-volume frequent flyers, list 1	A00601	B00601

Anne and Joanna now have everything in place to launch *Cruises Update*'s promotional campaign. Anne originally hoped that the promotion would bring in a total of 6,000 new orders. Joanna, however, convinces her that 6% was overly optimistic. They eventually agree that 4,000 responses is more realistic to expect.

Conversions and a Roll-Out Mail Campaign

It takes seven months to accomplish Anne's test mailing, process the orders, and analyze the results. Fortunately, subscriptions really are coming in: *Cruises Update* now has approximately 4,000 subscribers from the direct mail effort (as predicted) and 1,000 orders from the website. Anne has to begin converting her new subscribers into longer-term customers. She hopes to get 60% of her original subscribers to continue to subscribe. Sixty percent is an optimistic expectation, but not impossible: Many newsletters convert that many new subscriptions when their product is good, their niche very promising, and they have no competition.

With Joanna's help, Anne develops a five-letter conversion offering each original subscriber a second year's subscription at $32, or one-third off the full price. Anne begins sending out conversion promotions three months before the trial subscription period ends.

At the same time, Anne begins to roll out her second direct mail campaign using the information she gathered from her test mailing. This time, she will mail only about 50,000 letters to names from the top-producing lists. And this mailing will include the most productive promotion package, which, as she suspects, is the one containing the sample copy. On the basis of her results from the first mailing, Anne expects to generate 2,500 new orders from the roll-out mailing. She doesn't expect this mailing to generate as many orders as the first because she's already begun to saturate her market. As before, she'll support her Web and direct mail campaign by running ads and conducting a publicity campaign in travel industry trade publications. Also during this period, Anne will attend the annual travel agents' convention, renting a tiny booth there and handing out free copies of her newsletter. Being at the convention will also give her a chance to do some market research. Her total costs to attend, including her own travel expenses, the cost of printing extra newsletter copies and shipping them to the show, plus having the booth, are about $5,000.

Anne's plan as a whole is a success. She receives 6,500 responses to her two direct mail campaigns and 3,000 from her website in the first year. This is enough to sustain the newsletter and drive her business forward. Anne sets a date to analyze the state of her subscription business again, 18 months from the beginning of the promotional campaign. At that point she'll revise her plan based on what she has learned. If results continue to be good, then she will keep growing by planning additional mail campaigns and continuing her conversion and renewal programs. If results stop meeting her expectations, she will have to make a new plan.

But Anne won't have much spare time, since this will also be the critical time when her earliest subscribers near the end of their conversion period, making it time for them to renew. Anne will need to focus attention and promotion money on getting them to renew while also coaxing her second group of subscribers to accept her conversion offer. ●

Subscription Budgeting and Profitability

Can your publication sell subscriptions profitably? This chapter will help work you through the calculations necessary to make a budget that will tell you—yes or no.

What if your budget doesn't come out right? For example, what if your projected subscription revenues won't cover your estimated publishing expenses? You have several ways to try to bring your budget into balance. One is to abandon your publishing idea. Another is to go back to the drawing board and look for other sources of income, such as advertising sales or spin-off products that might enhance their profitability. (Ad sales are discussed in Chapter 5 and spin-off products in Chapter 6.) A third option is to modify one or more of your basic publishing ideas, such as how often you will publish, how much you will charge, or how you will distribute your periodical.

When you begin to create a budget, you'll have to make some guesses about what's going to happen in the future: How much will you have to pay someone to design and manage your direct mail campaign? How many orders will you get from that campaign? How much will the price of paper go up before you're finished printing all of next year's issues? Because you have little experience in many of these areas and you know your guesses are likely to be far from perfect, you may be tempted to skip the entire budgeting process. This would be a mistake. By gathering good information and the best advice you can get, you really can produce a pretty decent budget projection—which, of course, you should regularly revise as you get new information. Just do your best.

The budgeting process—and this chapter—begin by concentrating on converting and renewing trial subscribers, including pricing mechanisms publishers commonly use for these purposes. Conversions and renewals are critically important to your long-term profitability. Next is a discussion about ways to make reasonable guesstimates about your future subscription incomes. Then you'll learn how to estimate your publishing expenses. Finally, you'll find a simple financial tool called break-even analysis that should help you test your financial expectations and actually create your budget.

Renewals and Conversions

Every subscriber who leaves forces you to go looking for someone else. Furthermore, people who stick with you for a long period of time usually turn out to be your best customers because they will buy other products down the road. If you view renewals and conversions as your best methods for keeping your bucket full, then you'll understand why experienced publishers spend so much effort on renewal and conversion programs.

Many new publishers very reasonably create their own conversion and renewal letters by adapting ones from established publishers. If this is your approach, two suggestions may help you in tailoring the letters to your own needs: First, try to look at the whole three- to nine-letter renewal series you intend to imitate, not just one or two letters. This will give you the publisher's whole program, not just one or two pieces. Look at how letters are timed, how the sales pitch changes from one letter to the next, and how many different types of offers they make. Second, give lots of thought to changing the copy so it reflects both your own publication's style and that of your targeted audience. If you run into trouble developing your own conversion and renewal promotions, look for help from the publications listed in Chapter 14 or from a circulation marketing consultant.

The chart below illustrates four different conversion and renewal pricing strategies publishers commonly use, based on a normal subscription price of $18 for 12 issues, or $1.50 per issue. There are variations on these strategies, but these four are the basic ones you will find in wide use.

The simplest strategy is to charge one price for every customer. But you could also offer a discount for new readers, gradually raising the price as they stick with you. This second plan encourages lots of new orders and then weeds out people who don't have a long-term interest. Alternatively, you could charge new readers the highest prices—and then give a break when people loyally come back for a renewal.

Common Subscription Pricing Strategies			
Strategy	**New Orders**	**Conversions**	**Renewals**
Keep It Simple	$18	$18	$18
Introductory	$12	$18	$18
Stepping-Up	$9	$12	$18
Rewarding Loyalty	$18	$15	$14

Source: The newsletter *Subscription Marketing*

Let's look at Anne's circulation plans for *Cruises Update* to demonstrate the stepping-up strategy. Anne obviously hopes that most subscribers will find her newsletter so useful that they will keep subscribing even though the price creeps up. She decides to closely monitor conversions and renewals to see what actually happens. If a large number of subscribers drop off when prices increase, then she'll switch to a different pricing strategy.

Anne has already decided to charge a regular subscription price of $4 per issue, $48 per year for 12 issues of *Cruises Update*. Using the stepping-up strategy, her prices are as follows.

- Retail price: $4/issue and $48/year. This price is actually printed on the *Cruises Update* masthead.

- Introductory price: $2/issue and $24/year. Anne's direct mail campaign, website, and display ads offer a one-year trial subscription for $24, a 50% savings from the retail price.

- Conversion price: $2.66/issue $32/year. Anne's conversion promotion offers 12 more issues for $32 to new subscribers when their introductory term expires. This price is 33% off the masthead price.

- Renewal price: $3.60/issue $43/year. After a subscriber has converted to the $32 price, Anne offers to extend that subscription for another year for $43.

At this stage, Anne's promotion letters emphasize the newsletter's value rather than price. The renewal price is only about 10% less than the retail price.

A subscriber who accepts each of Anne's offers will pay a total of $185 for *Cruises Update* over five years, or an average of $37 per year.

Just like every other aspect of your subscription plan, how you will sell conversions and renewals will depend very much on your specific circumstances, especially your expectations for how long your best subscribers can be expected to keep subscribing. Some publishers send out a dozen renewal letters and get positive responses, even to the twelfth letter. Other publishers quit after sending only one or two renewal letters because they've learned that a third letter won't sell enough additional renewals to cover the expense of mailing it. It depends on the audience, the nature of the publication, and to some degree, on how the subscribers signed up in the first place.

A circulation problem has no single solution suitable for every publishing situation. But there are some general rules about selling conversions and renewals that will be of great help no matter what type of publication you plan.

Start Early

Many publishers start trying to convert an introductory order into a longer-term subscription with their very first billing letter, which typically arrives after the reader has received one or two issues on a "trial" basis at a very low introductory price. By simply offering to extend the introductory price for a longer term (from 18 to 52 weeks, for example) in the billing letter, the publisher can often accomplish an important step—converting that new reader from a trial reader to a full-fledged subscriber. This tactic is called "renewal at birth" and it has many advantages. All you do is offer to extend the subscription term in the first bill you send people or on the original order form.

Promote Your Good Qualities

Some publishers treat conversion or renewal notices like bills: "Your subscription's expiring, please renew." But you can usually be more effective if you remind your readers why they made a good choice to read your publication in the first place and tell them how they can continue to gain from reading it in the future. One good approach is to include testimonials—for instance, anecdotes about problems readers solved by relying on information your publication has provided.

Use Email

Email has become a very popular way to sell renewals because it is so cheap and convenient. There are no printing or postage costs, and many people prefer email for tasks like publication renewals. Remember to collect subscriber email addresses whenever possible so that you can handle at least some of your renewals in this way.

Be Persistent

Always remember there is plenty of competition for your readers' attention (and their discretionary income), and they have many other important relationships to deal with besides the one with you. It follows that many subscribers, even those who want to keep reading your publication, won't renew their subscriptions without a lot of prompting. That's why publishers sometimes approach each reader six or nine or even 12 times before finally taking them off the active subscription file. Although this may seem costly, it's really not when you compare the higher cost of getting a new subscriber.

Vary Your Messages

Different readers have different reasons for appreciating your publication, so your subscribers won't respond the same way when you ask them to keep reading. You have to try several different approaches and keep fine-tuning them until you find the most successful ones. For example, some people always wait until the last minute before renewing a subscription, even on their favorite publications, on the theory that there is no need to pay until the subscription really has expired. To persuade them to renew quickly, you may need to offer a discount or a slightly longer subscription for the regular price. Other subscribers who don't want to miss an issue are so glad to get the renewal chore out of the way that they will jump at your first renewal notice. Gift subscriptions are unique: Publishers usually send renewal promotions to both giver and receiver.

Pay Attention to Details

How you behave toward your readers is as important as what you say to them. The last thing you want to do is annoy them. For example, as soon as they respond to a renewal or conversion request, make sure you quit asking them to renew. No one respects a periodical that continues to bug people who have already renewed. Other potential bugaboos include setting deadlines a reader can't possibly meet to qualify for a discount or gift, or asking for intrusive information or information you already have (or should have) in your files.

Many publishers now offer online renewals and other customer service tasks such as address changes. As this becomes even more the norm, you may have to offer it too to keep pace with industry standards. This is a good reason to keep up with other publishers' customer service systems.

EXAMPLE: Anne's conversion program for *Cruises Update* includes three letters. The first one is mailed with the bill that new subscribers receive soon after they get their first issue. This letter offers to add on a second year for the same introductory price of $24. The letter also goes out by email halfway through the one-year trial subscription period making the same offer. The final letter is mailed with the last of the 12 trial issues and it emphasizes that it is the reader's last chance to buy additional issues at the discounted price. Anne hopes to convert 60% of the trial subscribers to a second one-year subscription.

Anne's renewal program includes five letters and emails, the first being mailed about five months before a subscription will expire and the last two months past its expiration date. She plans to use the same renewal letters as long as they continue to produce results. She hopes to achieve an average renewal rate of about 80% every year.

Estimating Subscription Revenues

Now that you are armed with the marketing plan you developed in the last chapter and a pricing strategy for new orders, conversions, and renewals, you can start to estimate subscription revenues. Be cautious: It's easy to overestimate revenues. For example, conversion rates can be as low as 15% and as high as 75%, depending on many factors, including who ordered the original subscription, how much they liked your publication, and how much they really need the information you provide. Even an experienced circulation person can't always predict what will happen in a new market with an untested publication. Their guesses might be somewhat better than yours, but only because their experience has taught them that finding and keeping subscribers is not easy.

The rule about subscription budgeting is to hope for the best but plan for the worst. But many new publishers are doggedly optimistic. For example, Anne asked her circulation consultant, Joanna, to help develop revenue assumptions, but then fought against Joanna's cautious recommendations. Anne estimated that she would get a 6% overall response from her first direct mail campaign, reasoning that she was tapping into a large universe of highly motivated readers with a product she felt they truly needed. Joanna pointed out that to be safe, Anne should plan on about 3%. Joanna also pointed out that over time, as Anne began to saturate her market, the response rate would likely drop below 2%, since she would have already found the most motivated readers in her universe.

Joanna also recommended making conservative estimates as to the number of new orders Anne would get from her website, ads, trade shows, and publicity campaigns. The two women reached some compromises, and finally agreed on some estimates for new orders of *Cruises Update*, as illustrated below.

Assumptions About New Orders for *Cruises Update*			
Source	Number of Orders	$ per Order	Total Revenue
Direct Mail (from the first 100,000 mailing)	3,200	$24	$76,800
Website sales	550	$24	$13,200
Ads	200	$24	$4,800
Trade Show	50	$24	$1,200
TOTAL	4,000	$24	$96,000

In terms of the second and third years' revenues, Anne had to predict conversion and renewal rates. Joanna suggested 50% for conversions and 60% for renewals, but Anne again insisted that those estimates were too low. After an extended conversation and argument, they agreed to use Joanna's numbers in the budget but hope for Anne's. The revenue projections that they reached for Anne's first three years of publishing are illustrated below.

Revenue Estimates for *Cruises Update*			
Subscription Income	Year 1	Year 2	Year 3
New Orders			
Number	4,000	3,500	3,000
Revenue/order	$24	$24	$24
Total new order revenue	$96,000	$84,000	$72,000
Conversions			
Number (60% of last year's new orders)	0	2,400	2,100
Revenue/order	$32	$32	$32
Total new order revenue	$0	$76,800	$67,200
Renewals			
Number (80% of last year's new orders)	0	0	1,920
Revenue/order	$43	$43	$43
Total new order revenue	$0	$76,800	$82,560
Total number of subscribers	4,000	5,900	7,020
Total subscription income	$96,000	$160,800	$221,760

Estimating Publishing Expenses

By now you should have some notion of how much income you are likely to take in during your first few years as a periodical publisher and will be ready to look at the expense side of your ledger. There are three kinds of expenses that you'll need to estimate: start-up costs, fixed operating costs, and variable operating costs.

Start-Up Costs

Start-up costs include all the one-time investments that you'll need to make before you publish your first issue. These include hiring consultants to develop your business plan, design your publication and website, or help you raise start-up money; traveling to research your market or meet prospective investors; buying computers and other equipment; and administrative and legal expenses, such as obtaining a business license, establishing your business entity (corporation, partnership, or limited liability company, for example), and checking out your trademark.

Anne budgeted $52,500 for start-up costs. She expected to spend:

• $30,000 for developing direct mail, conversion, and renewal promotion materials, and for consultants to help plan and execute her promotions

• $5,000 for editorial, design, and production consultants who would help her develop her newsletter

• $5,000 for website design and set-up fees

• $9,500 for computer and office equipment including new telephone lines and furniture (desk, files, bookcases), and

• $3,000 for administrative expenses like setting up her books with an accountant, reviewing her business agreements with a lawyer, and obtaining a trademark and a local business license. This relatively low fee is based on her decision to do much of the form-preparation work herself, using professionals in the role of advisors and coaches.

RESOURCES

A good resource for leading you through the complex maze of trademarks is *Trademark: Legal Care for Your Business & Product Name*, by Stephen R. Elias (Nolo). It discusses how to choose a distinctive mark, search for possible conflicting marks, and register the name you choose with the U.S. Patent & Trademark Office.

Fixed Costs

Fixed costs include essential staff salaries, utilities, rent, and office expenses, as well as debt repayments if you borrow money. These costs are called "fixed" because they remain the same no matter how many copies of your publication you print and distribute or how many subscriptions you sell.

Typical Fixed Costs

For most peiodicals, fixed costs will include:

- salaries and payroll taxes
- health insurance premiums
- other insurance premiums, including liability and disability
- rent, utilities, and other costs to maintain office space
- equipment rentals or leases
- debt payments
- office supplies
- fees paid to accountants, bookkeepers, or administrative consultants, and
- marketing expenses such as attending trade shows and hiring publicists.

For every publishing expense that you know about, try to pin down a reasonable cost estimate. Start with the costs that are easiest for you to estimate, like rent and utilities. Then challenge yourself to think about more. (You'll need to buy paper for the computer and fax machine, for example.) Where relevant, get help from vendors so that your estimates are as accurate as possible. For example, you can ask an insurance broker to spell out the probable costs of health, disability, and other necessary insurance policies for the number of employees that you expect to hire.

It's easy to underestimate costs. One way to reduce your risk of being overly optimistic is to check your numbers with knowledgeable people. For example, Anne asked her husband, Tim, to review her budget with her. Even though he is neither a publisher nor an accountant, Tim has some business experience. As a result, he helped her avoid one of the most common mistakes among solo operators—underestimating her own salary. Aiming to show profits as soon as possible, Anne originally decided not to pay herself a salary. Tim vigorously argued that she should plan to pay herself from day one rather than waiting for elusive profits to materialize. For one thing, Tim pointed out that the family could not live for an extended period without some income from Anne's business. For another, he argued that unless the newsletter could provide a reasonable salary for Anne in addition to the other expenses, it was not really a viable business. They talked it over at length, and finally settled on a compromise: Anne would create a budget including a salary for herself, but she would start very low, increasing it only as her business grew.

Anne was optimistic when making her fixed cost assumptions. For example, she believed she could control her expenses so well that they wouldn't increase from one year to the next, apart from her own salary. That may or may not be true. A small increase in the postage rate, for example, would have a big impact on her costs. And, of course, she is vulnerable to any increases in paper prices. Publishers periodically suffer when cyclical paper shortages quickly drive paper prices way up. In short, Anne might have been smarter to be more conservative and build some price increases into her budget.

Anne, like most new publishers, has also probably completely overlooked some expenses. It probably would not be a big deal if she left out a few small items, because she was careful enough that there wouldn't be any huge surprises. And, of course, she kept track of her actual expenses so that she could change her plans if something significant came along.

When Joanna reviewed Anne's numbers, she was satisfied that Anne had done a conscientious job. Nevertheless, her long experience in the publishing business caused her to recommend that Anne add a "fudge factor" to her overhead expense estimates—a few thousand dollars per year that would be available if needed to cover unbudgeted expenses.

Here are Anne's overhead expense estimates for her first three years. Notice how start-up marketing costs are figured in Anne's budget. Anne wants to recapture the $52,500 she spent on start-up costs over five years, so she divided that amount by five and charged $10,500 to each of the first five years.

Estimated Fixed Costs for *Cruises Update*			
	Year 1	Year 2	Year 3
Overhead Expenses			
Anne's salary	$20,000	$35,000	$45,000
Editorial freelancers	$12,000	$12,000	$12,000
Fixed marketing costs	$3,500	$3,500	$3,500
Office expenses	$9,000	$9,000	$9,000
Fudge factor	$1,500	$1,500	$1,500
Total overhead costs	$46,000	$61,000	$71,000
Start-up marketing costs	$10,500	$10,500	$10,500
Total fixed costs	$56,500	$71,500	$81,500

Variable Expenses

Variable expenses are the ones that rise and fall if you add or subtract subscribers. Most publishers include postage, printing, paper, and fulfillment—all of which are costs associated with delivering a year's worth of issues to readers. Anne, for instance, after talking to many printers and mailing services, estimated that it would cost $6 per subscriber per year to print and mail 12 issues of her newsletter.

Typical Variable Expenses

For most periodicals, variable expenses will include:

- printing charges
- paper
- postage and distribution costs
- fulfillment: mailing labels and letter shop services
- selling costs such as commissions
- promotion costs such as printing renewal or direct mail materials, and
- renting mailing lists.

If you have trouble calculating your production costs, here's a trick: Find a publication that looks similar to the one you want to publish and ask two or three printers to estimate how much it costs to print and mail that publication. Most printers can tell you exactly what the printing costs are, and they can also give you tips about how to spend more or less on the same kind of publication, for example, by choosing a different paper.

Publishers also treat sales expenses as a variable cost. This helps them to understand how much they spend to obtain each subscription. To make this calculation, they add up the total costs of the promotion and divide by the number of orders it produced. Anne divided her variable sales expenses into two categories: promotion costs for new orders, and promotion costs for conversions and renewals. Anne's variable sales expenses for new orders included printing promotion letters, renting mailing lists, plus postage and handling for her direct mail campaign. The total for a mailing of 100,000 letters came to $38,000. If the mailing generated 3,200 new subscriptions as Anne predicted, then each new subscriber would cost $11.88 in variable selling expenses.

Anne's variable promotion costs were much lower for renewals and conversions, since she didn't have to buy lists and mail to many thousands of people who would never subscribe. In addition, since her conversion and reward packages were much simpler—just a letter and an order form, or in some cases, just an email—she would spend far less on printing. In fact, she planned to spend only about $2.25 on an average of three letters to sell each conversion or renewal order. Of course, fulfillment costs for conversions and renewals would be the same as for new orders.

Anne's total variable costs are summarized below.

Variable Cost Estimates for *Cruises Update*	
Type of Order	**Amount**
New Orders	
Selling Costs	$11.88
Fulfillment Costs	$6.00
Total Per Order	$17.88
Conversions & Renewals	
Selling Costs	$2.25
Fulfillment Costs	$6.00
Total Per Order	$8.25

Using Break-Even Analysis

Now that you have guesstimated your revenues and expenses, you are in a much better position to answer the fundamental question: Can this publication produce any profits? Or to ask the same question in a different way: Can I recruit the number of subscribers it will take to achieve solid profitability? To actually answer these questions, use break-even analysis.

Fortunately, once you've estimated your revenues and expenses, break-even analysis is a relatively simple task. Here are your next steps:

1. Look at the revenue you will get from each subscriber.

2. Subtract your variable expenses for every subscriber.

3. The resulting number tells you how much every subscriber contributes toward your overhead costs. In accounting jargon, it's called the net overhead contribution per subscriber.

4. Divide your total overhead expense number by the net overhead contribution per subscriber.

5. You now know how many subscribers you need so that your revenues and expenses will balance. In short, you know how many subscribers you need to break even.

Anne's break-even numbers for *Cruises Update* are noted in this chart.

Break-Even Analysis for *Cruises Update*						
	Year 1	Year 2	Year 3	Year 4	Year 5	Average
Revenue per subscriber	$24.00	$32.00	$43.00	$43.00	$43.00	$37.00
Variable costs per subscriber	($17.88)	($8.25)	($8.25)	($8.25)	($8.25)	($10.18)
Net contribution per subscriber	$6.12	$23.75	$34.75	$34.75	$34.75	$26.82
Overhead Expenses						
Anne's salary	$20,000	$35,000	$45,000	$55,000	$65,000	$44,000
Editorial freelancers	$12,000	$12,000	$12,000	$12,000	$12,000	$12,000
Fixed marketing costs	$3,500	$3,500	$3,500	$3,500	$3,500	$3,500
Office expenses	$9,000	$9,000	$9,000	$9,000	$9,000	$9,000
Fudge factor	$1,500	$1,500	$1,500	$1,500	$1,500	$1,500
Total overhead expenses	$46,000	$61,000	$71,000	$81,000	$91,000	$70,000
Start-up marketing costs	$10,500	$10,500	$10,500	$10,500	$10,500	$10,500
Break-even number of subscribers	9,232	3,011	2,345	2,633	2,921	4,028

As you can see, Anne's break-even analysis covers a five-year period because her expense and revenue figures change significantly from year to year as her business develops. If you look at the break-even number of subscribers, you'll see Anne needs an average of 4,028 subscribers per year, each paying an average of $26.82 per year, to break even.

Two critical pieces of new information can be gleaned from Anne's break-even analysis: *Cruises Update*'s net contribution per subscriber, and the number of subscribers *Cruises Update* needs to break even.

Net Contribution Per Subscriber

Note that Anne has a good business profile with which to achieve profitability relatively quickly. That is, she has a good product in a strong market with no competition and an audience that is relatively easy to find. Many new publishers will not have all these advantages and therefore will take longer to get enough subscribers to make a profit. Some, of course, never will.

For some publications, the net contribution per subscriber is always a negative number: The publisher profits by relying on other revenue sources, usually advertisers. However, many small magazines and most newsletters depend primarily on subscription income for their profits. Recognizing this, most new publishers should strive to come up with a marketing plan that shows a positive net contribution from each new subscription. Otherwise, the publication has little chance of ever making a profit.

You can see that for *Cruises Update*, the net contribution per subscriber starts at $6 and jumps to nearly $24 and finally to almost $35 where it levels off. That pattern is very typical of a newsletter that depends on subscribers for all its income and relies on direct mail for new business. If your publication can find subscribers using a cheaper method or if it follows a different pricing strategy, you may see a more level pattern.

Subscribers Needed to Break Even

If your break-even number is too high, you can obviously bankrupt yourself trying to reach it. Look at Anne's situation. Since her first-year subscribers contribute only $6.12 towards her overhead, Anne would need to sign up over 9,200 people to break even. Since her variable costs are $17.88, this means she would need to spend over $165,000 to have a shot at breaking even that year. Anne doesn't have that much money.

But if Anne can sell just 4,000 paid subscriptions in the first year, and maintain that many throughout the whole five-year period, she'll be profitable in year three. Even better, she'll recapture all of her early losses by the end of the fifth year. After that, she can make a good living by holding steady at 4,000, although of course she'll do far better if she adds more subscribers or captures more revenue per subscriber by developing ancillary products. (See Chapter 6.)

Can *Cruises Update* cross the 4,000 subscriber threshold? On the basis of her audience research, Anne is confident that it can. There are more than 50,000 travel agencies in the U.S. and 17,000 cruise company executives, tour packagers, and cruise organizers, all of whom are relatively easy to reach by direct mail. That puts nearly 60,000 in the center of Anne's target. When she includes people who take at least one cruise every year and other avid travelers, Anne finds that her universe of prospective readers numbers well over 175,000 people. She also has learned that two other specialized travel-industry publications with similar potential audiences have over 30,000 subscribers apiece. Granted, her subject is more specialized than theirs and will probably appeal to only a quarter or a third as many readers. But still, this is good news since it tells her that people who are very involved with travel will purchase helpful periodicals.

Every publishing situation isn't as straightforward as Anne's. You'll need to take a hard skeptical look at your own circumstances. If you do a break-even analysis that indicates your business may not be profitable, maybe you need to significantly revise your overall publishing plans. Consider raising your prices or adding extra products, especially if your audience is highly motivated and has enough money to pay for what you offer. For example, to raise more money Anne might consider offering to fax or email her newsletter for a premium subscription price. Her direct costs would be about the same, but her net income from those subscriptions would be higher. And a dedicated core of her readers (perhaps 20% or so) might be glad to take advantage of the offer. Another possible revenue option is for Anne to sell advertising. (See Chapter 5.)

WARNING

Beware of changing a poor projection. It can be tempting to make a poor projection look better by lowering your overhead estimates or pumping up your projected income. Without a compelling reason to do so, this is a sure recipe for disaster. If you do a break-even analysis that looks bad, you have to consider that your publishing idea is somehow broken and look to see if you can fix it. Go back to your key strategic choices: frequency, distribution, pricing, and design. You may have to significantly change one or more.

Making a Budget

Now that you know how many subscribers you will need to break even, the last question you have to answer is: How many subscribers do you want to have? Consider Anne's situation: Anne needs only 4,000 subscribers to break even, but if she wants to have any profits, she should sell more. If we asked Anne how many subscribers she'd like to have, she'd probably say, "As many as possible!" But, like every publisher, Anne's options are limited by two factors: her pocketbook and her marketing prospects.

Before you can make a reasonable budget for your business, you need to consider these last two factors: What can you afford to spend to expand your circulation? And what can you hope to accomplish given the size of your audience and your competitors?

As you work your way through these two issues, remember this: Every budget number is flexible. You'll probably make lots of changes as you try to bring the whole picture into balance. Expect to try several different budgets until you find the one that works best.

Consider Your Prospects

If you plan to sell advertising, your circulation goals will be based on what your future advertisers will expect, plus your own anticipated revenues from advertising sales. For example, most computer magazines need to have well over 300,000 paid readers before advertisers in that market will take them seriously. Advertising pricing is discussed in detail in Chapter 5, but for now it's important to note that advertising rates are based on readership. In some markets, advertisers pay seven to ten cents per reader for their ads. Before you decide how many subscriptions you want to have, you must look at the other publications in your market and consider any advertising income you may get by adding new readers. Your advertising sales prospects may significantly influence your subscription sales goals.

Even if you don't care about advertisers' expectations, your growth potential can be limited by your market. Some markets don't have very many prospective readers, period. The medical profession is a good example: There are only so many heart surgeons, oncologists, and obstetricians, and their numbers are not growing very quickly. If you target a slow-growing group, then your publication must be able to function profitably with a relatively small number of subscribers. You'll have to find a way to keep expenses in line with your revenue expectations.

Get to know your market well to determine a reasonable circulation goal for your publication. How quickly are people getting interested and how long are they staying active? How and why are they leaving? How many people are out there at any given moment? And what percentage of them is likely to read a publication like yours? You will find it very hard to grow fast in some markets.

Consider Your Pocketbook

Most new publishers don't have enough cash to acquire as many subscribers as they would like as fast as they would like to get them, especially if they depend on direct mail. As you should now realize, it's not only expensive to get direct mail subscribers, but because introductory subscription rates are often steeply discounted, it can take a long time to make a buck on each new subscriber. Even if you eventually make money on your mailings (and some of them are sure to be miserable failures), you'll probably have to wait a while before you can afford to do another one. In short, many new publishers grow slowly because their available cash limits how fast they can reach their markets. Some publishers borrow money, but many resist it because they don't like taking on lots of debt or selling a share of their publication to investors.

Some publishers scrimp on their circulation and wind up losing the whole business because a competitor comes along and pushes them out of the market. There's a real danger to being too careful.

A Sample Circulation Budget

As Anne makes her budget for *Cruises Update*, she really begins to see how the leaking bucket dynamic of any publishing operation will affect her business. Even with her optimistic assumption that 60% of her first year's subscribers will stick with her for a second year, she'll have to replace the 40% who leave. This means if she starts with 4,000 subscribers in the first year, she'll need to get 1,600 new orders in the second year to maintain 4,000 total subscriptions. And of course the bucket will continue to leak subscribers in each succeeding year, although Anne hopes it will leak more slowly. In the third year, Anne assumes she will keep 60% of the new people from the second year, and 80% of the ones still on board from the first year, so she only needs to get 1,120 new orders to keep a constant 4,000.

So much for a quick review of Anne's circulation assumptions. The question is, should Anne try to keep a constant 4,000 subscribers? If she does, her dependence on direct mail will diminish every year. But, as we learned earlier, while 4,000 subscribers is enough to put Anne's operation in the black, her profits will be modest. And there is always the risk that another publisher might come along with a similar product and a more aggressive marketing strategy and steal her existing customers.

After trying out several different budgets, Anne decides to try to maintain about 6,400 subscribers in her subscriber bucket. That's enough to guarantee a good level of profits once she gets beyond the start-up period, but not so many that the cost of acquiring additional subscribers eats up too much of her profits.

To achieve this goal Anne will try to sign up 4,000 subscribers the first year and reach for 5,900 the next. If she reaches 7,500 subscribers by the end of the five years, her average for the period will be 6,390. Again, trying to grow faster than that would cost so much for direct mail that it would be beyond both her tolerance for risk and her ability to raise start-up money. And as noted, growing more slowly would leave her too vulnerable to competitors. Here is Anne's final budget for *Cruises Update*.

Cruises Update Profit and Loss Budget for Five Years						
Subscription Income	Year 1	Year 2	Year 3	Year 4	Year 5	Average
New Orders						
Number	4,000	3,500	3,000	2,500	2,000	3,000
Revenue per order	$24.00	$24.00	$24.00	$24.00	$24.00	$24.00
Total New Order Revenue	$96,000	$84,000	$72,000	$60,000	$48,000	$72,000
Conversions (60% of last year's new orders):						
Number	0	2,400	2,100	1,800	1,500	1,560
Revenue per order	$32.00	$32.00	$32.00	$32.00	$32.00	$32.00
Total Conversion Revenue	$0	$76,800	$67,200	$57,600	$48,000	$49,920
Renewals (80% of last year's conversions and renewals):						
Number	0	0	1,920	3,216	4,013	1,830
Revenue per order	$43.00	$43.00	$43.00	$43.00	$43.00	$43.00
Total Renewal Revenue	$0	$0	$82,560	$138,288	$172,559	$78,680
TOTAL Number of Subscribers	4,000	5,900	7,020	7,516	7,513	6,390
TOTAL Subscription Income	$96,000	$160,800	$221,760	$255,888	$268,559	$200,600

Expenses						
Variable Expenses per Subscriber						
New orders ($17.88)	($71,520)	($62,580)	($53,640)	($44,700)	($35,760)	($53,640)
Conversions & Renewals ($8.25)	$0	($19,800)	($33,165)	($41,382)	($45,481)	($27,966)
TOTAL Variable Expenses	($71,520)	($82,380)	($86,805)	($86,082)	($81,241)	($81,606)
TOTAL Overhead Expenses	($56,500)	($71,500)	($81,500)	($91,500)	($101,500)	($80,500)
TOTAL Expenses	($128,020)	($153,880)	($168,305)	($177,582)	($182,741)	($162,106)
NET PROFITS	($32,020)	$6,920	$53,455	$78,306	$85,818	$38,494

An experienced publisher might argue some with some aspects of Anne's budget, in part because her assumptions are so optimistic. As noted earlier, she has given herself every possible break—high response rates on new orders, conversions, and renewals, and expenses that don't creep up very much from one year to the next. And she has probably overlooked some costs altogether.

However, most publishing pros would probably agree that Anne's simple budget is a pretty good one. Lots of people only budget one year at a time, but Anne's budget looks at five years. Looking at a five-year period and separating her subscribers into three different groups shows how her readers are likely to come and go. It's a dynamic budget with a long-range viewpoint.

The budget is a tool that will help Anne remain in touch with the lifeblood of her business: subscriptions. For example, if her conversion rate falls below her expectations, Anne will be able to see the long-term effects well in advance, so that she can adapt her plans before running into serious trouble. In that situation, she might change to a different pricing strategy, increase the size of her next direct mail campaign, add extra conversion promotions, or even try all three. For another example, if her direct mail response rate for new orders falls below 3%, increasing her variable costs from $17.88 to some higher number, she may need to plan for less growth altogether. Maybe she's reached a saturation point and she should not keep investing in direct mail.

Key Budgeting Variables

If you decide to model your budget more or less on Anne's, pay close attention to the following areas where your projections are most likely to be wrong. Or put another way, any negative changes in these variables will quickly raise serious problems for you. So make sure your accounting systems and subscription processing software will give you all of this information regularly and in detail. (Financial reports and bookkeeping systems are discussed in Chapter 8.)

- *Direct mail response rates*. The percentage of people who respond positively to your direct mail solicitation will obviously have a huge influence on your cost of acquiring each new subscriber. It's common for response rates to fall over time as you mail to less-likely prospects. At some point, most niche publishers find that their circulation has grown as much as their market will allow. As soon as you experience a significant drop in the percentage of new direct mail orders, be warned that you may be reaching the limits of what direct mail can achieve. At this point you should either look for alternative sources of new orders, or retreat to a plan based on growing more slowly.

- *Pay-up rate*. Publishers sometimes ask for payment up front on new subscription orders. But when their order card says "bill me," it obviously takes an extra step to complete a new order. The pay-up rate is industry-speak for the percentage of new people who finally pay for their subscriptions after you've started fulfilling their orders. If this rate is below 50%, you may be wasting money getting the wrong people to order or getting people to order for the wrong reasons. You might want to switch to a different offer on new orders.

- *Conversion rate*. As discussed, this means the number of people who renew after their introductory offer expires. You will almost surely experience a range of conversion rates depending on the source of the original orders. For example, direct mail subscribers are likely to convert at a lower rate than someone who buys an issue on a newsstand and then sends in one of the subscription cards from inside the newsstand issue. Your circulation manager (or fulfillment software) should be able to report the rate for each subscriber by source, not just the average for all of them. That way, you can fine-tune whom you decide to approach in the first place, and structure your marketing plans so that you focus on subscribers who consistently convert at a higher rate.

- *Renewal rate*. If the percentage of your readers who renew is higher than 60%, it indicates that your publication is really meeting its editorial objectives. However, if it begins to drop off it may mean there is a problem either in the kind of information you're providing or the way you communicate it. Obviously your renewal rate will have a high impact on your financial situation, which is why you'll want to establish a good system to track it closely.

• *Variable expenses per subscriber.* Any change in the amount of money you spend to find and provide your publication to a subscriber will immediately impact your overall financial picture. If postal rates increase, for example, you will need to have more subscribers to break even because each one of them will contribute less toward your overhead expenses. Many publishers pass along variable cost increases to subscribers by raising their prices, but sometimes this isn't possible. Then the publisher has to cut back on expenses, find more subscribers to support the business, or look for additional revenue sources.

• *Overhead.* Many publishers focus on overhead when they are creating a budget. Since overhead is usually such a big piece of the total picture, this makes sense. (If you look back at Anne's budget, for example, you see she will spend almost as much on overhead as she spends on variable expenses every year.) But it is a mistake for a publisher to over-focus on overhead, ignoring, for example, subscription sales, which are ultimately what will be most important to the success or failure of the business. If your direct mail response rate or your conversion rate is too low, your business will fail, no matter how little you spend on rent or computers. You may be able to compensate a bit by cutting overhead, but doing so ignores far more important underlying issues. In fact, it is probably better to pay attention to your real problem by revising your promotion package or your subscription prices, redesigning your newsletter, or adding more desirable content. (For more about how to get out of trouble, see Chapter 13.) In the meantime, just remember: While it's always wise to keep your overhead as low as possible, it's essential to keep your eye on your subscription marketing program, which, after all, is what drives your whole operation. ●

Building Your Advertising Business

This chapter describes how to build a solid advertising sales business from the ground up. First, it looks at how to build a comprehensive ad sales program, which usually involves three stages:

1. crafting an overall strategy

2. putting together a strong marketing message, and

3. building the essential one-to-one relationship with each advertiser.

Through these three tasks, the chapter will look at all of the basic tools publishers use to manage their ad-sales business, from media kits to sales commission plans. It will also cover how best to create these tools for your publication. Finally, it will help you look at the benefits all parties—publishers, readers, and advertisers—get from a well-thought-out advertising program. Some publishers are surprised to realize that successful advertising yields more than just profits.

You can develop your advertising marketing strategy using many of the same broad concepts you used to sell subscriptions, since your goals are very much the same:

- to find the best customers and form a mutually rewarding bond that lasts as long as possible

- to develop a plan to replace advertisers who will inevitably drop out, and

- to continually develop new products and services that you can profitably sell to existing advertisers.

The big difference between subscribers and advertisers, of course, is that advertisers spend a lot more money. It follows that because an advertiser is worth many thousands of dollars to your business over time, you will give each one much more attention than you give to individual subscribers.

TIP

Borrow good ideas from more experienced publishers. A media kit is a publisher's basic ad sales tool (see "The Media Kit: A Guide," below). Each one reveals the fundamental publishing strategy driving the publication, from its editorial mission to its pricing and competitive positioning strategies. As you work out your own sales strategy, collect and study the media kits of established publishers. Many media kits are now accessible online or available upon email request, so be sure to check magazine websites when looking for media kits.

The Media Kit: A Guide

A media kit is a package of sales literature that publishers present to their advertisers and advertising prospects. The kit is usually created by or under the supervision of the marketing director and delivered to individual advertisers by salespeople. It should contain all of the information an advertiser normally needs to decide whether or not to buy ad space, how much space to buy, and how to meet a publisher's production specifications for printing ads. Here are the common elements of a good media kit:

- RATE CARD. The rate card summarizes a publisher's prices for ads of different sizes, colors, and positions in the magazine. It indicates the discounts a publisher will give to advertisers who buy ad space in advance or who agree to advertise regularly. The rate card also commonly includes the publisher's credit policy and other terms and conditions under which ads are accepted.
- CIRCULATION STATEMENT. Publishers must document how many readers they have and how their publication is distributed. A typical circulation statement will show the number of paid subscriptions, single copies and newsstand copies sold, and a geographic breakdown of the audience.
- EDITORIAL MISSION STATEMENT. This is a publisher's brief explanation of what his or her publication does for its readers. (See Chapter 2 for several examples.)

- EDITORIAL CALENDAR. Publishers try to tell advertisers in advance about topics that will be covered in future issues. In addition to helping advertisers decide when to advertise specific products, the calendar illustrates the publication's editorial mission.
- READER PROFILE STUDY. Many publishers regularly survey their readers to learn more about their reading habits and preferences. The studies also probe basic attributes like age, income, occupation, and education. These studies help advertisers match a publication's audience with their own target customers.
- MECHANICAL REQUIREMENTS FOR ADS. Prepared by the periodical's production department, this information describes the measurements of ads and all other production guidelines, including deadlines for each issue.
- MARKET ANALYSIS. Publishers often include information about the growth and development of their market in the media kit. Here, the publisher presents any relevant information about consumers in his or her niche, recent technical developments that impact the field, and overall market trends. For example, an Internet magazine would try to help advertisers understand how the Internet is developing, who is using it, and so forth.
- PUBLISHER'S CONTACTS. This information tells an advertiser how to reach the appropriate salespeople, editors, and other staff at the publication.

Creating Advertising Relationships

There are three steps necessary to build a profitable relationship with advertisers: creating a publishing strategy, describing the publication's market position properly, and convincing individual people to buy advertising space. In larger companies, the work is divided among the publisher, the marketing director, and the salespeople. But sometimes one person handles all three jobs, especially in smaller companies. Whether it's one person or three, the jobs break down roughly as described below.

Creating a Publishing Strategy (The Publisher's Job)

Just as editors have to know their readers' tastes, publishers have to know their advertisers well enough to define a workable relationship with them. For a new publication, this normally involves research into your market, your competitors, and your advertising prospects. Your campaign to sell ads will fail unless you can accurately and honestly determine who really should be advertising in your periodical. This, in turn, means figuring out what prospective advertisers are trying to accomplish, and how your publication can help them accomplish it. And often it also means establishing why you can do the job better than your competitors.

Developing a Marketing Plan (The Marketing Director's Job)

Marketing people take the publisher's broadly defined strategy and fill in the details. They develop information that explains what the publication offers in language that is meaningful to advertisers. This requires listening to advertisers' needs and wants, and crafting a message that speaks to them. Doing this well is extremely important, because when the marketing wing fails to effectively communicate with advertisers, the advertisers are left on their own to decide whether your publication can help them. A few may conclude that advertising in your publication will be profitable for them, but most won't even take the time to consider it.

Some of your marketing can be offloaded to online advertising networks, which will do the bulk of the selling on your behalf. Most of them pay 60% to 75% of the revenues back to publishers. They should be included in every marketing plan. (You'll find a list of these networks in Chapter 14.)

Tailoring the Message (The Salesperson's Job)

Advertising salespeople personalize your relationship with each advertiser. They tailor your broad advertising program and marketing services into customized packages designed to meet each client's specific needs. The best salespeople are good relationship builders: They listen well, empathize with other people, advocate for them, and help them solve problems. You'll need to find personable salespeople, arm them with appropriate marketing tools, and put them to work using their skills to build a lasting advertising business, one advertiser at a time.

Three Kinds of Advertisers

Focus on the niche and mail order advertisers who commonly support start-up publications (described below), and build your strategy around converting most of them to long-term customers.

Local and national advertisers fall into three basic categories. Most publications and websites concentrate on two of the three, but not all of them. *PC* magazine, for example, has never been able to capture any branding ads, even with a million readers of every issue, but carries lots of endemic and mail order ads, both in print and online.

- **Endemic or niche advertisers** promote products aligned with the editorial focus and audience behavior—meditation cushions for a Buddhist magazine, for example, or the local pub for a college newspaper. These niche advertisers come in large and small sizes, and you should make room for all of them: classified print ads and cheap Web listings for the little ones; and for the big ones, bundles of ad products that include a mix of full-page print ads, sponsored content on your website, plus some banner ads.

- **Direct sales or mail order advertisers** sell products directly to consumers via a website or toll-free phone call. These advertisers select media strictly on a cost-per-order basis. Check the back of any computer magazine and you'll see the mail order dealers advertising there. Every niche magazine and website has its equivalent. Nearly all of the companies advertising through online search or banner ad networks, such as the Google AdSense network, are direct sales companies. They want your site visitors to click through from the ads at your site to a shopping cart on theirs. If the content on your site is conducive to this kind of shopping, these advertisers will provide significant financial support.

- **Generic or branding advertisers** sell mass-market consumer products such as cars and credit cards. These advertisers aim to reach the largest possible audience at the lowest possible price. It is nearly impossible for any niche publication to compete effectively against the mass-market consumer magazines, websites, and radio and TV programs that capture 98% of all branding ad dollars.

As noted, in a tiny company, one or two people may have to do all of these tasks rather than a whole team of people. But even if you plan to do all the work by yourself, it is important to look at each task separately to see how they fit together. The rest of this chapter will cover in detail each of these aspects of building a successful advertising business.

The Publisher's Job: Strategy

Chapter 3 introduced the leaking bucket and bull's-eye analogies to understand how publishers create subscription marketing strategies. These analogies are also useful in creating an advertising marketing strategy. For a profitable advertising business, you'll need to keep a certain number of advertisers in your bucket. Study the broad market in your field so that you understand those prospective advertisers. Just as you need enough prospective readers to make a subscription business viable, don't expect your publication to be profitable unless and until you have identified enough potential advertisers to support it.

Like readers, advertisers are not all alike. Establish criteria to define who your best potential advertisers are and then learn as much as you can about them. Create and position your product as best you can to win advertisers' loyalty and keep them happy for a long time.

As a publisher, start building your overall strategy by asking yourself the following questions:

- Are there enough advertising dollars spent in my market—or likely to be spent in the near future—to support my publication?

- Within my niche, which companies will have the greatest need for my publication and how much support can I expect from them?

- How much competition for these ad dollars is my publication likely to face now or in the near future? What spot should I claim among competitors and advertisers?

• How can my publication's prices support the competitive position I choose?

Each of these issues is discussed in detail below.

Finding a Growing Market

It's hard to start a new publication in a no-growth or mature field, since existing publications probably have already captured most advertising dollars. But if you can spot an emerging or fast-growing market, it's much easier to start a publication that can grab some of the new advertising dollars.

When considering whether to launch a new periodical, some publishers approach the growth question by looking at advertisers rather than at the market. They track every company that currently advertises in a market and then forecast how much each advertiser's spending is likely to increase.

The trouble with this approach is that it misses new or changing markets. A better way to predict whether a periodical has the opportunity to round up enough advertising dollars is to look for events such as social, political, or technological changes that can cause new markets to emerge and often grow explosively. When new technologies become available, for instance, there is generally a net increase in advertising spending —even in relatively mature industries—as companies try to persuade customers to embrace new habits. For example, when low-cost video cassette recorders brought feature movies from theaters to our homes, the net effect was an increase in movie industry marketing budgets, which allowed several new film magazines to thrive.

Here's another example of an advertising market created by a significant social change. *Home Education Magazine* (www.homeedmag. com) and *Practical Homeschooling* (www.home-school.com) both speak to the growing community of parents who use the Web and other new technologies to teach their kids at home. These publications help advertisers reach an audience that never existed before in such large numbers. And they seem to understand both what the home schooling families want to know, and why advertisers want to reach them. Both print magazines also have rich and robust websites.

If you think you have found a growing market, don't get too excited until you investigate further. Follow the lead of many established publishers and interview prospective advertisers before you commit to your publication's launch. The idea, of course, is to see if these companies really are developing products or services for the audience you plan to reach. On the basis of these interviews, you may wish to fine-tune your circulation strategy so your publication will reach an audience that matches the needs of the largest possible group of advertisers. Or, you may decide to change your plans and focus on the needs of a smaller group of advertisers who want to target a specific kind of customer.

Finding the Best Advertisers

Assume that you have found a new or poorly served niche and have identified a substantial group of companies that are likely to purchase advertising. Your next task is to identify those companies that will have the greatest need for your publication. This means understanding how each of these companies—or at least, a representative sample of them—are planning to grow and how you can help them. Armed with this information, you should be able to find ways to induce them to advertise with you. Remember: Your advertising sales strategy will work only if it meets the fundamental needs of your advertisers.

This task involves researching the market, usually by talking with representatives from a number of companies and asking questions. If you are very involved in and knowledgeable about a particular market, you may be able to limit your interviews to several companies in the new field, but don't skip this step. No matter how much you think you already know, chances are you don't know enough. The more familiar you are with the needs of your potential advertisers, the better your chances of success will be. Especially in a field that is brand new, don't overlook smaller companies, since some are likely to grow into the new industry's biggest players.

What follows is a list of questions you can use to identify prime advertising prospects and, eventually, to begin building a relationship with them. Choose companies you think are the most influential in your field—the ones other companies are likely to follow. For example, when we launched *PC World* and *Macworld* magazines, we started out by interviewing the leading computer manufacturers and the major software vendors: IBM, Compaq, Dell, Apple, Microsoft, and Lotus. Here are some of the questions we asked to find out what our prime advertising prospects were thinking about the computer market:

- *Who are your customers?* You need to understand how your advertisers identify their best prospects. To do this, gather as much information as you can about each company's target customers: age, income, gender, occupation, lifestyle, interests, and activities. Then compare this information to the bull's-eye map of your target audience discussed in Chapter 3.

- *How do your customers buy products?* For example, do most get them directly from the manufacturer, or from retailers, or from mail-order dealers, or catalogues? Understanding how your advertisers' customers actually purchase their products will tell you a lot about what the advertisers hope their ads will accomplish.

- *What kind of growth do you expect your businesses to achieve?* To speak to your advertisers in their own language, you need to understand their overall business objectives and the day-to-day pressures they experience. One good way to do this is to ask about their competitive situation, as well as the strength of their market in general.

- *What products are you currently developing?* This will help you understand where they think their market is headed and how they are planning to develop new business for themselves. This is information that can also help you fine-tune your editorial plan.

- *What is the life-span of each of your products?* Industrial equipment or appliances have a relatively long life; other products, such as toys or video games, come and go very quickly. You want to understand your advertisers' time-frame for selling products, so ask how much time they need to recapture their investment from a specific product line.

- *How do you make media-buying decisions?* Here the key bit of information is whether a potential advertiser makes advertising decisions in-house or with the help of an ad agency. Obviously you need to know exactly who is involved in media buying decisions so that you know where and how you will have to deliver your own sales messages.

- *Where are you currently advertising?* You need a rough idea of how much your prospective advertisers are already spending and where, because in some cases, you'll get their advertising money into your publication only if you can take it away from other media.

We launched *PC* magazine into a market that was so new nobody knew where it would go. Although it seems obvious now, the biggest question on everybody's mind in the early 1980s was this: Will businesspeople bother to learn how to use computers on their own, or will they continue to rely on computing specialists located in centralized data-processing departments? Since, at the time, many business managers and executives didn't even know how to type, let alone how to install and manipulate word processing programs, the answer to this question was very important to us. After all, our best hope of creating a successful magazine was to understand how vendors planned to persuade people to buy their products.

To get the answers we needed, we did extensive interviews with the marketing and distribution managers at companies like IBM and Microsoft. By the time we launched our first issue in January 1982, we knew that these companies had decided to target their ads to individual business users, whom they hoped would embrace personal computers. Based on this information, we concentrated on reaching business readers and giving them a magazine that was technically complete, but friendly, easy to read, and really helpful in figuring out how to use this powerful new technology. It turned out to be a winning strategy.

Defining a Competitive Position

Assume you have identified a new or fast-changing market that you believe will produce a healthy demand among companies for new advertising opportunities. Chances are that other publishers have noticed the same publishing opportunity and that several of them are already planning to modify existing publications or create new ones to capture some of the same advertising dollars. Some of these potential competitors may even be a few months ahead of you in their planning efforts. So your next question is, what are you going to do about competitors?

The answer is that you must define a viable competitive position that you can reasonably expect to claim and defend, based on your resources and the resources of your competitors. There is generally room for several different players in every market. Typically, the most successful periodicals are able to define a publishing strategy that is different from the others in the field. Several ways to think about this are examined below.

First Place Is Too Expensive for Most Publishers

The publication with the largest circulation and broadest audience nearly always captures the largest chunk of the profits in a given market. The reason: Advertisers always put the number-one publication first on their media schedules, spending pretty much whatever is necessary to maintain a highly visible presence in that publication. When a company is launching a new product or a new advertising campaign, it will make the biggest splash in the number-one publication. And, conversely, when a company's sales start to decline, it will cut back spending in other publications, but not in the leading one.

It usually takes big money to win a first-place position in a growing market. Not only does the eventual winner have to do nearly everything right—from editorial content to circulation strategy to accounting—it usually must invest lots of money very quickly. Especially in a new, fast-growing market, advertisers that are themselves trying to cope with rapid, unpredictable growth and fierce competition will have many questions and problems. Because of this, they will tend to look for publishers with the resources to provide lots of help and reassurance. Or, put another way, most advertisers will put their ad dollars in the hands of publishers who seem the most stable, experienced, and well informed.

Specifically, this means advertisers will favor a publisher with a proven circulation record and a sophisticated marketing and selling style. Smaller publishers that have neither often find it very hard to compete. Matching the big companies' programs costs a lot of money—money that small companies simply don't have.

Assuming there are two or three big publishers trying to capture first place in a particular broad new field—a very common situation—one thing is sure: Costs for all publications in the market will go up as each large publisher tries to outspend the other. Eventually, one or more of the big companies may drop out, since they know there are plenty of other opportunities in other fields.

Your own options depend on your resources. If you don't have the resources to fight for the top spot, you will need to adopt a different strategy. Fortunately, experience has shown that growing industries often have room for a second-place and sometimes even a third-place general-interest publication. And most industries have many more specialized niches that a smart small publisher can claim, for a lot less money than it takes to become number one.

Big Companies Overlook Good Opportunities

It is not worthwhile for giants such as Hearst and Time, Inc., to maintain less-than-mass products. Recently, for example, Hearst shut down a magazine called Victoria, claiming that the shelter title wasn't generating enough ad revenue even with 950,000 paid circulation. As one Hearst executive told me: "Given our overhead and corporate expenses, we can't go out for a cup of coffee without spending $5 million." Of course, the only magazines that can hope to achieve 1 million paid copies per issue are the mass-market titles aimed at the widest possible audience. That leaves hundreds of ideas open to any entrepreneur planning to launch something with more modest goals—say, up to 500,000 circulation. If you find something smaller than the mass market, you need never fear that a corporate publisher will compete with you.

Second and Third Place Can Be Profitable

If you study any mature publishing market, you are likely to find a leader plus two, and sometimes three, publications serving the most important readers in that market. One reason why the number two and three positions in a particular publishing market are usually also fairly profitable is because many advertisers don't want to become totally dependent on only one publication to reach their customers. By spreading their ad dollars around a little, advertisers can keep the leader on its best behavior and influence it to keep ad prices at a competitive level.

Some publishing companies are happy with the second-place position in a good-sized market, reasoning that they can offer a product that is just as good as number one and take in plenty of advertising dollars, but not have to spend as much on big-name writers, promotions, and salaries as they would if they were the market leader. Incidentally, although the second-place and third-place publications will publicly position themselves relative to the number-one publication, they privately worry most about competing with each other, knowing that if a market contracts even a little bit, the publication in third place may begin to bleed red ink.

Many Competitive Positions Exist

Fortunately, in most good-sized markets, a small publisher has a chance to carve out a specialized niche. Since this strategy can be successfully accomplished with far less money than it takes to launch a broader-based publication, it's often the best choice for small players. A few of the most common "niche-within-a-market" positions publishers typically claim for themselves are described here.

Specific Consumer Groups

Pick a selected group of readers who are highly desirable from an advertiser's viewpoint. For example, parents who send their children to pricey private schools might be a more profitable submarket for a publication about parenting than public school parents. By focusing your publication on a selected group within a wider market, it's far easier and less expensive to target and reach likely readers.

Industry Suppliers or Distributors

Target industry activists such as retailers or manufacturers who need access to specialized insider information. Our model railroading publisher could launch a magazine for hobby shop owners, for example. This is the classic strategy for business or trade magazines and newsletters, which provide specialized information to a relatively small group of businesspeople for a relatively high price.

One Region or Location

Instead of trying to capture a national audience, thousands of publishers focus on a local one. Aside from the lower costs involved in reaching a smaller market, these publications often cater to advertisers—like restaurants, country inns, or shops—who don't need or want to reach a national audience. If this idea works well in your town, often you can expand into other towns, too. A good example is parenting magazines. You will find a handful of glossy parenting magazines that enjoy nationwide distribution, but if you check the neighborhood preschool lobby, you may also find a local parenting magazine. Almost every community has one. The national magazines are published by huge media companies, and they carry expensive ads from big manufacturers and nationwide chain stores like Toys'R'Us. The local publications are generally owned by a small company and they carry ads from local, mom-and-pop businesses like private schools, camps, and day care providers.

Specific Products or Services

Publishers commonly find profitable niches by focusing on very select groups of products within a larger market. For example, many crafts publishers created profitable niche publications by focusing on specific hobbies—quilting, knitting, or woodworking. Similarly, in the travel business, there are many publications that focus on specific kinds of vacations—such as cruises, wilderness adventures, train trips, and health spas, to mention just a few. Of course, applying this strategy to a new market area requires successfully identifying submarkets that are big enough and growing fast enough to support your publication.

If you know a market well, you can probably think of several possibilities. But before you commit yourself, consider the market from an advertiser's point of view: Are there advertisers who are not being served by other more general publishers? Do enough advertisers want to reach the niche on a regular basis? Are products about to come onto the market that will fuel future growth for your specialized publication?

Setting Prices

Establishing appropriate advertising prices involves learning how to use two critical sales tools: CPMs and rate cards. If you are new to the publishing business, perhaps you've never heard of either one. Here's a quick introduction.

CPM means "cost per thousand" (M being the Latin symbol for 1,000). It is a tool advertisers use to compare the price of different media. You can calculate the CPM of any media by dividing the price of the ad by the total number of people who are predicted to see or hear it. For example, a 30-second radio spot that is broadcast to 750,000 people at a cost of $7,500 has the following CPM: $7,500 / 750,000 = $10/1,000 or $10 per thousand listeners. Most print publishers follow generally accepted guidelines for measuring their readership.

A publisher's rate card lists prices for different types of ads. These can be fairly complicated documents, since publishers typically offer a wide range of prices based on an ad's size, color, location in the periodical, and the number of times it runs in a given time period. The rate card reports all of these different pricing choices so that advertisers can make their own calculations for a particular ad. (See the discussion below, "Create an Advertising Rate Card," for more on this.)

Establish Your Own CPM

If your publication has only 5,000 readers and you want to charge $600 for a full-page ad, then you're setting your CPM at $120. As you can see from the following chart, $120 is a very high CPM for some markets and very low for others. CPMs generally reflect the different values publishers and advertisers place on different audiences. Don't be afraid of setting a high CPM for your publication, just be prepared to explain your choices.

CPM Examples: One Black-and-White Page in One Issue				
Title	**Audience**	**Total Circulation**	**Ad Price**	**CPM**
TV Guide	Television viewers	9,000,000	$95,600	$11
Teen People	Teenage girls	1,450,000	$79,500	$55
Careers & Colleges	High school seniors	750,000	$34,900	$47
Family Handyman	Homeowners	1,100,000	$57,300	$52
American Way	Airline passengers	344,000	$20,500	$60
ABA Journal	Lawyers	364,000	$20,060	$55
Barron's	Private investors	300,000	$30,100	$100
California Dairy	Dairy farmers	5,040	$1,500	$300
Institutional Investor	Investing professionals	100,700	$33,500	$335

Source: *SRDS*, April 2006

Your CPM is vitally important, because some advertisers decide whether or not to advertise in your publication solely on the basis of it. Indeed, some will plug your CPM into a computer, push a button, and decide whether you get their ads or you don't, based entirely on the number that emerges.

EXAMPLE: Harold was the marketing director for a company that sold wooden toys. He had a yearly advertising budget of $400,000. By doing research among his own customers, Harold determined that people who were attracted to his toys tended to be college-educated parents with household incomes above $60,000 who lived in urban areas. Harold naturally wanted to spend his advertising money to reach people who matched this profile. To help him do so, Harold consulted a syndicated research service provided by MediaMark Research Incorporated (MRI). (Syndicated research is discussed in more detail later in this chapter.) On the basis of face-to-face interviews in 10,000 American households every six months, MRI developed a detailed profile of the products and services people bought in various types of households. Using this material, MRI could project reader characteristics for any participating magazine, including what kind of toothpaste they were likely to use and where they were likely to go on their next vacation.

Using MRI statistics concerning the type of person he was trying to reach, Harold determined which magazines his target customers were most likely to read. Next, Harold called each publication and asked its lowest price for a half-page color ad for 12 issues. He also asked each magazine how many readers it reached. Harold plugged these numbers into a spreadsheet which calculated the CPM for each magazine—price divided by circulation. Finally, based on this information, he bought ads in the magazines with the lowest CPM, until his $400,000 was used up. That was it. Incredibly, Harold didn't even ask to see any sample issues or media kits.

Many publishers very sensibly argue that MRI statistics can contain enough measurement errors that they should always be used with caution. Even the sponsors of the MRI research would doubtless counsel to use their statistics more carefully. For instance, they might suggest comparing MRI figures to information gathered from a variety of sources.

Understand that advertisers depend on CPMs to make their buying decisions, and fix your own CPM to reflect your audience and the spot you want to claim among your competitors. Look at what CPMs other publishers have chosen for audiences similar to yours. And of course, look at your potential competitors. The sample competitive ad strategies discussed below present a whole group of publications in the golf field, and you will see how each one created a competitive positioning strategy and chose an appropriate CPM.

Create an Advertising Rate Card

Your advertising rate card contains the most important rules that will govern your relationships with your advertisers. It spells out the prices for every conceivable ad variation and also lays out your credit terms, publishing schedule, copy deadlines, placement policies, and mechanical requirements for printing ads. Ideally, your production, sales, editorial, accounting, and marketing people should all be involved in creating your rate card, since the rules it sets down will affect all of them.

Once you have published your rate card, try not to make major exceptions unless, of course, you decide to publish a new card. Advertisers may pressure you to charge less for ads or give them other sweetheart deals—for example, the back cover for the price of a regular page—but you will rarely gain in the long run by accommodating them in this way. Once the word gets around (and it usually does) that you don't stick to your rate card, you'll end up having to negotiate your basic prices with nearly every account. Needless to say, that's a real headache.

RESOURCE

You can find thousands of rate cards from other publishers in the Standard Rate and Data Services (SRDS) database. The SRDS publications also offer a long list of the rules publishers commonly use on their rate cards, called Contract and Copy Regulations in industry jargon. You'll find them in every issue of the SRDS directories. See Chapter 14 for details about getting access to these directories.

TIP

Study the competition's rate cards. Make sure you know what all other publications in your market charge. Then go further and check out publications in other fields that you regard as being similar in some important way. For example, if your magazine is aimed at pet store owners, you might not only look at the rate cards of direct competitors, but also at publications aimed at hobby shops, toy stores, gift shops, and other specialty retailers.

When you look at other rate cards, notice how different types of ads are priced. It will help if you understand that the basic price from which all other prices are figured is for a one-time, full-page, black-and-white ad. Smaller ads are priced in relation to a full-page ad, and ads that run more than once in a calendar year are normally given a "frequency" discount from the one-time rate. Color ads, either two-color or four-color, are charged a premium to cover their extra production costs. The covers and other choice locations within a magazine are also generally sold at a premium rate.

Here is how to break down a rate card. First, put all of the publisher's rates onto a spreadsheet, like the simplified version, below, of the rate card for *Golf Digest* magazine. This trimmed-down example leaves out the fact that *Golf Digest* offers several regional editions, each with its own rates, and more frequency discounts, up to an 18-time discount.

Golf Digest Rate Card					
Black & White Ad Rates	**1 Time**	**3 Times**	**6 Times**	**9 Times**	**12 Times**
1 page	$73,340	$70,407	$68,940	$66,740	$63,806
2/3 page	$56,227	$53,978	$52,854	$51,167	$48,918
1/2 page	$42,087	$40,404	$39,562	$38,299	$36,616
1/3 page	$28,114	$26,989	$26,427	$25,584	$24,459
1/6 page	$14,056	$13,494	$13,213	$12,791	$12,229
4-Color Ad Rates					
1 page	$91,675	$88,008	$86,175	$83,424	$79,757
2/3 page	$70,284	$67,473	$66,067	$63,959	$61,147
1/2 page	$52,609	$50,505	$49,452	$47,874	$45,770
1/3 page	$35,142	$33,736	$33,034	$31,979	$30,574
1/6 page	$17,571	$16,868	$16,516	$15,989	$15,286

Source: *SRDS*, April 2006

Look at how *Golf Digest* structures its ad rates. First, notice that a color ad costs 25% more than the same ad in black-and-white. Color pages cost more to produce, and the publisher is passing along these extra costs to the advertisers. Also notice that a 2/3 page costs about 77% of the full-page ad price, not 67%. This means that a solid page of partial-page ads will generate more revenue for the publisher than a single full-page ad. Why? Because it costs the publisher more to produce several smaller ads than one full-page ad, so the rates are set to cover these higher costs. The pricing structure also encourages fractional page advertisers to upgrade. Finally, note that advertisers receive a discount of almost 13% when they sign up for a monthly ad contract instead of buying ads one page at a time. Again, *Golf Digest* rewards advertisers for behaviors that are more profitable for the publishing company.

Golf Digest's rate card reflects its particular publishing strategy. Other publishers' cards will be significantly different. For instance, if you want to encourage full-page ads instead of partial pages, you may elect to charge disproportionately more for partial pages, as *Golf Digest* has done. But if your market is made up of small companies that can't afford full-page ads, you may need to give partial-page advertisers a better deal. Or you may decide to give higher frequency discounts to encourage long-term contracts. Many publishers do this by offering as much as 18% or 20% off for a 12-time contract, as opposed to *Golf Digest*'s smaller 13% discount. Should you want your publication to be flashy, you might decide to charge a smaller premium for color ads, too.

Sample Competitive Ad Strategies

The golf publishing industry is old and well established. Many of the major publications in this field have been around for decades, and have long since settled into a fairly stable competitive position. Although your own publishing situation is probably less settled, looking at the golf field will provide some useful information, as this is the kind of long-term situation you can look forward to as your publishing field inevitably matures.

General-Interest Golf Magazines

In all, there are more than a dozen reasonably healthy magazines and hundreds of specialized newsletters in the golf field. The top two magazines are *Golf Digest*, originally published by the New York Times company and now owned by Conde Nast, a large media company, and *Golf* magazine, published by a division of Time, Inc. As of 2006, *Golf Digest* had 1.6 million paid readers and a CPM of $47. It costs $73,340 to run a black-and-white full-page ad in *Golf Digest*. It costs $86,800 to run the same full-page black-and-white ad in *Golf* magazine, which has only 1.4 million paid readers and a CPM of $62. These two magazines are unchallenged at the top of the niche. The Golf Digest Company owns three magazines in the niche: *Golf Digest, Golf for Women,* and the biweekly tournament newspaper, *Golf World. Golf* magazine's owner, Time, Inc., is the largest media company in the U.S., with at least 45 magazines, including other golfing magazines. Between them, these two companies control about 75% of the advertising money spent in golfing magazines. As an added bonus, golfing advertisers can get special discounts when they buy ads in more than one magazine from the same company. Thus, when there is a downturn in the economy or a slowdown in golf advertising, advertisers will keep buying from these bigger companies—and cut back their spending with smaller companies—to preserve the multititle discounts.

Golf Magazines from Big Publishing Companies			
Title (Owner)	Circulation	1-Time Color Ad	CPM
Golf (Time, Inc.)	1,400,000	$124,000	$89
Golf Digest (Conde Nast)	1,550,000	$91,675	$59
Golf for Women (Conde Nast)	500,000	$40,809	$82
Golf World (Conde Nast)	200,000	$23,851	$119
The Met Golfer (TPG Sports)	100,000	$13,375	$134

Source: *SRDS,* April 2006

It would be very hard to compete head-on with either one of these publishing companies. But several smaller companies publish successful magazines for more specialized audiences.

Golf Magazines Targeting Specific Groups

Six targeted consumer publications focus on specific kinds of golfers, all from relatively small publishers. Notice how some of the publishers who have chosen a more targeted audience charge a higher CPM than *Golf Digest* and *Golf* magazine. These publications no doubt make a case to advertisers that their readers spend more money than the average golfer, and are therefore more valuable.

Targeted Golf Magazines From Smaller Companies			
Title (Audience)	Circulation	1-Time Color Ad	CPM
Executive Golfer (Private club golfers)	100,000	$11,000	$110
Golf Connoisseur (Private club golfers)	235,000	$29,375	$125
Golf Illustrated (Avid players)	140,000	$8,000	$57
Golf Tips (Avid players)	238,000	$21,025	$88
Golf Week (Competitive golfers)	155,000	$24,407	$157
The Golfer (Avid players)	151,000	$16,300	$108
The Green (Ethnic golfers)	152,000	$21,000	$138
T&L Golf (Affluent, avid players)	625,000	$66,940	$107

Source: *SRDS*, April 2006

The magazines for "avid players" are well-established titles from independent companies. *Golf Illustrated* is almost 100 years old, and published by a company with three other sports instruction magazines onboard. The publishers of *Golf Tips* and *The Golfer* also publish other how-to magazines on sports topics. Because they can spread their publishing costs among several magazines, these companies are well positioned to endure a passing downturn in any one niche. The private investors launching *The Green*—for Hispanic and black golfers—also plan to start a companion television show. Their start-up budget, for the magazine alone, is a reported $2.5 million. The other titles on this list come from single-title publishers that don't publish other magazines, but may have other ancillary businesses. In any event, their golf magazines are so targeted that they don't compete head-on with the bigger companies.

Regional Golf Magazines

In the golf world, hundreds of courses are eager to promote their business to local customers. As a result, several regional golf magazines in good-sized metropolitan areas focus on this local market. Most of these regional and local publications are owned by small publishers who are intimately connected with the local golf scene. Their CPMs are relatively high, primarily because golf is such an upscale activity; their readers are often financially comfortable people who spend large amounts of money in restaurants, golf shops, and country clubs. Obviously, if we were looking at a less affluent market—teens, for example, or PTA members—we would find CPMs much lower than these.

The listing below shows what several of the regional golf titles charged in 2006.

Regional Golf Magazines			
Title (Owner)	Circulation	1-Time Color Ad	CPM
Arizona Golf (TPG Sports)	46,000	$4,585	$100
Chicagoland Golf (Independent)	55,000	$2,900	$53
FORE (Southern California Golf Association)	149,000	$8,250	$55
Metropolitan Tee Times (Independent)	25,000	$1,170	$47
Texas Golfer (Independent)	40,000	$3,025	$76

Source: *SRDS*, April 2006

There are many other regional golf titles which, like the ones above, are usually owned by independent, single-title publishing companies. Sometimes the local golf association will sponsor its own magazine, like *FORE* from the Southern California Golf Association. One company, TPG Sports, has made a business of publishing four regional golf magazines. In addition to Arizona, it publishes regional magazines for Chicago, Minnesota, and Virginia.

This survey of golf magazines points out the many different positions a title can hold within one large niche. The main point here is that smaller companies can succeed if they choose a unique subject and then cover it very well.

The Marketing Director's Job: Communicating

Fortunately, many advertisers consider a whole range of issues in addition to CPM when they're trying to decide where to advertise. They generally will look at information you provide about your audience and make their own assessments of the quality of your editorial coverage, and, if relevant, of other services you offer. In fact, because they're already actively involved in your market, many of your advertisers will also be your readers. And since they probably also read your competitors' publications, chances are they can quickly judge how well your publication will serve the market they want to reach.

Still, marketing a publication—especially a new one—is above all a teaching and communicating occupation. Advertising decisions are often made by people who deal with many different markets and don't have an in-depth understanding of any one. This is especially true if the advertiser hires an agency to make its media buying decisions. An advertising agency media buyer is supposed to study all the magazines in a field and recommend which ones are appropriate for any given product. Conscientious media buyers try to learn as much as they can about every market. Over time, some become expert within a specific industry or product category. But most have far too little time and too few resources. As a result, they commonly depend heavily on publishers for the information they need to make smart buying decisions. The marketing job of any periodical, then, is to create a simple message that can penetrate the clutter and confusion in a typical media buyer's mind.

Advertising salespeople are generally the ones who deliver your marketing message to individual advertisers and media buyers. However, most publishers don't depend on salespeople to create the information in the first place; instead they rely on editors, circulation directors, and others. It's analogous to the teaching profession, where some people write the textbooks and other people do the teaching. The skills of each group are related, but not identical.

There are always four basic marketing tasks to accomplish:

1. Help advertisers understand your niche and put it into the context of the overall market.

2. Explain your editorial mission so that advertisers understand the usefulness of your publication to its readers.

3. Prove that your readers are valuable from the advertiser's viewpoint, and design tools within the publication itself and within your company to help readers and advertisers connect.

4. Prove that you have the number of readers you claim to have.

RESOURCE

For more information on innovative and affordable marketing techniques, see *Marketing Without Advertising: Inspire Customers to Rave About Your Business & Create Lasting Success,* by Michael Phillips and Salli Rasberry (Nolo).

TIP

Marketing doesn't have to be complicated. Even if you're publishing largely on your own, you can benefit from the marketing work described in this section. Go through the process as best you can, cutting out difficult or expensive steps if you need to save time or money. For example, ignore the circulation audits and reader research studies until your business is big enough to justify those expenses. In the meantime, understanding how professional marketing people handle these issues will help you communicate more effectively with your advertisers, even if you wind up using simple tools to speak to them.

Helping Advertisers Understand Your Niche

Publishers have a unique perspective because they study a subject, but generally don't participate in it. For instance, sports magazines study their sports from every angle, but their editors, writers, and other staffers don't usually join a major league or professionally play the game. This position, which is in the middle of something but still on the sidelines, gives publishers a special point of view. Even when they interview people who are directly involved in a sport, or print ghost-written articles under a famous player's name, the publication itself remains above the fray.

Typically, advertisers will see your market from a more narrow perspective than you do, because they are participating more directly and experience a different kind of pressure. For example, an advertiser who sells dog food may worry more about immediate sales problems rather than the long-term trends in the market, which will probably be of far more interest to you. You may be surprised to learn that many myopic manufacturers may not even know much about overall trends and preferences among dog owners. In short, a given advertiser's view of the market may be pretty foggy.

You can clear up misapprehensions and also help advertisers understand a larger picture of the market by sharing your broader perspective with them. Who are your readers? What are they doing? What products are they buying? And how are they participating in your market? (Chapter 12 covers the many ways publishers can study a market and use what they learn to develop their own long-range strategies.) In the advertising context, remember that all of your strategic information can be as helpful to your advertisers as it is to you. Sharing your good market data with advertisers is an excellent way to bind them to you over the long haul.

EXAMPLE: *Silent Skier* was a monthly cross-country skiing magazine published by Kate Macdonald and her partner Ben Wiggins. Kate and Ben were young skiing enthusiasts who started *Silent Skier* after leaving their publishing jobs, writing up a business plan, and raising some start-up capital. They employed nearly 40 people, most of them young skiing enthusiasts like themselves. Because they were eager to make a success of their magazine business, Kate and Ben collected a lot of information about the cross-country skiing industry. Their research really paid off when one of their big advertisers, MegaTravel Co., came to them looking for some help.

Irene, a travel agent at MegaTravel, had an idea to sell several new skiing tour packages exclusively to women. This was a new area for MegaTravel, which had traditionally focused on selling outdoor adventures to men and to couples. But Irene believed that there were many women who would like to vacation with their female friends without having to deal with the complications that can develop in mixed-gender groups.

Irene approached Kate Macdonald, the publisher of *Silent Skier*, to get information about the skiing habits of women. Looking through the information *Silent Skier* had collected about its subscribers in annual subscriber profile surveys, Kate found the age and marital status of female subscribers and even some information on how much single females spent on past tours compared to males. Kate also went back over the past few years to see if there were any significant changes in the number of women reading *Silent Skier* or in the interests or activities they reported in reader surveys. Here are some of the interesting details Kate was able to share with Irene:

- *Silent Skier* had fewer female subscribers than males, but individual women subscribers generally spent a little more on skiing vacations than men, and took more packaged tours.

- The women who reported taking the most tours tended to take shorter trips but booked more upscale lodges and resorts.

- The women who reported taking the most tours were 43 years old, or 14 years older than the average *Silent Skier* subscriber.

Kate's information was obviously of critical importance to Irene. She had planned to create low-cost tours, under the assumption that women had limited money to spend on vacations. But she rethought both her plan and advertising campaign. After doing additional research (with Kate's help) among older, professional women to explore their interest in women-only vacation packages, Irene created an attractive upper-middle-market package. And Kate benefited as well: The revenues from the successful tours allowed Irene's company MegaTravel to increase its ad budget in *Silent Skier*.

Explaining Your Editorial Mission

Many publishers don't provide enough information to advertisers about their editorial accomplishments, thinking that the publication speaks for itself. But, it usually doesn't. For starters, some of your advertisers may not even read your publication. And even when advertisers are avid readers, few are savvy enough about the magazine business to articulate what the publication does for its readers, let alone what it can do for its advertisers. In short, it's up to you to educate your advertisers about how your publication can help them.

First, write a good editorial mission statement and include it in your media kit. (See Chapter 2.) Yours should be concise (about 200 words) and tightly focused on what you do for your readers, and why your publication is important.

Go on to describe your publication. Show how the various sections, departments, and articles meet the needs of your readers. Show a close connection between your editorial mission and your audience.

Next, tell advertisers about stories you plan to run in the future. Many publishers provide a complete editorial calendar to alert advertisers about upcoming articles and special issues. The calendar helps them plan what kinds of ads to run and when to run them.

Finally, demonstrate how enthusiastically your readers are responding to your publication. You can use a combination of things to prove that readers appreciate your work: testimonials from subscribers; circulation statistics, including newsstand sales successes; and responses to fax polls, contests, or other interactive features in the publication. In addition, some publishers conduct surveys among subscribers to gather evidence about how much readers like their publication.

Proving That You've Got the Right Readers

After explaining your market niche and your publication's editorial mission, your next marketing task is to explain clearly how your readers match the advertiser's target customers. Most publishers also need to document how many readers they reach and how they reach them. These are two very different challenges, as explained below.

Showing Advertisers How Readers Match Their Target

Remember that advertisers are always looking for a specific kind of customer. Some advertisers know precisely whom they want to reach, while others may have a more intuitive, less scientific idea. Either way, it's up to you to convince advertisers that your readers are the ones they want to reach. To do this, you need accurate, convincing information. Create it by conducting what the publishing business calls a subscriber profile study.

A subscriber profile study asks a small percentage of your readers about themselves and their behaviors, not about the publication or how they like it. The purpose is to develop a profile of your typical subscriber, including age, income level, gender, and educational background, as well as details about the readers' interests and activities.

In addition to basic demographic questions, you can also ask readers about their activities. For example, if your advertisers are selling computer games, you can ask your readers what kind of computers they have, how much they use their computers for recreation, and whether or not they have children who also use the computers. A tennis magazine can ask readers how often they play, where they go to play, and how much money they spend every year on tennis equipment and activities.

 TIP

Niche publications may not need a subscriber profile study. Sometimes, it is so obvious who your readers are that a survey may be unnecessary. For example, if you publish a highly technical magazine about heart surgery, and your readers are paying $150 per year to subscribe, most advertisers who sell medical equipment won't need to see a subscriber profile study. They'll already know that your readers are important to them.

Helping Readers Connect With Advertisers

Another way to assure advertisers that your publication reaches the right readers is to offer ways to directly link them together. Technologies like faxes, voice mail systems, and the Internet offer fruitful opportunities for readers and advertisers to interact. For example, some publications let readers send an email to one central location to request brochures or other information from several advertisers. Publishers can link readers directly to an advertiser's home page from their magazine's website. You can judge all of these options by one simple rule: Does the service help readers locate the products they want and make appropriate contact with the manufacturer? From an advertiser's viewpoint, that is your most important function as a publisher. If your company fosters strong connections between consumers and advertisers, you will have the foundation for a solid advertising business.

Advertisers will make their own independent judgments about how well your readers respond to their ads. Sometimes they ask readers for some direct action—to visit a Web page, call a toll-free number, or send in a coupon. But when an ad does not suggest a direct response, advertisers will look for other results from their ads, if only an overall increase in the sales of a specific product that they can generally attribute to an advertising campaign.

Assuming that your publication provides the right audience for the advertiser's message, what else can you do to help the advertisers get good results? Publishers have developed many creative answers to this question.

- *Design reader navigational tools.* Design your publication so that ads are easy to locate. Look at the problem from readers' perspectives to see whether you've done a good job helping them find the ads they want to find, where they expect to find them. For example, put mail-order ads in a special section. Or include an advertiser index by product or by manufacturer. These and other design features will increase reader responsiveness to ads. *Macworld* is one excellent example of a magazine designed to help its readers find the ads they want to read. Study a copy to inspire ideas for your own publication.

- *Use your website to encourage reader interactions with advertisers.* You can put information on your website that helps readers find products from your advertisers. Comparing complex product features is an excellent use of Web technology, and many magazine publishers have put searchable product database tools on their sites. *Opera News* magazine, for example, posts an online calendar of performances that is a very popular page among site visitors. Meanwhile, the calendar directs people to visit the websites of opera houses and promoters, who are also advertisers in *Opera News.*

- *Tell advertisers about the tools you've created.* Your reader-friendly designs and services will not always be obvious to advertisers, who may not be reading your publication regularly. It follows that you should tell them about the tools you've created and how they work. Use testimonials from other advertisers if you can get them.

Proving That Your Readers Exist

In the magazine world, there are two organizations that will examine the distribution of a publication and produce audited circulation reports for your advertisers. The Audit Bureau of Circulation (ABC) generally focuses on publications written for the broad consumer audience, while as its name suggests, Business Publications Audits, Inc. (BPA), looks at publications for business audiences. Like the Nielsen ratings, each company attempts to provide an independent, objective measure of publication distribution. (See Chapter 14 for contact details.) Both also measure website traffic.

Circulation audits are similar to tax audits (except you have to pay for a circulation audit). First, you file a sworn statement describing your circulation. Later on, an auditor shows up to look for inconsistencies or other errors. Auditors normally compare printing bills, fulfillment documents, postage receipts, and other records to verify the number of copies you are printing and how they are distributed. If everything adds up as it should, then the auditor will certify that your circulation is what you've reported. Audits cost several thousand dollars, depending on your circulation size.

Circulation audits can be expensive, not only because the audit itself costs money, but also because of the more stringent circulation accounting rules you will need to follow to meet auditing standards. For these reasons, many publications are not audited. According to the Magazine Publishers of America, an industry trade association, only a fraction of all 18,800 U.S. magazines are audited, either by ABC or BPA. Most publishers simply issue a general statement about their circulation and forgo the audit. Check to see whether or not the other publications in your niche are audited, and let that information help you decide whether or not to audit.

Audit Status	Number of Publications in 2004	Percent of Total
ABC Audited	708	4%
BPA Audited	208	1%
Total, All Publications	18,800	100%

Source: Magazine Publishers of America, Fact Sheet

Whether or not you audit your circulation, you should understand circulation audit reports and sworn publishers' statements so that you know what your advertisers may be seeing from other publications. Start by asking the ABC and BPA for literature that explains basic circulation reporting conventions. You'll want to offer the same information about your own publication, whether or not you choose to be audited. Not only will this help prepare you to enter an auditing program in the future, it will also help answer your advertisers' questions and prepare your own nonaudited circulation statement.

The Sales Job: Building Relationships

A salesperson puts a face and a personality on your publication. From an advertiser's perspective, the individual salesperson represents your publication. Therefore, to put the best face possible on your business, you should find excellent salespeople. Chapters 9 and 10 detail how to find talented and experienced publishing people. They also cover training and performance appraisals. The next section describes how to organize good people into an effective selling team.

When you have completed all of the research, planning, and marketing tasks that a publisher and marketing director must do, the last remaining task is to make a personal connection with each advertiser. Assuming you have hired good ad salespeople or set up a positive relationship with an independent sales agency, you have made a good start. In addition to finding talented people, you have to develop a structure that helps them sell ads effectively. You need to organize your sales team so that each salesperson gets the support he or she needs to create and maintain personal connections with advertisers. Some time-tested tips are offered here and discussed in detail below.

- Give salespeople clear instructions and the proper tools to carry them out: a viable publishing strategy plus the marketing tools to sell it. Develop your rate card, media kit, and other materials long before making your first sales call. These are the products of your publishing and marketing groundwork.

- Assign each salesperson specific advertiser accounts to manage and help establish specific goals for each.

- Make sure your commissions and other rewards properly motivate people to accomplish your goals.

- Participate in the sales process. Go along on occasional sales calls. Ask for information and suggestions from your salespeople as to how your publication can be improved.

Advertising Mistakes You'll Want to Avoid

Inexperienced publishers often make three ad selling mistakes that you can easily avoid.

1. They neglect to lay the groundwork of a good advertising program as discussed earlier in this chapter. Before you can successfully sell ads, you have to carve out a competitive publishing position, with a strategy that you can earnestly and honestly defend (the publishing task), and then carefully put together material that tells your story the way you want it to be told (the marketing job).

2. They refuse to listen to bad news. Often salespeople will be the first ones to learn about problems brewing among your advertisers or potential advertisers, problems that may seriously depress your revenues in the near future. If you are willing to listen to them, your sales staff can alert you to oncoming problems before they become full-blown disasters.

3. They scapegoat their salespeople. Selling ads is just the last step in a long dance that involves creating compelling editorial products, a good circulation strategy, and sharp marketing programs. If ad space is difficult to sell, you could just as easily have problems in one or more of these areas as with your ad sales team.

RESOURCES

A good resource for finding independent advertising sales firms is the National Association of Publisher's Representatives (NAPR), a professional association of sales firms. Its website includes a database of firms by location and valuable tips on hiring and managing someone who sells ads for your publication (www.naprassoc.com). You can also download the free standard agreement form offered there if you are a publisher looking for representation.

Finding Good People

Your salespeople need to be secure in their jobs. You can't ask individual salespeople to help you build long-lasting relationships with advertisers when they aren't sure about their own long-term relationships with you. Be sure of this: their relationship with your advertisers will reflect your relationship with them. If you've made a commitment to the people you've hired, they'll convey that same level of commitment and conviction to your customers. If you create an atmosphere of fear and chaos, it too will be passed on.

Many small publishers can't afford to hire a full-time sales team. Still, there is much you can do to make part-time salespeople feel secure. Start by choosing them carefully, and follow up by making it clear that you will work closely with them to help them be successful. (See Chapter 10, Managing Employees, for more detail on this.) Once people prove themselves, make it clear that yours is a long-term relationship. Finally, do your best to make them full-fledged members of your team by including them in meetings and strategy discussions and giving them meaningful responsibilities.

Once you've got good people who are committed members of your ad sales team, make sure they understand what you want from them. The chances are that your ad sales goals will change significantly over time. In your first year, for example, you may just want to get enough ads into your magazine so that it looks and feels like a survivor. To do this, you might sensibly decide to make special price concessions for new advertisers. Later on, when you feel more secure, you will probably want to stick to your rules. Make sure that your salespeople understand your plans and goals at any given moment, and are clear about why you have adopted them. Talk about the market with them. Tell them about the competition and how you want to deal with it. As best you can, share your long-term perspective with them, but make the goals for each issue as explicit as possible.

There were only four of us selling ads when we launched *PC* magazine in 1981: the publisher, David Bunnell, two freelance salespeople, Mark Doss and Noreen St. Pierre, and me. I was the marketing and sales director. David and I were on salary, and the others were paid a very small stipend plus a sizable commission. We did our best to make Mark and Noreen feel like part of our family. For example, even though our funds were very tight, we provided them with the best furnishings and equipment we could afford. The setting wasn't fancy, but they could see that we were doing our best for them. Of course, we gave them business cards, but we also listed them in *PCs* masthead. Above all, we did our best to stay closely involved with what they were doing and to truthfully answer all of their questions about our business.

All four of us met before we started selling every issue to go over our goals: which advertisers we hoped to bring in, what we were willing to offer to get them, and how we were going to approach them. Even though our situation was changing constantly (because the personal computer market was growing so fast), we were determined to keep everyone up to date on our team goals and our plans for achieving them.

We were so anxious to have IBM run an ad in our first issue, we joked about paying them to advertise. It was a big day when they signed up. Then, to our horror, their advertising materials didn't arrive on time. Rather than leave them out of the issue, we held it up and missed our printing deadline. That move cost us a bundle, but it was worth it to us: Because we ran that IBM ad and one from Microsoft right up-front in our first issue, many other companies decided to advertise in the next one.

Once we'd published a few issues, our sales style changed dramatically, and we were much less willing to make concessions, even to IBM and Microsoft. To avoid looking inexperienced or desperate for new business, we gradually tightened our rules and our policies. And, we never again held up an issue for an advertiser.

RESOURCES

New publishers can find a number of helpful tools for managing the sales process.

- *Magazine Manager* is an Internet-based program for maintaining your database of advertising prospects, recording contacts with them, and tracking their ads, bills, and payments. The program also has capacity to manage editorial workflow and circulation. It costs about $1,500 to set up and $200 per month to maintain (www.magazinemanager.com).

- *Sequel Ad Sales Management Software* is another Internet-based program delivered on a subscription basis and priced so that smaller publishing companies can afford to subscribe (www.publish2profit.com).

- *Smart Publisher* is another integrated, Internet-based suite of programs to manage advertising contacts, ads, and editorial workflow (www.pre1.com).

- Fake Brains has a program called *AccountScout* that handles the same general features online (www.fakebrains.com).

- *Ad2Ad* is a program specifically designed to handle classified ads in community publications and on websites (www.ad2ad.com).

Setting Up the Right Boundaries

Every good relationship depends on a set of rules that the participants agree to follow. Salespeople are no exception. They need two kinds of boundaries: a client list or territory and a rate card. As mentioned, it pays to make good decisions about both and then stick to them. Otherwise, your salespeople will wind up wandering all over the place, making unwise deals with individual advertisers, fighting each other for the better accounts, and generally wreaking havoc in your business.

There are many different ways to define sales territories. The best ones are usually the simplest. A few examples include:

- by geographic location
- by product type, and
- by the alphabet.

Sure, questions will always come up—for example, what happens when Company X moves its headquarters, or when Company Y, which had long been in your shoes category, also starts making purses? As long as your categories are clear and simple to start with, the occasional adjustment should be easy to handle.

Advertisers always ask for favors—to extend their credit terms, for example, or to put an ad in a special spot in the magazine. Many will try to get price concessions. To keep your sales department working well, it's key that the same rules apply to everyone. This means making sure that all advertisers live by the same rules. If you find you can't stick to a specific rule, it's time to discuss why and change to one with more holding power.

It's not just advertisers who need to respect rules. Never allow yourself to play favorites among salespeople by allowing one to offer advertisers special accommodations.

Establishing Effective Rewards

Because good salespeople will give you what you pay them for, you must be very careful about how you pay them. For example, if you pay commissions on pages sold, without regard to the creditworthiness of the customer, you may wind up with lots of deadbeat advertisers. Similarly, if you don't pay a bonus to salespeople for advertising contracts or for year-to-year growth within their territories, you will be less likely to achieve these valuable results.

Remember, you want long-term relationships with healthy advertisers who are influential in your industry. You also want all of your advertisers to pay their bills on time, meet your deadlines, and otherwise behave dependably. To help accomplish this, structure your commission schedule appropriately. Here's how:

- *Pay a lower commission for ads that run only once or twice.* And pay a bonus whenever an advertiser signs a contract for multiple insertions. Contracts are harder to sell, but you'll get more of them if you pay for the extra work involved.

- *Don't pay commissions until you've collected the money from the advertiser.* This discourages people from selling space to advertisers who can't afford it.

- *Pay a commission for every advertiser in a salesperson's territory.* And do this even if he or she didn't directly make the sale. That encourages salespeople to take good care of all the customers in their territory, no matter how they were sold in the first place.

- *Create an extra bonus to reward sales results that meet any important immediate need.* For example, if your primary problem this year is to gain a lead in ad pages vis-a-vis a specific competitor, you can pay a bonus for every page your sales team moves from that competitor to your own magazine. Save a little of the money you use for commissions to fund these bonus programs. They can be very effective.

- *If you can afford it, pay your salespeople a base salary in addition to commissions.* Similarly, if possible, share other employment benefits such as medical and retirement plans with the sales force. People will generally repay you with their loyalty and hard work if you make the best commitment to them that you can afford to make.

- *Give out other perks and rewards besides money as freely as you can.* Be sure that such benefitts reward appropriate behavior. Run contests, hand out trophies, throw parties, and take people out to dinner. Selling is tough, and people can get tired or discouraged. They need your constant appreciation.

Listening to Your Salespeople

Listening to your salespeople is so cheap and easy, it's surprising how many publishers fail to do it. Don't make the same mistake.

Your sales team looks at your market one client at a time. Its job is to understand the individual problems and prospects for each client. As a publisher, your job is to add up each of those individual portraits into a complete picture of your industry. You don't need to hold hands with every advertiser, but through your ad salespeople, you do need to hear what all of them have to say about your market.

Demonstrate to the people on your sales team that you are interested in what they have to tell you. This will help them look at their clients from your perspective (as best as they can) and give you the information you need to make good strategic decisions. A few specific strategies may help.

- Before you launch a new product or start a new promotion, make sure you know what your sales team thinks about it.

- Bring your team members together regularly to talk with each other and share insights. The ensuing conversations—or even arguments— will help you spot trends within the mix of individual situations they handle.

- Give a hand when advertisers raise problems with your salespeople. One advertiser's problem may point to some fault in your services or publishing strategies. Listen carefully to every complaint until you understand what's at the bottom of the problem.

- Thank people for telling you bad news, even when you hate to hear it. Then people will be willing to tell you what you most need to know.

In 1985, IBM introduced a new computer designed for families called the PC Junior. We were running *PC World*, and our publisher, David Bunnell, considered launching a magazine for this new computer called *PC Junior World*. Our sales team reported that advertisers were not enthusiastic about the PC Junior. The entire sales team felt that the new magazine would be a failure. David compromised and he created a special section about the new computer that we inserted into *PC World*. If the PC Junior turned out to be a winning product, we planned to go ahead and launch the new magazine. If not, then the special section would quietly disappear. Guess what? The computer was a flop and we saved a bundle of money because David wisely listened to our sales team. It cost a lot less to eliminate a special section in *PC World* than it would have cost to fold a separate magazine.

The Publisher/Advertiser Relationship

An advertising business offers many benefits to publishers, advertisers, and readers. But you must face the fact that it takes a whole lot of work and money to forge relationships with advertisers, even just a few of them. A healthy advertising business depends on building and maintaining relationships with advertisers, not just on selling ads. So before you jump into an ad sales plan, it makes sense to think about what you want from advertisers—that is, define specifically how their presence will strengthen your publishing business. And of course, it's also essential that you consider what advertisers want from you so you can do your best to meet their needs.

The Benefits of an Advertising Business

Executed correctly, your advertising business can be not only profitable, but can develop relationships that will be valuable later on. In other words, there's more to a successful ad program than just the immediate ad dollar. Here are some of the benefits publishers derive from their relationships with advertisers:

Your Publication Connects With Its Market

When publishers sell advertising, they link their own economic well-being to their market more directly than they would if they only sold subscriptions. This happens because a publication that accepts ads brings consumers (subscribers) and vendors (advertisers) together. Since a publication will suffer if there are obstacles to the reader/advertiser relationship, its publisher is strongly motivated to look out for the well-being of both groups. In short, they will work to support healthy commerce within their markets.

! WARNING
    A few publications shouldn't take ads. Some publications face an obvious conflict of interest if they take ads, especially those whose editorial mission is based on putting readers' interests ahead of advertisers. *Consumer Reports* is probably the most prominent example of this type of consumer-first periodical, but there are others. *Ms.* magazine has gone back and forth over the years about selling—or not selling—ads. Gloria Steinem wrote a fascinating article about the ad sales headaches she faced as editor of a feminist magazine, called "Sex, Lies and Advertising." After trying it both ways, Steinem concluded that ads for cosmetics, fashion, and other products targeting women as consumers could not comfortably travel side-by-side with articles targeting women as citizens, political activists, and change agents. (The article is available at www.publishingbiz.com/html/articles.html.)

Readers Enjoy an Economic Benefit

In almost every instance in which a publication sells advertising, its readers—not just the publication—enjoy an economic benefit. Because the publisher has more money to spend, editorial content tends to be broader and deeper than would be true if there were no advertisers helping to pay the bills. Readers pay less for the publication than they would have to if it had no advertising revenues to support it.

Of course, there are strings attached to that subsidy. The largest one is that publishers who depend on advertising money can be tempted to censor editorial content key advertisers might find objectionable. For example, a teen magazine might hesitate to tell young women they look just fine without make-up because that message would undermine the cosmetic industry which buys so many ads. On balance, though, the value of the ad subsidy to readers is generally far greater than its cost: Even teens who aren't offered enough content about a lipstick-free existence are given useful information about health, fitness, and relationships that most couldn't or wouldn't afford to buy without the advertising subsidy.

Readers Appreciate Ads

Advertising lets companies speak directly to your readers as consumers, without passing through the editorial filter. Done well, this direct link is appreciated by both parties. Most readers like to see product ads when they buy publications—even when they are primarily interested in a publication's editorial content—because ads provide additional information. Fashion, travel, and hobby publications are only three of many types of publications in which advertising pages routinely make up more than two-thirds of each issue, and lots of readers buy these periodicals primarily for the ads.

What Advertisers Want From You

It should almost go without saying that all advertisers want to sell products or services. Most will have very specific goals in mind when they buy space in magazines or newsletters, including whom they want to reach and how much they are willing to spend to reach them. They appreciate publications that can be counted on to consistently deliver their message to the right people for the right price.

To help advertisers succeed, your publication can:

• locate prime prospects efficiently

• cultivate an atmosphere of trust and enthusiasm, and

• educate consumers to buy smart and use products appropriately.

Syndicated Audience Research

Just as television has its Nielsen ratings service, magazines have polls conducted by several different syndicated research services that measure their audiences. "Syndicated" simply means that the studies are financially supported by dozens of publishers, advertisers, and advertising agencies. The largest syndicated research firms are Simmons Market Research Bureau (SMRB) and MediaMark Research Inc. (MRI). (See Chapter 14 for contact details.)

Although their survey methods are slightly different, the goals of Simmons and MRI studies are the same: to develop a detailed picture of the people who read magazines. To accomplish this, researchers poll people to find out what products they use and what magazines (among participating publications) they read. In short, they collect a small library of data for every person surveyed. When they mix and match all this information, the result is a remarkably precise profile of each periodical's readers, covering a thousand details from their religious preferences to the toothpaste they use. Advertising agencies buy these syndicated studies to help them find the magazines that are popular with their target customers.

Unfortunately for small publications, it takes about 100,000 subscribers, minimum, to participate in a syndicated research survey.

Additionally, small publishers usually can't afford the big bucks the services charge, ranging from $5,000 to $25,000. The result is that thousands of excellent small magazines are excluded.

Locating Prime Prospects

When your audience overlaps an advertiser's targeted market, everything you do to locate your most profitable subscribers—testing various distribution methods and marketing techniques—helps advertisers target a bigger market than they currently have. Think of it this way: By assembling an interested audience, you allow the advertiser to speak to both current customers and future prospects.

Most advertisers are intensely interested in studying their customers and prospects. Knowing this, smart publishers routinely conduct their own research about the purchasing habits and plans of subscribers, which they share with their best advertisers. The largest publishers can also afford to participate in syndicated surveys. (See "Syndicated Audience Research," above.) Often, information you collect in the normal course of your business can also be of help to your advertisers. This might include the geographical distribution of your subscribers—such as whether most avid golfers really live in warm-weather states—demographic information about them, or even the kinds of questions they ask in the letters they write to your editors.

Cultivating Trust and Enthusiasm

Your publication does more than simply find prospective customers for advertisers. Your focused editorial coverage of the issues and opportunities in your market puts readers into a mindframe receptive to an advertiser's messages. For example, computer magazine articles help people feel comfortable about using the Internet. As a result, advertisers in computer magazines have a receptive audience to whom they can sell the hardware and software products that make the Internet accessible. There are many other examples: Travel magazines encourage people to take trips, business magazines help people make good decisions, and parenting magazines help families develop healthy lifestyles and habits. Advertisers hope that some of the trust and credibility editors establish with readers will rub off onto them.

Educating Consumers

You help advertisers by teaching your readers to be good consumers. For example, if you review products, report on how other people have used products intelligently, or show consumers how best to enjoy their hobbies or to accomplish their professional objectives, this information can save advertisers the time and money they would otherwise have to spend doing much the same thing. Even when manufacturers receive criticism in the form of a mediocre product review or poor rating, their resentment will be tempered by the fact that, after all, you are teaching consumers what to look for and encouraging them to buy products in the particular category.

What You Want From Advertisers

Just as the best way to develop a long-term profitable relationship with readers is by getting them to subscribe for an extended period, you want to bond with advertisers by having them sign a contract calling for a series of ads. Your overriding ad sales goal is to create a business relationship that will last for many years, not just to sell individual ad pages. Accomplishing this goal is extremely profitable because it lets you spread your ad sales costs over a long period of time, much like spreading the costs of acquiring a new subscriber over many years.

There are, of course, major differences between subscribers and advertisers. With subscribers, you generally offer the same subscription deal to every person. Not so with advertisers. For all advertising clients, you create a semicustomized business arrangement based on several considerations, such as the amount of space they buy from you, how often they run their ads, and, sometimes, what kinds of ads they run. Each advertiser decides what ad sizes, frequencies, colors, and other options are right for them, with the help of your advertising sales representatives. While the rules are the same for everybody, each advertiser will have a customized agreement with the publication. In the best circumstances, each deal is recorded in a formal, legally binding advertising contract.

A formal advertising contract typically provides advertisers a discounted price in exchange for a commitment that they will run a certain number of ads over the course of a year or more. If they fail to run the specified number of pages, they are responsible for paying you the difference between the discounted rate and the actual rate for the number of ads they did run. Most advertisers appreciate not only the discount, but also the way a contract helps them budget their marketing costs ahead of time.

By industry custom, many advertisers sign contracts for the next year during the fall, when marketing budgets for the coming year are often approved. Others, who for some reason are on a different budget cycle, buy contracts at other times. Naturally, you want to understand when key potential advertisers make their commitments so you can pitch your ad sales at the appropriate time.

TIP

Patience is key. It takes time to sell ads—even to the most promising advertisers. Nike, for example, took four years to decide that it should advertise its running shoes in *Runners' World* magazine. You must have enough cash to keep publishing during the frustrating weeks, months, or even years it takes to build up ad sales income.

Besides price and frequency, contracts cover other important issues—for example, where an ad will run within the magazine, how you will bill them, when ad materials are due, and how to submit them.

Like subscribers, advertisers often expect special discounts or promotional prices for new publications or first-time orders. Later on, you can convert them to a contract, but at first you may need to offer them a trial advertising deal, like a trial subscription for readers. For example, you could offer first-time advertisers three ads for the price of two, which is a common practice among start-up magazines. Or you could give them half off on their first three ads. Avoid giving away your ad space completely for free, but it's fine to be flexible about discounts and promotional prices during your first year.

The Essential Elements of Your Ad Sales Plan

A plan is a relatively simple thing to create, but many people skip this step. Here's a list of the essentials any advertising sales plan should cover.

- **A target list of advertisers.** If you can't list companies by name, then describe the kinds of products and services people are likely to advertise in your magazine. The more detailed you can be, the better.

- **A very specific budget.** Specify the number of ad pages you believe you can sell to each of your target advertisers.

- **A rate card.** Make yourself notes about why you picked your CPM, including a brief explanation of your competitive position.

- **Ad page forecasts for each issue.** Add up the pages from each advertiser plus any classified ad pages, trades, and house ads to project the total ad pages for each issue. Forcing yourself to make specific projections may prevent wishful thinking.

- **An advertising revenue forecast by month.** This figure is simply the number of pages times your revenue per page plus your website ad revenues. Because advertisers typically pay a range of prices, most people use an average price to predict their revenues. Some publishers use a one-time rate, and others use a four-color rate. You can use whatever you want, but be consistent.

- **A budget describing your selling costs.** Outline your commission structure and all of your sales expenses.

A well-constructed sales plan offers a number of benefits.

- **It will help to organize your sales efforts.** You will find it easier to negotiate commissions if you've done some detailed planning, because you'll have realistic expectations about what you want from your sales team. And you can use your target advertiser list to define sales territories and to parcel out sales responsibilities.

- **It will help to fine-tune your overall publishing strategy.** The planning process will help you find any errors in your overall publishing strategy. You may find, for example, that there aren't enough advertisers in the market to support your publication. If that happens, then you may need to find a different audience, or redefine your editorial mission so that you can attract more advertisers.

- **It will help to raise money.** Chapter 7 discusses start-up money in detail. For now, you should know for certain that lenders and investors will want to see a detailed advertising plan. A good plan will always help you raise money from outsiders. ●

Adding More Products

Look around at all the most successful and longest lasting publishing companies and you will find one common feature: They all have multiple streams of revenue. No successful publisher depends entirely on one magazine or one newsletter for 100% of his or her business income, and neither should you. As soon as you can, it's a good idea to build more revenue legs under your publishing table—the more, the better. You can often secure the future of your company by starting out with plans for these ancillary—that is, add-on or spin-off—products, right from the beginning.

Indeed, ancillary products are often very profitable, providing you build them on the strong base of your publication. *The Bark* magazine, for example, is founded on the simple idea that great writers will write unique articles about their dogs, and every issue carries wonderful, literate stories that are wildly popular with dog lovers. Collecting those articles into a series of gift books makes perfect sense for *The Bark*, and makes good profits, too. The publishers also plan a series of cards, calendars, and gift books using the fine art and photographs they're collecting in the magazine.

But as with everything else in life, rewards and risks go hand in hand when you introduce ancillaries. Not only does each new product or service you introduce risk losing money, if executed poorly, ancillaries can damage your reputation with your subscribers, or overtax your staff and resources. Before examining several types of ancillary businesses in more detail, this chapter will take a closer look at the opportunities and dangers of ancillary product lines in general.

Strategies for Adding Products

Smart publishers are careful to develop ancillary products that capitalize on their competitive strengths. For example, *ReadyMade* sells plans and kits based on the unique do-it-yourself projects featured in its magazine.

The Bark, for another example, sells books. When done well, the company continues to grow based on a unified and unique publishing strategy. Unfortunately, some publishers follow poorly focused ancillary strategies that waste time, make little money, and may even damage their reputations. Before you launch any ancillary product, take the following steps to make sure it will be a successful venture.

Analyze Your Opportunities

You must accept the fact that not every idea for an ancillary product is a good one. You are especially vulnerable to failure when your company is young, your market uncertain, and your cash short. Each major move you make at the beginning has the potential to damage your business and possibly even cause it to fail, especially if you try to do too many things all at once. Your long-term success depends on focusing your resources on your core business, and then carefully adding ancillary ventures that promise to be solidly profitable without using up too much of your time or resources.

Make a Complete Plan

People almost never hop on a plane for an unfamiliar location without making a travel plan. But a surprising number of entrepreneurs will leap into a new business idea with less planning than they do for a vacation. Planning how you are going to develop ancillary products doesn't have to be elaborate. Sometimes all you need to do is to mentally walk through the start-up process, making notes about the resources you'll need and the opportunities you expect to have when the business actually gets underway. Fill any information gaps by reading or asking questions of knowledgeable people. Then define your expectations, line up the resources, and make sure you can afford the unavoidable start-up costs.

Do It Yourself

Many inexperienced publishers underestimate how much time, energy, and money it actually takes to develop an ancillary venture. They don't plan for the extra fixed costs that come along. For example, if a solo operator like Anne Cox decides to publish a book for her newsletter readers, she may decide to do all of the extra work by herself, a plan that looks pretty profitable on paper. But if she overtaxes herself, she's asking for trouble. And besides, someone else may have better book editing skills than Anne.

Recognizing correctly that they can't do the whole job of creating ancillaries alone, a surprising number of people will make a different mistake by signing over an important new business venture to the first person who offers to help. No matter how busy you are, this is a mistake. Especially when your company is young, you will often have only one shot at a new business venture. If it fails, you probably won't have the resources to try again. And, of course, there will always be others ready to compete with you. No matter what your ancillary plan—books, trade shows, special issues—take the time to find the best collaborators. These are people whom you enjoy working with, who understand your mission, and who can be trusted to do a top-quality job. (For more about finding and working with collaborators, see Chapters 9 and 10.)

Test Before You Invest

Even when you've decided that an ancillary idea is a good one, don't bet the bank on it until you are certain that it will contribute to your overall profitability. You don't want to fritter away money and energy on marginal ventures. Testing is the time-honored way experienced publishers use to find out if a proposed venture will really work. For example, make one test issue of a potential spin-off publication to see if it's a hit with readers before committing yourself to a series of issues.

Introducing even a well-conceived ancillary product can be dangerous to your company if your market isn't growing as fast as you hope. For example, if you add a host of new products during a growth spurt, you will have to support them all, even when your market starts to decline and they are no longer profitable.

Duplicate Your Strengths

As mentioned before, it's wise to study what other publishers do and to imitate their best ideas. To do that well with ancillary ventures, you first decide what types of ideas are appropriate for you, and which are best left to someone with a different set of strengths and weaknesses. For example, if your overall publishing strategy is to be narrowly focused on a small but profitable niche, look for ancillary product opportunities that reflect this general strategy. For instance, you might decide to sponsor a small, select conference for the most influential people in your market, letting somebody else spend all the big bucks and take the big risks associated with sponsoring a major trade show that aims to draw thousands of people.

Manage Growth Carefully

Growing companies can be great places to work, since they often attract energetic, committed employees. With a superior staff, you can focus your own time and energies on the most important tasks with confidence that others will be done well. Unfortunately, growth can sometimes be painful, especially if you grow so fast that your employees become overtaxed. In this situation, introducing ancillaries can be a terrible idea, heaping stress upon people who are having trouble keeping up with their core jobs.

Before you commit to any new product, it's best to seek the enthusiastic support of your key employees. If people already feel overworked, they will resist new products. With new periodicals in particular, start-up staff is often hoping for a breather at just the moment the owner gets visions of grandeur and wants to launch a bevy of new products.

You can avoid staff overload by communicating openly with your helpers. At bottom, your team usually wants to know, "Do you care about us, or only about making more money?" If they see that the company's growth plan also includes adding new personnel and resources, not just handing out more tasks to the same busy workforce, they are far more likely to cooperate. For instance, many publishers bring in fresh people, or promote an enthusiastic junior person to manage ancillary activities. Others find an outside vendor willing to manage these separate operations.

Remember that ancillary products work best when they reflect the strengths of your original publishing venture. As long as they do, it will be relatively easy to integrate them with your original operation, and to encourage a close working relationship between the people who will develop the new products and the people working on your original publication. But if for any reason your key staff believe that a particular ancillary idea is a poor one, stop and rethink it. It's almost impossible to succeed with an idea your staff hates.

Also realize that staff harmony can break down during the development of ancillary ventures—even successful ones—unless you actively nourish it. For instance, if you have a staff of editors and designers who have helped to create a successful look and feel for your publication, you are likely to face a revolt if you unilaterally decide to sell a line of ancillary products they don't like. Far better to get your key people involved from the beginning, allowing their creative input in all the new ventures.

Keep Pace With Your Market

Your ancillary products can help you understand your market by providing your staff new ways to communicate with industry insiders and trendsetters. For example, when a publisher sponsors a trade show it gives key industry people a chance to meet together and with you in person. Not only do you interact with vendors and customers, but you often get a great opportunity to see what your competitors are doing. Business directories and online databases—two other common ancillaries—can also help to expand your market, especially when the field is highly specialized and participants have a hard time finding each other without your help.

But even in a growing market, adding products may not be the answer for every publisher. Some publishers, especially solo or very small operators, may want to control their growth according to their personal goals. Especially if the core publication starts to strain at its moorings, a small operator may sensibly choose to narrow the focus of the business rather than to expand the product line.

Of course, too much caution doesn't make sense either. If you miss a rising tide that your competitors catch, you may never catch up. If you are hoping to grow as big as you can get and stay in step with your market, then you'll need a mechanism for correctly gauging the tides. (See Chapter 12 for a discussion of publishing strategies.)

Strengthen Your Competitive Position

You can make your company less vulnerable to competition by using ancillary ventures to distinguish yourself from competitors. Larger publishing companies very often capture a leading position in a small niche by following this strategy: They buy a good periodical from its creators and then invest in a batch of supporting ancillary products such as trade shows, books, and online services. In this way, they can pull a small publication out from a crowd of competitors and make it a star. For example, if you start a periodical about a fast-growing new game— let's call it "bosh ball"—and you also establish the first international bosh ball competition, any competitor will have a harder time establishing credibility.

Growing one magazine or newsletter into a publishing power by using its clout to set up ancillary ventures is exactly how many of today's most successful publishing empires got started. But beware: This approach presents a danger for small publishers that is not shared by the big companies. As a small company creates more and more ancillaries, its whole life and livelihood is invested in a single industry. Bigger publishers, on the other hand, routinely spread their risks by diversifying. So, for example, if bosh ball starts to lose popularity, a big publisher will simply transfer its resources to roller lacrosse, ripple racket, or some other trendy sport, while you watch your bosh ball ventures rapidly lose profitability.

On the other hand, the special strength of small publishers is their deep, personal knowledge of their own markets. This often helps them understand when to hold back from making further investments and when to push forward. If you're in close touch with your industry, you'll also have the opportunity to design the best products that are most suited to the unique needs of your customers. Big publishing companies often fall into the ancillary formula trap—they try to apply the same tricks in every market. As long as you are more selective, quicker, more creative, and more responsive to the special interests of your audience, it's often possible to run rings around the publishing giants.

Win Financial Security

Since well-chosen ancillaries ride piggyback on the customer bond you have created with your original publication, they often allow you to capture solid profits. You've already earned the respectful attention of a willing audience of readers. They are likely to buy more of what you are selling, so long as you respect your original relationship with them and offer products that are useful. In short, when you sell ancillaries, you don't have to spend time and money finding customers. You already have them.

Choosing the Right Products

Smart publishers have invented a host of successful ancillary products. The key thing to remember about all ancillaries is that each time you offer something new to your customers, you have an opportunity to increase their dependence on you, but you also risk alienating them if your product or service is poor. Adopting a good ancillary strategy is a lot like using wooden blocks to build a tall structure—the whole thing will topple over if each new level isn't planned and executed well.

What follows is a discussion of the most common types of ancillary businesses, describing how they work, and how publishers usually integrate them with an established periodical publishing operation.

Spin-Off Publications

A spin-off publication is simply another periodical that you create and distribute to a different slice of the same or a very similar market. If you publish a newsletter for softball coaches, for example, you could create another one for players. Or you could create a spin-off for an audience different from but closely related to your original audience—for example, a publication for environmental activists could create a second publication aimed at reporters who cover their activities, perhaps an email newsletter.

Publishers can also introduce spin-off publications that come in a different format from the original—CD-ROM, fax, PDF, digital, or email versions, for instance, targeted at readers who want information in a hurry or in electronic form. For example, some subscribers of a biotechnology industry newsletter such as stockbrokers or professional traders may be willing to pay a premium for daily delivery by fax or email, while individual investors or people making fewer trades would be content with a cheaper version of the same news, mailed weekly or even monthly.

RESOURCES

Publishers are currently selling single articles in PDF formats for downloading through Amazon.com. For example, the site offers a 3,000-word feature article from *Bank Marketing* magazine selling for $5.95. Go to www.amazon.com/publishers to learn about selling your articles through this outlet.

As you think about spin-offs, remember that many different groups participate in every market, often including consumers, vendors, manufacturers, investors, regulators, technicians, distributors, suppliers, employees, educators, and professional consultants such as lawyers, accountants, business advisors, and the like. (See Chapter 3 for a discussion of evaluating and ranking your audience.) Each of these groups has a slightly different connection to your subject and therefore might be interested in a specialized spin-off, delivering information of interest only to them.

You are likely to find that spin-offs are the easiest new ventures to execute well, precisely because you already understand both the periodical publishing business and your particular market. It follows that this is probably the type of ancillary business you should first consider. Stop and think about what your best spin-off options might be. And then consider how much help you will need to execute one of them. If you are typical, you will probably conclude that while you need to add new editorial and advertising salespeople, your spin-off can share circulation, production, and management staff with your original publication.

The Newest New Thing: Email Newsletters

Lots of publishers are finding new sources of advertising income by creating email newsletters supported by an advertising sponsor. You can find many examples, particularly if you look at *PC World* or *Macworld* or some of the other computer magazines. E-letters are always sent only to people who have requested them, and they tend to be very specialized. For example, *PC World* has one just for Web designers. Delivered weekly, each newsletter has one or two commercial sponsors that place live links in the newsletter back to their own websites. This idea works well if you have lots of advertisers looking for new ways to reach your readers. So far, readers have not proved willing to pay for e-newsletter subscriptions, but you may want to try that, too, depending on your audience.

Special Issues and Free-Standing Reports

When you operate in a small but deep niche, you may find a great demand for your published material within your own audience. Indeed, the more specialized your focus, the less likely your readers will have many alternative information sources. That's why niche publishers so frequently and successfully repackage information they've published before in a stand-alone format, often adding some fresh material to attract long-term readers.

A free-standing product such as a subject-specific report or a users' guide can also offer a publisher the opportunity to experiment with different market segments, perhaps in anticipation of launching a spin-off periodical. Or you can use it to promote your original publication, giving your editors an opportunity to show off their own best work all over again in a new, fresh format.

Here are several common examples of special-issue publications.

- *Annual reviews*, which encapsulate a year's worth of articles about specific subject areas or issues you cover. A good annual review can help to establish your authority within your field. For example, a copper mining industry newsletter's annual review might simply summarize all of the previous year's articles and organize them by geographic region, as well as provide a forecast of future mining activity written exclusively for the annual report.

- *Beginner's guides*, aimed at people who are just entering your field or market (such as new parents, or first-time investors), and which help introduce them to your publication. A good beginner's guide succinctly demonstrates to new readers how valuable your publication can be to them. Publishers often use them to attract newcomers and to sell subscriptions. For example, a newsletter about children's health might publish a special report about caring for newborns. The publisher can either sell the newborn report— through ads in parenting magazines, a website, or direct mail, for example; or give it away—perhaps through diaper services or baby product tie-ins.

- *Technical reports*, aimed at the most active participants in your field and often covering a single topic. This is another way to bond with select groups within your larger audience, while at the same time demonstrating that you are an authority within your field. For example, a women's health newsletter may publish reports specifically for health insurance providers on menopause, breast cancer, or dieting, which include cutting-edge information on those subjects.

- *Seasonal or event-related issue*s, the classic example being the Christmas or Thanksgiving issue of a cooking magazine. Every field has events or seasons when most people in that industry are focused on specific situations—the upcoming football season for sports periodicals, the tax season for accountants, and so on.

- *RSS feeds and blogs* are new ways to reach out and bring readers into your website. They can generate some income if you allow advertisers to sponsor them. And your material can be published through aggregators who will see that it reaches a wider audience. (See Chapter 11 on Internet publishing for more on this.)

When business is tough, as is often the case in an economic recession, you can use special issues to effectively lower your subscription prices without appearing to do so—thus delivering 13 or 14 issues for the same price as 12. In good times, you can put a substantial price on these special issues, significantly increasing your revenues without spending much more on overhead or other fixed expenses. And in boom times, you can use special issues to capture extra ad revenue.

Whether you sell them or give them away, the key to success with freestanding products is to execute them well. To do this, copy the best ideas you can find from experienced publishers and avoid the worst mistakes you see in clumsy products. It is always a mistake, for instance, to do nothing but reprint old articles in a new binding. Your dedicated readers will recognize the material instantly, realize how little effort you put into the product, and think less of you for selling them recycled material. By contrast, if you reedit, update, and add new features to your existing material, most readers are likely to be pleased.

The annual buyer's guide published by *Consumer Reports* is a well-known example of a special issue, and a good one to emulate. The *Consumer Reports* editors always create new material that explains significant issues involved in buying certain types of products, and then provide a year's worth of specific product evaluations taken from the magazine. They offer a good combination of new and old material in a useful package, and it consistently sells well on newsstands and in bookstores. Their guide not only brings in substantial revenues, but it helps them increase subscriptions by introducing their magazine to new consumers.

Organic Gardening and other Rodale magazines use another sound approach. Their editors create excellent single-subject booklets on topics of special interest to their readers—composting, plant propagation, organic pest control, and so on—by drawing material from the magazine, then expanding and reorganizing it to read well in report form. These reports are generally sold through ads in the pages of their own magazines, or distributed free as subscription premiums. In both cases, the special reports help to strengthen the bond between the original publication and its subscribers.

Books and CDs

It's no surprise that there are many different book-publishing strategies. For periodical publishers, the three most common are to publish an occasional book, keeping the business as simple as possible, to find a book-publishing partner, or to create your own stand-alone book-publishing company. It may be wise to get help in deciding which of these strategies could be a good fit for you or in modifying one or more to fit your needs. Just as with periodicals, your odds of making any profits with your first book or CD are slim unless you really understand the business.

RESOURCES

To learn more, take a look at some of the excellent guides to book publishing cited in the Resources for Publishers chapter: for instance, *Publish It Yourself: Five Easy Steps to Getting Your Book in Print*, by Alton Pryor (Stagecoach Publishing).

Whatever your strategy, it's most important to realize that a book or a CD has a limited shelf life. Especially when it covers a fast-moving topic like how to select a personal computer, or how to invest in a bullish stock market, a book may only have a few months to recapture the money you put into it. This means your initial marketing and distribution strategy must be good. If you fail to get your book into retail stores quickly and support it with publicity, you may never get another chance. Unlike the periodical business, you won't have the opportunity to learn the market and refine your product and circulation strategies over time. This is another reason it's so important to let knowledgeable people help with your publishing efforts, whether as staff, outside partners, or consultants.

Many publishers hire experienced book editors, CD developers, or freelance writers to successfully translate periodical articles into a full-fledged book or CD product. Others try to do most of the repackaging themselves, with less outside help. But it's rarely possible to go it entirely alone. You'll need to assign skilled people to rework their existing material before you try to sell it in a new form, a job that can take considerable time, money, and energy.

Now, consider the three good book-publishing strategies described below. You can move from one to the other over time as you learn more about the book business. Your choice at any given time should be based on these questions: How much time do you have to learn the book business? And how much room do you have to make mistakes while you are learning?

Keeping the Business Simple

Perhaps the most common book-publishing strategy among periodical publishers, and certainly the least complicated, is to market your books almost exclusively to your own readers, never attempting to distribute them through retail channels. Not only does this strategy allow your books to maintain a specialized voice since they don't have to address an uninitiated audience, but it frees you from the need to learn and create a whole new distribution strategy.

Finding a Book-Publishing Partner

If you want to venture beyond your core audience and into the more complicated world of retail book distribution, one approach is to form a partnership with an established book publisher, especially one that is already familiar with your industry or subject area. A well-chosen publishing partner will already know how to distribute a book or CD through the complex network of wholesalers, chain store buyers, libraries, and independent booksellers, saving you a great deal of time, worry, and money. The key to your successful partnership is finding a publisher that is knowledgeable about your market, has independent information to offer, and is excited to work with you.

In exchange for their distribution expertise, book publishers may demand a hefty share of your book profits. Many will treat you like an author, giving you royalties amounting to only 10% or 15% of their net profits. You'll do better than that only if the publisher agrees that your material is highly valuable.

You are probably already familiar with many of the publishers most active in your field. Start with them. To look for other candidates, check *Writer's Market*, in print or www.writersmarket.com online, which lists publishers by the subjects they cover. (See Chapter 14 for information on this and similar directories.) Some writers' guides also offer useful tips about how to negotiate with publishers. It is important to understand how your partner's business makes money so that you know what to expect from it and what kind of help it will need from you. (Chapter 9 covers this in more detail in discussing working with vendors.)

Creating Your Own Book-Publishing Company

Periodical publishers who have the resources often create their own book-publishing businesses. The best-known computer magazine publisher—IDG—follows this strategy. Its periodicals came first and established the company's credibility within the field. Then, IDG created a book division operating independently from its periodicals, but benefiting from being in the same corporate family. This strategy lets IDG keep all of its book profits, rather than sharing them with a publishing partner. It also gives IDG a chance to hand-pick the individual people it wants to work with and to develop a company that will reflect its own publishing style.

Naturally, the financial risks are great if you follow this strategy, meaning that it's usually a poor approach for many smaller publishers with limited financial resources. But as with any other strategy, there are different ways to implement this general approach, one of which is to start small. You can even begin with one book idea, one editor, and one part-time book marketing expert, and grow from there. As with any venture, the key is to get the best help you can find and afford and to focus your resources where they'll have the greatest impact. That obviously means choosing the book or CD ideas that are most likely to win favor among your own audience and the people who will need your products down the road.

Database Products

You probably never thought you were headed into the database business when you started your periodical publication, but that might be exactly where you land. The information you gather for your own purposes may become very valuable to others in the form of specialized databases, especially if you plan ahead and pay attention to how you gather and store it. That's why it's a good idea for all periodical publishers to understand a little bit about databases.

A database is simply a collection of information that has been collected in a consistent manner. Periodical publishers often develop databases for editorial purposes that can be sold to readers. For example, a retirement newsletter that runs a regular feature reporting the average monthly cost of living in assisted living facilities by city is gathering information that might be sold to several groups of interested people: families looking for retirement homes, managers of retirement homes, government health care policymakers, and private health care industry analysts. Even though the newsletter publisher gathers this information from public sources that are free and available to everyone, by tracking the information over time the publisher creates a unique and valuable database product.

Many periodical publishers who are just starting out don't realize that they have the opportunity to build a database business. Only after a few years do they see that they have inadvertently created a valuable collection of information. Even something as humble as their Rolodex of phone numbers and addresses may be an example of a marketable product. Other examples include back issues, articles stored away in electronic form, information about companies, or products that have been covered in a newsletter, and government statistics. In short, by consistently gathering and organizing information that is meaningful to people in your market, you almost automatically create a database.

Many publishers sell database information in printed form, a format that is still very useful for libraries, schools, and other institutions. For instance, you may start your database-publishing efforts by simply offering customers a three-ring binder to store back issues of your newsletter plus an annual index to your articles. Next you will want to consider more sophisticated ways your information might be organized and sold. As you do so, take a look at successful directories and other printed database products.

RESOURCES

One good example of information packaged this way is Bowker's *Books in Print*, which lists nearly every book from every publisher available to consumers. Another is *Peterson's Guide to Colleges and Universities*, which reports on the course offerings and admission requirements of undergraduate and graduate schools. You can find both of them in any bookstore or behind the reference desk at any public library. Notice how their publishers organize information, what they charge for their products, and how they are distributed.

Nowadays, most publishers are eager to publish database information in electronic form because of lower production costs, and because many customers prefer to use and store information digitally. One big advantage, of course, is that electronic storage and retrieval systems allow users to reformat and customize the information as they wish.

Many traditional database publishers now provide their information electronically, both through online networks and on CD-ROM. For example, you can buy Books in Print and the Peterson's College Guides on CD, and you can also access both of them through online networks.

Whether you publish your database in printed or electronic form, you will have to make it useful to people outside of your company. But be sure the information is accurate, well organized, and easy to understand. And, of course, you'll need to figure out who might want to buy it and accommodate their needs.

To make the information useful, you must also develop a way for the user to efficiently retrieve needed information. In print this means a good index. In electronic form it means a search system that lets users easily pinpoint the information they need. You may need to get outside help to develop an electronic database that has a powerful and easy-to-use searching capability.

There are a few key points to remember about creating and marketing your database.

- *Make it a truly useful product.* Customers need to quickly understand what the database contains and how to find what they need out of it. Package the data in a way that makes sense, given your market. Once you've created a useful database, look for opportunities to customize it for sale to different markets.

- *Maintain your data as efficiently as you can.* Like a periodical publication, a database product requires your ongoing commitment to collect and organize information consistently. Think ahead to create a product that is relatively easy to maintain, ideally one that serves in-house needs as well as being a good candidate for outside sales.

- *Find the most interested people.* Look for the people who most need your information and concentrate your energy on selling your database to them. If they suggest ways to change or add to your product, take them seriously.

- *Get the best marketing and distribution help you can find.* Whether you decide to market your data yourself or to work with distributors, find helpers with experience and savvy.

EXAMPLE: *Vermont Life* magazine has created a quality database product. The magazine put all of its advertisers into a well-organized online database of destinations, products, and events in Vermont. Access to the database is free for site visitors, but the advertisers pay a modest fee for their listings, boosting the magazine's ad revenues.

Common Database Products

Publishers accumulate many different kinds of information. Here are some of the common ways publishers package and sell their own database products.

SUBSCRIBER MAILING LISTS. Your subscriber list may be your most valuable database.

BACK-ISSUE DATABASES. Publishers commonly offer article reprints in full or in abstract form distributed in print, online, or by fax. One of the best systems for selling back-issue material I've seen is *Inc.* magazine's "Inc. on Demand: The Small-Business Information Database." Readers call in for a free index of articles which they receive by fax. They order specific articles, pay by credit card, and receive them by fax the same day. Some publishers are experimenting with the same idea online. Several vendors distribute articles from hundreds of magazines, newsletters, and journals in a common database. One of the largest vendors is Information Access Databases, which pays a royalty to publishers when their material is downloaded by subscribers. Their databases are available on the CompuServe network and others. Another vendor is LEXIS-NEXIS, which specializes in online computer services for law firms and media companies. Contact these vendors to find out how they might distribute your articles.

PRODUCTS, PEOPLE, AND COMPANIES LISTS. Databases you've created to track people, products, or companies can be marketed to your readers and advertisers, as well as to people outside your field who need information about your industry. Here are some examples: A magazine for writers compiles a database of regional writing workshops, another of publishers and small presses arranged by specialty, and a third of literary agents. All three databases are sold in printed form as annual books and electronically on CD-ROMs. In a similar vein, *The Kiplinger Letter*, an insider's newsletter about the federal government, publishes a Washington, DC, Insider's Contacts Directory, which includes the people its own reporters turn to for stories and information. And the Newsletter Clearinghouse, a publisher of newsletters about the newsletter business, sells a directory of newsletter publishers and also operates a newsletter brokerage business.

NEWS OR EVENT COMPILATIONS. When you record or report events regularly, you always have the opportunity to develop a database showing historical trends—so long as your records are up-to-date and accurate.

An example: A newsletter might publish a table of the daily stock prices of software companies. This information could also be available in a database distributed on disk to industry analysts and investors. A ski magazine might keep a database tracking weather conditions by date at ski resorts around the country and sell it to tour promoters.

MARKET AND DEMOGRAPHIC INFORMATION. Information you collect to help you make strategic plans or marketing decisions, including government statistics, company sales figures, stock prices, and other relevant indicators for your industry, can often be published in the form of market reports. For example, *Inc.* magazine publishes its own regional market reports.

Another example: A golf magazine might publish an annual profile of its subscribers in printed form, which could also be stored in an electronic database and sold on disk to golf equipment manufacturers.

Bulletin Boards and Chat Rooms

Chat rooms and online bulletin boards let your readers and website visitors communicate with you and with each other. Some services, such as message boards and electronic mailing lists, allow people to post notices that other people can read. Other services, such as private bulletin boards and chat rooms, offer "live" contact among everyone who logs onto the service at the same time. At their best, all of these services function like electronic conventions or conferences: people pose questions, exchange ideas, and engage in dialogues with other people who share common interests.

You can use interactive services to sell products or to post unique information that will attract readers and enhance your bond with them. From a user's viewpoint, these services are beneficial because they are selective—participants have been screened (often by themselves) to ensure that they have a common interest. Scientists, technicians, and other professionals have been using interactive communications services for years. Millions of other people now also find them interesting, too.

Some publishers create and staff their own bulletin boards. Others use a commercial online service like AOL to provide the electronic meeting spaces. Each service has a different method for screening participants and collecting fees. Whatever service you choose, try to match your audience's needs: Where is it likely to want to meet? For example, are your subscribers AOL members or not? How much are they willing to pay for a chance to interact with each other (and with you)? How can you add value to the service so that it reflects your mission and expertise? (Chapter 11 contains some detailed considerations about Internet opportunities for publishers.)

EXAMPLE: One good example of a magazine's online chat room is Mac 911 hosted by *Macworld* magazine. Other computer websites are intimidating to many users because they're populated with techies who get impatient when people ask basic questions. But the Mac 911 chat room is hosted by a *Macworld* editor who sets a civilized, accepting tone that works well. The discussion topics are well organized—and the site is easy to navigate.

Advertisers Without Ads

Even without running ads within the pages of a publication, there are several ways to profit from advertisers. The possibilities may be worth considering, especially if you need more revenue to make a better editorial product.

Inserts

Many newsletter and association or nonprofit publishers insert a freestanding page or two of promotional literature into the mailing envelope with their publications. The inserts are usually clearly differentiated from the publication itself, by differences in layout design and paper stock. Sometimes these inserts promote only the publisher's own products, but it is also common practice to promote unrelated products and services, or even to insert a page of classified ads from a number of outsiders. Some publishers control production and design of inserts, while others leave it up to the customers to produce their own inserts, according to any guidelines the publisher might have. Because inserts are such an easy way to bring in extra revenue, they are particularly popular among people with limited sales resources or too few subscribers to attract major advertisers.

The Newsletter Clearinghouse, whose *Newsletter on Newsletters*, available online at www.newsletterbiz.com, is subtitled "News, Views, Trends and Techniques for the Newsletter Professional," offers an excellent example. With about 25,000 subscribers, each monthly eight-page issue comes with a single-page insert of classified ads. Often a flyer offering books of interest to writers, editors, designers, and publishers is also included. This advertising page, which is printed on a loose sheet not bound into the newsletter itself, stands apart from it and is easy to discard if a subscriber isn't interested.

Of course, inserts work best if they contain ads for products or services related to your niche. Especially in esoteric fields where products and services are hard for newsletter readers to locate on their own, these targeted ads meet a genuine need.

Card Decks

These are packages of promotional postcards featuring other products and services that you produce and mail to your subscribers. Sometimes an outside vendor produces a card deck that it pays to distribute to your subscribers. Many publishers handle their own card decks because they want to control how the cards look, what kinds of products are included, the scheduling of mailings, and other quality-control issues. Usually the publication identifies itself as the card deck sponsor by including language such as, "Here are some quality products and services brought to you by *XYZ Magazine*."

Card deck advertisers are typically charged for the production costs of their postcards plus an advertising rate based on how many people get the deck. As a rule, you need to have 10,000 or 20,000 subscribers before you can profitably publish a card deck. And you generally need 25 to 35 participating advertisers. Publishers operating below those minimums may still participate through an independent card deck broker.

RESOURCES
You can find card deck vendors in the *Folio: Super Book* and the *SRDS Direct Marketing List Source,* both listed in the Resources for Publishers chapter. The *Folio: Source Book* also lists printers who specialize in printing and distributing card decks for publishers.

Print and Online Catalogues

Some publishers create their own catalogues of products and services from many different companies. The publisher distributes the catalogues among its subscribers or posts it on its website. Sometimes the publisher buys the catalogue products wholesale and then sells them to consumers. More often, the periodical forwards orders directly to the vendors who then handle their own order-processing and fulfillment. Either way, the catalogue publisher's primary service to subscribers is deciding which products to include and how the products will be represented. Many niche publishers have signed on as associate vendors for online retailers like Amazon.com. The retailer handles all transactions, paying a commission to the publishers. (See Chapter 12 for more information on associates programs.)

> ⚠ **WARNING**
>
> **Don't shortchange your subscribers.** If you allow advertising of any type, you will constantly be challenged to guard the sometimes conflicting interests of two constituencies—readers and advertisers. For example, if you become dependent on advertising income, you may be tempted to accept ads for products you don't like or services you would never recommend to a friend. To say the least, boundaries between acceptable and unacceptable advertisers can be difficult to define. Several publishers have sold inserts and other services to advertisers and then backed away from that business because they found it impossible to control. Far better to establish strict ground rules limiting your ad sales to companies with quality goods and services.

Conferences and Trade Shows

If your publication is well regarded, your market is expanding, and there are not already many opportunities for your audience to meet together, you might consider putting on a trade show, small conference, or other group event. Done well, you can simultaneously establish or solidify a leadership position in your market and earn a good profit.

When you think about it, putting on a conference or trade show is a natural extension of the publishing business. Attending a well-produced event feels a bit like walking through the pages of a three-dimensional magazine or journal: You can meet your favorite writers and editors, attend conferences run by distinguished people in your field, and interact with advertisers in person and try out their products. Conferences allow people who share a very specialized set of concerns to meet and exchange ideas.

As the organizer of a conference, your job is to establish the agenda, set up a meeting space, and invite people to attend. In this way, the work is very similar to what you're familiar with as a periodical publisher. But when you actually set out to organize a conference or trade show, you'll quickly learn that putting on a live show is much more complicated than publishing a periodical. Producing a show involves:

- negotiating sites and services with convention centers, hotels, airlines, trade unions, freight companies, and contractors
- marketing and promoting the event among prospective attendees
- providing customer services—taking care that attendees are housed, fed, transported, registered, and informed about schedules and events
- marketing the event among prospective exhibitors and selling exhibit spaces
- assembling speakers and organizing conference programs, and
- providing accounting, communications, and management services.

Realizing how difficult and time-consuming all this can be, many publishers find an outside promoter to help them execute a conference or trade show. The publisher retains responsibility for creative and marketing decisions while the promoter is responsible for taking care of all the details involved in putting on a first-class event. Sometimes the outside manager is paid a flat fee and sometimes a percentage of the profits.

Conferences and events can be quite profitable if handled properly, so get the best help you can find, especially during the conception and planning stages. It is crucial that a conference accurately reflect the character and quality of your publication, because that's what your readers will expect. Be careful not to disappoint them.

Software

There are many examples of periodical publishers successfully venturing into the software business, especially now that so many people have access to computers. For example, computer magazine publishers often use computer maintenance software (utilities programs) as free subscription marketing premiums. Sometimes they simply sell these programs. For example, the publisher of this book, Nolo, primarily publishes self-help law and business books. But it also has created a number of successful software products, including one for writing a will or a living trust (*Quicken WillMaker Plus*) and another one for creating a limited liability company (*LLC Maker*). These products are sold to the same people who buy its books.

Despite many successful examples, periodical publishers should think twice before getting into the software business. Selling software is tougher than marketing other ancillaries because it requires a fairly complicated product, good user documentation, and excellent customer support services. A program that works well for experienced insiders can be a customer service disaster if it's hard to learn or to use. Especially if your price is relatively low, having to field even a moderate number of customer calls for help can quickly put you into the red.

On the other hand, done well, selling software can create an important and irreplaceable bond between you and your audience. For one thing, you will learn more about your audience through the software registration process. You can use what you learn to develop and sell more and better products. You can get help dealing with the details of the software business from the Software Publishers Association, which was formed several years ago precisely because so many programs are interrelated and interdependent. The association has been working to help its members cooperate by pushing for technical standards and universal licensing agreements. You will find their work very useful. (See Chapter 14 for contact details.)

WARNING

Don't tread on someone else's copyright. Be careful not to tread on somebody else's legal rights when you develop software products. For example, if your program uses someone else's database or spreadsheet program, make sure you have the owner's consent, which may involve paying a license fee. On the plus side, having the support of a major database or spreadsheet company can mean a lot to a smaller software publisher, so find out what kind of help these big companies offer.

Other Paraphernalia

Readers are often surprisingly pleased to have a coffee mug, a T-shirt, or other small item from their favorite magazine or newsletter. While these products are rarely big moneymakers, they can be valuable by virtue of their ability to add some humor and warmth to your relationship with your audience. You can buy these products from hundreds of different manufacturers and offer them to your subscribers. Look under "Advertising Specialties" in your Yellow Pages and you will likely find dozens of local firms. Naturally, you should choose vendors who make quality products, so make sure you examine their work before placing orders with them. And get competitive bids, because prices vary considerably.

Publishers typically use these products as premiums and give them away free to subscribers and advertisers, but you can also sell them.

List Rentals

Even if you don't run advertisements in your publication, you can profit by renting your subscriber list to advertisers. Sometimes publishers make substantial profit from the list rental side of their businesses. People who rent your mailing list are looking for customers with a certain interest and specific demographic characteristics, just as you were while building your readership. Marketers often pay handsome prices for lists of people who closely match their targets in a growing market. You can also trade names with other list owners.

To successfully rent or even trade your list, you must be able to tell prospective list renters about your readers. Sometimes it's enough that they read your publication—from that, a renter will assume your readers are interested in the right subjects or products. But often you must provide additional information, such as the results of reader profile studies indicating your average reader's age, income, occupation, and so on. (Reader profile studies are discussed in Chapter 5.)

List renters often want to know how you sold your subscriptions in the first place. Since they usually rent lists to conduct direct mail campaigns, they obviously want to find people who respond to these offers—that is, habitual direct mail responders. But they'll also rent other lists, as long as you can identify the sources of the names.

For example, when a pregnant woman picks up a free magazine in the doctor's waiting room and mails in a subscription card, she's demonstrating a sufficiently high interest in her pregnancy and imminent parenthood to become a first-class prospect for thousands of baby products. So even though she didn't respond to a direct mail pitch to begin with, the fact that she took the trouble to send in a card means her name is a hot prospect. Marketers pay big money for lists full of hot names like hers.

In addition to correctly identifying your subscribers and proving their interest in your subject, a successful list-renting business also depends on good service to the list renters. This means your lists must be accurate, up-to-date, and free of duplications. A profitable list-rental business typically involves hundreds of very detailed orders every year, and each order must be handled without error. That's why many publishers hand over their list-rental business to an outside vendor who promotes the list and handles all of the orders in exchange for a share of the rental income.

Even if you use an outside list manager, you should use your own unique knowledge of your market to develop ideas about how and where to market your subscription list. A good list manager will listen to and follow up on your marketing ideas.

You will need at least 5,000 subscribers, and preferably many more, before most list-rental managers will be willing to handle your business for you. If your list is smaller, you may need to handle the business yourself. But call the list-rental managers anyway to see what they tell you; some are interested in smaller lists if the market is a good or growing one. You can also try to find out what kind of list-management software they use, where they promote lists (what directories and periodicals), and what they generally charge—information that will help you manage your list business yourself.

TIP

Email is hot. These days, list renters are eager to use emails. And your subscriber list will be that much more valuable if you can offer both postal addresses and email addresses. So be sure to collect email addresses from your subscribers.

RESOURCES

You can locate list managers in the *Folio: Super Book*. (See Chapter 14.) The *2006 Folio: Super Book* is a great example of a highly successful ancillary product. You will also find useful information about mailing-list brokers, compilers, and managers in the bimonthly SRDS publication called *Direct Marketing List Source*. This enormous publication lists over 10,000 mailing lists, giving a detailed description of each one. (Both publications are detailed in Chapter 14.)

While you will probably want to maximize your income from renting your list, you don't want to do this at the risk of offending your readers. For this reason, many publishers prohibit certain kinds of advertisers from using their lists and others insist on reviewing all promotional literature before it is sent to their subscribers.

TIP

Let them opt out. Every publisher who rents his or her list must offer individual readers an option to opt out. Check with the Federal Trade Commission, which administers rules about advertising and privacy issues. It posts some of the rules about mailing lists on its website at www.ftc.gov/privacy/protect.htm.

> ### "Seeding" Your Subscription List
> ### Before You Rent It Out to Strangers
>
> Organizations that rent your list are only supposed to use it once, and
> are supposed to mail only the material they've described to you or to
> your broker. However, purchasers sometimes cheat by mailing to your
> list more than once, or by mailing different materials than promised.
> That's why publishers nearly always seed their lists with their own names
> so that every time a list is used, a publisher will automatically receive the
> mailings either at home or at the office.
>
> A seed name is simply one you create exclusively for your list. For
> example, Lisa Sherer might add the phony name Leslie Stevens or Lynn
> Smith to her list, using her own home address. Every time Lisa gets mail
> for Leslie or Lynn, she knows that the mailer used her mailing list. By col-
> lecting this mail and comparing it to the legitimate list orders that have
> been handled by her list manager, she can easily spot any cheaters.

Some Well-Executed Products

This section offers some examples of publishers doing good jobs and
realizing good profits with ancillary products. You can find other
excellent examples if you pay attention to what good publishers do.
Rodale, a publisher of sports, organic gardening, and health periodicals,
is often recognized for skillfully developing ancillary businesses. The
Newsletter Clearinghouse is another excellent publishing company to
look at, having added several successful ancillaries to its own newsletter
operation. The Newsletter and Electronic Publishers Association can help
you find other, perhaps less well-known but equally skillful newsletter
publishers, too.

Cruises Update on the Web

Anne Cox's travel newsletter turned out to be very popular among travel agents, frequent travelers, and tour operators. Her database of cruises was such a unique and useful product that people began asking for direct electronic access to it. Anne was reluctant to put her database onto an online network, since doing so would pressure her to make updates and corrections every day, rather than every few weeks, which was her normal schedule. As a solo operator with limited time, this would necessitate hiring someone. Even if the potential revenues were enough to cover the cost of an employee or freelancer, Anne would have to spend her own valuable time supervising that extra person.

After carefully thinking about her options, Anne decided that the best approach would be to post the database on her website, update it monthly per her usual schedule, and simply send out an email announcement for each update. Access to the Web database would require a password, allowing Anne to charge an extra fee for it. All subscribers to Anne's print newsletter would get access to her Web database for an extra $5 tacked onto their subscription bill. Other people could access the database for $20 per year.

Fortunately, Anne found a local vendor who agreed to manage her email newsletter for a reasonable price. The vendor also introduced Anne to a programmer who helped her reorganize her database slightly so that it would be easier for a user (other than Anne) to read and manipulate the information.

To announce the new Web version of *Cruises Update*, Anne created a flyer and began inserting it with her printed monthly newsletter. After six months, 23% of her subscribers also signed up for Web access to the database and 43 nonsubscribers bought Web access. After all costs were subtracted, about half of the gross income from the website was pure profit for Anne, who, of course, was delighted.

Silent Skier's Winter Getaways

The managing partners of *Silent Skier* magazine, Ben Wiggins (editor-in-chief) and Kate Macdonald (publisher), both had a passion for exploring wilderness areas on cross-country skis. When they started the magazine, each agreed that having employees actively participating in the sport would be good for their company and so they encouraged everyone who worked for *Silent Skier* to continue taking ski trips. To accommodate all the time and travel involved, Ben developed a unique editorial production schedule: Most feature articles and some columns and departments were written, edited, and designed during the summer months and put in the can for publication during the winter, thus giving editors and contributors more time for winter skiing.

In one of their periodic business development meetings, someone suggested that *Silent Skier* should publish a catalogue promoting group ski trips which could be led by the magazine's writers and editors. Kate was quick to see that the idea suited their company well, since many employees already had experience as travel organizers and the initial financial investment would be minimal. The trips would also offer a wonderful opportunity for *Silent Skier* employees to spend time with readers, advertisers, and ad agency people in a pleasant, noncommercial situation. Kate asked for a volunteer task force to develop a business plan.

The planning team quickly reached an important decision: In addition to creating their own trips, *Silent Skier* would include trips with outside sponsors, so long as the sponsors met high standards of quality and service. By including outside tour operators, the team hoped that *Silent Skier*'s online catalogue would quickly become the preeminent guide to cross-country ski vacations, not just one among several others. They created a budget for staffing and promotions, and outlined a marketing plan that they circulated widely among employees. With so many experienced travelers among the staff, they collected some excellent ideas and suggestions.

With a good plan in hand, Kate hired a full-time staff of two and began negotiating with trip promoters who might want to be included in the online catalogue. They spent the better part of a year completing negotiations with outsiders and developing and testing new trips sponsored by *Silent Skier*. All of the work was done by *Silent Skier* employees. The finished website went live about 18 months after the original idea had surfaced.

The website was not only a comprehensive guide for cross-country skiers, it was a big moneymaker for *Silent Skier*. The *Silent Skier* company collected a 10% commission whenever someone signed up for an outside operator's trip through their site. The site was loaded with subscription offers for Silent Skier magazine, and became a very good source of new subscriptions for them.

The tours that the *Silent Skier* staff organized were only marginally profitable, but wildly popular among the employees.

The *Tracks* World Expo

After a couple of good years with *Tracks* magazine, Tony Thomas felt that there should be a national trade show for model railroad enthusiasts. There were dozens of local and regional model railroading conventions, but no one had created one big annual convention that would bring all major industry players together—including established vendors, new product developers, other publications, and, of course, all prominent advertisers. Tony believed that model train enthusiasts, who'd already demonstrated a willingness to attend conventions, would travel to desirable cities for a chance to see what was going on in the whole industry at one location.

In trying to pull off a successful national trade show, Tony's small magazine faced possible competition from several larger, richer media companies that had been publishing model railroad magazines much longer than Tony had. He knew he could not afford to match the investment his bigger competitors would be able to come up with if one of them developed the national show. But, if *Tracks* could move quickly and develop the first national show, the *Tracks* World Expo might become so important even his competitors would participate, complete with big booths and impressive sales staffs. In short, their presence would add to the influence of *Tracks* magazine, not diminish it.

Trying to get the *Tracks* World Expo started would amount to a big financial risk for Tony. Indeed, it would take such a huge chunk of his resources that if it failed, he might very well lose everything, including the magazine. With so much at stake, Tony decided to look for two partners to share the risks with him. First, he wanted to find an established player in the model railroading industry who might offer financial support in exchange for top billing. And then he wanted to find an experienced trade show promoter who would run the event for a share of the profits.

Tony was lucky. A German manufacturer of model railroad equipment was looking for an opportunity to increase its sales in the United States market. It had ambitious goals and money to back it up. The German company had relatively few connections in the U.S. and the *Tracks* World Expo idea was very appealing to it. None of Tony's publishing competitors had proposed the same idea. Tony and his German partners drew up an agreement to do one show, sharing any profits and giving Tony's partners product line lots of exposure. If the show was a success, they would proceed to make it an annual event. Next the two partners went looking for a third—a trade show promoter with the track record and resources to make their test show a success.

Tony met with seven different promoters before choosing one. In the process of interviewing different promoters, Tony learned more and more about how trade shows operate. He went to see the shows each promoter was managing for other clients, and asked a million questions.

The promoter/partner Tony finally selected agreed to rent the exhibit space and manage the event, including handling promotions and selling exhibitor spaces. She would be an equal partner and share all profits with Tony and the original partners. Tony and his magazine staff were responsible for developing the agenda of the convention, scheduling speakers, workshops, and conferences, and developing a look and feel for the convention exhibit spaces. The German manufacturers provided financing and marketing support as well as lots of hot new European-style train models and computer operating systems that would guarantee that the show would be genuinely exciting.

Since everyone in his company would be involved, Tony spent a lot of time talking about the idea with all of them and listening to suggestions. It was agreed that each *Tracks* department would have specific responsibilities for the Expo, to be carried out in cooperation with their partners. Editors were given creative control over the conferences and workshops. Marketing and ad salespeople took responsibility for reviewing publicity materials and promotions to exhibitors. The magazine circulation manager was responsible for developing a comprehensive marketing plan for attendees. Tony also added one full-time person to his own staff who would be the show coordinator at *Tracks* magazine and the primary liaison between the three organizations. The in-house coordinator was charged with keeping everyone well informed, actively involved, and hopefully reasonably content with the development of the Expo. To help inspire enthusiasm, Tony proposed sharing a small percentage of *Track's* portion of anticipated Expo profits with his employees. Sometimes *Tracks* employees had to push hard for their ideas, especially with their trade show organizer/partner, who feared they might be too expensive to successfully accomplish. But they worked out their differences, and each group contributed its best to the Expo, making it a hit.

The *Tracks* World Expo turned out to be even better than anyone had anticipated. Tony's editors created an imaginative central theme: linking the history of modeling to the future by using technology. Personal computers were everywhere, demonstrating modeling design programs, running multimedia exhibits about train lore and history, and helping attendees find their way around the exhibit hall and conferences. The European angle—especially the gigantic train layout that dominated one end of the hall—was a huge hit with attendees. Speakers and workshop organizers came up with fresh, innovative discussion topics. The *Tracks* World Expo became an annual event, and over the years contributed as much to Tony's profits as his magazine. ●

Raising Money and Working With Investors

This chapter and the next one look at money—how to get enough to start your business, how to keep track of it once you do, and, most important, how to spend it wisely. The discussion begins by looking at the way periodicals normally evolve from start-up through maturity. If you understand what's coming next in the financial life of your publication, you'll be better equipped to manage your current situation. For example, cash tends to be terribly tight during start-up, but in just 18 months or two years, cash flow usually improves greatly.

This chapter will help you create an effective plan to raise the money you'll need to get your publication started. But before you worry about actually raising money or approaching potential investors, you should deal with a basic question: What are your personal financial goals? The reason that you need to put your own goals first should be obvious: To succeed in the long run, you want to find investors whose financial needs are compatible with yours. It's best to define your goals in terms of these critical issues:

- How much money do you want to make from the business?
- How much financial risk are you willing to accept?
- How open are you to allowing investors to participate with you in the running of your business?
- What financial and personal rewards do you ultimately want out of the business?

After giving you some pointers about how periodicals typically raise and spend money and discussing various funding sources you might explore, the chapter will walk you through the steps necessary to develop a fundraising strategy that matches your personal goals. It will then conclude with some examples of successful fundraising campaigns.

The Financial Stages of Publications

You will find it easier to develop a long-range vision about the financial side of your business if you know how publishing companies generally start up, grow, and become profitable. Although every publication is different, there are several typical developmental stages you can expect to encounter, explained here in detail.

Testing the Idea

It can be extremely hard to raise money for a new publication, especially if you have no track record and few connections within the publishing business. Part of the reason for this is that hot-sounding publishing ideas are relatively easy to come by, but few really turn out to be winners. To help demonstrate that their publishing ideas are likely to succeed, people who need significant start-up capital often conduct a market test. Whether or not a lender or investor asks you to do this, it is still wise to test your publishing idea before you make a long-term commitment to it.

Fortunately, there are many different ways to test a publishing idea. The most traditional method is to conduct test mailings through direct mail and measure the response. This may sound expensive, but in fact a limited direct mail test for a small newsletter may cost you only a few hundred dollars. Other more expensive testing methods have also become popular in recent years. One is to publish a single issue and to actually test it on the newsstands. Another is to start a fairly low-cost annual or quarterly publication and then increase the frequency if public response is good. And finally, some people now use the Internet to test new publishing ideas, offering free newsletters online, and then converting their readers to paying subscribers later on.

The value of a test, of course, is that you need to raise only enough money to measure reader response to your publication, which will be just a fraction of the money it would take to launch a regular periodical. Many aspiring publishers fund a quick low-cost test out of their own pocket. Others raise money for their testing from a small group of investors, which may include family members and friends. Then, if the test results are good, they will approach more affluent investors to raise the much larger sums of money necessary for full-scale publication. Some people raise the initial seed money by forming partnerships, which can be dissolved when the test is complete. If results are good, each original partner can get a small share in the ongoing publication, which would then include additional investors. But if the idea is a flop, each partner would lose only the seed money he or she put into it.

Most circulation tests can be accomplished in less than a year, sometimes considerably less. (See Chapter 3 on circulation marketing.) Even a fairly thorough direct mail test, for example, can usually be accomplished in seven or eight months. And, of course, running a test isn't a full-time job. During the test period, you can hang on to your day job while spending time promoting your idea among potential collaborators and financial contributors. Indeed, this is a very common strategy. Then, if the results of your tests are good, you are in a good position to bring together the resources you'll need to move into a regular publishing schedule. If the test results are bad, you have a good excuse for gracefully withdrawing from the project, and you haven't lost too much time or money chasing a bad idea.

Establishing a Foothold

The next stage starts when you begin a regular publishing schedule and typically lasts for about two years. It includes the hard work of building relationships with readers and advertisers discussed in Chapters 2, 3, and 5. During this stage, your potential customers will decide for themselves whether they like the publication enough to pay for it. For instance, if you are on course to succeed, many or even most of your subscribers will renew their subscriptions at least once during this stage. A significant number of advertisers will also get hooked by signing up for long-term advertising contracts, or at least choosing to run a predictable volume of ads in the publication on a regular basis.

In both cases, the key to establishing a secure foothold will be converting your customers from your introductory prices and irregular publishing schedule to a higher price for their regular subscriptions or ad contract. Most periodicals begin to see profits only when they reach this stage.

Although reaching profitability is an important milestone, it offers only a temporary respite from financial worries. New publications typically find that their profitability is extremely tenuous for several reasons, one of the most important being that they are vulnerable to competition at this early stage. After all, since you have proved your publishing idea is a good one, lots of other publishers may be tempted to jump in. The need to fend off competitors helps explain why so many publishers find that they need to raise more cash as soon as they get a foothold—either to cope with increasing competition or simply to keep up with the growing demands of readers and advertisers.

How Competitors Drive Up Your Costs

If you have a market all to yourself, then you can run your business with a great deal of freedom—depending, of course, on your resources and your publishing objectives. But nobody ever gets to keep a profitable publishing niche to themselves for long. Competitors will appear, with the result that your cost of doing business will go up and your choices will begin to narrow. Here are a few of the common ways competitors are likely to cause problems.

- You will lose some of your good subscribers. This means you will have to go after less desirable subscribers, those in the outer rings of your subscriber target who are less interested in your publishing mission, and therefore more expensive to acquire and renew.

- The amount you charge advertisers and subscribers will drop if competitors undercut your prices, making it harder for you to profit even from your most loyal readers and advertisers.

- Your advertiser-related marketing and promotion costs will increase. An experienced publisher can often oust an inexperienced one simply by spending more on advertising sales and marketing efforts.

- Your costs will be driven up as a result of producing extra products and services you feel compelled to provide to retain reader and advertiser loyalty.

TIP

Consider selling out when your business becomes profitable. Once you have reached a profitable position that will make your publication attractive to prospective buyers, and, if your niche is a good one and your publication has good growth prospects, you may be able to set an extremely profitable price. Many established publishing companies grow by buying viable publishing properties from outsiders and building upon the foothold already created. After a sale, some buyers will ask you to stick around indefinitely, but this is usually negotiable. Some purchasers actually want to take over completely, and fairly quickly.

Building an Empire

Once you have a strong foothold in your market and can cope with competitors, you may want to relax a little and enjoy your success. After all, many publications never make it this far. But you probably have another option. If your niche is a good one, you can use your original publication as a springboard from which to build a bigger business. In addition to ancillary products or new related publications, there will surely be many ways to strengthen your original publication. For instance, you could recruit more top-notch editorial contributors, or offer new services for readers and advertisers by expanding your website. However you decide to grow, your initiatives should be designed to strengthen the bond between your company and your customers.

Managing growth can be tricky. Publishers who follow this approach must grapple with how fast to grow, how to stay focused on the best opportunities, as well as how to deal with competitors trying to move in on your expanding territory. All this is complicated by the fact that most fast-growing publications need to raise more money during this stage. And as is true at all growth stages, chances are your periodical will need new and probably different kinds of help during any period of fast growth. For instance, it is common to change vendors, or add new ones, and to hire more professional employees at this time.

This publication stage can last for many years, depending on how your industry grows and on the overall state of the economy. You'll have some control over the rate and direction of growth, but much of what happens will be influenced by external forces, especially the demands of your audience and the efficiency of your competitors. You reach the end of this stage when your business begins to consistently generate enough profits to support its own future growth, whether that pace is fast or slow.

Shaking Out

Sooner or later, the growth in your market will slow down. When this occurs—and it always does—some of the publications in your niche will likely close down. It's often hard to predict which publications will survive and which will perish because so many different factors contribute to success or failure. For example, during the big magazine shakeout in the late 1960s, some of the biggest failures, including *Look, Life, Collier's,* and *The Saturday Evening Post,* involved the largest and most experienced publishing companies. The lesson is that even experience and deep pockets don't guarantee success when a market falls off a cliff.

During the last several decades publishers have generally prepared to survive hard times by carving ever more narrow niches for themselves. The heart of this strategy is focus. That is, publishers find a subject they know intimately and then try to become recognized as either the best— or the second-best—source of credible information about that subject. Publishers who are likely to survive a shakeout also tend to be those who pay close attention to the bottom line—that is, they concentrate their energies on the parts of their businesses that generate the greatest financial returns.

Being able to retrench quickly during hard times is another key to survival. When business dries up, you need either to cut back or to redirect your spending. Agile publishers who have kept fixed overhead to a minimum are particularly likely to be successful. Fortunately, many of the business practices that are common among small publishers today— outsourcing, for example—increase financial flexibility and allow for quick cutbacks if necessary.

It's also important to realize that a shakeout can be fast and furious, or it can last a long time. Often your market will never regain the growth pattern it once enjoyed. Again, the publications that will survive tend to be the ones that adapt quickly to the new market reality.

The Dot.Com Market Shakeout

The first technology business magazine, called *Upside*, was founded in 1989. Another one, *Red Herring*, launched a few years later, and the two magazines competed side-by-side for six or seven years without any other competitors. Then the dot.com market began to heat up. Venture capitalists invested millions of dollars into new technology companies and several new magazines jumped into the fray. By 1999, there were four magazines besides *Upside* and *Red Herring*, including *Wired*, *Fast Company*, *Business 2.0*, and a weekly called *The Industry Standard*, each fat with dot.com advertising. In early 2000, *Red Herring* increased its frequency from monthly to biweekly. That same year, *Upside* hired about 25 people and launched a daily online news service plus a radio program.

Initially, entrepreneurs created all of the technology business magazines, but the big publishing companies quickly started buying their way into the market niche. Conde Nast bought *Wired*. Time, Inc., bought *Business 2.0*, and later folded it. And a huge multinational publisher, Gruner and Jahr, bought *Fast Company*, which is still in print. Each deal was sweeter than the last and everyone felt like geniuses.

Then—the bubble burst. Overnight, the market went from honey to handouts. Technology ad spending fell by 75% in just nine months during the last part of 2000. *The Industry Standard*, published weekly, had the most to lose and the least to spend and immediately folded. So did *Upside* and *Red Herring*. *Business 2.0* lasted a year or so after the bust, and *Fast Company* is still in print. The whole amazing boom-to-bust cycle started and ended in about five years.

Reaching Maturity

Mature publications can be very profitable because, by definition, they have claimed a solid spot in their market, a spot that is relatively secure against competitors. In other words, you won't reach maturity unless you have prevailed against at least some competitors and survived the shake-out stage.

A mature market typically supports two or three profitable publications. Each one has a loyal following large enough to sustain the publication for many years. Competition is relatively calm because relatively few publishers will think it worthwhile to sink lots of new money into mature markets. You can find examples of maturity in any well-established market, such as model railroading, sewing, gardening, or weekly news magazines.

Mature publications strive to keep expenses under control and learn to live profitably within a slow-growth or even a no-growth market. Since revenues in a mature market are usually fairly stable and predictable, publishers can generate healthy profits simply by controlling their costs.

Some publishers relax into a comfortable groove once their enterprises reach maturity. They pay off debts, put their profits in the bank, and have a bit of fun. But others want to keep growing. These publishers seek new ventures in younger, growing markets where they can invest their profits and keep expanding their empires.

Death or Rebirth

Some publications live a very long time. For instance, many business publications were founded long ago, including *Publishers Weekly* (1872) and *Advertising Age* (1930). General-interest publications like *Harper's* (1850), *The Atlantic Monthly* (1857), *The Kiplinger Letter* (1923), and *The New Yorker* (1925) will probably go on for decades more.

In recent times, for example, many publishers launched and then abandoned print magazines about the Internet—including one called *Yahoo Internet Life,* and another called *eBay* aimed at users of that site. For a short time, readers and advertisers liked having print magazines about the Internet, and many of them flourished, such as *Wired* and

Business 2.0. But after a time, people became more interested in reading about the Internet or advertising Web businesses *on* the Internet rather than in print magazines. The print editions of *Wired* and *Business 2.0* have been trimmed down significantly—and the other print magazines have folded.

From a publisher's viewpoint, a rapidly declining publication represents a big liability. Even though less money is coming in each month, you must still fulfill your obligations to subscribers, so the very business that has sustained you in good times becomes an increasingly heavy burden. Even if you stop publishing, you have an obligation to give a cash refund for undelivered issues, or at least to offer something of equivalent value and hope that most subscribers will agree that it's a fair trade. In desperation, some publishers simply stop sending issues and turn off the telephones—not a recommended course of action.

The rebirth of a publication thought to be dying—or dead—is sometimes possible. There have been dramatic examples of this phenomenon—the brief rebirth of *Life* magazine is perhaps the most noteworthy. In that case, the weekly periodical quit publishing altogether, and then was completely revived in a monthly format years later by a whole new crew of people. Another example is *Harper's*. After *Harper's* failed as a profit-making enterprise, The MacArthur Foundation and the Atlantic Richfield Company joined forces to give the magazine a totally new life subsidized by a new nonprofit organization called The Harper's Magazine Foundation. *Ms.* magazine went through a similar transformation.

In the small-magazine and newsletter world, a far more common form of rebirth consists of a major makeover, where publishers who see their market shifting change their publishing strategies accordingly. For example, a disco dancing magazine might drop the disco angle and simply speak to single people who go to nightclubs. Or a skiing periodical might switch a major part of its coverage to the faster growing sport of snowboarding. In short, if you want to keep on publishing, there is often a way to do it, if you move quickly enough so that your original market hasn't completely dried up. But you will often need both new money and energy to do it, and it can sometimes be hard to find investors who are willing to gamble on a makeover.

The main point to remember about a dying publication is that if you wait until the situation gets truly bad, you'll have lost your chance to reclaim value from your business by selling it or changing strategies. At that point, you may even find yourself saddled with the unhappy burden of settling the legitimate claims of your subscribers at a time when your own resources are depleted. Although you might be able to offload your subscription obligations to a competitor who's looking to acquire new subscribers, they'll pay you very little, if anything. In short, you'll want to exit from the business long before your publication reaches this terminal stage.

When Can You Take Out Profits?

Many publishers are willing to work hard, but in exchange want to cash in big at some stage. So the question arises, When can a publisher typically take out profits? The answer is, if you plan to sell your business, or shares of it, the best times are usually during the empire-building stage—when you've established a strong and profitable foothold and the future of your enterprise is bright, and at the beginning of reaching maturity—when your publication is mature and profitable. Not surprisingly, at these moments you can expect to find many willing buyers if you want to sell, or agreeable new investors if you want to expand the business yourself. For guidance on taking out profits, see *The Small Business Start-Up Kit*, by Peri H. Pakroo (Nolo).

Your Financial Attitudes

If you reflect on the predictable publishing life cycle just described, you should see the value of developing a fairly well-defined long-range plan to cope with each stage. Doing this will help you marshal the resources you will need to succeed as your publication faces different market conditions.

Before examining the many sources of money that are available to publications in each developmental stage, focus on your own attitudes toward money so that you don't waste your valuable time looking for financial help in the wrong places.

Ask yourself these four questions:

1. How much does money matter to me?
2. How much personal financial risk can I withstand?
3. How much do I need to control my own business?
4. What financial and personal rewards do I really want out of this business?

The following sections discuss the significance of these questions to your fundraising strategy.

How Much Does Money Matter to You?

Big profits are hard to come by. If money is a top priority, you must organize your publishing business to be profitable all along the way. Of course, many people who start publications have other goals that are more important to them than producing a large financial return. For example, some people become publishers because they want to influence the world in some way. Others think the job is fun, romantic, or prestigious.

Although most of us are probably motivated by some combination of both altruism and greed, let's take a quick look at how people who want lots of money, and those who barely think about it, might go about finding investors.

If Wealth Is Your Primary Goal

Some folks get into publishing simply because they want to make a ton of money. They hope to come up with a good idea, build up a loyal following among readers and advertisers, and then either sell the publication for a huge profit or use it to build a publishing empire.

But very few people succeed at the big money strategy. It only works when lots of things go right: your chosen market grows, your publication perfectly matches reader needs, and you can run your business with maximum efficiency. Especially for inexperienced people, achieving a big success will also involve good luck on all three levels at the same time.

If wealth is your primary objective, then you should look for investors and collaborators who share your sense of risk-taking and adventure. Also, try to find people who might bring some needed expertise to your business.

If Doing Good Is a Greater Goal Than Money

Of course, some people don't get into publishing to make themselves wealthy. Instead, they launch periodicals to do something useful, or to communicate a particular point of view, or for other reasons. Sometimes people with this approach will even restrain their publishing business if it threatens to take over too much of their lives, as would be the case if it started to drain their finances, cut into family time, or interfere with their involvement in their field of interest—protecting the environment, for instance.

If you don't want to worry much about money, you certainly don't want to work with debtors or investors who care significantly more about profits than you do. If, despite this advice, you do go into debt or take on partners, look for lenders and investors who understand and support your goals. So long as you have a good publishing idea and an articulate mission, you can sometimes raise money from private individuals or nonprofit organizations that support your fundamental vision and are not greatly interested in big profits themselves.

To see this approach at work, look at *Mother Jones* magazine, for example, or any of the other 500 magazines that belong to the Independent Press Association (www.indypress.org). Most of them make just enough money to stay in business—and no more—but each serves a unique political, social, or artistic mission. Many of these publications get financial support from private individuals who support the mission and don't care about profitability.

TIP

You might be a better publishing employee than entrepreneur. If you find that you don't care a great deal about making big bucks, have little tolerance for financial risk, and have no great need to be in control of your own publishing business, perhaps you are better off job-hunting than trying to raise money for a start-up. In the best circumstances, you can land a job at a good publishing company that focuses on a subject you love, or one that you can learn to love. The upside of this approach is that you get to do work you enjoy without having to spend time agonizing about the business.

How Much Risk Can You Withstand?

Generally, the more money you risk, the more money you stand to gain. Although there is no absolute correlation between risk and reward (some people take risks and fail and others sleepwalk their way to riches), there is definitely a connection. And one thing is sure, since publishing is a very risky business, risk-takers have plenty of opportunity to shine.

The risks come in many forms besides money. For instance, you can gamble your reputation on a publishing idea and lose not just the business, but possibly your ability to take advantage of other opportunities, too. For example, if you persuade all of your colleagues and professional allies to invest in your new periodical company and then fail spectacularly, you may have trouble working with those same people later on and tarnish your reputation within the publishing field.

One way to control your risks is to share them with other people. Find partners and collaborators who will strengthen your business and shoulder some of its burdens. Another way to manage risk is to start small: Test your market and your ideas, and move forward only if and when you get strong, favorable results from your tests.

When you have some idea about your tolerance for risk, you can review all of the various funding sources and consider not only how much each source demands that you risk on your own, but how you can use the different sources to diminish your personal vulnerability.

How Much Do You Need to Control?

Often, your need for control is related to the level of risk you are taking. You likely trust yourself more than you trust other people, so you won't likely let somebody else make all of the critical business decisions if you've staked everything you own on this business. It's important to realize that people who invest in your business are likely to have the same thoughts. That is, the more money they contribute, the more control they are likely to want.

It follows that if you have a strong need to retain most operational control, you should look for a number of small investors instead of one or two big ones. Or at least be aware that control is likely to be a major issue if you deal with larger investors and make sure everyone understands how decisions are going to be made right from the beginning.

What Rewards Do You Want?

Lots of new publishers ask, How will I get my big payoff if my publication succeeds? Basically, there are two options for getting your money out of the business: keeping the business or selling it. And, of course, there are variations on these two possibilities.

Using Your Publishing Business to Support Yourself

For many publishers, the greatest reward is simply to make a decent living from their publishing business. They understand what the late media critic A.J. Liebling meant when he said, "The only real freedom of the press is to own one." Their dream is to earn enough income through publishing to support themselves and perhaps some other people as well.

Ideally, as your business grows, it will produce enough profits that you can invest some back into the business to reach more subscribers, add new products, or collect your own rewards. It is worth noting that although many publishers never achieve much financial success from their publishing activities, when they do, they usually have a choice as to how to reward themselves financially:

- they can pay themselves and any other investors who work in the business a high salary and generous employee benefits, or
- they can distribute cash dividends to partners, shareholders, or employees.

And, as mentioned earlier, freedom is another type of dividend; many publishers never sell shares or take on investors because they value their freedom more than anything else.

Options for Selling the Business

Assuming your publication is profitable, or soon promises to be, it is easy to find business brokers, investment bankers, or mergers and acquisitions experts who will help you sell your business (see "Specialists at Buying and Selling Publishing Businesses," below). Broadly speaking, there are four options for selling out: selling the company to a new private owner, going public, working with a venture capitalist, or selling to an employee stock plan.

Finding a New Private Owner

Often, a new owner will pay your price and take complete control of the business, allowing you to walk off into the sunset. But especially if your publication is highly specialized or dependent on your expertise, you may have to agree to stick around for one to three years as part of a transition plan.

Going Public

Very few publishing businesses ever grow to the point where they can go public, because they generally need annual revenues of $10 million or so before a public offering is possible. Few publishing companies ever earn that much.

Going public means that you give control of the business over to a board of directors and the corporate officers elected by the board who are responsible for protecting the interests of shareholders. As long as you retain a significant ownership interest, you'll still have some control, but you'll always be accountable to the shareholders.

Working With a Venture Capitalist

Venture capitalist firms inject new money into a business with the idea of expanding it quickly and then selling it for a big profit in a few years. They typically contribute some management expertise as well as their investment dollars. If you can find a compatible venture firm, this may be a smart way to go—especially if your ultimate goal is to sell your business in the short term. For example, when you are ready to retire, you might look for a venture firm to help you develop your business so that it will command the highest possible price when you sell it or take it public.

> **TIP**
>
> **Most start-up publications are not attractive to venture capitalists.** Most venture capital firms avoid working with start-up publishing companies. Their goal is to quickly turn a profit on their money, and it typically takes too long for publications to reach profitability. Venture capital firms will invest only in the rare publication that makes a big enough splash that they can go public very quickly, or find a private buyer. In recent years, the only examples have been in high-technology markets like multimedia or Internet publishing. Very few run-of-the-mill publications produce big profits fast enough to attract venture firms.

Sell the Business to Its Employees

Sometimes an owner sells a business to an employee stock ownership program (ESOP) or to a group of managers who form a partnership and borrow money to buy the company. Whether all employees or a small group of them are involved, this option is fairly common among smaller, privately held publishing businesses that are producing enough profits to repay the loans. There are professional consultants who can help to organize an employee or management buy-out (see "Specialists at Buying and Selling Publishing Businesses," below). These same consultants can help you establish employee stock option plans as you build your business so that your employees will benefit from its growth along with you.

> ### Specialists at Buying and Selling Publishing Businesses
>
> There are several investment banking and consulting firms that handle most of the magazine mergers and acquisitions among established companies. They look and act like bankers, but these knowledgeable folks are very friendly to entrepreneurs. Contact them to help you figure out whether or not you can sell your publishing business.
>
> - Berkery, Noyes & Company, 165 Broadway, 13th Floor, New York, NY 10006, 212-668-3022. Website: www.berkerynoyes.com.
> - DeSilva & Phillips, 475 Park Avenue South, 22nd Floor, New York, NY 10016, 212-686-9700. Website: www.mediabankers.com.
> - The Jordan, Edmiston Group, 150 E. 52nd Street, 18th Floor, New York, NY 10022, 212-754-0710. Website: www.jegi.com.
> - Bay, Sherman, Craig & Goldstein, 11845 W. Olympic Boulevard, Los Angeles, CA 90064, 310-477-1400. Website: www.magazineconsulting.com.
> - Veronis, Suhler, Stevenson, 350 Park Avenue, New York, NY 10022, 212-935-4990. Website: www.veronissuhler.com.
>
> There is also a national clearinghouse for information and assistance setting up employee ownership programs. Contact it or tell your accountants and lawyers about it if you are interested in this form of ownership:
>
> - The National Center for Employee Ownership, 1736 Franklin Street, 8th Floor, Oakland, CA 94612, 510-208-1300. Website: www.nceo.org.

Writing Your Business Plan

No matter what your attitudes toward money or long-term goals, if you want to raise money you'll need to draft a business plan that clearly and convincingly presents your ideas to prospective lenders, investors, and other supporters. Many people dread the prospect of doing this, sometimes because they've looked over the textbooks and they see what a massive job it can be. Take heart. Your business plan is merely an efficient way to organize and communicate information you need to gather anyway.

RESOURCES

For guidance with the task, see *How to Write a Business Plan*, by Mike McKeever (Nolo). Several other excellent books that will help you do the job are listed in Chapter 14. I also sell a business plan tool kit on my website at www.publishingbiz.com. This is a tool I created for my students at the Stanford Professional Publishing Course, who are required to write a complete magazine start-up plan in just ten days.

General Tips

Whether you write a long, formal document or you scribble your plans on scrap paper, here are some specific suggestions that will help you write a useful business plan.

- *Sell the idea to yourself.* As you create your business plan, it's wise to adopt a somewhat skeptical attitude. If your publication idea has a major flaw, you have a huge interest in finding it out as early as possible. Face it; experience shows that lots of start-up businesses in any field, including publishing, should never have opened their doors. If, on the other hand, you can produce financial and other information to sell yourself on the idea, chances are you'll also be able to convince others to support you.

- *Pitch your business plan to likely supporters.* Don't waste time creating a plan for people who are unlikely to invest. Instead, decide early who your best prospects are and create a plan containing the information you believe they will want. Many people go so far as to create a separate business plan for each key prospect by customizing their general information. For example, if you're approaching someone who already knows your market, don't bore them by extolling its terrific prospects. Concentrate instead on the details of your publishing idea and why you have the savvy to make it work. On the other hand, if your prospective investors know nothing about magazine publishing, then your plan had better include some basic information about the publishing industry to help them understand your ideas in a broader context.

- *Keep it short.* Often, the less you say the better. Not only will you save readers time and increase the chances they will actually read your material, but you will also be able to share your understanding of what information is truly important. For example, it's better to simply but convincingly explain why you are the best person to launch this publication in a punchy, thoughtful paragraph or two, than to write a long and elaborate history of your education and work experiences.

Essential Elements

The periodical publishing business is significantly different from other manufacturing or service businesses. Many prospective investors or lenders may not understand how the business works. The ones who do understand publishing will expect to see that you understand it too. Here are the essential elements to include in your plan.

- *Editorial mission statement.* Include some sample pages if you have a designer already onboard. Otherwise, just describe the kinds of information you plan to provide for readers, and who will develop the contents. Use this section of your plan to inspire investors— describe a publication they'll want to read so badly that they'll give you gobs of money to get it started. (Refer to Chapter 2 for info on editorial mission statements, and also look at some of the editing books listed in Chapter 14.)

- *Circulation marketing strategy.* Explain who your target readers are and why they need your publication. Describe your pricing and competitive strategies, and outline your circulation marketing plans—which sources you plan to use and why. (Refer to Chapter 3 for details.)

- *Potential ancillary products.* People who are not familiar with the publishing business often overlook the great potential for ancillary revenues that periodicals enjoy. You will be smart to include this subject in your plan. (Refer to Chapter 6.)

- *Advertising sales strategies.* If you plan to sell ads, explain who the advertisers will be and why they will be excited about your publication. Note where these prospective advertisers are currently advertising and why they might switch to your publication or increase their marketing budgets appropriately. Also detail how you plan to sell ads: who will make the calls, how you will set up selling territories, and how much you will spend on marketing and sales support services. (Refer to Chapter 5.)

- *The stages of your business.* Prospective investors need to know how much time it takes for publications to build a foothold and achieve profitability. Explain your strategies for dealing with each developmental stage. (Refer to Chapter 12.)

- *Experts who will help you.* Luckily, there are many people with sound publishing expertise who you can add to your team as advisors, consultants, and part-time contributors without having to hire them as full-time employees. Investors will be reassured to know that you have publishing experts on board, even on a part-time or consulting basis. (Refer to Chapter 9.)

As this chapter describes potential sources of money, begin to make up your own list of prospects and decide which sources look best for your business. Try to concentrate on the people who are most likely to help you. If you aren't careful, you can waste lots of time chasing the wrong people.

EXAMPLE: Ben Wiggins and Kate Macdonald were trying to raise money to start *Silent Skier*, a cross-country skiing magazine. One lead was Kate's brother George, who worked for a venture capital firm. Even though George's bosses had never invested in a magazine, they agreed to meet with Ben and Kate as a favor to George. Ben and Kate worked hard to prepare for their meeting: They wrote an elaborate business plan, including detailed budgets and cash flow and income projections. George provided a little advice, pointing out that unless their projection showed that the business would produce a 20% profit or more within the first few years, his bosses would reject their plan.

Ben and Kate struggled to come up with a forecast that would honestly show a 20% profit in the early years of a new publication. Unfortunately, they found it impossible to accomplish. The best they could do was to find a few examples of established publications that earned 20% profits, but none that had earned that much profit at the beginning. They soon realized they had a serious ethical dilemma: Should they manipulate their profit forecast to produce the result the venture partners want to see, or should they draft a plan they believe is truly achievable? In the end, they decided to do a little of both—to offer a plan that presented a very optimistic profit projection but one that was nevertheless below 20%.

At the meeting, the venture partners listened politely, asked a few questions, and declined to invest. Later, going back over the meeting with George, Ben and Kate realized that it was a waste of time to have approached George's firm in the first place. Venture firms typically want to put money into a business, develop it for a short while, and then either sell it to a larger company or go public with it. In contrast, Ben and Kate's plan was to build a publishing business and keep it until both of them decided to retire in 20 years or so. In short, even if they had successfully persuaded the venture firm to help them get started, they would certainly have run into conflict with them as soon as the business got underway because of the fundamental difference in long-term objectives.

Raising Money Takes Time

On average, people spend two to three years trying to raise enough money to start a glossy national magazine, and it can take much longer. It took ten years to get funding for *Fast Company*, even though the founders had publishing experience at the *Harvard Business Review* and lots of ripe investor contacts. As a rule, the more money you need to raise, the longer it will take, even with great contacts and an excellent business plan. My suggestion is to develop more than one plan—a big-money plan and a budget plan for a back-up. After all, if you are trying to raise $3 million and you only come up with $2 million, will you quit, or will you try to see what you can accomplish with what you have?

Allow three to four months of diligent work to develop a comprehensive business plan, including all of the market data and financial projections, plus a dummy issue or graphic representation of the magazine. I have often worked with clients who hope to start publishing two or three months after we finish putting their business plan together. Instead, you should allow 12 to 18 months after you have completed your buisness plan for making the rounds with investor prospects.

Persuading Lenders or Investors

Now that you have an idea about how publications typically mature, and have confronted your own long-term goals for your business, you can thoughtfully consider how best to finance your start-up. For example, you should now understand that you don't need to raise the large sums needed to take your planned periodical from a start-up to a mature and profitable business. As long as you can raise enough money to successfully establish a foothold, you should be able to raise further money as you need it. Often, this is the best approach, since it allows you the opportunity to switch from one kind of funding to another—for example, from borrowing money to selling shares. The examples provided at the end of this chapter illustrate several different ways to raise cash.

Lenders and Investors Have Different Claims on Your Business

It's important to understand that while investors own a piece of your business, lenders don't. Unless you pledge your business assets to secure a business loan, the lender has no ownership interest in your company. Therefore, when you don't need lenders anymore, you can simply repay them. It's harder to shake an investor. So why deal with investors? There are usually two reasons: No one will lend you enough money, or if they will, you don't want to pledge the security (collateral)—such as your house—they demand.

If you do want investors, don't take them on too soon. At the beginning your publication won't be worth much, meaning you'll have to give up fairly hefty shares to tempt investors. Self-finance or borrow to get started and grow your business until its value increases. Then, investors may advance you far more money for a smaller interest in your business.

Your relationships with lenders and investors are important and you should choose them as carefully as you would employees or vendors. Try to find people who make you feel comfortable so that you can easily communicate with them about your business. Ask them about their business goals and expectations so that you understand each other.

Even though they are different in many ways, lenders and investors have some common concerns. To varying degrees, every prospective lender or investor will want information from you that will help them answer these basic questions.

- What are the risks that they'll never get their money back?
- How much money will they make if they lend or invest it?
- How will they get their money back (plus a profit)?
- How long will it take to get back their money?

In addition, you will have to address the following issues with every one of them before you can persuade them to get involved with your business:

- *Can they trust you?* Every appeal for money must include some evidence that the borrower or principal business partners are trustworthy individuals. If you have any problems with your credit history, you must either completely wipe the record clean or be ready to explain fully.

- *What do they know about publishing as a business?* Potential investors may know lots about publishing, perhaps more than you do. But many will be attracted to your ideas for other reasons (for example, they may see publishing as being glamorous), and know little about its business side. If you encounter people like this, you'll need to educate them about how publishing works before they'll be likely to part with much money.

- *What do they know about your market?* Insiders who understand your market are more likely to appreciate its growth potential. It follows that outsiders will need information from you to understand the potential you see in the market. While the information you provide should reflect your optimism, it should also be realistic.

- *Do they believe in your publishing idea?* You need to be able to explain your editorial mission convincingly and enthusiastically: what your publication will do for its readers (and advertisers) and why your target audience will support it. It may help to point out profitable publications performing the same editorial mission in different industries. Also, you will want to sell some sizzle—that is, convince potential financial supporters that your publication, no matter its size and target market, really is destined to do well. This sort of pitch is often based less on hard facts than on charisma. Just the same, convincing investors of the magic of your idea should be part of any sales pitch.

- *Do they think you can carry it off?* Finally, you need to persuade prospective financial supporters that you can do what you say you can, either by yourself or with the help of others. Be prepared to name any others who will help you, and clearly explain how they will contribute to your success. Convincing people that you can follow through is a question of character as well as one of experience and training. Many people trust their own immediate impressions more than they trust résumés, so you need to think carefully about how you will make a positive impression. Every encounter with prospective lenders or investors is an opportunity to convince them of both your personal and professional strengths. It may seem obvious, but people will be judging you at least as much on what you do as what you say—so keep your promises, be on time, be well prepared, and communicate clearly about your plans. The less someone knows you, the more you must attend to these basic professional details.

Sources of Money

When considering who is likely to help finance your publication, it is usually wise to begin with the following approach.

1. Start with people who know and respect you. Tell your friends, colleagues, and acquaintances what you are trying to do and invite them to get involved. Obviously you'll want to concentrate on friends you think may be able to help most—those who have money or business talent or publishing connections—but don't stop there. Remember that your friends have friends, too. So even if one friend can't lend you money or open doors for you, perhaps he or she knows someone who can. Don't be afraid to ask.

2. Look for natural supporters. Seek out people who will benefit from your business, and for whom making money isn't the only reward. For example, if you are starting a city or regional magazine, contact businesses, educational institutions, or others who may directly benefit from your publication once it gets going. Also talk to civic groups and cultural institutions that share your enthusiasm for your city.

3. Look for aid within your market. People already doing business in a new market are likely to understand its prospects. Some, such as major vendors or retailers, will consider helping you get started because they share your enthusiasm for the industry.

4. Don't expect to find all the money you need in one place. Most independent publishers start out with a mixture of several funding sources in addition to their own savings: family, banks, borrowing on their credit cards, and outside investors.

The rest of this chapter will look at how to work with lenders and investors, and will wrap up with sample fundraising strategies.

Working With Lenders

Lenders like predictability. They negotiate all the terms of a loan in advance and they expect everything to work out as agreed with the borrower. They hate surprises. Here are some tips for working with lenders.

- *Figure out how much money you need.* It's your job to figure out how much you need to borrow, how long it will take you to repay it, and how much interest you can afford to pay. Establish your needs as clearly as you can before you approach prospective lenders.

- *Negotiate everything.* The price you pay for any loan is the interest rate plus any fees or points the lender charges to set it up. In addition to the price, other characteristics of the loan—for example, its term, its repayment schedule, the securities or guarantees you offer —should be negotiated carefully. A surprising number of people are so grateful to get any loan that they settle for the first terms they are offered without even attempting to bargain for better ones and without shopping around. They wind up paying too much for the money they need. If you need cash for a relatively short period of time—to finance a direct mail campaign, for example—don't agree to a 15-year home equity loan with a hefty prepayment penalty, because it will cost you far more than you need to pay. Assuming you need money for two years at most, you'd either pay interest for about 13 years longer than necessary, which could amount to thousands of dollars, or if you prepaid the loan, you'd have to fork over a chunky penalty. Far better to ask your banker for a shorter-term arrangement or make sure you have the right to accomplish the same thing by paying back the loan early with no penalty.

> **TIP**
>
> **Tough negotiating won't cause a lender to say no.** Lenders lend for one reason: They are confident you will repay their money with enough interest or other payments that they will make a profit. Hard bargaining will not cause a lender to evaluate your business prospects or loan repayment prospects differently and refuse to lend to you.

- *Understand your lender's goals and the rules under which it operates.* Every lender is different. Private lenders are much more flexible than institutions or government loan programs, which are limited in their options by laws or regulations. You may have to mix and match loans from several lenders to get all the money you need. The more you know about each lender, the better you can choose the best ones.

- *Tell lenders the truth and keep them informed.* Contrary to what some sharp operators apparently believe, it's a poor policy to lie to a lender. If you have trouble making a payment or keeping up with a loan agreement, the first person you should talk to is the lender. Explain your situation and be prepared to negotiate. The sooner you bring up a problem, the easier it will be to find a workable solution. Don't let your lender relationships go bad if you can avoid it, because you never know when you might need the same lender's help again in the future.

Family and Friends as Lenders

Private lenders—your family, friends, and others who know you personally—are generally willing to lend you money because they believe in you and have faith in your ability to repay them. They can be very willing lenders, assuming they have extra money on hand. But there's an obvious danger: Turning those you know into lenders will complicate both your personal relationships as well as your business. Of course, the greatest risk is that your business will fail and your closest allies will have to suffer the consequences with you. Borrowing from family and friends may add to the other pressures you feel about making the business into a success. Here are some ways you can at least keep problems to a minimum when you borrow money from your intimate friends and relations.

Borrow Only What You Need

Repay the loan in stages as you accomplish specific goals. For example, borrow money to finance a direct mail campaign. When the project is completed and the revenues are collected, repay the loan plus interest. Then, if you still need cash, borrow just enough to achieve your next major goal—perhaps enough money to develop sales materials and a prototype issue so that you can sign up a dozen advertisers. In this way, you can avoid piling on more debt than you can handle.

Pay a Commercial Rate of Interest

Even if you borrow from family, pay a commercial interest rate, as you would for a bank loan. This should guarantee that your lender receives a fair return and will help defuse any idea among your siblings or other family members that you are a charity case or are being treated too favorably.

Follow Normal Business Procedures

Whenever you borrow money from private individuals, especially your relatives, treat the loan as seriously as you would treat a bank loan. Draw up an agreement that specifies the terms of the loan and a repayment schedule and then stick to that agreement. Otherwise, you or others can easily lose track of what was included in the agreement, damaging your relationships as well as your business.

RESOURCES

You can find downloadable sample loan agreements online at www.nolo.com as well as a book, *101 Law Forms for Personal Use*, which you can download from that site.

Get Them Out of the Loan Loop as Fast as Possible

Finally, switch your borrowing to public lenders as soon as you can. Not only does this reduce the likelihood of future misunderstandings, but it also allows you to build up a credit record—something you can't do if you stick to private lenders. When your business grows beyond the lending capabilities of your family or friends, you will be glad to have a track record with public institutions that will improve your access to bigger loans. So as soon as your business is established enough that you can get credit from banks or other financial institutions—even credit cards—you should switch to them.

Public Lenders

Public lenders such as banks, credit card companies, and government loan programs judge your creditworthiness on the strength of your past borrowing activities and by their own assessment of your ability to earn money in the future. They are trained to measure risk by a fairly standardized set of criteria which they believe increase the chances that their loans will be repaid with interest. One of their rules is to demand some kind of collateral or security they can turn to if you fail to repay. Equity in a house or other real property is the most common kind of collateral. Obviously, lenders don't insist on this type of security because they want to own your home, but because they want you to repay the loan.

Most public lenders will want to see a business plan, but again, before you write up an elaborate one, check with each lender you plan to approach to find out specifically what it requires. If you try to take out a business loan from the Small Business Administration, you will need a fairly detailed business plan, including extensive financial projections, following the SBA's exacting guidelines. On the other hand, many small publishers start out by charging business expenses on their credit cards. Even though this is a high-cost and generally poor way to borrow, credit card companies won't ask to see business plans, which makes this option easy for many new publishers.

Working With Investors

Like lenders, investors want to use their money to make money. But that's where the similarity ends. People who invest in small business ventures are usually willing to accept the relatively high risks involved, but in return hope to enjoy big rewards. Some of them will take a much more active role in your business than lenders do, and others will expect you to keep in close contact—something that can consume both time and energy. And some investors can contribute expertise as well as money to your business.

Investors—with the exception of close family members and friends who are simply trying to support your dreams—generally require an ownership position in the business and some control over critical decision making because they expect to share in your growth and profitability as the business develops over time. For example, although your parents may invest without wanting active participation, chances are your entrepreneurial uncle Dave—and certainly a venture capital group—will want a seat on your board of directors and some say in how you make major decisions. How much ownership and how much influence they get is usually something you negotiate with every investor.

Private Investors

Private investors can be anybody—wealthy individuals, privately held companies, partnerships, and even employees who invest their money, time, or expertise in exchange for shares in the company. You should sit down right now and make a list of the individuals you know and respect who may have the personal wealth to help you get your business started. Think about people who have made some money in your market already, or people who have worked with you in some capacity in the past.

Many successful entrepreneurs look at their private investors as mentors as well as sources of financial support. You may be able to do the same thing. If you can find moneyed people who also have expertise or wisdom, and then structure a relationship with them that allows for a continuing exchange of information and ideas, you'll truly be making a good deal. One way to do this is to ask them not only for an investment, but to serve on your active board of directors, which periodically meets to review major business decisions and develop strategies for the future.

Conversely, it is a mistake to take on an investor you don't trust or have good personal rapport with—for example, a person who has made quick money in a business you don't respect—even if he or she is willing to give you the money your business needs to get started. The reason is that it can be very difficult, even impossible, to get rid of someone who holds a share in your business if your relationship goes sour. Even a minor shareholder can cause trouble for you, and a major shareholder can cause major trouble, so pick your investors carefully.

Public Investors

Public sources of investment money include venture capital firms, investment banks, the stock market, and mutual fund or retirement fund shareholders. By definition, public investors are people with whom you don't have a personal relationship, but they are willing to invest in your business because they judge that it will be profitable.

It's very rare for a start-up publication to involve public investors, but much more common for them to become involved when the business is more mature. You may, nevertheless, find yourself trying to explore this possibility if you cannot develop any personal funding sources. In that situation, find a banker or business broker who will help you develop the necessary business plans, contracts, and other documents you'll need to approach prospective investors. Business brokers normally will expect an up-front fee as well as a percentage of the funds they raise for you.

Before most public investors will be interested in investing in your publishing business it will need to be taking in at least $5 million to $7 million, or better yet, $10 million or more, in annual sales.

> **WARNING**
>
> **Going public involves a steep learning curve.** Running your business with public investors, especially if you sell stock, can be complicated, because there are strict laws regulating how you make business decisions and how you communicate with investors. You will need professional legal and accounting help managing a company that has public investors.

Working With a Parent Company

If you want to be a publisher, but don't absolutely need to own your own publishing business, you have several other possible options to raise start-up money. In each of these scenarios someone else, such as an existing publishing company or nonprofit organization, will own the business. But, assuming you will be involved in a major role and paid well, you may nevertheless find that this is a good way to bring your publishing idea to life.

Publishing Companies

Obviously, you don't have to start your own publishing company just to start a publication. If you already work for a publishing company, consider asking your employer to publish rather than quitting your job and looking for start-up money. Of course, if you take this route, the company will own the publication, not you. But it will also have all the financial headaches to worry about, while you still receive a paycheck. What's more, if your parent company is good at what it does, you can expect the publication to benefit from its expertise.

Keep in mind that it's unlikely an established publishing company will support your magazine idea if you don't already work for the company. Most companies simply don't accept ideas from outsiders. On the other hand, publishing companies will buy established magazines from independent entrepreneurs. It's certainly a reasonable strategy for you to start your magazine with private funds, then try to sell it to another publisher. This happens all the time. In this case, you can sell it outright and walk away from the magazine, or become an employee of the publishing company when it buys your magazine.

> ### One Reason Why Publishing Companies Don't Buy Ideas
>
> Someone from the Hearst corporation once told me about an entrepreneur who met with Hearst executives to discuss his idea for a new magazine. The executives told the man that his idea was not new to them, and that in fact, they were already well into the process of developing their own magazine on the same topic. Even so, the man sued Hearst when its magazine came out months later, claiming that Hearst had stolen his idea. He lost the suit, but the process was so disagreeable to the company that it quit meeting with outsiders about new magazine ideas.

Since the parent company will most likely retain 100% ownership and therefore exercise ultimate control (including the ability to give your idea away to someone else), the more you know about it the better. In particular, find out how it has handled other ventures in the past. Make sure you understand what it will expect from you and what you can expect from it.

Nonprofit Organizations

There are thousands of successful publications operated by nonprofit organizations (NPOs). One of the world's largest publications, called *AARP: The Magazine*, is sponsored by the nonprofit American Association of Retired People; there are 22 million subscribers in the United States. And, of course, many other widely read magazines and newsletters are also sponsored by NPOs, including *Sierra*, which reaches about 700,000 members of the Sierra Club nationwide, and *Mother Jones*, with 230,000 subscribers, published by the Foundation for National Progress. There is even an association for people who work at sponsored publications, called the Society of National Association Publishers. (See Chapter 14 for contact details.)

Don't be put off by the term "nonprofit." Nonprofit publications operate much like their profit-making brethren: selling ads and auxiliary products and hopefully making money for their parent organization. The big difference between a for-profit and nonprofit organization (NPO) is the way profits and assets are handled. A profit-making venture pays out the profits to its owners. An NPO keeps the profits and either uses them to improve the publication or hands them over to the parent organization to further its mission—helping senior citizens, improving young girls' self-esteem, fighting pollution, combating child abuse, or whatever its goals might be. Senior people working for nonprofit organizations are typically paid in the same general ballpark as other publishing professionals.

An NPO has one huge advantage over other publications: In lean times, you can ask individuals and institutions to donate money instead of looking only to subscription or product sales for income. Indeed, a publication that is not viable as a profit-making venture might succeed as a nonprofit precisely because people are willing to contribute to support the cause.

RESOURCES
You can find many examples of successful nonprofit publications in the online membership directories of the Independent Press Association (www.indypress.org) or the Society of National Association Publications (www.snaponline.org).

Corporate Sponsors

Many profit-making companies that aren't primarily in the publishing business nevertheless sponsor publications. American Express's *Travel & Leisure* magazine is one example that is distributed among American Express card-holders and even sold on newsstands. *Friendly Exchange*, published by the Farmers Insurance Group and sent to policyholders, is another. And, of course, many corporations publish newsletters they send to customers, dealers, and investors, sometimes on a fairly large scale.

Consider whether your publishing idea could be promoted to a corporate sponsor that would share the financial risks with you. For example, if you want to publish a magazine about trading, collecting, and maintaining classic Ford automobiles, you might approach the Ford Motor Company for sponsorship.

"Custom publishing" is the term used for publishing an entire magazine or a portion of it for a sponsor. Companies that specialize in custom publishing put out magazines for a variety of corporate sponsors. The sponsor owns the magazine, and pays the publisher for creating it.

> **RESOURCES**
> The Magazine Publishers of America (www.magazine.org) publishes a booklet about custom publishing, which includes a list of companies and their capabilities.

Sample Fundraising Strategies

A Solo Operator's "Good Life" Strategy: *Cruises Update*

Anne Cox wants to build up a publishing business that will make a decent profit, engage her creative energy, and be a good candidate for sale when she is ready to retire. She is willing to take some financial risks because if her business fails, she is young enough to recover her losses before retirement, and because her husband is capable of supporting the family for a few years if necessary.

While outright failure is Anne's worst nightmare, she is also afraid of simply failing to thrive. She doesn't want to expend her time (which she considers to be her most valuable asset) for years without a significant financial reward. Anne's business, then, has to be profitable enough to pay her a decent salary and must be capable of growing in value so that she will have something to sell when the time comes.

Anne needs about $80,000 to start her newsletter, *Cruises Update*: $52,000 for one-time start-up expenses and $30,000 to cover her first-year's operating losses. She raises the money by dipping into her retirement savings ($38,000), taking out a home equity loan ($20,000), and borrowing from her parents ($22,000). She also has four credit cards which give her access to another $24,000 that she can reluctantly use for emergency cash shortages.

Anne's first direct mail campaign generated $96,000 in gross revenues. She uses some of that money to repay her parents, and then she turns to her local bank to request a business line of credit to help her get through her first year's operating expenses. She shows them the excellent results of her direct mail campaign, her own impeccable credit history, and her business plan which details how her business will operate and how she will earn the money to pay off her debts. The bank agrees to extend a to-tal credit line of $20,000, but the interest rate it offers is fairly high, three points above the prime rate. Anne checks with a few other banks, learns she probably can't do better, and accepts the proffered line of credit.

During her first year and a half, the cash flow in Anne's business is hard to predict. As a result, there are a few weeks when her debt repay-ment obligations combined with other expenses means there isn't enough left in the bank to cover her own salary. But after a couple of years, cash flow improves and Anne's business starts to make a small profit. When it does, Anne goes back to her banker and asks to renegotiate the credit line. Anne's banker agrees to give her more credit on slightly easier repay-ment terms.

After five years, Anne's business is debt-free and is generating more than $50,000 per year in profits over and above her salary. This allows Anne to begin putting money back into her retirement savings. In addition, she invests some of her profits back into the business, adding a few ancillary product lines such as the online version of her database, and hires a few part-time freelance helpers to improve *Cruises Update*. She also knows that the business will be more valuable to an outside buyer if it is not en-tirely dependent on her, so she gives thought to developing products and services that other people can produce just as well as she can.

With all of her growth funded from profits or bank loans, Anne has retained complete ownership of *Cruises Update*. After about 12 years, her revenues are over $300,000 per year, her salary is $65,000, and her profits are $45,000.

At this point Anne decides to sell the business. She hires a mergers and acquisitions consultant who helps her locate three prospective buyers, all of them newsletter publishers in the travel field. However, even with the broker's help it takes Anne nearly a year to work out a sale that meets her goals. Eventually, she is able to find a buyer who sees a significant growth potential in the business and is willing to pay nearly $475,000 (equal to ten times her average annual profits), to be paid in equal installments over a period of five years. During the first year after the sale, Anne must make herself available part-time to the buyers for a reasonable fee, but after that her responsibility is over.

Publishing as a Sideline:
Computer Advertisers' Media Advisor

Jack Edmonston spent over 25 years as a marketing executive for publishing companies, first at International Data Group (IDG) and later for Cahners. Now he consults with marketing executives in the computer industry, advising them about developing effective ads for their products, managing advertising budgets, and selecting appropriate media. Jack's newsletter, *Computer Advertisers' Media Advisor (CAMA)*, covers these same topics. In this way it is a lot like thousands of other newsletters that grow out of a consulting practice or professional service company and provide a secondary business for their publishers. *CAMA* subscribers pay $195 per year for 12 eight-page issues.

Jack views the newsletter as an excellent way to keep in touch with prospective consulting clients as well as to provide useful information to a large group of people. He sees the newsletter as a sideline to his other activities because he can earn more money as a consultant than as a publisher. Still, Jack wants his newsletter to make enough money to make doing it part-time worth his while. If the newsletter ever fails to make a profit, Jack will quit publishing it. The newsletter, in existence for more than a decade, has consistently returned a small profit.

Because Jack wanted to control his own operation, he started *CAMA* with $10,000 from his own pocket, involving no outside lenders or investors. Jack had some experience in the publishing business, and so he knew he could start out with very little capital if he grew the business one step at a time. He used the first $10,000 to finance a direct mail test campaign that he wrote and organized himself. Nine months after the mailing went out, Jack had taken in 300 orders for a sample issue which he eventually converted to 100 paid subscriptions at $195 each. After paying the mailing costs and delivering sample issues, but without paying himself for any of his own time, Jack made $9,000 on the first mailing. He decided to continue publishing the newsletter.

After three years (and two more mailings), subscriptions leveled off at about 300, enough to be profitable, but not enough to pay all of his bills and finance future direct mail campaigns. So Jack quit doing mailings and focused on retaining the subscribers he accumulated during the first three years, and trying to get more by word of mouth, his modest website, and the subscription coupons he includes in each issue. Jack also generated some extra money by selling group subscriptions and reprint orders among the current subscribers.

By the end of the third year, Jack's revenues were $60,000 and his costs (without any more direct mail campaigns) were less than $35,000, so he could take out about $25,000 for himself. He considers this reasonable given that he spends about one week a month on the newsletter and the rest of his time on his thriving consulting practice. He continues to enjoy publishing *CAMA* and believes it keeps him in touch with interesting, important people while contributing to the success of his consulting practice. ●

Gathering and Using Financial Information

This chapter will help you collect and analyze financial information that you can use to make smart business decisions. Obviously, managing your publishing business is easier when you have reliable, easy-to-understand financial information. Yet many small business operators make do with poorly organized bookkeeping systems and incomprehensible financial reports. As a result, some of them struggle for years with problems they could have solved quickly if only they had the right information. As soon as some of these publishers fix their bookkeeping systems and financial reports, they are quickly able to fix nagging business problems, too.

Solo operators often find it especially hard to simultaneously keep the books and run the business. For them, creating a good financial information system is difficult because they don't have enough time or experience to do the job themselves and can't afford to hire—or aren't willing to pay for—competent help.

The good news is that useful bookkeeping systems don't have to be complicated or expensive. Low-cost accounting software combined with the occasional advice of a professional will allow you to develop a financial information system that meets your needs as well as your budget.

RESOURCES

Working From Home, by Paul and Sarah Edwards (Putnam Publishing Group), offers excellent advice about managing money for small businesses and solo operators. With suggestions included here, you can create a simple accounting system that is easy to maintain.

Another excellent book for solo operators is *Small Time Operator*, by Bernard Kamoroff (Bell Springs Press), which includes ledgers and worksheets, and instructions on how to use them.

Legal Guide for Starting & Running a Small Business, by Fred S. Steingold (Nolo), clearly explains the latest in law, business, and taxes for owners new to small businesses. And *The Small Business Start-Up Kit*, by Peri H. Pakroo (also published by Nolo), shows you how to launch a business quickly, easily—and with confidence.

All of these books will help you understand what you need from your accounting system, even if you hire someone else to run it. And there's a bonus: All of these books provide great tips for solving other important business problems like marketing, selling, and managing your time.

Financial Challenges

Beyond the basic goals of being efficient and profitable, periodical publishers have some additional financial concerns that are somewhat unique to the publishing field. This chapter explains how to get and use good financial information to help you handle these issues.

Cash Flow

Most manufacturers fill up a warehouse (or retail shelves) with products and then find customers to buy them. Subscription publishers do the opposite: They collect a bundle of paid-up customers and then create and deliver a series of products to them. That is, unlike customers in most other businesses, your subscribers pay you before your product is fully created.

While it's great to get money up front, it can be difficult to make the cash last until you have created and delivered the product. When the revenues from a direct mail campaign come in—perhaps even hundreds of thousands of dollars—you may feel rich for a few weeks. This feeling of prosperity will soon pass, however, as you deal with the reality of delivering the issues you've promised, and making a profit to boot. To stay afloat, you must carefully and accurately predict your future cash needs and save up to meet them.

Measuring Profits, Not Cash

Given the irregular cash flow endemic to the publishing business, it's not always easy to distinguish between cash in the bank and profits. For start-up publishers, there can be months between the time money comes in and expenses go out, or vice versa. Even if you're bringing in more cash than you're currently spending, you may not be running a profitable business in the long run. For one thing, costs of paper, printing, or mailing may increase between the time you sell a new subscription and deliver the final issue. And, as discussed in Chapter 3, you may lose money if most of your current subscribers don't renew, because you'll have to spend so much money to build a new relationship with replacement subscribers. Obviously, to avoid those kinds of problems, you need to know how to measure both your profits as well as your cash flow, and make necessary adjustments to your business as you go along.

The Battle of the Details

Publishers make decisions every day, many of which have financial consequences. To take just one simple example, suppose you decide to hang on to nonrenewing subscribers a little longer by sending them a few extra issues while you try to persuade them to renew. This decision will increase your production, fulfillment, and delivery costs, but may also produce some revenue if you accept ads and can base your rates on a larger number of readers. And of course, if some of the lapsed subscribers eventually renew, this, too, will increase your revenue base. Obviously, it's best to understand these extra costs and revenues before you make your marketing decisions.

In the course of any month you will make dozens of small decisions that can have a significant financial impact on your business, and your finances may get out of control if you don't have a good system to project the consequences of your decisions.

Special Tax Considerations

Periodical publishers have unique tax issues. The IRS allows publishers to defer the taxes they pay on subscription profits until all issues have been delivered. In effect, the tax code lets you keep the cash that you collect from subscribers in reserve and to pay it to yourself to cover the expenses of actually delivering issues. So any profits you end up with after you sell a 12-issue subscription aren't taxable until you deliver all of the issues.

The deferral of taxes is a benefit that comes with a price: Keeping track of deferred income is a bookkeeping headache. Fortunately, the same software that you use to manage your subscriptions will generally handle deferred income for you, too.

Why Fulfillment Often Isn't Fulfilling

"Fulfillment" is a term that covers the whole process of receiving subscription orders, entering them into a subscriber database, and generating mailing labels. In addition, fulfillment systems track renewals, deferred subscription income (an accounting idea unique to publishing), and all subscription promotion efforts.

Obviously, publishers want as few errors as possible in their fulfillment operations, and most systems include cross-checks to eliminate mistakes. As a result, many fulfillment systems are very inflexible: You have to use them precisely the way they were designed to be used, or the whole system won't work. For example, the publishers of *Bioworld Today*, couldn't find an off-the-shelf fulfillment program to use because they needed to update their subscriber list every day—theirs was a daily newsletter delivered by fax. Most software was designed to handle weekly or monthly publishing frequencies. The problem was finally solved when the publication was acquired by a company that had its own fulfillment software that could be modified to handle the daily frequency.

Since a subscriber database is so valuable to publishers, the choice of an appropriate fulfillment system is always very important. A few off-the-shelf fulfillment programs are listed in Chapter 14. You can also refer to *Folio: magazine's Source Book* issue—it's also listed in Chapter 14—to find service bureaus that handle fulfillment. It's a good idea to look at several different options before making any decision. Better still, ask other publishers what software or outside vendors they use. Publishers post questions like this on message boards all the time and get really great responses. Check out the Independent Press Association message board at www.indypress.org, or the Western Publications Association, Ask-the-Experts section of the website at www.wpa-online.org.

Using Numbers to Make Good Decisions

Accounting and financial information will help you understand your business and, as a result, run it better. While this point may sound obvious, it is lost on a surprising number of entrepreneurs. Too often, people use accounting information only to produce numbers that satisfy the IRS or their bankers, and not to teach themselves. They wind up with accounting reports that cover taxes and cash flows, but do little to illuminate the inner workings of their businesses.

Another problem: Standard accounting reports are not generally designed to help you measure your progress toward long-range, strategic goals. So even if you are careful and set up a good bookkeeping system, you won't automatically get all the key strategic information you need. For example, every accounting program will track your revenues, but none will track your market share. That's a big problem. Your accounting program will tell you if your revenues are lower than they were last year but it won't say anything about the revenues of other publishers in your niche. Let's suppose that their revenues are all down too. Without this information, you may be tempted to try and fix your publication, when in fact the problem is that your entire market is slowing down or headed for a shakeout.

Luckily, the strategic numbers you'll need usually aren't hard to find, once you decide to look for them. So in addition to organizing the same kind of general-purpose accounting system that all businesses need, you also need to define some key numbers—like market share—that are unique to your business situation, and find a way to regularly collect and review them.

Key strategic variables are numbers that measure your progress toward long-term goals. They help you determine whether or not your business is moving in the right direction. Since each business adopts different strategies at different times, you'll have to decide for yourself which variables are most useful to you.

Ultimately, all of the information you collect must help you accomplish three basic business goals.

1. To be able to focus your attention on your most profitable products, you need to know how much each contributes to your bottom line.

2. To be in a position to choose the most efficient marketing and selling tactic, you must be able to monitor the effectiveness of each one.

3. You must stay in touch with your market so that you can quickly understand changing circumstances. Strategic financial reports can help you stay focused on the future, quickly spot developing trends, and rapidly understand their significance.

Some Common Financial Variables and What They Indicate

AD/EDIT RATIO. This is the ratio of advertising pages to editorial pages. Most publications that accept ads establish a target ratio between the number of pages they produce and the number of pages they sell to advertisers. It can range from 20% advertising in a technical journal to more than 75% advertising in a high-fashion magazine.

AD PAGE COUNT. This is the number of ad pages you have sold for specific issues. Publishers generally look at upcoming ad pages as a way to budget a total page count for future issues. Obviously, this is also an important indicator of advertising demand and ad sales effectiveness.

ADVERTISING CONTRACT RATE. This is the percentage of your advertisers who are buying space according to long-term contracts. The rate can be measured per issue: how many pages in each issue are running under contract. Or, you can look at the average revenue you receive per advertising page, a number that will automatically reflect the frequency discounts advertisers qualify for with long-term contracts. Both numbers tell you not only a lot about whether you are operating profitably and efficiently, but also whether advertisers are satisfied with your publication.

BAD DEBT RATIO. This is the percentage of your advertisers or subscribers that fail to pay all or a portion of their bills. Bad debt numbers over 15% or 20% can signal real problems with your choice of customers or your selling tactics. You may need to adjust your credit policies, your sales strategies, or both.

CONVERSION RATES FOR SUBSCRIBERS. What percentage of your new subscribers sign on for a longer-term subscription or a second term? This rate indicates whether each of your promotions is reaching the right audience and whether your publication meets their expectations.

COSTS OF SALES. This is the total overhead costs for ad sales (travel, payroll, employee benefits) as a percentage of ad revenue. The result is a measure of sales productivity that you can compare across publications or with other publishing companies.

EDITORIAL, ART, AND DESIGN COSTS PER EDITORIAL PAGE. This is a dollar amount showing how much you spend to create the number of pages you are publishing. The number lets you develop meaningful budgets for creative expenses and compare your publishing expenses to those of other publications and industry norms. For a small newsletter, these costs may not be significant, but fat, glossy magazines need to control them tightly.

MARKET SHARE. This is your percentage of the total pages (or advertising dollars) sold by all publications in your market. Market share indicates competitive strength as well as the strategic positioning of each publisher. It can also help you track your own performance vis-a-vis that of your competitors.

NEWSSTAND SELL-THROUGH RATES. What percentage of the copies you distribute to newsstands or other retail outlets are being sold? Sell-through not only indicates whether you are distributing your copies in the right places but can help you determine what types of covers and editorial content sell best.

PAY-UP RATE FOR CREDIT-SOLD SUBSCRIPTIONS. This is the percentage of people who ordered a trial subscription and immediately received a few issues on credit and later paid up. The pay-up rate tells you a lot about whether your promotions are targeted to an audience that values your editorial content. If they canceled or wouldn't pay, they weren't the right prospects or didn't like your publication.

PER COPY PRODUCTION AND DISTRIBUTION COSTS. This is a dollar amount arrived at by dividing each issue's total spending on printing, paper, and postage by the total number of copies you print. Especially for magazines with high printing and distribution costs, this figure is a key to overall profitability, and one that publishers watch closely.

PER UNIT CONTRIBUTION TO OVERHEAD. This is a break-even number that reflects how much profit you are earning from each individual ad or subscription. It is measured by subtracting all of the variable costs (promotion, sales, production, and distribution expenses) from the revenues associated with each new ad or subscription you sell.

PROFITABILITY PER EMPLOYEE. This measures how much each of your employees is contributing to your profitability. Some publishers, for example, measure sales per employee or overhead as a percentage of revenues. When compared to your own baseline—or industry averages—these measurements help indicate your overall productivity.

RENEWAL RATES. What percentage of your subscribers continue to subscribe after a year or more of reading your publication? Since renewal subscriptions are almost always your most profitable ones, your renewal rate is a key to your long-term profitability. The percentage is usually measured for each group of subscribers—such as all the people whose subscriptions expire with your January issue—but analyzed over a longer period of time—for 12 months or more. The rate can also be used to analyze effectiveness of individual renewal letters against each other.

SUBSCRIPTION PROMOTION RESPONSE RATES. This is the percentage of your direct mail, bind-in cards, renewal solicitations, or other promotions that result in a sale. The response rate to each of these types of promotion indicates its effectiveness and allows you to make the best choices in the future.

Understand and Control Profits

Break-even analysis is a method for calculating your profits from each product you sell. (See Chapter 4.) This type of analysis asks you to identify all of your costs associated with making each sale, including selling, production, and delivery costs. These are called direct or variable costs because they increase every time you sell an extra unit. (By contrast, overhead costs like rent or salaries remain the same no matter how many units you sell.)

Variable costs are your key to profitability. Paired with your prices, variable costs can tell you exactly how much you earn (or lose) every time you sell another ad or subscription. Once you figure out your variable costs, you have a chance to adjust your expenses and fees so that every sale brings in a solid profit.

There's another benefit to using break-even analysis. Paying attention to your variable costs teaches you to stay in close touch with the business issues most important to your success. With editors, salespeople, and customers all demanding your attention, and problems sprouting up like mushrooms, it's not easy to stay focused on your long-range goals. Luckily, a break-even analysis can save lots of time because it points directly to the problems that you have to fix.

EXAMPLE: Anne Cox decided to offer her travel newsletter, *Cruises Update*, in three formats—an online database, a daily "hot list" delivered by fax, and the original printed biweekly newsletter. She arranged for online access through a vendor who charged Anne $1/hour for the time *Cruises Update* subscribers accessed her database. Figuring that each subscriber would only use about four hours per month, Anne estimated her online costs at about $48 per year per subscriber. As a result, Anne decided to charge them $65 per year for unlimited access, giving her a projected profit of $17 per year per subscriber.

After a year, Anne's three products were selling very well, but her profits were poor. Despite studying all of her sales and marketing reports, and controlling every nickel of expenses, she was still making a very meager profit. She hired a consultant named Sarah to help her figure out why.

Sarah's first step was to calculate the variable costs for each product by adding up all of the variable expenses associated with each and dividing the three totals by the number of people who subscribed to each format.

In doing so, Sarah ignored Anne's overhead expenses and focused only on the costs that rose or fell with the number of subscriptions Anne sold: printing and postage for the newsletter, telephone bills for the faxed editions, and online service fees for the database product.

It turned out that the faxed hot list and the printed newsletter were both profitable, but the online database product—which was very popular—was not. The problem, which of course Anne already suspected, was that some subscribers were spending way more than four hours per month accessing the database. On average, Anne paid $102 to the online vendor for each subscriber and only collected $65. She was losing nearly $50 per year on each subscriber. The database losses were totally wiping out her profits on the other two products.

Once Anne understood the problem, she moved quickly to fix it. She didn't want to raise the database subscription price because some customers had already complained that it was too high (and many customers used it only a few hours per month). Instead, Anne chose to look for a cheaper way to provide online access. She struck a good deal with a well-known commercial online service that was much less expensive. Her subscribers would join the online service and pay hourly access charges directly to the online service, which in turn would pay Anne 50 cents per hour whenever anyone used her database. Subscribers would like the arrangement because many of them already subscribed to the commercial service, which offered a host of features such as email, Internet access, and access to dozens of other databases.

Under the new deal, Anne collected less money initially from each subscriber, but her revenues increased the more they used her database. Some heavy users spent hundreds of dollars a year, but the average user spent much less. So under the new arrangement, everybody won: Subscribers got more access for less money and Anne's online product became more profitable.

Analyze Marketing and Sales

Let's assume now you have used a break-even analysis to show exactly where your greatest profits are generated so you can concentrate your business on these areas. Having found that profit focus, you now need a way to monitor your marketing and selling efficiency so that you can find new customers as profitably as possible. In other words, you need a way that you and your employees can keep score.

Many publishers are too busy chasing down new customers and making sales to stop and measure whether or not they are growing efficiently. And yet efficient growth is a key element in every successful publishing venture. For example, every direct mail campaign you conduct should tell you a great deal about how to make the next one more efficient and profitable. The same is true for every ad sales effort, renewal promotion, or telemarketing campaign.

Chapter 4 emphasized key marketing variables to watch. "Some Common Financial Variables and What They Indicate" earlier in this chapter, lists several other variables publishers commonly monitor. Your task now is to set up your accounting system to automatically collect as many critical marketing efficiency numbers as possible, so that you can routinely monitor them. When your strategies change, you'll have to change your financial reports to match your new strategy.

EXAMPLE: Kate Macdonald planned to grow her cross-country skiing magazine, *Silent Skier*, primarily by selling more copies on the newsstand and in specialty ski shops rather than by attempting to lure new subscribers through expensive direct mail campaigns. Kate knew that she could collect about $5 in additional advertising revenues for each copy that she sold to a subscriber or a newsstand customer, in addition to the income that she collected directly from the reader. Naturally, Kate wanted to sell as many copies as possible. But there was a problem: her magazine was chunky and colorful, so it was relatively expensive to print and distribute.

Given her circumstances and her growth strategy, Kate needed her financial reports to give her information about the following issues.

Sell-through rate. Kate had to carefully monitor the sales for the copies of *Silent Skier* she placed at every retail outlet. Because unsold copies went to a paper recycler, this variable was key to Kate's profitability. Using sell-through numbers, she could fine-tune her distribution, putting more copies in the most productive outlets and eliminating those where *Silent Skier* simply didn't sell.

Market share. Because *Silent Skier*'s long-term growth and profitability depended on capturing and maintaining a healthy share of the advertising dollars in her niche, Kate had to keep close tabs on how her publication was doing as compared to its competitors. Using market share data by advertising category—ski equipment, clothing, resorts, and the like—would also help her focus her sales efforts on the categories where she needed to gain or protect her market share.

Unit production. Because her magazine was costly to produce, unit production and distribution costs amounted to a big percentage of Kate's total expenses. Every penny she could shave off in that area would make a big difference in determining how profitable *Silent Skier* would be.

Use Simple Financial Reports

Once you've identified the information most important to your business, organize it into easy-to-use reports. Your accounting software, which provides reports that are handy for tracking budgets and expenses, monitoring cash flow, and paying your taxes, will contain some of the raw data you need, but won't do the whole job. You'll have to design the unique financial reports that deal with the key variables you've identified. The best ones are short, tailored to your current strategic situation, and easy to understand: a financial scorecard.

Step One: Decide What Numbers You Need to Watch

As we've seen, different bits of information will have different significance depending on your situation. For instance, if your business is new and your resources limited, cash may be more important than profits. If so, you will probably be eager to sell a subscription to anyone, regardless of his or her long-term value as a subscriber. During this period, you might have a financial report or scorecard that tracks new subscription orders and revenue—how many orders for how much money you are getting compared to what you expected. Later, as your cash situation improves, you will probably want to be more selective about selling subscriptions, realizing that it makes the most long-term financial sense to focus on those new subscribers who are most likely to renew when their subscriptions expire. Then you'll want to know how many subscribers in each target category are renewing, at what rate, and for how long.

> **TIP**
>
> **Focus on a few big issues.** Be selective about the variables you include on your current scorecard. Since you can't watch too many things at one time, pick the items that are either crucial to your survival in the short-term or that you believe will have the greatest overall impact on your long-term success.

Step Two: Set Goals for Every Key Variable

It's wise to include on your scorecard a projection of what you want your key numbers to be a year or more from now. This will allow your scorecard to accomplish an important function—keeping track of whether you are reaching your monthly and yearly goals. (See Chapter 3 about creating a long-term strategy for subscriptions, Chapter 5 for more about your ad sales strategy, and Chapter 12 for information about making strategies in general.) Assuming you have worked out your strategies, it's usually easy to identify the goals you'll need to meet to accomplish them. But if you don't have a strategy, don't make up arbitrary goals. Goals are useless unless you (and your collaborators) believe they can be achieved.

Setting specific goals can be a useful way to explain an overall strategy to employees and other helpers. For example, tell your sales staff that you are tracking advertising market share on your financial scorecard, not just ad revenues, and that will help them to understand your advertising sales goals. Once they see why market share is important to your business, brainstorm with them about how to win targeted advertisers away from specific competitors. And as part of doing this, ask them to help you project how much your market share might increase in the next year and then set a precise goal.

Similarly, you can use your scorecard to let key people know whether or not they are meeting their goals. To help accomplish this efficiently, most scorecards should track performance and compare it to budgeted goals on a monthly basis.

TIP

Track key numbers for a reasonable period of time. Real progress usually takes time. The gains that you will make in dealing with major publishing challenges such as circulation, ad sales, and market share won't happen overnight. So don't jump to quick conclusions until you track key numbers for long enough to allow real trends to develop. For instance, one terrific renewal campaign is great, but it's more significant if your renewals remain where you want them to be for the whole year. To avoid becoming confused by temporary fluctuations, most publishers look at annual averages or long-range trends for key variables.

Get Numbers You Can Trust

Let's face it: record keeping, budgeting, and paying taxes are headaches. But since you already realize that you must invest time and money to set up your accounting system, do it as efficiently as possible. Get someone competent to help you find the best and most automated solutions. It's probably obvious that if you make the effort to establish a good system to begin with, you'll save time and money down the road.

Find Competent Help

Because of publishers' special cash accounting and tax considerations, it makes sense to get help in setting up a good bookkeeping and tax accounting system from a professional who knows the periodical publishing ropes. Accountants with such specialized expertise may be hard to find. Still, even if you operate a small newsletter on a shoestring budget from your home, it will be a wise expenditure to make. If you can't find an accountant with publishing expertise, then look for a good small-business accountant, period. When you find one, ask him or her to study Section 455 of the IRS Tax Code, which explains the deferred subscription income rules that we described earlier.

The Importance of Getting Good Financial Advice!

I helped Hank Resnick make the painful decision to stop publishing his magazine, *The Berkeley Insider*, in Berkeley, California. By all accounts, *The Berkeley Insider* was a terrific magazine, but it was nevertheless a financial disaster for Hank and his partner, Bert Dragin. For four years they kept *The Berkeley Insider* going by scrimping and saving. In the end, there simply wasn't enough advertising revenue to support them, no matter how frugally they produced their magazine.

As we talked about closing *The Berkeley Insider*, I asked Hank what he thought had contributed the most to its downfall. Knowing how careful Hank is about money, I was surprised when he said, "If there's one thing I regret most it's that I never had someone holding my feet to the fire about spending money. My accountant managed my taxes pretty well, but he never suggested that I was spending too much money, or spending it foolishly. In short, he never challenged the wisdom of my expenditures. Maybe that's not an accountant's job, I don't know. But I think every publisher needs someone who will really insist that you ask the tough question, 'What am I really getting for all of that money?' I'm convinced we could have saved this magazine if only I'd had someone asking me those tough questions."

A good accounting system won't advise you about business or financial strategies, but at least it will place at your fingertips the kind of information you'll need to communicate with the people who can advise you about marketing, management, and strategic planning issues. And it should make it easier for you to see if you are heading for a financial abyss early enough to take corrective action.

There are several ways to find a reliable accountant with experience working with publishers.

- *Publishing referrals.* There are sure to be periodicals based in your area. Make a list of those you consider to be most efficiently run, and ask those publishers or accounting managers for referrals. You may be lucky enough to find an affordable local accounting professional who specializes in this area.

- *National organizations.* If you can't get any local referrals, you can ask the following national organization to help you locate publishing specialists. (See Chapter 14 for contact details.)

  - The American Accounting Association in Sarasota, Florida, can provide you with a membership directory; its website is at www. aaahg.org.

- *Publishing associations.* Join one or two of the publishing associations listed Chapter 14, and then use their message boards to ask other publishers for referrals.

  - The U.S. Commerce Department operates local Small Business Development Centers where you can get much useful advice and information.

> **TIP**
>
> **Make sure you like and respect your accountant.** It's worth the time and effort to look for an accountant who makes you feel comfortable about accounting information. You'll get better service if you are comfortable with your accountant and able to confide in him or her.

Automate the Process

In a typical publishing business, a complete accounting system contains all of the following pieces of software.

- *General business accounting programs* to handle bills, receipts, debts, payroll, and inventory. Your accountant can probably recommend the best accounting programs for your business. These days you can buy excellent small business accounting software for a few hundred dollars or less. Two of the most popular are *QuickBooks* from Intuit and *Peachtree Accounting* from Peachtree Software. These programs have a wealth of accounting expertise built right into them. Both contain pop-up help documentation that will explain basic accounting concepts as you work through a task. You can learn a lot about accounting just by using either one. Accounting programs range from under $50 to many hundreds of dollars, depending on their complexity.

• *Database programs* to maintain information about each subscriber and advertiser, generating individual invoices, renewal notices, and mailing labels. Subscriber databases are generally managed by fulfillment programs or outside fulfillment service bureaus. When linked to your other accounting programs, subscriber and advertiser databases can help you to predict revenues, analyze the results of sales campaigns, and monitor variables like renewal rates. There are several customized database options for publishers and you can find them through *Folio:* magazine's *Source Book* issue. (See Chapter 14 for contact details.) You can also find fulfillment software for your office computer. And there are personal computer database programs designed specifically to manage advertiser databases. You can find these specialized programs through ads in *Folio:* magazine or the *Newsletter on Newsletters.* Some are also listed on the website links page at www.publishingbiz.com.

• *Spreadsheet programs* such as Microsoft Excel or Lotus 1-2-3 that can import information from your accounting system and then allow you to generate customized reports, such as a monthly sales report. You can also use these powerful tools to explore different "what if" scenarios and to bring together many different kinds of information that will allow you to do the type of analysis of your business that we discussed earlier in this chapter. If you don't already know how to use them, you may want to learn.

Tips on Buying

It's essential to purchase programs you can learn to understand and feel comfortable using. Look for these general characteristics.

- READABLE REPORTS. Before you settle on any accounting system, look at the management reports it generates. Does the language make sense or is it full of jargon and unintelligible abbreviations?

- ACCURATE INFORMATION. Most good accounting programs build in checks and balances to flag simple bookkeeping mistakes. Look for these automatic safeguards.

- EFFICIENCY. Keeping the books is labor-intensive, and each time someone enters new information into your accounting system by hand, mistakes can happen. Programs that allow for lots of accurate automatic links will require less work on your part, and leave less room for error.

- LOGICAL CONNECTIONS BETWEEN VARIABLES. An ideal accounting system would automatically connect all related entries—for instance, as you add new subscribers, your program should automatically increase your production and distribution budgets. Look for programs that do this.

- GOOD USER MANUALS. Someday, you may turn over your bookkeeping chores to someone else. Make sure your software comes with the kinds of top-notch instructions that will make it easy for an outsider to step in and run your system.

TIP

Build your system around the strongest individual element you can find. If you find a program that you like very much—for instance, an advertiser database program—look seriously at buying other programs that link to it, even if they are not your first choices in their own categories.

EXAMPLE: Tony Thomas, publisher of the model railroading magazine, *Tracks*, found a subscription fulfillment program called *QuickFill* that ran on the Windows operating system. He decided to buy it, even though all of his other publishing programs operated on Macintosh computers. He chose *QuickFill* because it was easy to install, handled all the functions he needed, and provided sensible reports. In addition, it came with good technical support from the vendor, including a training manual that was very thorough.

Tony paid about a thousand dollars for a top-of-the-line version of *QuickFill* that could handle several publications in one database. Naturally, he also had to buy an IBM-compatible computer that would run Windows. After going to the trouble of buying a new computer and putting all his subscribers into the new *QuickFill* database, Tony took the next step and moved all of his general accounting files and spreadsheets into Windows programs so that he could link them. He spent about $700 buying a new Windows accounting program and spreadsheet software. The transition took him several months to accomplish, but the end result was well worth the effort: Tony's data flowed so seamlessly from one program to the others that he ended up with better information and, as a result, more control of his business.

A Sample Publisher's Scorecard: *Cruises Update*

Remember Anne Cox, our fictitious home-based newsletter publisher? The table on the next page shows Anne Cox's scorecard for her newsletter business after she's been publishing for five years. Because her primary concern at this point is profitability, that's the focus of her scorecard. It highlights the profits from each product so that she can see which ones are generating the bulk of her income. Notice that while it covers a lot of ground, it nevertheless fits onto one page. This example shows only the month of June, but notice that Anne's scorecard shows the whole first half of the year, not the individual months. She designed her scorecard this way because she wants to be able to look at six-month trends in addition to the results of a single month.

Annes Publishing Company
MONTHLY SCORE CARD
MONTH of: June

		YEAR TO DATE			YEAR-END FORECAST		
		Budget	Actual	Variance	Budget	Actual	Variance
	Cruises Update (Print Newsletter) RENEWAL INCOME						
1.	Revenue per Renewal	$43.00	$43.00	100%	$43.00	$43.00	100%
2.	Direct Costs per Renewal	$8.25	$8.65	105%	$8.25	$8.60	104%
	Overhead Contribution Per Renewal	$34.75	$34.35	99%	$34.75	$34.35	99%
4.	Renewal Rate (%)	85%	82%	96%	85%	82%	96%
5.	Number of Renewals	3800	3649	96%	7800	7490	96%
6.	Total OH Contribution From Renewals	$132,050	$125,343	95%	$271,050	$257,656	95%
	NEW SUBSCRIPTION ORDERS						
7.	Number of Orders	1500	1050	70%	2500	1694	68%
8.	Overall Response Rate	1.80%	1.26%	70%	1.80%	1.22%	68%
9.	Revenue Per Order	$24.00	$24.00	100%	$24.00	$24.00	100%
10.	Direct Costs Per Order	$18.00	$19.25	107%	$18.00	$19.25	107%
11.	Overhead Contribution Per Order	$6.00	$4.75	79%	$6.00	$4.75	79%
12.	Total OH Contribution From New Orders	$393	$389	99%	$393	$384	98%
13.	NET OVERHEAD CONTRIBUTED	$141,050	$130,331	92%	$286,050	$265,703	93%
14.	Per Subscription Served	$27	$28	104%	$28	$29	104%
	Cruises Hot List (Faxed)						
15.	Number of Subscribers	636	658	103%	1236	1378	111%
16.	% of Print Subscribers	12%	14%	117%	12%	15%	125%
17.	Revenue Per Fax Subscription	$498	$498	100%	$498	$498	100%
18.	Direct Costs Per Fax Subscription	$393	$389	99%	$393	$384	98%
19.	Net Overhead Contributed	$66,780	$71,707	107%	$129,780	$157,046	121%
20.	Per Subscription Served	$105	$109	104%	$105	$114	109%
	Cruises Database (Online)						
21.	Number of Users	1500	1437	96%	3000	2937	98%
22.	Average Hours per User per Month	8.00	9.35	117%	8.00	10.00	125%
23.	Total Access Hours	12,000	13,436	112%	24,000	29,370	122%
24.	Revenue Per Hour	$0.50	$0.50	100%	$0.50	$0.50	100%
25.	NET OVERHEAD CONTRIBUTED	$6,000	$6,718	112%	$12,000	$14,685	122%
26.	Per User	$4	$5	117%	$4	$5	125%
27.	Total Overhead Contributions (From All Products)	$213,830	$208,755	98%	$427,830	$437,434	102%
28.	OVERHEAD EXPENSES	$175,800	$184,600	105%	$351,600	$369,200	105%
29.	NET PROFIT	$38,030	$24,155	64%	$76,230	$68,234	90%

Most of Anne's income comes from her printed newsletter, *Cruises Update*, and the most profitable source of income for the newsletter is renewals. So her scorecard begins by looking at renewal incomes (lines 1 through 6). If you look at line 5, you can see that Anne's renewals are down slightly for the year's first half. On line 2, you can also see she's spending more per renewal than she planned, probably because she's working harder to sell each one. The net effect is that Anne's renewals will generate $257,656 instead of the $271,050 she budgeted (see line 6). That's $13,000 less income than she had expected for the year unless, of course, she can turn this situation around.

New orders for the printed newsletter should generate about $15,000 income per year (line 12). Anne sells nearly all of her new subscriptions through direct mail, and there are two keys to profits from new orders: the response rate to direct mail solicitations and the direct costs of fulfilling an order. As you can see on line 8, Anne's overall response rates are dropping from 1.8% to 1.26%, probably because her subscription market is approaching saturation. And on line 10 you can see that her direct costs for new orders are going up. If these trends continue, Anne will earn significantly less money than she had planned from new orders before the year is out (line 12, year-end forecast).

Anne's daily faxed hot sheet product is very profitable. You can see on line 14 that she earns about $100 from every subscriber. Since she only promotes this product by running ads for it in her printed newsletter and on her website, her promotion costs are very low. As you can see on line 16, only about one out of seven subscribers to the printed newsletter also buys the faxed hot sheet. But since each subscription is so profitable, Anne might be wise to spend more money promoting the fax service. For example, she might print colorful flyers to insert with the newsletter instead of simply running an ad.

Anne's scorecard next shows the key variables for her online database product. This product is managed by a commercial online service that pays Anne a 10% commission for the hourly access fees it collects from people who use her database. The net revenue to Anne from this arrangement is 50 cents per hour of access. The 10% commission rate seems low, but the service handles all of the billing and collection headaches, as well as marketing the product to its many millions of subscribers. Thus, it's a hassle-free product for Anne. For her, the way to make more money with the database is to make it more useful so that people spend more time looking at it. She tracks the number of users and their average access time per month (lines 21 and 22).

On line 28 of her scorecard, Anne records all of her overhead expenses in one lump sum. The figure represents dozens of details, from office supplies to insurance premiums. She doesn't need to look at each detail regularly because her overall strategy is the same for all of them: spend as little as possible.

Anne uses this monthly scorecard to make decisions about her day-to-day operations. In particular, since the scorecard compares the profitability of the three publications (lines 8, 16, and 24), Anne can use it to consider shifting resources from one publication to another (more profitable) one.

Anne doesn't have any employees, but if she did, she could share this scorecard with them and use it to keep everyone marching in the same direction. Anne also doesn't have any debt, which may be unusual for a small business owner. If she had debts to repay, her scorecard would probably track her cash flow so that she could be prepared to keep up with payments when they come due. And if she had any partners, lenders, or outside investors, Anne would certainly use this scorecard to keep them informed about her business. ●

Getting Help From Other People

Inexperienced publishers sometimes waste money and miss important opportunities because they make mistakes while learning about the periodical business. While some business blunders are to be expected in any new business, many publishers overlook a vital fact: Getting knowledgeable help at the beginning of a publication's life really can help you make better decisions.

Fortunately, you don't have to live without needed expertise just because you can't afford to hire a stable of pricey publishing experts. This chapter explains how to get low-cost, effective help from experienced people when you can't afford to hire a full-time staff. And even if you have generous funding, you should be able to use these measures to get the most for your money.

Making Limited Resources Work

A few big publishing companies have all the resources they need for any project, but most new publishers have to manage with much less. Like many other small business owners, most novice publishers are tempted to go it alone, or to involve a small group of relatively inexperienced helpers.

Fortunately, there are better approaches. Among the ways to get experienced help at an affordable price are to:

- borrow good ideas from other publishers
- outsource—that is, hire experienced companies to handle jobs you don't know how to do by yourself
- take advantage of free advice from your allies and supporters, and
- hire professionals and other experts as part-time employees or independent contractors.

Borrow Good Ideas

Always keep in mind that somebody, somewhere, has already solved every conceivable publishing problem. It follows that you can usually save time and avoid errors by borrowing good ideas from other publishers. Because most publishers face similar problems, you can often imitate innovators with good results.

But suppose you have a specific problem that you can't solve by observing what others do. One approach is to contact other publishers and ask for help. So long as you are not directly competing with them, other businesspeople will often respond positively to direct and simple questions like:

- How have you organized your advertising sales staff?
- Why do you limit each advertising salesperson to 30 accounts?
- Has this arrangement increased your sales results?
- Can you recommend anyone to help me find and train advertising sales employees?

EXAMPLE: The American Buddhist Society's directors decided that they should try to expand their nonprofit organization membership by selling their magazine, *Sitting Well*, at bookstores and newsstands. Publisher Lila Keene was willing to try it, but she had no experience with single-copy sales. She told the board that she would research this potential market and report back to them. Then she consulted the Standard Rate and Data Services databases (see Chapter 14), looking for magazines that were similar in purpose to hers—especially those published by nonprofit associations—that distributed a significant number of copies on newsstands.

Lila found 13 publications more or less similar in size and frequency. She then called their publishers asking for information about newsstand distribution. Three never returned her calls, four refused to help, and two referred her to their circulation managers—who also left her calls unanswered. Four publishers, however, were very helpful. They gave her the names of their distributors and explained how their distribution contracts worked. Since *Sitting Well* didn't directly compete with any of them, all were willing to tell

Lila very specific information. They also told her about the Independent Press Association (IPA) and the Society of National Association Publishers (SNAP)—both listed in Chapter 14—where she could get additional advice and information. After joining IPA and SNAP for a total investment of only $500, Lila was able to sign onto the online message boards for both groups. She posted her problem on each list and got several good suggestions from other publishers whose practical advice was based on their own experiences. Now, she goes back to both message boards whenever she needs help.

As it happened, several publishers raved about the same newsstand distribution consultant, Raoul. Lila called him, explained the *Sitting Well* situation, and asked for a detailed proposal about how he could help and what his services would cost.

Based on what she learned, Lila presented a report to her boss which detailed what it would take to get *Sitting Well* onto the newsstands. She also presented Raoul's proposal as well as other information she had gathered from her publishing contacts about the potential benefits and costs associated with newsstand distribution. Both Lila and the society's directors agreed that newsstand sales might be profitable if handled by an outside professional, so Lila began to work with Raoul to develop a newsstand circulation plan.

One Friendly Publishers Association

The Independent Press Association (IPA) is one I can heartily recommend, especially for very small companies and startups. Its mission is to promote progressive and alternative media.

That said, I encourage publishers of all stripes to check out the IPA. The organization helps with newsstand distribution, a revolving loan fund, technical reports, conferences, and grants for short-term consulting services. No other publishers' association has the same mix of services and its member publishers are extremely generous with one another. Dues are very reasonable. Membership details are posted at the IPA's website at www.indypress.org.

Give the Tough Jobs to Outsiders

Hiring outside business services instead of employees is one of the favorite cost-saving strategies of small businesses. Name any business service—bookkeeping, computer programming, collections, graphic design, copywriting (to mention just a few)—and you'll find small firms willing to do it for you.

In addition to saving money for their clients, which they usually do, outside services offer these important benefits to new publishers.

- *Flexibility.* As mentioned, your needs are likely to change over the life of your business. This is particularly true in the first year or two when businesses often grow the fastest. Outsourcing lets you easily switch to different, and probably more sophisticated, service providers as your needs evolve.

- *Expertise.* Besides getting expert help from outsiders at a reasonable price, outsourcing allows you to gradually learn their skills which you can later implement in-house. For example, the agency that processes your subscription orders and generates mailing labels can also teach you how to keep track of promotions and how to save money on postage.

- *Simplicity.* A service company handles all of its own administrative headaches: hiring and firing people, keeping up with technology, paying taxes. Freed from all of those concerns, you can concentrate on the core tasks of your business.

If you find the right service companies, you can make them permanent members of your team. Many small business owners use the same outside services for decades because the relationship works so well for both of them. The next section gives tips on how to find good services and manage your relationships with them.

Solicit Free Advice

Good, free advice is often readily available from people with an interest in your success. Examples include vendors who want to sell you their services (printing, subscription fulfillment, even a long-distance telephone company); people who lend you money or invest in your business; and any others who stand to benefit from the success of your publication such as family, readers, even potential advertisers. For example, a bulk-mailing company that wants your business may explain new or emerging technologies that could provide more affordable solutions to your direct mail problems.

Because your business allies are busy with their own affairs, they will appreciate a straightforward approach that lets them provide the most help in the shortest time. Tell them what you are trying to do, and ask them simple, direct questions like these:

- Is there a better way to organize my direct mail campaign?

- How can I test several different subscription offers in this mailing while still getting the total number of new orders I need?

- Should I set up this mailing all on my own, or should I find a more experienced person or organization to do it for me?

- If you think I need expert help, can you recommend someone and suggest what I should pay for it?

EXAMPLE: Tony Thomas had four employees helping him publish *Tracks*, his magazine for model railroaders. Tony knew that he and his staff could keep costs down by producing *Tracks* on schedule and cutting back on last-minute changes, but neither Tony nor his employees had much experience in doing this. So Tony had a talk with Paul, his printer:

Tony: "What can we do to keep our printing costs down?"

Paul: "Hire a seasoned production manager who knows how to meet deadlines on time, every time."

Tony: "I can't afford to add any new employees for at least another year. Hiring someone now just isn't an option. What can *Tracks* do in the meantime?"

Paul: "One thing I can do is give you an overview of the printing process so you can appreciate the impact of your decisions. Press time is expensive; to save money, you need to schedule it in advance and then live by that schedule to the minute. I suggest that you hire a part-time production consultant to help you create schedules and procedures that will keep you out of trouble until you can afford to hire full-time help."

Tony, his editor, and his advertising director went to the printing plant for an intense, but informal, course in printing. They worked their way through the plant, studying every step in the printing process. Back home, the *Tracks* group developed production schedules together and then reviewed them with Paul.

Paul also introduced the *Tracks* staff to Marsha, the veteran production manager at *Bayside Boating* magazine. Marsha invited them to visit her offices where she explained her work to them and gave them copies of the production forms and schedules she used. She also agreed to spend a Saturday consulting with them, for a fee. In the process, Marsha earned her pay twice over by suggesting some simple design changes that would allow Tony to produce *Tracks* for less money. A year later, when Tony hired a consultant to streamline his production operations, his whole team understood more about what they needed from the consultant—and what they should expect her to do—because of the advice they got from Paul and Marsha.

> **TIP**
>
> **Pay fairly for good advice.** Many people are willing to help new publishers get started, but nobody wants to be taken advantage of. If you want to ask more than a half dozen direct questions to someone who doesn't stand to benefit directly, offer to hire him or her and pay a reasonable hourly fee. All advisors, paid or not, will appreciate your acknowledging the value of their time.

Vendors

Certain vendors may be more important to your success than your employees, investors, or customers. Printers, newsstand distributors, subscription fulfillment agencies, advertising sales firms, and direct marketing agencies can all make critical contributions to your success, especially for small or new publications. There have been many situations in which vendors saved publishers tons of money and kept them from making deadly business mistakes. And the opposite also happens—a vendor stands quietly by while the publisher self-destructs. The point is, you need to choose your vendors very carefully and then build a solid working relationship with them.

If yours is a small business, you may find it hard to get your fair share of attention from a vendor who deals with lots of bigger clients. Sometimes you can cut through this indifference; other times you will have to seek out another vendor who will work with you to grow your business.

Choose Carefully

Printing and postage are the biggest expenses for most newsletters and magazines. There is only one post office, but luckily, there are many printers to choose from, and you should talk to several before you pick one. Make a mock issue and then ask all of them to bid on it. The bidding process will teach you loads about each vendor, and also about the printing business generally.

Choose each of your printers and vendors as carefully as you would choose a permanent employee. Shop around, get references, look over their work, and ask a lot of questions. And remember that while price is a major concern, it is not the only one. Service is equally important.

Finally, if everything else is equal, choose the people you like the most over the ones who just don't inspire you. If you like the people you work with and they like you, loads of unexpected benefits are likely to flow from your relationship.

Learn Their Business

Try to understand the business of all the vendors you deal with so that you can use them the most effectively. For one example, your vendors need to be paid, just like you. If you understand their cash flow needs, and always get your check to them before they have to call and beg for it, chances are you'll be treated as a preferred customer.

EXAMPLE: Ben Wiggins, the editor of *Silent Skier* magazine, hired Patricia's small company, Pre-Press Productions (PPP), to transfer *Silent Skier* articles and ads into digital files to be sent to the printer. The files were due at the printer's plant on Monday morning.

Ben's articles were due at PPP at 9:00 a.m. on Fridays, but it was often well into the afternoon before he made the delivery to PPP. One Friday afternoon after delivering the articles to PPP, Ben stayed around for a few minutes and watched Patricia sit alone at a computer screen while her employees left for the weekend.

"Want to go have a beer?" Ben asked her.

"Can't," said Patricia. "I'll be here till 10 o'clock finishing this job and then setting yours up right behind it."

"But what about your staff?" said Ben. "Aren't they staying around to help you?"

"Hey, it's the weekend. If I ask them to stay, I'll have to pay overtime, and I just can't afford that right now," Patricia replied.

"Hold on," said Ben. "Let's talk about this. I'm making your life miserable, aren't I?"

They talked for a while and Ben learned a lot about Patricia's business problems. For instance, he learned that many of her clients were, like Ben, chronically late delivering materials. She often had to pay her staff overtime or make up for the delays by herself. Hearing this, Ben decided to rearrange his editorial schedule so that he would be sure to always get his materials to Patricia on time. After a few weeks of this, Ben was surprised to receive a thank-you note and a case of his favorite beer from Patricia. Later, when he reciprocated by taking her to lunch, the two of them were able to figure out a couple of additional efficiencies that would end up cutting Ben's bill.

Review Contracts

Even if you love your printer and never want to switch, you may have to anyway. What if his plant burns down? What if his accountant runs away with the money and he's forced into bankruptcy? What if he sells the business to someone you don't want to work with? Under any of these circumstances, you'd be stuck if you didn't know any other printers. The same is true for every vendor you depend on, and that's why you should always know about your options.

When your vendors' competitors call or want to stop by and bid for your work, let them. Get to know who they are and what they can do for you. There have been many technical innovations in the printing business in recent years, most of which save time and money for publishers. Some printers keep up with these changes better than others do, so it's important to connect with many different printing vendors. In the process, you'll learn many things about printing that may prove useful, even if you stick with your current printer.

> **TIP**
>
> **Always check print prices.** Periodically, you should sit down and review every important vendor contract—especially printing, which will probably be your biggest bill. Even experienced publishers with long-term vendor relationships put their printing contract out to bid at least every three years, sometimes more often. In between, they take time to meet with other printers and to learn about new developments in the printing industry. That information helps them to negotiate wisely at contract renewal time.

Foster Good Relationships

Spend time with your vendors. Ask them about trends and developments in their businesses, and tell them about your plans. Never assume that a vendor knows about your market or your products the way that you do. You must be prepared to educate them. For example, tell them about your customers and how your publication helps them. Share your successes with them. If you put up a website offering sample issues and thousands of people respond, make sure you tell your newsstand distributor about it so it knows your magazine generates that kind of interest.

An Experienced Publisher Talks About Vendors

John Griffin is president of *National Geographic* magazine. Here's what he told me about vendors:

"Vendors are key contributors to any publishing business, but especially to a new one. The newsstand distributor is a typical relationship that can make the difference between succeeding and failing. If you are a small magazine with a relatively small distribution and you think you have big potential, well, you've got to realize that there are a thousand other magazines out there who think they have big potential, too. You've got to demonstrate your willingness to work to make things happen. Don't just yell at your distributor, go out into the market. Visit retail stores and wholesalers to find your success stories so you can use the good news to get your distributor excited about your magazine. That kind of attention is very important and it really pays off. You're only going to get as much as you put into these relationships, regardless of your size."

Consultants and Independent Contractors

Much of the time, a new publisher can make and implement good decisions with common sense and hard work. Sometimes, though, you really need expert help. Experienced people often have tools you don't know about, as well as information resources and unique skills you haven't had the time to develop on your own. In short, they can often achieve superior results in much less time than you can.

The business of periodical publishing is complicated, and many times a single problem (for example, a shortage of operating cash) can be fixed only by making changes in several areas of your operation simultaneously—perhaps rescheduling renewal promotions, modifying advertiser credit policies, and working with creditors to restructure debts. Sometimes you may need the advice of several different people to help you solve a major problem.

Fortunately, you can often get the expertise you need by hiring consultants and independent contractors. And often, one savvy expert can direct you to others.

Get the Best From Outside Experts

Sometimes helpers aren't helpful. In many instances publishers follow bad advice that results in wasted time and money pursuing the wrong solutions to their problems. Knowing what you should expect from the people you turn to for general business advice as described below, can help you avoid those wasted hours and dollars.

- *They should ask lots of questions and sincerely solicit your input.* A surprising number of consultants are like magicians with only one rabbit up their sleeve. They pull out the same old bunny no matter what the situation. Obviously, this doesn't work well in the publishing business, where there are loads of possible problems and no one solution to any of them. How do you spot a one-trick consultant? Anyone who is really going to help you fix your troubles has to start by asking you a lot of questions: How do you perceive the problem? What have you already done to try to fix it? What other possible solutions have you identified? In short, your helpers should be at least as curious and open to new ideas as you are yourself, and probably more so.

- *They should be willing to admit to what they don't know.* Nobody has all the answers. Because publishing is such a specialized business, you will often encounter people who are experts in one area (like circulation) but have only very general knowledge about another (like finance or ad sales). Good advisors will tell you right away if they can't help you solve a particular problem, and might direct you to more qualified people.

- *They should be willing to educate.* Good helpers should be willing to teach you what they know so that you can be less dependent on them in the future. Like a good physician who helps you avoid medical problems by teaching you how to stay healthy on your own, they should work to empower you to the maximum extent possible. If, instead, they treat their techniques and information as secrets you are expected to pay for over and over, choose someone else.

- *They should tell the truth.* Often, an expert is called in to solve a particular problem and then discovers that others need fixing as well. For instance, a publisher might ask for help with developing a new promotion to improve renewal rates. But the hired consultant may conclude that weak content is the real reason renewals are lagging. If that's the situation, a good expert will say so, even if it means risking the ire of the publisher who believes his or her periodical is nearly perfect.

Beyond finding the right consultants in the first place, there are many ways you can make the most of your relationships with your consultants.

Act Promptly

If you know or suspect you'll be out of cash in July, don't wait until June to deal with the problem. This advice may seem obvious, but it's human nature to procrastinate and hope a looming problem will fix itself. It's far better to start working on a problem as soon as you see or strongly suspect it. This will typically afford you (and your consultants) many more options to cope with it. By contrast, if you wait until you face a true emergency, you'll be forced to accept a last-minute solution—one that is highly likely to be unsatisfactory.

EXAMPLE: Kate Macdonald, the publisher of *Silent Skier* magazine, called in a consultant named Carl to help her find a new ad sales team shortly after the last of her three salespeople quit. As it turned out, Kate's first signs of trouble with ad sales had surfaced a year earlier, when ad pages started falling off and her sales team began to push for a new rate and commission structure. Although they raised the yellow flag as soon as they saw they were losing accounts and having trouble replacing them, Kate refused to take their warnings seriously and didn't change her rate card or sales pay structure. Before long, the ad salespeople started looking for other work. It took nine months, but eventually they all moved on.

Carl flatly told Kate that waiting a year to deal with the falling ad sales might cost Kate her business. While she had been arguing with her salespeople and using up her operating capital, advertiser relationships had fallen apart. He told Kate it might well turn out to be too late to create a new selling strategy, find qualified people, train them, and have them repair the damaged relationships.

Carl also urged Kate to face a larger strategic problem: Why did her advertising sales fall off in the first place? Was her niche in trouble? Were competitors skimming off good accounts? If so, unless changes could be made quickly, a new ad sales team would likely face exactly the same problems that had discouraged her former salespeople.

Luckily, Carl could help Kate. Together, they met with 15 of Kate's top advertisers and, instead of focusing on selling ad space, they interviewed the advertisers about the evolving cross-country skiing market. They learned enough from those meetings to quickly develop a new strategy for *Silent Skier* that many advertisers greeted enthusiastically. Carl also helped Kate change her commission schedule and find seasoned salespeople who were willing to pitch in and help turn the situation around. Within a year, they had *Silent Skier* back on track.

Be Open to Unpopular Advice

Getting to the root of your problem may mean facing some unpalatable facts. Although it's tough to do sometimes, it can help if you are willing to let others define your problem as broadly as possible and then really listen to as wide a range of advice as you can find.

EXAMPLE: Tony Thomas, the publisher of *Tracks* magazine, suddenly began to have trouble selling ads. To cope with this he hired Rachel, an experienced freelancer, to create new advertising sales materials, including a media kit. It didn't take Rachel long to see that the tactical solutions Tony wanted wouldn't solve his larger strategic problem, which was that his core market was shrinking. In Rachel's view, Tony's first problem was to adapt his target audience so that he could attract different kinds of advertisers.

For example, he might be able to attract Amtrak, BritRail, and EuroRail ads if he could include active train travelers in *Tracks'* readership. This advice wasn't what Tony wanted to hear, so he fired Rachel and hired Iris, another marketing consultant, to redesign his sales materials.

Fortunately for Tony, Iris gave him the same advice as Rachel had. She urged him to investigate his market more carefully so that he could develop an appropriate new strategy, and she offered to help. Eventually, Tony agreed to Iris's proposals. With her help, Tony discovered that segments of his market—such as retirees and older hobbyists—were decreasing in number and interest, but that there were some pockets of growth and stability within the model railroading industry such as families with young children. A reader survey proved that young families were avid consumers of train-related products, including railroad vacations, books about train lore, and replicas of historic trains. Tony crafted a new circulation strategy to expand his readership among families, and Iris developed a new ad sales campaign to match. The work took several months to complete, but the result was very good: *Tracks'* subscription and ad revenues first leveled and then began to climb.

Don't Hesitate to Reject Ideas

You don't owe anything to an expert except a fair, open-minded hearing. It makes no sense to follow inappropriate advice, no matter how experienced the advisor. After you have done your best to filter out your own biases and open yourself to new ideas, you may nevertheless conclude that a particular expert is wasting your time.

Unfortunately, many inexperienced people are intimidated by experts. They jump into relationships too quickly, pay more than is necessary, and expect too much. The result is almost always disappointing.

EXAMPLE: Anne Cox, publisher of *Cruises Update,* hired Charlie, a well-known copywriter, to create a new series of letters to promote renewal subscriptions. They agreed on a fee of $7,500. Unfortunately, Charlie, who was obviously enthralled by his own portfolio of award-winning direct mail packages, didn't really listen to Anne. Even though she explained what she believed her readers expected from *Cruises Update,* and what tone of voice they seemed to respond to, Charlie presented her with over-slick copy recycled from other jobs. It was so unacceptable that Anne rejected the material, which, of course, precipitated a bitter argument about paying Charlie's bill. Finally, after lawsuits were threatened, the copywriter settled for a 50% payment for his time. Anne was left with a smaller bank balance and no usable renewal letters. She wished she had paid Charlie to write one trial letter before giving him the whole series. Or maybe she could have drafted her own letters and then hired someone to polish them, for a much lower fee.

TIP

Don't be afraid to negotiate fees. Just because an expert quotes a high hourly fee doesn't mean you have to accept it. Each job is unique. Even highly experienced people who quote a firm hourly rate for their work will often work for less, depending on the circumstances. This is especially likely if you tell them that you hope to continue to use their help in the future, for example, to lay out each issue of your newsletter. And of course, if the expert is short of work when you call, this, too, may induce him or her to agree to a lower fee. In short, any expert may be willing to work for less if you ask.

Tell the Whole Truth

You must be clear about what you want from consultants and what the facts of your situation are if you expect them to help you effectively. A surprising number of people shade the truth when talking to consultants and other advisors. Of course, lying is never a good idea. If you're broke, say so. Otherwise, people will likely suggest solutions you can't afford, wasting your time and theirs. If you're open with people about your situation and what you hope to achieve, you stand a far better chance of receiving the help you need.

EXAMPLE: Marjorie, approaching age 55, had been publishing *Family Nursing*, a newsletter for pediatric nurses, for 12 years. Stressed out and overwhelmed by the workload, she decided to try to sell her newsletter. To help get the highest possible price, Marjorie hired a consulting group that specialized in selling publications. The consultants warned Marjorie that some buyers would demand that she remain as editor and publisher after the sale. Marjorie decided not to reveal how desperately she wanted to quit the business because she didn't want to discourage potential buyers.

In short time, the consultants found a buyer willing to pay a good price. Because they had no editors with pediatric nursing experience, however, the owners-to-be wanted Marjorie to remain at the helm for a couple of years. Before the sale was completed, Marjorie belatedly admitted her burnout and balked at signing a two-year employment contract. "I haven't had a vacation in five years—how will I keep going for another two?" she asked. The deal fell apart. Even when Marjorie reluctantly agreed to sign the employment contract, the buyers-to-be had lost their trust in her and they shied away from the deal altogether.

Had Marjorie been honest with her consultants in the first place, they might have helped her find a different buyer or a different remedy for her distress. For example, in exchange for a slightly lower price, they might have negotiated Marjorie's employment agreement so that she'd have less responsibility and more time off, since the money shaved off the sales price could have gone to hire a new editor.

Treat Independent Contractors and Employees Differently

The distinction between independent contractors and employees is very important to the IRS. In general, the government prefers to classify someone as an employee, making you (the employer) responsible for withholding income taxes, and paying Social Security taxes, workers' compensation insurance, and unemployment insurance premiums for them. Employers are also required to maintain a safe, healthy working environment and to comply with a wide range of governmental regulations designed to protect employees' rights.

The IRS and state governments routinely investigate to see if employees have been misclassified as independent contractors. If an audit reveals that an employer has inappropriately assigned contractor status to employees, they impose stiff fines and penalties. If you have any doubts about the correct status of a specific worker, it's a good idea to get more information.

RESOURCE

Sample contracts for freelancers are readily available and you can use them to avoid legal disputes that arise from creating your own contracts, without hiring a lawyer. Here are three excellent sources.

- *Consultant & Independent Contractor Agreements*, by Stephen Fishman (Nolo), is a book that includes many different examples.
- The Editorial Freelancers Association maintains a directory of freelancers and also provides a sample writers contract at www.the-efa.org.
- The National Association of Publishers Representatives provides similar information for freelance ad salespeople at www.nprassoc.org

To make sure that people who do occasional work for you are properly classified as independent contractors, take the following simple steps right from the start of your relationship.

- *Draw up a contract.* Spell out their responsibilities and deadlines, and how they will be paid. (You can find good sample contracts in *Consultant & Independent Contractor Agreements,* listed above.)
- *Let the contractors use their own tools.* Contractors should supply their own tools, equipment, and materials—whether word processors or wrenches—plus provide for their own insurance. Don't reimburse them for overhead expenses or costs not directly attributed to your project.
- *Don't let contractors work in your offices.* Except for meetings, contractors should do most of their work at their own place of business, not yours.

- *Make sure contractors are free to work for other clients.* Independent contractors are always free to offer their services to other clients. If people work solely or mostly for you, chances are the IRS will treat them as employees.

- *Pay for work completed.* Pay by the job, not by the hour, and make sure that contractors submit invoices for each job before you pay. It's okay to pay in installments as long as they are tied to work-completion goals.

- *Don't withhold any taxes.* You are not required to withhold taxes from the money you pay contractors, and you don't have to pay their Social Security or Medicare taxes. You do have to file a Form 1099-MISC with the IRS at the end of the year if you paid any contractor more than $600 during the year. Send copies of this form to the IRS and to the contractor. ●

Managing Employees

Publishers work with and manage lots of people, many with highly specialized skills. Some of them are employees, while others are freelancers, vendors, or outside contractors. If you are new to the publishing business, the inherent difficulty in putting together a good publishing team could be compounded by the fact that you won't always understand what your specialists are doing for you. This chapter will describe how you can effectively manage people, even when their contributions are highly specialized. It also discusses how to avoid some of the mistakes publishers often make when hiring employees and building a publishing team.

How to Find Experienced People

You may start your publishing business with untrained workers simply because you can't afford higher-priced, experienced people. For some specialized tasks, however—designing covers, organizing a direct mail campaign, or setting up your accounting system—even a start-up with a tight budget will need to find and work with skilled employees. Finding them will be one of your most important tasks.

Finding Good Employees

John Griffin is president of *National Geographic* magazine. He explains how he finds good publishing people:

"Trying to find good people, keeping the excellent people you already have happy, and helping them grow is a 24-hour-a-day job. Everything you do every day should reflect these goals. If you meet a good person from another company, make a note of that for future reference. And ask your employees, suppliers, and competitors to recommend good people. I've recently come to appreciate good headhunters, too. But even when I use one, I take the time to meet the people they recommend myself. I probably interview 20 or 30 people over the course of a year, even when we don't have any jobs, just to get to know them."

You may not have the resources of an established, well-financed publishing company to rely on, but you can still use some of the same recruiting tactics. The trick is to gather personal recommendations from people in your network whom you trust. Even if you haven't worked side-by-side with Molly and Frank, the two applicants for your ad sales job, someone else has. If those people are willing to advise you and have good judgment, they can make a huge difference in whether or not you hire the right person.

When enlisting others to help you find employees, be as clear as you can about your needs. For example, what responsibilities are you planning to give the person? How much independence will the person have? How much will you pay?

Here are several resources for finding competent helpers.

- *Suppliers.* Ask suppliers for recommendations, especially for circulation, production, and design people. Printers and other vendors often work very closely with employees from other publications in your area. Often they can steer you to the best ones— and away from people who are sloppy, inefficient, or otherwise tough to work with for some reason.

- *Advertisers.* Advertising sales is a relationship business, and for most new niche publishers, there is nothing more valuable than a good salesperson who already knows the advertisers in the market. People who plan to advertise with you can probably recommend ad salespeople from other publications. An experienced person with established relationships can bring important new advertisers to your magazine in short order.

- *Consultants.* Publishing consultants often work in a fairly narrow niche such as newsstand distribution, direct mail copywriting, or magazine design. When they start, they may not know people outside their own specialty, but over time they generally meet a broad array of publishing people. Busy direct mail copywriters, for example, may work for 15 circulation directors in a year's time. If you need help in circulation, they should be able to direct you to a few good candidates. Some consultants even make a side business of finding talent. When they do, they generally charge a recruiting fee, which can be a wise investment for you.

- *Trade groups and media professionals.* Media people in most major cities have professional associations to help them network, solve problems, and find new jobs when they need them. Make yourself and your publication known to them. When you need editorial contributors, reporters, or consultants familiar with your subject area, a local association will be a good place to find them.

Recruiting People

At larger publishing companies, good people sometimes get stuck below well-entrenched top executives who rarely give up their jobs. Except in publishing centers like New York, this means top jobs don't open up often. As a result, many capable, well-trained people are waiting for a chance to move up. Commonly, the only way for them to advance their careers is to go somewhere else. They often do.

While many publishing professionals are often looking for new opportunities, lots are understandably wary of start-up situations because so many start-ups fail. When you talk to skilled people with decent jobs about joining you, they may want assurances about the solidity of your funding. Be prepared to provide the same information to key prospective employees as you would to your investors.

There are also compelling reasons for talented people to join a start-up, however. They include:

- *Broader challenges.* In a corporate publishing environment, people get stuck doing the same job again and again—something which can be intensely frustrating and uninspiring. At a smaller company, each person naturally assumes wider responsibilities. People develop a wider range of skills as they expand their attention and activity, and grow professionally.

- *Being in at the beginning.* The start-up of a new business is often the most creative time, simply because there are no long-established footprints to follow. Some people long to leave a mark on fresh sand.

- *Personal influence.* Skillful people with experience will be very important to a new publication, especially if the publisher is new to the business. As a publisher, you can often entice them to work with you by pointing out that they will have more power in your organization than they might in a larger company.

- *Flexibility.* Smaller companies and start-ups typically are more open to offering flexible work schedules and an informal working environment. This appeals to many people, including those who want to work primarily, or at least part of the time, from their homes.

- *Personal preference.* Some people will be attracted to your subject or editorial mission because they share your passion for the topic. Even when they don't care so deeply about your editorial mission, many people will have other personal issues that you can appeal to: a short commute, an office with a window, or flexible hours. Don't be surprised if production, circulation, finance, and even sales professionals seem unmoved by your editorial mission but are eager to work with you for other reasons.

- *More money.* Most new publications don't have the resources it takes to pay hefty salaries. But they may be willing to part with something many key employees feel is even more valuable—stock. In the heady 1990s, companies commonly handed out stock options to key employees, promising them the chance to earn a large chunk of profits if their efforts paid out later. But the results proved less favorable than everybody hoped they would be: Many companies failed to make a profit or went under, leaving the workers without the promised riches. Now, employers and employees alike are more cautious about stock options.

Because few start-up publishers have deep enough pockets to hire a whole new team of experienced employees, they gradually assemble a mixture of independent contractors and part- and full-time employees. By adding employees only when they can afford them and accepting the fact that it may take several years to build the team they really want, these publishers learn to bootstrap their businesses into decent-sized organizations.

Building a Publishing Team: An Illustration

In practice, publishers find people in many different ways. To identify many of them, consider our imaginary publisher, Tony Thomas.

Tony's model railroading magazine *Tracks* starts out as a solo operation he runs from his home. At first, Tony uses many outsiders to get his business started: freelancers, consultants, service bureaus, and other vendors. But after a year of modest success, Tony rents a small office space near his home and begins to look for regular freelancers and full-time employees.

Tony's printer, Paul, has dozens of catalogue and small magazine clients. Following leads he gets from Paul, Tony is able to find an experienced, freelance magazine designer.

Realizing that he can't write and edit every word in *Tracks* himself, Tony next begins looking for freelance editors and copy editors. He decides to check with the established publishing companies in his city, hoping to obtain referrals from them. A few people are very helpful to him. For instance, the managing editor of a local college alumni magazine helps Tony find an excellent self-employed copy editor and two very good freelance photographers. Another local publisher can't help Tony with writers, but introduces him to a magazine accountant who, in turn, helps Tony find a part-time bookkeeper.

From the very beginning, Tony wants to hire experienced ad salespeople because he expects to devote most of his own time to writing articles and managing the business. But it takes several years before Tony is really able to hand over the advertising sales job to anyone else and he winds up selling ads himself. In the meantime, he hires and fires a dozen freelance salespeople, something which, naturally, becomes a major source of frustration for him.

At first, Tony tries using an independent ad sales agency. Going back to the *Folio: Source Book* for leads, he asks a succession of different agents to work for him, but without much success. Probably because *Tracks* is new and small, the independent agencies refuse to take the assignment. They point out that it will take time to develop relationships with Tony's advertisers. Without other clients in the model railroading field, they aren't particularly motivated to build long-term relationships in that market.

In frustration, Tony finally contacts several of the biggest advertisers in his field, some of whom he knows personally, and asks them, "Who is your favorite advertising salesperson?" Three names are mentioned, and Tony tracks down all three. One of them works for an independent ad sales agency which will not represent *Tracks* because it handles a competitor. Although both of the others work for other publishers in the field and live in cities far removed from Tony's, he calls them. One isn't interested, but the other, Angela Marlar, has just learned she is pregnant and is looking for an opportunity to change her lifestyle. When Tony agrees that Angela can work from her home office and offers to buy her a computer, modem, and a fax machine, she signs on. To Tony's great delight, Angela quickly taps her existing relationships to bring in a whole new group of advertisers. Despite living 1,000 miles away and caring for her baby, she turns out to be one of Tony's best employees.

Tony also needs to find someone who can process subscription orders, generate mailing lists, and maintain his subscriber databases. In *Folio:* magazine and the *Newsletter on Newsletters* (both listed in Chapter 14) he finds ads from companies that handle subscription fulfillment and from companies that sell software that allows publishers to handle their own subscriptions. While he is investigating these leads, Tony also asks Paul, his printer, for ideas. Since Paul works with publishers who fulfill their subscriptions in several different ways, he has some good suggestions. In particular, Paul urges Tony to hire an experienced fulfillment bureau rather than attempting to buy software and handle subscriptions in-house. "You'll get cutting-edge technology and unparalleled expertise if you work with an outside vendor," says Paul.

Tony also finds consultants by referral from a publishing association. Mary, a marketing consultant who specializes in creating strategies for ad sales, is also a member of the Independent Press Association (IPA). Mary helps Tony and Angela make decisions about ad pricing, competitive positioning, advertiser services, and creating a database of advertising prospects. Because of her experience with other IPA members, she is able to help find other freelance marketing helpers. In particular, Mary helps Tony find someone to write and design his media kit and a moonlighting college student to help Tony develop a home page on the Web.

Because he treats them well and listens to what they have to say, each of the people Tony hires becomes an advocate for *Tracks,* and through them, Tony meets other useful individuals. For instance, William, who created Tony's website, helps Tony find Tom, a local technical consultant who makes himself available to resolve any problems with computers or software.

Tony can see that he will also need to develop a network of professional contacts in his city. To accomplish this, he becomes active in several publishing associations and attends their conferences. He routinely posts job listings with these associations and the local college employment offices. And he collects résumés from the good people he meets in each association. Later, when *Tracks* needs a business manager and a managing editor, Tony finds them through his local professional contacts.

Encouraging Collaboration

Publishing involves many people with different specialized skills, from artists to accountants, working together. Successful collaboration depends on finding the right people for each job and then creating an environment that encourages each person to contribute his or her best efforts to the success of the whole. A collaborative environment is so important that when it's missing, there's sure to be trouble. A clear signal that a publication is likely to fail is when its key people bicker and undermine each other's work in struggles for power or control. In such an environment, the normal everyday clashes that come up—for example, between editors and ad salespeople or circulation and accounting people—never get resolved.

In a healthy publishing business, on the other hand, employees focus their attention outward. They are curious about their market and actively engaged with their constituents (readers, advertisers, industry participants). They seek out information and share it with each other. People have fun, and they get the job done, too.

The following practical recommendations about encouraging healthy collaboration among the skilled people you'll work with can help you avoid many trouble spots common to new publishers.

Define What You Want

Depending on your market and the stage of your business, your day-to-day goals may change rapidly. This makes it doubly important to tell people exactly what you need from them at any given time. You can't always control whether or not people will meet your needs, but you can control how well you communicate your priorities and expectations to them.

To accomplish this, large employers typically write job descriptions for employees, and sign contracts with very specific task descriptions and timelines with freelancers. It is rare for small business owners or solo operators to have the time to be so careful. But, you can nevertheless reap the same benefits by spelling out what you expect from people as clearly and thoroughly as possible.

Make Teams Accountable as a Group

People usually will learn to work together if you make it meaningful for them to do so. Unfortunately, many publishers never give teams a chance to coalesce because they don't hold them accountable as a team. For instance, a salesperson who is only responsible for bringing in a certain number of ad pages, but not for achieving an overall profit or any other larger goal, doesn't have much motive to think beyond his or her own job. However, if you give people a common responsibility—increasing monthly ad revenues, for example—most will take the time to figure out how their own efforts can contribute to the group's success.

EXAMPLE: Kate's magazine, *Silent Skier*, was chronically over-budget on production expenses, and she was at a loss about how to solve the problem. No matter how much she cajoled the editors, they couldn't stick to their schedule. And her sales team was just as bad: the people on it were always trying to hold up an issue while they frantically tried to bring in a few more ads. Kate appreciated their enthusiasm, but constantly missing the printer's deadlines was costing thousands of dollars every year.

Over lunch one day, Kate's friend suggested a solution: Kate should figure out how much money she could save if the magazine reached the printer on time, and then offer to share some of the savings with employees. Kate created an ad hoc committee of editors and advertising salespeople and charged them with solving the scheduling problems. She agreed to pay 20% of any money they could shave off the printing bills into an employee benefits fund. In the very first year, the team not only saved *Silent Skier* a bundle of money, but learned a lot about cooperating with one another. On their own, the team members suggested useful ways to work together to smooth out other bottlenecks.

Focus on Tasks

In a publishing business, there is room for all kinds of people, from a shy, introverted editor to a people-pleasing ad salesperson to a hard-nosed production manager. Inevitably, however, some personal styles will be easier for you to live with than others. The best approach is to focus on what people do for you, not on how they do it. Especially when you deal with experts who, by definition, are supposed to know how to do the job, you'll usually want to focus more on whether the desired outcome is achieved than on the process by which it's accomplished.

EXAMPLE: Allison published a modestly successful newsletter about women and motorcycles called *Wind in Her Hair*. At a stable point in her business, she hired a business consultant named George to help her start a side business organizing motorcycle tours for women. She asked George to put together a financial package that might interest potential investors and, assuming some were found, to help with negotiations about sharing ownership in the new venture.

George started to put together a formal business plan for Allison, but almost immediately ran into trouble with her. George was appalled at how poorly Allison's accounts and records were kept, and tried to reorganize the financial side of her business. Allison resented his criticism and promptly fired him.

Too late, Allison realized that George had been right in many ways—if she was going to have outside investors involved in her business, she would need better financial records. Her prejudices against "MBA types" like George prevented him from helping her, and she never overcame her accounting and bookkeeping problems. As a result, she had so much trouble communicating with potential investors that she eventually abandoned the tours idea.

Give Honest Feedback

It's inevitable that at some point, you'll be unhappy with the work of one of your employees. A publisher should always speak up pleasantly but directly if someone's work doesn't meet true needs or expectations. Don't wait for an improvement that may never happen. Be candid right from the start and you'll set a tone that others will follow. There is no need to feel guilty about occasionally being critical as long as you take pains to be constructive and not to embarrass people in the presence of others. Remember, honesty is the best way to achieve your goal of building a network of productive relationships that will satisfy each participant over the long term.

Developing Your Own Experts

Many small publications start out with inexperienced people because that's who they can best afford. Although beginners will make mistakes, the good ones who are both open-minded and eager to learn should be a great asset to your business. By providing them time to learn, solid educational opportunities, and strong leadership, you can quickly transform your beginners into a creative and well-focused team. Here are some tried and true suggestions.

- *Help employees take advantage of educational opportunities.* There are many wonderful and reasonably priced opportunities to learn about publishing. (See Chapter 14.) In addition to courses and seminars about every aspect of publishing, and self-help books and magazines, you can learn a great deal by judiciously hiring outside experts and consultants to train your permanent staff.

Employers frequently pay for their employees to take skill-developing programs. Some give people paid time off to take classes, and others give the time off without pay. The choice depends on your circumstances and your budget. If a loyal employee has the opportunity to increase her productivity, meet new people in her specialty, and strengthen her contributions to your company by taking a class or a seminar, then it's obviously in your interest to support her any way you reasonably can.

- *Budget time to learn.* As a new publisher, no one has less free time than you. But don't jump to the conclusion that you don't have enough time to learn about the business. The only way you'll get more time is to work more efficiently, and the only way you'll do that is to improve your skills. Even if it's only 30 minutes on a weekday and two hours on Saturday, make the commitment to devote regular chunks of your time to improving your knowledge and skills.

EXAMPLE: Partially because he had such a hard time finding good advertising salespeople, *Tracks* publisher Tony Thomas personally handled much of the magazine's advertising sales alone at first. To free up time for other pressing needs, he urgently needed some ad sales help. Eventually, he hired Angela, but he still needed another rep. Sharon, *Tracks'* office manager, had no sales experience, but Tony believed she would be great at selling ads. She listened well, paid attention to details, followed up on her commitments, and could be persuasive when she believed something was the right thing to do.

Sharon was reluctant to try ad sales, but Tony urged her to give it a shot, explaining how much more money she could earn in sales and how much the magazine needed reliable salespeople. They reached a compromise: Sharon would try ad sales for six months if Tony would pay for her training. During Sharon's training period, they would hire a part-time secretary—a temp—so that she could spend half of her time learning.

Sharon started her training by attending an advertising sales seminar. Tony also made time to train her himself. He took her with him on personal sales calls and let her listen in on telephone calls, showing her how he prepared for the calls and how he followed up afterwards. They spent an hour per week together talking about sales and advertisers. After a few weeks, Sharon jumped into sales, ahead of schedule and full of confidence. Tony could finally focus on other critical business issues.

Avoiding Common Hiring Mistakes

So far this chapter has focused on ways for you to identify, hire, and manage good people. Because it's always best to learn from other people's mistakes rather than your own, consider some of the most common errors publishers make when hiring people.

Paying Too Much

Conserving every nickel of spare cash will help you bounce back from the inevitable beginner's mistakes or just plain bad luck that can strike a new publication. Oddly, many first-time publishers are too generous with compensation, often because they expect their publication to succeed faster than is likely. Another common mistake is to put lots of energy into creating a profit-sharing scheme that never pans out because there isn't enough time left to create a profitable publication. Handing out ownership shares to people who haven't yet proved themselves is still another all-too-common pitfall.

TIP

Don't undervalue your stock. Although it's very hard to predict what your stock will be worth when your business gets off the ground, don't sell yourself short. While it can make sense to offer small ownership shares to people who really will help you succeed, many people give stock away too freely, too soon. Far better to assume your publishing venture will be a winner and value your stock accordingly. Parcel it out sparingly, as if it were the precious commodity that you hope it will become.

You can protect yourself from some of the worst compensation mistakes by being cautious. Make new employees prove themselves over a reasonable period, giving them pay increases or stock down the road instead of right up front. And don't sign long-term employment agreements except in extraordinary circumstances, such as luring a highly experienced editor to join your team.

Paying Too Little

It's far better for a new publication to pay too little than too much. Just the same, parsimony can be expensive if it prevents you from recruiting good people or if it causes them to leave just when they have become highly valuable. Talented people will save you money in the long run if they work smarter and accomplish more than others. When you find people who are extraordinarily capable, pay them as well as you can.

> **EXAMPLE:** Tony hired a part-time receptionist named Ryan when he moved his business out of his home and into an office. Ryan turned out to be very skillful at handling customer complaints and resolving problems. When Ryan proposed that he receive the new title of Customer Services Manager with a small increase in pay, Tony said he couldn't afford it, preferring to let Ryan keep on doing the customer service job at a receptionist's pay. Only after Ryan had left the company for greener pastures and Tony was faced with hiring a replacement from a field of underwhelming applicants did Tony realize his mistake.

Hiring a Hero

Many new publishers look for an expert to fix things even though they don't fully understand or can't specifically identify their most important problem. It's easy to push the panic button when faced with a revenue shortfall, production problems, a low subscription renewal rate, or a disappointing direct mail return. If a clever person with a terrific-looking résumé and an "I can fix it" attitude comes along at such a time, you might be tempted to make a generous deal and wait for a miracle to materialize. Don't yield to temptation. You can rarely hire a hero to fix a problem you don't understand yourself. Instead, gather your wits and ask yourself, "What's wrong? What can I do about it?" For example, if renewals are down, examine whether your market is changing, whether you are facing more competition, and whether your editorial content is compelling. Enlist all of your supporters in identifying the problem. Keep exploring the situation until you are confident that you understand what's happening and why. Only then can you sensibly look for a long-term solution. Chances are, you won't need a hero, just a new strategy that can be carried out by ordinary—and probably far cheaper—mortals.

Putting People in the Wrong Positions

Besides having technical publishing skills, the people you hire must be able to work together. True, some publishing jobs require less collaboration than others—and as mentioned, there is room for people with different personal styles—but most publishing tasks demand good communication and social skills. Before hiring someone, evaluate him or her based both on technical proficiency and the ability to work well with others. In doing this, many experienced publishers use a simple technique—they involve all employees who will work with the potential new employee in the hiring process. If a particular candidate doesn't impress this group, he or she won't get hired.

Another strategy is to give people a trial run before making a major commitment to them. Try to see both the quality of their work and how you like working with them. When dealing with outside contractors, this is usually easy since you can nearly always break a big project into stages and assign a small piece to the new person. For example, agree to buy one sketch, not ten full-color illustrations. If you like the result, give the contractor a bigger assignment.

Setting up a meaningful trial is harder when dealing with a new employee, since the person usually will be coming to your workplace and interacting with others from the first day. Still, it's a good idea to establish a probation period—commonly three to six months—before you award people a permanent job. That way you have an opportunity to ease misfits out before they join your permanent staff.

Trusting a Resume

There are loads of stellar résumés attached to unimpressive people. In a business where turnover is fairly common, incompetent people can keep themselves employed simply by moving from one company to another. In these litigious times, few employers will tell a potential new employer why they were disappointed in an employee. Just the opposite: Realizing that an employee with a new job is far less likely to sue, the old employer will adopt a "take him, he's yours" philosophy.

Fortunately, you can protect yourself from the trauma of hiring a dishonest, incompetent, or abrasive employee for a key position. First, diligently search for impartial, independent references. Talk not only with the person's former boss, but also to vendors, consultants, or colleagues who have worked with the person. And after at least three interviews, don't be afraid to trust your own instincts and those of key staff members. Does the person's style and manner impress you as much as his or her résumé? Do you look forward to your next meeting or does the thought of it make you tired?

In addition, being sensitive to personal issues, develop a practical test for candidates to take. For example, if you are hiring a writer, ask each candidate to write something under time pressure. And if you are hiring a graphics person, give each candidate the same one-hour design assignment. In both cases, the results of the test are likely to speak volumes about whom you should hire.

EXAMPLE: Lila Keene, the publisher of the Buddhist magazine *Sitting Well*, was looking for a managing editor. There wasn't a big publishing industry in the town where the magazine was located, so Lila's prospects were limited. Plus, she hoped to avoid the added hassle of hiring someone who would have to move to the area.

Then Jason, a local person, applied. Jason had a great résumé, and all the right experiences and qualifications, but for some reason Lila didn't like him. She couldn't say what the problem was, just that she didn't warm up to Jason. Still, since Lila needed someone right away and Jason had experience, she was tempted to hire him. But first, Lila was determined to find somebody who knew Jason well, such as a vendor or a consultant who had worked with him.

When she tracked down several such people, she was surprised to find that nobody was willing to talk freely about Jason. Even Jason's former employer was reticent, saying he had once been sued after giving a poor reference which led him to adopt a strict policy against making any comments about former employees.

Finally, feeling frustrated, Lila organized a lunch meeting with Jason and two of Lila's favorite contributing writers—people with whom Jason would have regular contact if he got the job. Neither of the writers liked Jason. Their judgments and her own mistrust persuaded Lila to keep looking for a better candidate. Much later, Lila learned that Jason was fired from a job with another publication after repeatedly failing to do quality work.

Hiring People You Can't Fire

The worst thing you can do to a struggling new publication is to load it down with unproductive employees or contractors—your brother-in-law, your best friend's daughter, or anybody else you hire out of compassion instead of normal business considerations. A new business simply doesn't have the luxury of carrying unproductive people and as its leader you'll have more than enough problems to face without having to worry about your sister who can't do much good work but still tries to lord her relationship with you over others.

Think of it this way: While nepotism isn't necessarily bad, it won't take many underperforming employees to quickly kill an otherwise good business. In short, if your brother-in-law is terrific at his job, willing to live by the same rules as everybody else, and just as devoted to your success as you are, hire him. If not, hire somebody who is.

Failing to Help Employees Grow

It's a good idea to periodically review your relationships with your employees. Are your employees still happy and productive? Are you helping them to grow and earn a better living? Is it time to change your leadership style?

As your publishing company begins to grow, you will probably find that your expectations from your employees will change. Now it will no longer be enough to publish a competent journal. You'll want every aspect of what you do to be truly excellent. To get this to happen, one of your most important jobs will be to help your veteran employees meet your new goals or, if they can't, to help them find decent jobs elsewhere. As discussed in the next section, the way to do this is to help key employees improve their skills.

But it's not just your expectations or your employees that will change. As your publication becomes increasingly successful, your employees will expect to share your success in tangible ways: stock options, retirement savings plans, and other employer-funded employee benefits such as health care, education, and paid leaves.

EXAMPLE: In their fifth year, the *Silent Skier* executive team realized that salary inequities had begun to creep into the company. In particular, some of the original employees who had joined the company in its poorer days were not making as much as several skilled newer people brought in to solve particular problems. True, early birds had come to their jobs with less experience, but they had learned a lot along the way and were annoyed that even with raises and improved benefits they were not being fairly treated. The problem was compounded by the fact that some of the original employees had worked hard to improve their skills, but others had not.

When one key employee shocked Kate, the publisher, by telling her she was looking for another job, Kate hired an outside consulting firm to review salaries and to recommend compensation guidelines for every job in the company. The process took several months. All of the middle- and senior-level managers were involved, since the consultant wisely advised Kate to make sure every critic had a hearing, and that every problem was brought forward.

The consultants used independent information, such as the *Folio:* magazine annual compensation survey, to determine how much people were earning in comparable jobs at other companies. They also did a quick private survey of salary ranges at ten publications similar to *Silent Skier* in size and profitability. The *Folio:* survey was particularly helpful, since its salary information is organized to take into consideration important factors, like geographical location, magazine size, and the number of people an employee supervises. (See the salary survey, below.) The Magazine Publisher's Association and Newsletter Publisher's Association publish similar information.

The consultants concluded that some *Silent Skier* salaries needed a major adjustment and recommended a raise of $20,000 for one key staffer and smaller, but still substantial, raises for several others, including the person who had threatened to leave. In other cases, however, the consultants concluded that employees were being overpaid and suggested that they not receive future raises until they upgraded their skills. Nearly all recommended adjustments involved increases to the *Silent Skier* payroll, but it was impossible for the magazine to increase its expenses so fast. Kate developed a plan to bring the undercompensated employees' salaries up to the recommended levels over two years. All those affected were pleased, including the person whose threat to leave had initiated the process. For the first time in more than a year they were confident that *Silent Skier* was willing to treat its veteran employees equitably.

A Summary of the 2005 *Folio:* Salary Surveys

Basic Salaries for Magazine People
(excluding bonuses, commission, or profit-sharing)

Position	Average Salary	Lowest	Highest
Editor-in-Chief	$97,000	$40,000	$250,000
Editor	$65,600	$24,500	$98,000
Managing Editor	$48,500	$20,000	$85,000
Art Director	$57,500	$43,500	$85,100
Ad Sales Director/Publisher	$90,600	$56,500	$124,000
Ad Sales Regional Manager	$64,400	$48,500	$78,200
Account Executive	$49,200	$27,500	$71,300
Production Director	$73,100	$58,000	$83,000
Production Manager	$50,000	$45,000	$67,700
Circulation Director	$83,200	$49,400	$94,600
Circulation Manager	$51,500	$33,900	$62,500

Folio: magazine has made a salary survey available as at its website, called the Salary Estimator. Using data from the surveys, you can choose qualities such as publication size and location, employee experience level and responsibility, and so forth. The Estimator will predict what a person in that position would be paid. To find the salary survey, go to www. foliomag.com; then type in "salary" at the Advanced Search prompt.

People Give Back What They Get

At troubled publishing companies, far too often, the main problem boils down to one thing: poor leadership. Unfortunately, some people think that running a business gives them license to indulge themselves, when just the opposite is true. Here are some of the worst examples.

- *Emotional volatility.* Employees should not have to deal with the emotional ups and downs of their bosses. Leaders need to handle their emotions privately. That means no temper tantrums, and no long-winded personal therapy sessions with your employees.

- *Deception.* There are many ways to rationalize keeping secrets or giving inaccurate information to employees, but deception is never a good idea. It only encourages more deception. For example, I worked with a fellow who believed in setting very high goals for his team, even when he knew for certain that the goals were unachievable. He claimed that people will accomplish more if you trick them into doing more than they believe is possible. His deception didn't fool anybody, and it often backfired on him. Instead of straining themselves to meet his unreasonable expectations, employees generally ignored him, lied to him, or joked about him behind his back. They wasted huge amounts of time and energy resisting him in a thousand different ways. He struggled to keep his business going despite rapid employee turnover, constant bickering among key employees, and outright sabotage.

- *Chaos.* Some people deliberately create chaos, believing that it signals creativity or an artistic nature. They do it by refusing to explain themselves, failing to consult with people or giving them conflicting signals, and generally generating confusion among their colleagues. That kind of chaos is always wasteful. By contrast, successful teams depend on effective communication, which requires significant effort from a leader who is determined to keep things as clear and simple as they can be.

- *Bullies*. Anyone who uses their power over employees to extract favors is a bully. That includes making people sit through long, unproductive meetings with you, asking them to do personal favors, or forcing them to work with your sullen teenage children who are getting paid as much as everybody else for half the work.

- *Greed*. Publications succeed through collaboration. That means everyone deserves some of the credit, including some of the financial gain. Some publishers have trouble sharing financial and emotional rewards with their collaborators. Resentment builds among people who are working hard for none of the credit. Like deception, greed engenders more greed. People will withhold their best ideas from you unless you can appreciate them properly.

The time-tested rule of leadership is this: An effective leader wins support from people by setting a good example.

John Griffin, president of *National Geographic* magazine, recently had this to say on the topic: "I have to be aware that every time I talk to somebody, it's the 'president' talking, not just me. It's amazing how many problems can come up if I forget myself and say the wrong thing. Even something as simple as saying that I'm worried about money…might cause some people to start to panic, thinking the business is going under, when actually I was just annoyed about a small financial issue. I've learned to recognize that my own behavior has more effect on the work people do for me than anything else."

You don't have to become a perfect human being in order to lead a publishing business and inspire people to work hard. You only have to be aware that people are looking to you for direction, and that your behavior has a real effect on theirs. So be as fair, honest, and uncomplicated as you can be. Do your best. Keep your word. Lead by example. For the most part, the people you depend on will do the same for you. ●

An Internet Publishing Strategy

We are well past the dot.com boom and bust phenomenon. For a short time, during the height of the dot.com mania, nobody wanted to invest in print magazines or newsletters anymore, believing that the whole world would move onto the Internet. Print publishers who had the resources spent gobs of money trying to transform themselves into Web-based enterprises. Today, however, most have retreated from that posture. And they're the lucky ones—some invested so much on their Web ideas that they forced themselves out of business.

This chapter describes an online publishing strategy tailored specifically to the needs of smaller players. A key concept to remember is that in the developing world of Internet publishing, being small is often to your advantage. Many experts have predicted that the most innovation will come from small companies that approach the Internet from a fresh perspective. With this in mind, don't try to copy what the bigger companies are doing, because you can't afford to, and besides, they may be way off base anyhow. And if you already have a print publication, don't be a prisoner of your own print history. Instead, use the knowledge that you have about your subject, your targeted audience, and the related advertising marketplace. Then, apply the best technical tools that you can find to build an online presence that is totally new and totally your own.

Getting noticed is the toughest challenge for smaller websites. While a hundred well-known sites get millions of daily visitors, most smaller websites struggle to reach a few thousand people every day. It helps if you have a print magazine or newsletter that promotes your website. If not, then you'll need a coherent strategy for bringing people into the site— and that is the major focus of the discussions throughout this chapter.

The Tunes They Have A-Changed

I first wrote about the Internet only a few years ago, in the first edition of this book. It doesn't seem that long ago, but the changes in the world of online publishing that have occurred since then are astonishing. In 1996, I spent months combing the Internet looking for publishing resources, examples, and tools that would help readers develop successful Internet publications. I started by looking at established print publishers to see what they were doing online. I thought they would naturally be first and finest at using the Internet to deliver information. After all, they're experts at gathering, packaging, and delivering information.

But I was dismayed to learn that print publishers were performing poorly online. With a few notable exceptions, in 1996 most print publishers were ignoring the Web. The ones who were active online (like *Wired*, *Playboy*, and *The Wall Street Journal*) were spending truckloads of money developing sites and running pricey promotions to drive traffic to them—a strategy none of my readers could possibly adopt for themselves. I did not find examples of good, low-cost Web publishing strategies, and what's worse, I found very few resources for small publishers. The software and hardware needed was expensive, hard to learn, and time-consuming to manage. I believed I had good reason to be skeptical about Internet publishing for small businesses, and so in the first edition of this book, I advised my readers to go slowly, be careful, and even to wait a while until the wild, wild Web could be tamed for them.

In a very short time, many things have changed. Most notably, there are now tools, services, supports, and proven Web publishing strategies that you can follow. Suddenly, it's safe for small publishers to launch a successful business on the Web, either in conjunction with a print publication or not. And now, nearly all publishers have websites. Indeed, you could not launch a print magazine these days without also launching a website for it, if only a very simple one.

> **Web Publishing Tips**
>
> 1. Define a mission for your site before you design it.
> 2. Take advantage of whatever content strengths you already have.
> 3. Expect to spend more time and money than you anticipated.
> 4. Focus on serving the needs of your audience, not making a flashy presence.
> 5. Understand the strengths of the online medium, which is timely, global, interactive, customizable, and deep.
> 6. Don't try to do everything at once just because you think you can.
> 7. Remember to include some fun, because most people are still looking to the Web for entertainment.
> 8. Quality and originality count even more on the Web than in print. So does personality, style, and a point of view.
> 9. Attract an audience; don't chase one. As any fisherman will confirm, you can't herd fish. Instead, you must make an attractive lure so they will come to you.

Essentials for Start-Up Websites

Today, you just can't launch in print without simultaneously launching online. There is no one-size-fits-all prescription, but some general guidelines are offered here.

- *Make it seductive.* A site that draws people into your project by inviting visitors to contribute questions, offer suggestions, or answer polls can enrich your publication at very little cost—much less than you would have to spend hiring writers or editors to develop thoughtful content. Collect their email addresses for ongoing communications, and those early contacts may become core supporters down the road.

- *Incorporate income.* Make room for ads in your initial site design, and also post information about how to advertise on the site. This is important, because your first ad income may actually come through the site, rather than the print publication. (Online advertising is discussed in detail later in this chapter.)

- *Get the best technology.* Outsource the site if you don't have technical experts on your launch team. In the same way that print publishers always hire outsiders to print their magazines and newsletters, Web publishers often successfully hire vendors to build and maintain their websites. Third-party Web developers keep up with rapidly changing technology and offer the latest tools at the lowest cost. (Vendors are discussed later in this chapter, too.)

- *Maintain momentum.* Many publishers launch at a low frequency in print—quarterly or even less. A lively website maintains relationships with readers, advertisers, and freelance writers and contributors between the print editions. Hire an inexpensive intern or freelancer to post fresh news, write a blog, or monitor, and edit and publish material coming in through your chat rooms and message boards. You can also subscribe to free news feeds and articles through a content aggregation site such as www.freesticky.com.

Niche Strategies Are Working

The Internet is a surprisingly personal place. A thousand people—each with unique personal interests—can spend the same 60 minutes online together and never come close to crossing paths. Recent studies show that 73% of all American adults regularly use the Internet. Not surprisingly, Web activity is highest among younger age groups.

Use of the Internet in 2006, by Age Group	
Age group	Percentage Using the Internet
18 – 29	88%
30 – 49	84%
50 – 64	71%
65+	32%

Source: Pew Internet and American Life Project

Among Internet users, 77% looked for information on a hobby or interest, and 79% looked for health information. Publishers launching sites that target dedicated hobbyists and interest groups—including people with specific medical issues—can succeed on a much smaller start-up budget than sites that strive to reach a mass audience. If you already publish a niche magazine or newsletter, then you're halfway home to building a successful website.

Shopping is also a major pastime: 78% of users researched a product before buying it, and 67% bought something online. Successful publishers are folding shopping into the core activities offered at their sites, as an extension to the information they offer in print.

Later, this chapter will provide examples of entrepreneurs who are succeeding by taking advantage of this phenomenon—and provide details about how you can do it, too. But for now, turn to the key elements of a niche strategy.

Start With a Niche You Know

Start with your own interests and expertise for two reasons. First, these are your strengths as a publisher. Second, niche-marketing strategies are the best option for Internet publishers. Study the information that is already available in your niche, looking for gaps you can fill. Then fill the gaps with valuable information nobody else provides. Go back to the first three chapters of this book about defining an audience, creating a compelling product, and attracting readers. The same principles apply to websites, newsletters, and magazines: You must create unique and valuable information that meets the needs of your targeted audience. The Web is different only because you can provide information in new forms that would not be possible in print. Publishers are finding many different ways to provide compelling information uniquely formatted to make use of the Internet's capabilities, like searchable, interactive databases, calculators, and encyclopedias.

EXAMPLE: Bill Moore is a computer magazine editor with a passion for electric vehicles (EVs). He started an online publication in 1998 about electric cars and vehicles called EV World (www.evworld.com). In his spare time, he uses his journalism skills to develop the EV World website and email newsletters. He travels to auto shows and test-drives cars, posting his reviews, photos, and recommendations on the website. He also works to develop friendly relationships within the small community of engineers, auto designers, environmentalists, policy makers, and other folks working on alternatives to gas-powered cars.

EV World has now come to be recognized by most people in the EV community as the leading website on the topic. Bill won a grant from a foundation and has sold some content to cover his expenses. He started charging $29 per year for subscriber-only access to some of his website feature content, but with limited results. He says, "Going to a paid subscriber model isn't a panacea. The site gets 38,000 unique visitors a week, but only a tiny fraction of them is willing to pay."

Bill offered the following advice to other publishers: "Pick a topic you're passionate about and stick with it, but also be realistic about what it will take in the way of commitment to make a splash in a universe of 36,000,000 websites. The days of people handing you money just based on an idea are long past. You'd better have a real-world business plan to make your Web business work."

In 2005, Bill upgraded the site and started offering new features, including podcasts, RSS feeds, and a unique "advertising-optional" service for paid subscribers, who can turn off all third-party advertising on the site when they log in. At the same time, ad revenues jumped significantly— and the site is finally profitable.

Encourage Users to Connect

Create a gathering place for people interested in your topic. Allow people to connect with each other. Invite your visitors to contribute articles and opinion pieces. Big sites don't do this because their traffic is simply too congested. They can't afford to sift through all the contributions they would get from the hordes who visit them. Niche publishers, on the other hand, can use their Web presence to attract informed, articulate people who by their presence and contributions will add value to the site for every other visitor

For example, consider the newsletter called Dollar Stretcher (www. stretcher.com). Subtitled "Your weekly resource for simply living," the publication offers folksy, homespun ideas for living better by spending less. In addition to chat rooms (which are very popular), this site asks visitors to supply their own ideas in a "reader tips" area, and lets readers pose questions in a section called, "Can you help this reader?" In this way, it encourages readers to connect with each other and with the publication. Dollar Stretcher generates income from advertising and sponsorship, and was profitable after only two years. (Both advertising and sponsorship are discussed in detail below.)

Develop Exposure and Connections

If you focus on something that already interests you deeply, the chances are good that you already have connections with other people in your niche. If you don't, you clearly need to develop them. On the Web, using your connections is an essential way to develop name recognition. Without connections, you'll have a very hard time making a splash even in a tiny market. But once people know who you are, you can make lots of noise with a small budget. There are several ways to do this.

First, look for every opportunity—both on and offline—to speak or write about your topic to people in your niche, always mentioning your site. Include the website address on every page of your print publication, for example, and also in your email signature. Writing a feature article or column in a print magazine also draws great attention, especially if the publisher mentions your site along with your byline. But even if you can only write a letter to the editor, make it a habit to regularly submit your ideas where they'll be noticed. And seize every sensible opportunity to reach your audience through trade shows, conferences, seminars, and even ads in print publications. Posting comments along with your Web address on online message boards and newsgroups is another good way to increase your exposure.

Second, trade links with other quality websites in your niche. Publishers who include well-chosen links at their sites universally report that their links pages are very popular. People bookmark and visit them often. Still, some publishers won't give visitors an exit from their site via a links page.

> **WARNING**
>
> **Link only to pages you can heartily recommend.** Links are like business referrals: You should only make links to sites you would enthusiastically recommend to a friend or a customer. In the long run you will lose more business than you might gain by linking to sites that don't meet your standards. If you do accept payment for links—and many niche sites follow this practice—make sure readers understand that links are paid ads, not personal recommendations.

Third, submit your material to other sites with a link back to yours. For example, *Dollar Stretcher* offers its most popular columns free to print and online publications that want to share its folksy, homespun money-saving ideas with a different audience. Put a page on your site describing your terms for sharing content with other websites. In a small niche, these information content-sharing relationships are commonly established through personal negotiation. Bloggers are also using a completely automated system to share either the headlines of their articles or the complete article. You can build this technology into your website, which is a common feature of every weblog program. You can also submit complete articles to independent content syndication services that will publish your material on other websites. You can find syndication services online at www.freeSticky.com and www.yellowbrix.com.

TIP

Make your documents into ambassadors. Sometimes a popular article gets copied and redistributed to thousands of people on the Internet. If every reader knows that the material originated with you, many of them will come looking to see what else you have to say. You may never get paid for the reuse of your material, but by labeling your work in the following ways, you'll get loads of free exposure:

- always include the following copyright information:
    a. either the word "copyright" or the symbol ©
    b. the name of the copyright holder, and
    c. the year the work was first disseminated;
- always identify the author and publisher and describe how to reach both of them (online and off); and
- always include your Web address somewhere on the document so that readers can find your site.

Finally, learn how the search engines such as Yahoo! and Google work. Most people find their way around the Internet through search engines, which crawl through the text at your site looking for relevant words, phrases, or ideas. You can dramatically increase the odds that search engines will deliver up your site to a seeker by including key subject words in your text. (Working with search engines is covered in detail later in this chapter.)

RESOURCE

You can learn more about copyright law from *The Copyright Handbook: How to Protect & Use Written Works*, by Stephen Fishman (Nolo). And you can learn more about search engine optimization from *The ABC of SEO*, by David George (Lulu Press).

Outsource Technology

Whenever established Web publishers are asked what advice they have to offer new publishers, they almost universally respond by saying, "It's harder than it looks." Their biggest headache is technology. This is understandable, because Internet publishing technology is changing so fast that nobody can keep up with it. People commonly buy software products that become obsolete far too fast.

To save time, money, and frustration, your best bet is to work with service bureaus and outside vendors who will handle many of the technical headaches for you. For about $100 per month (or less), you can hire a Web hosting service that will provide the features a successful website needs to have. And as new technologies become available, your host will seamlessly integrate them into your site for you. Hosts often offer reasonably priced design services, too.

Look for a vendor that specializes in sites like yours rather than a generic website construction company. For example, one Web developer called InfoSwell.com focuses on creating websites for print publications in small niches. By concentrating on the unique needs of small print publishers, InfoSwell has developed a bundle of services specifically for them. For instance, it created a product called iDigital Edition, which converts print magazines or newsletters into an enhanced electronic replica presented in an onscreen flip-the-page format, complete with ads.

And recently, InfoSwell created a sleek, money-making website for a niche magazine, *Southern California Physician,* at www.socalphys.com. The site has multiple revenue streams and a rich assortment of interactive content that, according to the publisher, has added new life to its publishing company. Through online classified ads, a job board, an event calendar, and banner ads, the publication is attracting new advertisers who are also choosing to run print ads in the magazine. And physicians appreciate the ready access to searchable article archives, a digital edition, and community forums. The publisher says, "The site brings new credibility to what we do—and we are building community through our online resources."

Having found the right developer, make sure he or she sets up a site that you can take over and maintain on your own as your business grows. This means that you should retain ownership of your content and get training in how to maintain the site if you decide to manage it independently. InfoSwell and a number of other developers offer a Web-based site administration panel so that publishers can add content without knowing HTML and without having to hire HTML programmers.

Get Paid

Niche websites are finally generating income for many publishers—and ingenuity is the key. These are the publishers who devote serious energy to thinking up new ways to repurpose existing content, or cool new products they can sell, based on the unique needs and interests of people in their niche. Here's where it really pays to be original: Figure out what your readers want that nobody else will ever think of doing for them.

One good example of this niche-based creativity is a publication called *ReadyMade,* at www.readymademag.com. Subtitled "Instructions for Everyday Life," the magazine appeals to people who like to make stuff, and features articles about projects like making furniture out of your old computer parts. Its editors created a series of kits for sale through the website—things that would not likely sell to any other crowd except *ReadyMade*'s readers—including a $35 kit to make a 100-square-foot building out of scrap materials.

The Worst Idea in Cyberspace: SPAM

Spam is any message that you send electronically to someone who has not specifically requested mail from you. Like a telemarketing call during dinner, spam is almost always offensive and annoying to those who receive it, especially when the message is commercial or impersonal. There are several more effective ways to use email to keep in touch with current and potential customers.

1. Invite people to subscribe to an email newsletter instead of sending unsolicited emails. Have a sign-up form on your website and explain that you'll send timely, informative emails to subscribers.

2. Include late-breaking, useful information in the emails you send to subscribers. Because it can be delivered so quickly, email is actually a perfect vehicle for alerting people who are already part of your community to new and interesting developments. Even a modestly self-serving message will go over well if you package it with enough truly unique and valuable content, and send it only to those who want to hear from you. Just keep the hype to a minimum.

3. Make it easy to quit receiving emails. Every message should include brief, friendly instructions for getting off your mailing list. Even people who keep subscribing will appreciate knowing that you've made it easy for them to say, "Enough already!" when the time comes.

Here are a couple of good email newsletter examples. Both are basically promotional, but their content is so interesting that each has collected tens of thousands of volunteer subscribers. To see these emails, go to the authors' websites and subscribe.

- Web Marketing Today (www.wilsonweb.com) is a free weekly email from Ralph Wilson, who sells design and marketing services to people who own and operate websites. I like how this newsletter combines Ralph's gentle self-promotion with useful information about developing and promoting websites. And the newsletter always includes links to free, in-depth articles posted at Ralph's site.

- Web Reference Update (www.webreference.com) is a free email newsletter from Andy King, who offers technical services to website developers. I like the short, newsletter-style articles in this one. Each is hyperlinked to more detailed information posted at websites, including Andy's and others. You could spend 20 seconds or 20 minutes reading Andy's emails, depending on how much of the linked information you want to explore.

New Revenue Opportunities Have Arrived

The biggest websites are still taking the lion's share of booming online ad revenues. In 2005, the top 50 sites captured 95% of online ad spending. Even in the highly concentrated print magazine world the big companies don't get such a huge share of ad spending. But a remarkable turn of events made the Web friendlier to small publishers than the print publishing world: The big companies decided to share.

For example, Google figured out how to make money by sharing its technology and advertising programs with smaller websites through a project called AdSense. Yahoo! and MSN eventually chimed in, and now every Web publisher has the opportunity to earn money from online advertising through one of these programs.

The details keep changing, so it is wise to check with Google, Yahoo!, and MSN for the latest scoop. But the general idea is this: The search engine company convinces its advertisers to buy ads that appear on your website and gives you a share of the resulting income. The search engine handles all the details and sends you a monthly check for your share. Even though the search company keeps 50% or 60% of the money generated on your site, it's a pretty good deal for a couple of reasons.

- *You can make money fast.* You can begin generating income in a few days just by signing up with one of these programs. You won't get rich on the $50 or $100 per month most publishers earn with low traffic levels, but it's instant and relatively effortless revenue.

- *You can attract new advertisers.* You're likely to encounter advertisers that would not otherwise consider advertising on your site under any circumstances. Every national brand you can think of is participating in the search ad programs—and running ads on niche websites—even though very few of them are advertising in niche magazines. In this way, the search companies are creating new income for niche publishers.

But there are drawbacks, too.

You have no control over what products are advertised. Although generally linked to the content at your site, search ads are not always niche related. You won't get ads from a direct competitor, or an unsavory class of business, because you can exclude them. But you may get totally unrelated ads and potentially distracting ads that drag your visitors away from your site before you're ready to let them go. For this reason, some highly targeted niche sites have decided not to participate in the search ad programs.

You have no direct relationship with the advertisers. Google and the others expressly prohibit you from contacting advertisers directly. This means that you lose the opportunity to sell print ads to your search advertisers, for example, or to "upsell" one of them from a small ad to a bigger one—even with companies closely tied to your niche—if they came to you through Google, Yahoo!, or MSN.

You are the little guy. The search companies dictate all the terms, and there is no negotiating with them, no matter how wonderful or unique your site might be. They can reject you if ads on your site do not generate enough business for them. And since high traffic numbers are not always compatible with niche websites or start-ups, some sites do get booted out of the programs.

The bottom line advice about search advertising is: Try it. But only while you are simultaneously making your best effort to directly sell online ads to all of your best niche-related prospects. (If necessary, reread Chapter 5 on advertising sales.) And create a package price for your print advertisers that includes online ads. You'll make the most money if you handle your best prospects that way rather than letting an outside sales company, such as Google, get between you and those prime prospects.

Luckily, there are new tools and services making it easier for niche sites to handle direct selling and management of online ads as well as the bigger sites do.

TIP

Make room for ads. Google limits publishers to two search ad spots, plus one or two banner ads per page. Breaking up long articles into multiple pages, just like you would in a print magazine, increases the ad space available to sell at your site.

Online Ads for Advertisers

Before you offer an advertiser space on your website, you must be ready to serve up the right ads, track how many people clicked on the ads or viewed them, and collect appropriate payment from the advertiser.

Ad management programs automate all of these details. This software runs on your server and displays and rotates advertisements on your Web pages. It can also track and target ads and users based on various criteria. Until recently, you would pay thousands of dollars for a good program, well beyond the budget of most niche websites. But several low-cost options are now readily available. Today, any small site can shuffle banner ads just like the big sites. In fact, it has become so much easier to manage online ads that every online publisher should consider doing it.

The first step is to ask the vendor hosting your website if it provides ad management capabilities—and what the cost will run. Most of them do. You can buy low-cost ad programs if your host is not already using one, as noted below. But it's best to adopt whatever package it is already using.

RESOURCE

You can buy these ad management programs to run on your own server:

- the program at www. adjuggler.com, a reasonably priced program popular with small sites
- the one at www.centralad.com is also a powerful, budget-priced program, and
- WebAdverts is freeware available at www.awsd.com.

You can also subscribe to centralized ad sales sites that will host your ads through their servers instead of yours at:

- www.mediabrains.com
- www.bannerserver.com, and
- www.orbitcycle.com.

Some additional advertising management programs designed for print magazines are discussed in Chapter 5, Building Your Advertising Business. A number of these programs also provide online ad management features, so check with them, too.

In addition to running your own direct selling efforts, it is a good idea to investigate advertising networks. These are companies that combine lots of sites together and sell ads on all of them. Most of them specify a minimum number of impressions—or page views—that you must deliver on your site every month, but these minimums are relatively easy for a niche site to reach. Like the search ads, networks help you reach advertisers you might not reach otherwise. Networks will pay you a bigger share of the dollars generated on your site through the network than the search firms are paying, and some niche publishers are earning a significant amount of money this way.

The earliest online advertising networks focused exclusively on really huge sites and would not accept any site with fewer than a million visitors per month. But now there are networks that specialize in niche sites, including those listed in the chart below.

Name	Minimum Impressions/Month	Percentage of Revenue Share
adservingnetwork.com	2,500	60%
burstmedia.com	5,000	50% to 55%
realtechnetwork.com	25,000	70%
valueclickmedia.com	3,000	Negotiable
adbrite.com	Not specified	75%
adengage.com	Not Specified	75%
experclick.com	Not Specified	65%

Because you know your niche, you may be able to create new advertising opportunities beyond the standard banner ads and links. Take, for example, Vermont Life Online (www.vtlife.com), which is the online extension of *Vermont Life* magazine, a quarterly publication of the state's Tourist Board. It is a modest site by some standards, but the unique content—including features from the current issue about things to see and do in Vermont, and a Web-only calendar of events—has made Vermont Life Online the leading Internet source of travel information for the state. Only advertisers in the print version of *Vermont Life* may advertise on the website, and online ads remain active for the three months that each quarterly print issue is current. The publisher has decided not to accept search ads or network ads, which might undermine the relationship with print advertisers. Some of the mom-and-pop restaurants, inns, and tour companies that advertise in Vermont Life Online had no other online presence until the magazine publisher created Web ads for them. The publisher is an important marketing partner for these companies. *Vermont Life* uses MediaBrains.com to manage online ads.

Classified Ads

Online classified ads have become popular with small business advertisers. These are the same companies who might buy a 1/6th or 1/9th page ad in your print magazine, or even a classified ad. You can readily accommodate these advertisers on your website these days using the same technologies described just above. Ad management programs often handle classifieds, too. And there are comparable networks that sell classified ads on publisher websites.

For example, Southern California Physician magazine runs a robust section of online classified ads that are highly targeted to its niche: legal services for physicians, plus medical equipment, office real estate, and even medical practices for sale. Advertisers are required to run classifieds in both the print and online editions, for a total price of $100 per month—that's a minimum, depending on the word count—and the ads generate about $4,000 of extra income every month.

Within the sort of specialized niches many small publishers occupy, classified ads can be especially lucrative. Imagine enthusiasts of a niche sport buying and selling used equipment, or collectors buying and selling antique toys, radios, or classic car parts. Whether from small businesses or private individuals, classified ads help your visitors form communities as much as any other kind of contact you might give them. As an added bonus, you can earn revenue at the same time.

For example, Reunions Magazine (www.reunionsmag.com), published in Milwaukee, Wisconsin, has both print and electronic editions. The magazine helps individuals find people such as college mates, lost relatives, or the birth parents of adopted children. Articles and handbooks that they sell in print from this site cover topics like how to organize a search for someone or how to manage a family or high school reunion. This website is very well organized and draws heavy traffic. The market is a good one for classified ads, judging from the large number on the site. Ads, in a "Reunions Resources" section, cost just $1/word per quarter and the exposure is huge. Categories include reunion-friendly places to stay, cruises, photographers, travel agents, and professional reunion planners. The site also participates in Google's AdSense program.

E-Commerce

Electronic commerce has arrived, at least in selected categories. People are becoming much more comfortable about buying products online and paying for them electronically. In 1997, only 10% of Internet travelers had purchased products online, but in a 2006 study, that figure jumped to more than 67%, revealing shopping to be among the most popular activities online. In 2006, 73% of Americans identified themselves as Internet users, according to that same 2006 survey, which you can find online at www.pewinternet.org.

So, how can you profit from the spending boom? Consider becoming a retailer. Most print publishers already sell ancillary products like T-shirts and coffee mugs to their subscribers. On the Web, publishers are selling those same items, and developing a whole new range of products they can sell and deliver completely online.

A small private company called Air Age Media has developed this idea to perfection. The family-owned business publishes seven print hobby magazines, and each one has a thoroughly developed website with a shopping area. One of these, the monthly *Model Airplane News*, was founded in 1929 and has 48,000 paid subscribers plus 22,000 newsstand buyers. Its website (www.modelairplanenews.com) offers a host of Web-only features, like video clips of model planes, discussion groups, and bulletin boards. In the Web store, you can buy books, buyer's guides, and T-shirts that are delivered offline, as well as downloadable products like model airplane construction plans. The publisher promotes its Web store inside the print magazine, and it generates a hefty chunk of revenue.

TIP

Information is a product, too. You'll make the most profit on information products that you can develop yourself rather than tangible goods you have to buy from someone else and ship to your customers. So look hard at the information you've already got to see if some of it could be packaged into products you can sell at your site. For example, rather than trying to sell seeds, a gardening newsletter could instead publish a special report about seed propagation, plus a directory of seed sources. Selling seeds would require paying a middleman to package and ship them, while the special report would be much more profitable and easier to do.

Commissions

If you don't have products of your own to sell (or even if you do) you can earn commissions by providing links to other online vendors and encouraging your visitors to buy products from them.

That's the idea behind the programs at Amazon.com and Barnes & Noble, called "associates programs." If you recommend books that your visitors buy from these booksellers, the bookseller will pay you a commission on the sale, ranging from 5% to 15%. Amazon recently announced that it has more than 500,000 associates in its program (including me). Other vendors have adopted this model, and it's easy to see why. These programs allow you to build new business relationships based on your expertise and your relationship with customers. Everybody wins, and you can make a few dollars without having to open a store. Check to see which vendors in your niche offer associates programs.

Print, Email, Ebooks, and Fax

The Internet is great for finding information, but not as good for reading it. Many people want to locate material and then read it offline. That's why it's often a good idea to offer the same content from your website in alternative forms like faxes, email, ebook downloads, and printed pages delivered through the mail. If you have an online archive, you can allow visitors to conduct free searches and read abstracts of the related articles, and then charge them for the complete article delivered by fax or email.

For example, *The New York Times* offers articles from its archives for $2.50 each. Another example: A recently launched website, www.talltalesaudio.com, sells recorded stories for children available as a downloaded MP3 file or delivered on a CD. The downloads and CD sales are outsourced to a vendor, cdbaby.com. Another delivery option: For a 50% or 60% fee, a broker such as cyberread.com or ebooks.com will handle downloads of your larger articles or books to the general public through their websites.

The Internet is also great for customizing information. Look into ways to allow visitors to search through your site, locate, and call up the unique information they're after. Then you can charge them for specialized reports. For example, a site called Investools (www.investools.com) lets visitors create a custom portfolio of stocks, and then delivers email, print, or fax reports about those specific companies for a fee. Investools uses many different ways to charge for the same information, depending on the needs and interests of each customer.

Pay-Per-View

Many publishers have created different access levels at their websites with limited access for nonsubscribers, and full access to all the site's resources only for paid subscribers. Some of the sites already mentioned have areas reserved for paid subscribers. Another example: The site at www.accu-weather.com offers "premium" weather reports for $79.95 per year, or $7.95 per month. The premium service comes without advertising and also includes more detail from more weather satellites than its free reports.

Apple's I-tunes is perhaps the best example of successfully selling small bites of content online. Charging just 99 cents per song, Apple recently reported selling more than 1 billion songs in three years. But lesser known companies are also profiting from online sales of content. A company called istockphoto.com sells "stock" photographs at $1 each. Another example: A site called MarketingSherpa.com provides how-to articles and business case studies in either PDF or html formats for about $9 each.

It's Getting Easier to Collect for Small Transactions

Credit card processing fees are still too high to justify transactions where only a few cents are involved. Below about $5, it just doesn't make sense for a merchant to accept a credit card, because the bank will charge a dollar or more just to process the sale. Some companies have come up with innovative solutions to this problem. PayPal (www.paypal.com) is the most popular third-party payment system on the Web right now. About 75% of those who buy items on eBay use PayPal to pay for them. You don't have to be a credit card merchant to use PayPal—in fact, only about 20% of PayPal merchants also accept credit cards. Merchants pay roughly the same fees to PayPal that they would pay to a credit card company, in the range of 2% to 3% of the transaction amount. It's easy to sign up as a merchant, and offers a significant convenience to your site shoppers.

As Internet commerce develops, new payment options are also coming along. Nonprofits can accept online donations through a new class of vendors that handle the transactions for them, for example. Ground-spring.org and DonateNow.org are two reputable nonprofit service providers. Kagi.com is a vendor providing the same kind of payment processing services for small publishers selling downloadable products such as software and PDF documents.

Building Your Online Business

Many tools, services, and resources have become available that make it far easier to become an online publisher than it was even a year or two ago. If you launched your site then, you would have had to use a hodgepodge of software products loosely tied together. Now, you can buy very decent off-the-shelf programs that efficiently manage the many aspects of a site, making it possible to put together a bigger and better online presence in less time.

There is a downside to the easy availability of Web publishing tools: They raise the minimum standards site publishers must meet. For example, since programs that measure site traffic became available, every site is now expected to provide sophisticated traffic measurements to advertisers. In addition, your customers will demand top-level service such as searching capabilities, customized information updates, and message boards, because the new tools that produce them are so widely used at other sites.

Here's a look at each step in the publishing process and a review of the tools you can use.

Studying Others

There are now lots of books, newsletters, magazines, sites, and news-groups about Web commerce and Web publishing. (See "Finding Publishing Directories Online," below, and Chapter 14.) While many of these resources are undoubtedly helpful, they're no substitute for experiencing and understanding the Web first-hand. Start planning your site by exploring lots of others. Pay particular attention to how they handle e-commerce and online advertising. Don't spend too much time on the extremely sophisticated sites of multinational publishing and entertainment companies. Instead, look for smaller niche publications like the one you want to do. This research will help you understand what is possible, what the potential obstacles might be, and what your customers probably expect from you.

RESOURCE

Look for Web publishing conferences. An excellent one is hosted in Monterey, California, each November by Stanford University (www.publishingcourses.stanford.edu). There's no better opportunity to learn about the latest tools and best practices of Web publishers. I can recommend the Stanford course from personal experience, but if Stanford is not convenient for you, check for others.

Finding Publishing Directories Online

Directories and databases come and go. You can still find publishers for free in several different ways. The easiest way is to use your favorite search engine, either by keyword or by browsing in the appropriate categories. Yahoo!, for example, has nearly 4,000 listings in the category News and Media > Magazines. Yahoo! also lists free online magazine directories such as PubList (www.publist.com), a general magazine site called All You Can Read (www.allyoucanread.com), and the Ezine Directory (www.ezine-dir.com).

You can also find excellent examples of magazine or newsletter websites by searching the member directories of the top publishing associations. The Independent Press Association (www.indypress.org), for example, maintains an online newsstand of its members with links to their websites and contact information. Like most, the IPA member directory is searchable by subject. (Additional publishing associations are listed in Chapter 14.)

Designing Your Publication

To get started with your online publishing career, it is tempting to buy a software program and just start making Web pages. Unfortunately, if you follow this haphazard approach, it's more likely than not that the pages you end up with won't meet your long-term needs. You'll need to redo everything many times over. And you certainly won't draw the audience you're hoping to attract. A better approach is to go through the four short steps described below. Spending just a little planning time early on will make your site much better in the long run.

Define Your Mission

As with designing a print publication, it's important to take the time to define your website's mission. Start with a statement that describes what you want to do for your audience, how it will interact with you, and what you want from it. Be as specific as you can about your goals.

For example, how much revenue do you hope to get, and from where? Clear goals will help you build those revenue options into your site. For example, assume that you want to sell banners and classified ads as well as a few special reports, books, and maybe videos. In addition, say you want to deliver an email newsletter and sell subscribers-only access to your database. It's important that you identify these goals at the beginning so that you can plan how your site will operate, both on a business and technical level.

List the Features You Will Need

With a good mission statement in hand, you can spell out a structure for your site and a list of features you'll need, such as chat rooms, message boards, shopping carts, spaces for banner ads, searchable databases, and other website building blocks. Once you develop this list of features, you'll be able to decide how your site will work. And with function in mind, you'll be prepared to evaluate different design and hosting options. For example, to accomplish the set of goals described above, you'd need the following features at your site:

- a database program for keeping your mailing list
- a shopping basket and secure server for taking online orders
- traffic analysis software to show advertisers who they're reaching
- software to manage the placement of banner ads
- access controls, and
- a private newsgroup for paying subscribers.

It might also be good to have an email auto-responder to give customers a quick reply to their inquiries.

Find an Appropriate Website Host

To be an online publisher, you don't have to set up your own server to handle the thousands (or millions) of browsers that you hope will visit your site. Most publishers hire an outside service to host their sites, with hosting fees ranging from $20 to $250 per month. Available services—and the fees for them—change rapidly. Generally, prices are falling while services are improving, so it's important to make a thorough search before you decide which host to use. Ask other publishers and get referrals. And watch out: Anyone who picked a host more than 12 months ago may be paying more for less service than what you can find today.

You can find a list of possible hosts by going to a search engine like Yahoo! and looking up "web hosting." There are also a number of useful online resources that offer help with choosing a host or designing your own site. At these sites you'll find articles about picking a host, directories of good ones, and information about what features you should have.

- c/net (www.cnet.com) is a leading source for technology information generally, and for Web management information in particular. For example, c/net has a section called Web Hosting 101, with instructions about deciding what features your site needs to have and tools to help you search for vendors offering those features at the best prices.

- Internet.com (www.internet.com) offers more than a dozen different channels of information organized for different audiences. There's something here for the most technical among us and the least, the deepest pockets and the not-so-deep. For example, there is a channel on Internet.com called Small Business Computing offering advice especially for typical small businesses (like most publishers).

It's important to realize that not all hosts are alike, and the cheapest one isn't necessarily your best bet. (See Chapter 9 for advice on working with vendors.) As with any other vendor, look for people you like, who are easy to work with and eager to make your site a success. Make sure you understand the capabilities they're offering you and their pricing structure. Find out from them which software you should use to design and update your site. Some hosts offer this software free. Others have definite preferences you should know about ahead of time. Look at their customers' sites and pick a host that is already managing sites similar to yours. If you can't easily communicate with them, or you don't like the sites they've created, take it as a sign that they're not right for you.

A Vendor You Should Know About: InfoSwell.com

InfoSwell (www.infoswell.com) helps print publications develop a comprehensive Web presence for a very reasonable fee. The company specializes in responding to the needs of print newsletters and magazines, which will be regularly translating content from print to the Web and back.

Its sites are database-driven, so that content is easy to store and repurpose. And its programs are specifically geared to generate online income from all the sources discussed in this chapter: downloads, pay-per-view content, and all kinds of paid ads.

The company also offers a product, idigitaledition, that creates a Web-friendly replica of your print publication, including the ads, in an on-screen flip-the-page format. Many publishers are using the digital edition to sell international subscriptions, and to generate additional income from their print advertisers.

You can see an example of the idigitaledition at www.hawaiianstylemagazine.com, a lushly illustrated print publication that uses the digital version to reach thousands of readers and subscribers outside of Hawaii. In fact, more outsiders read *Hawaiian Style* than locals, and most local advertisers need to reach an international audience of potential tourists. The digital magazine is a perfect fit in this situation.

Create the Design

You have at least two options for designing your site: You can use website design software to put your site together by yourself, or you can work with a professional Web designer.

There are some powerful desktop design programs like Adobe Live Motion, Macromedia Flash, and Dreamweaver that will do much of the design work of a Web page for you. (Several good books about website design are listed in Chapter 14.) If you spend time studying other websites, reading self-help design books, and doing a little experimenting, you can probably do a decent job of it on your own.

Still, this option is generally not wise because there are almost always more important ways for you to spend your time as a publisher. Instead, it is usually preferable to work with a professional website designer.

You may be able to get website design services from your hosting service, many of which employ skillful and efficient designers. You can also sometimes find good designers by looking for websites that you like and then contacting their designers to see if they are taking on more clients. Web designers usually charge from $35 to $50 per hour. Obviously, the more you know about what you need (like your mission and features list), the more efficiently a Web designer can work with you.

Whatever route you choose, remember your audience when you design your site. More than 73% of U.S. households access the Web, but many homes still use modems. Rapidly improving access is becoming available for ordinary people, but for now, if your market includes home-based workers, retired people, and families, then make sure to design your site for their equipment as well as yours. If the site is too slow or unwieldy for a home system, use fewer graphics and smaller pages. It's always a good idea to preview your site using other people's computers, just to see how it will appear to others. You can even go to the public library to take a look at it.

Government, education, and business users generally have much faster access, larger-screen monitors, and the highest quality software. If they make up your target audience, your site can include the latest graphics, sound, video, and multimedia features. In fact, since there are millions of sites competing for attention from businesspeople, you may *have* to include the jazzy stuff.

Market Research About the Internet Population

For the latest demographic information and discussions about Internet research issues, visit these sites:

- Web Marketing Today (www.wilsonweb.com). Ralph Wilson is a website designer and consultant to small businesses. His site is an excellent resource for people trying to make sense out of the Internet market. He offers links to a great number of resources, so you might want to start here.

- ClickZ Network (www.clickz.com/stats). This site is operated by a market research firm that includes its own surveys and a thorough rundown on related studies.

- American Demographics magazine (www.adage.com/americandemographics). This magazine offers feature stories and in-depth coverage of demographic and marketing information.

Gathering an Audience

It takes more work to gather an audience than it takes to design a website. Much more. And it also takes more time. You need to cultivate your connections within your niche so others will mention and link to your site. Here are the basic steps to bring an audience to your site.

Work Your Niche

Start by developing and working online relationships with others in your niche. Make a checklist of every site your prospective visitors are likely to visit on the Internet, and connect with each. There are a variety of ways to do this. Your best options include agreeing to write articles for other sites, or posting useful messages with your Web address on their bulletin boards. Send press releases and emails about interesting features on your site to print as well as online media in your niche. Trade links and ads with other sites in your field, and if you can afford it, pay to run your classified ads at related sites.

One niche publisher doubled her traffic by spending two months of her time (and a small amount of advertising money) working through all the sites in her niche in this way. Another hired and supervised a net-savvy high school student with similar results.

In addition to bulletin boards and websites, make sure to cover offline watering holes in your niche. List your Web address wherever you also list yourself—business directories, professional associations, chambers of commerce. Speak at trade shows or conventions.

Work the Search Engines

There are a few good online resources about marketing your site—in particular, about how to make your site stand out through search engines.

- Search Engine Watch (www.searchenginewatch.com) is an online newsletter that offers comprehensive, practical tips about making a site that search engines can find. There are also some good links for webmasters here.

- The Web Marketing Today newsletter (www.wilsonweb.com) has several useful articles by Ralph Wilson, a marketing consultant.

TIP

Putting advice to use. I read the articles in the resources recommended here and followed their advice. One key step was to include words on my Web pages that people were likely to use in a search engine when they're looking for information about newsletters and magazines. For example, I changed from saying, "business help for publishers" to "newsletter, magazine publishing consultants." In the month after I began using those keywords, my traffic increased by 45%.

Google, Yahoo!, and the other search engines now offer lead-based advertising plans—meaning ad dollars that you spend only when someone enters key word searches through the search engines. In 2005, U.S. advertisers spent $5.1 billion buying spots on search engines and the ads have proved to be extremely effective at generating traffic for websites.

Yahoo! calls its program "paid inclusion," because it allows your listing to arise whenever someone searches one of your key terms. Google calls its program "ad words," and your listing is clearly marked as an ad, separate from other search results. Although the details are slightly different, you can buy these ads in pretty much the same way at all the different search engines. You can dictate how much money you will spend for every lead you get, and you can bid a price for each lead—generally, from 5 cents and up. And you can complete the whole sign-up process in minutes entirely online.

Use Your Print Publication

These days, most publishers are trying to fully integrate their Web and print publications: using the website to find new subscribers for the print magazine, and using articles in the print magazine to drive people to a website where they can buy Web-only tools or ancillary products.

Truth is, full integration is not as easy as it sounds. You can't just put your Web address on the masthead and expect people to jump online when reading your print magazine. Instead, your website must be a constant presence throughout your print publication. Editors must create parallel features for both at the same time. For example, when you run an article about cooking with chili peppers in your magazine, put an up-to-the-minute schedule of cooking classes on your website, plus a directory of hot sauce mail order companies with links to their sites.

A few other suggestions: Ask for emails in your Letters department, print a website table of contents in your print magazine, and include email or Web addresses for your authors, advertisers, and staff. All of these measures will signal to your print readers that yours is a Web-savvy publication.

The *Utne Reader* does a good job linking print and online content. Its Web address, www.utne.com, appears at the bottom of every page of the magazine, next to the page number and issue date. There is also an entirely separate masthead for the Utne Reader Online crew, a staff of eight people plus four interns and a host of volunteers. In keeping with the *Utne Reader*'s mission—to keep readers abreast of new ideas and emerging issues by gathering and republishing thoughtful, stimulating articles selected from independently published newsletters, journals, and magazines—the Utne Reader Online offers hosted discussions about the topics raised in each print issue. Every print article includes an invitation to visit Café Utne online and join a discussion about the article's subject. One recent issue offered Café Utne discussions about terrorism, open-source electronic publishing, Arabic music, the GI Bill, homeopathy, South Africa, and the AIDS epidemic.

Send Emails

Email can be an effective way to bring people to your site. You can find outside vendors to handle all the details for you—from collecting addresses to broadcasting the emails—often for less than $500 per year. When you update your site just once a month or less, an email update system can be very helpful for your regular readers and loyal fans. It's also a good idea to send out a notice when you make major improvements to your site.

Remember that if you use someone's email address without permission, you are a spammer. As discussed earlier in this chapter, spam is sure to backfire on you, so only send emails to people who have asked for them. Be sure to include opt-out instructions in every email that you send, and always provide a reply address.

Finally, be prepared to handle incoming emails, if only by sending an automatic response. In other words, don't ask for correspondence unless you are planning to read and respond to it.

Keeping Your Site Fresh

Online information grows stale even faster than printed information does. And people won't come back if your site doesn't contain fresh, up-to-date information. While a site updated daily or weekly will get significantly more repeat visits than one updated less often, many small publishers have found that they can't maintain such a frequent update schedule. The key is to update and refresh your site as often as you reasonably can. Weekly or biweekly or even monthly updates are very common. Some publishers who update less than once a month use an email notification system to inform subscribers about updates.

Finally, be sure to get feedback from your audience. Fortunately, it's a lot easier to connect with readers on the Internet than with print readers. Many online publishers conduct surveys at their sites, or collect information in guest books. *Carolina Country* magazine, for example, runs a series of online contests and polls to boost reader feedback to its site. Recently, readers could complete the phrase, "You know you're from North Carolina if … ," and there is a feature in each issue of the print magazine called "Nothing Could be Finer" including stories submitted online by readers.

Profitable Sites on Modest Budgets

Now that you have a general idea about designing and launching your Web publishing venture, look at some great sites from smaller publishing companies. These sites are included here because each is accomplished with a reasonable investment, something within reach of typical start-up publishers. It's also a good idea look at more expensive sites for inspiration, especially considering how rapidly Web publishing technologies are expanding while costs are decreasing. The jazzy features that big companies are inventing today will become affordable for the rest of us sooner than you might think.

The sites described here may be quite different by the time you look at them for this same reason: As new features become commonplace, these publishers are likely to adopt them. The message is to stay tuned.

Copy Editor (www.copyeditor.com)

Copy Editor, a bimonthly newsletter with no advertising devoted to the finer points of copy editing, offers a beautifully designed and organized website. The site is rich with material that readers will find useful, including a job board and an extensive listing of workshops held all over the country. There is a members-only area with current, Web-only articles and access to a members-only message board. The site also does a great job of promoting the print newsletter: You can download a free sample issue and then, if you like it, sign up online for a print subscription at $69 per year for six issues.

Copy Editor is published by McMurry Newsletters, a division of the McMurry Company, which also creates custom magazines for corporate clients like Citibank, the University of Phoenix, and the Columbia Healthcare Corporation. In addition, McMurry offers full-service advertising agency services. This company, like many others, publishes newsletters that serve some other business mission. In addition to *Copy Editor,* which is designed to help professionals develop their skills, McMurry also publishes *Publications Management,* a newsletter for corporate and nonprofit marketers who have an in-house publishing program.

E Magazine (www.emagazine.com)

In 1990, the Earth Action Network launched *E Magazine,* a bimonthly print magazine devoted to environmental issues. The print magazine enjoys a total distribution of about 70,000 copies, including some 15,000 sold in bookstores around the country. Subscriptions cost $20 per year, and about 40,000 people subscribe. Another 90,000 people receive the weekly opt-in environmental newsletter, *Our Planet*, which is supported by banner ads. The site also participates in Google's AdSense program.

E Magazine launched its website Emagazine.com (www.emagazine. com) in 1996. This excellent site was developed by an outside consultant named Roddy Scheer, who maintains it with lots of input from the magazine's editorial and business staff. The nonprofit spends less than $12,000 per year on the site, mostly on hosting fees, list management, programming, and Roddy's monthly retainer. It's a minimalist site— there are no links, banner ads, or e-commerce features—but it works just fine for the Earth Action Network.

This site has many helpful features, and all of them are presented very well. The free trial subscription offer is hard to miss and easy to accept. There are searchable archives of past issues and thoughtful abstracts of the current issue contents. Advertisers support the site by buying ads in the print magazine, which also gives them exposure on the website. For example, anyone who buys an ad in the Marketplace section of the print magazine gets to post the exact same ad on the Emagazine.com website for no extra charge, with a link to the advertiser's own site. A typical advertiser, and there are now about 50 of them, would pay less than $3,500 for a full year's exposure in the print magazine and on the website.

Scheer emphasizes that the outsourcing strategy has worked well for this magazine. He says, "Of course, nothing is wrong with hiring an in-house webmaster if you can afford the extra payroll expense. But websites require a wide range of skills, from HTML programming to database management to graphics and design. One person alone may not have all of those skills, but you can get everything you need by using the right outside contractor, or a small network of outside vendors."

Thrasher magazine (www.thrashermagazine.com)
Thrasher covers skateboarding culture. It's an ideal niche for a publication because the audience is intensely involved in the sport, there are hundreds of advertisers hungry to reach them, and the subject is just the kind of timely, people-rich, active topic that works best in a magazine. Founded in 1980 in San Francisco, *Thrasher* is riding the wave of this popular sport, and is a huge hit with its readers and advertisers. Paid

circulation is more than 165,000, each issue is fat with paid ads, and the company has developed a broad mix of ancillary products from T-shirts to skating videos to backpacks.

The *Thrasher* site perfectly reflects the print magazine's irreverent style, but don't be fooled—it's a down-to-business website. There are options to buy something on almost every page and a host of Web-friendly features. For example, you can search a worldwide database of skate parks (there are eight in Australia, 114 in California, and three in Kansas). You can download clips of music or videos. You can search 20 years of magazine archives conveniently sorted into channels—interviews, product reviews, and feature articles. There is a message board, gaming area, ramp-building plans, and quotes from reader emails. There are no banners or button ads except on the home page, but print magazine advertisers get links to their sites from the *Thrasher* website, sometimes including their logos. Most of the links are reciprocated, helping to build traffic.

Thrasher's site is hosted outside and maintained by webmaster Greg Smith plus one other person. Smith estimates that total annual costs are around $7,000 for the *Thrasher* site plus two others operated by the same company.

Asked how he promotes the *Thrasher* site, Smith said, "We do lots of link exchanges; we advertise in music magazines; we sponsor events and put up banners with the Web address ... we are always trying to promote the site." Greg's advice to other publishers: "If you are going to sell things from your site (like we do) make sure that your site is user-friendly and secure. Also try to update the site as much as possible because the more you add, the more people will want to come back. Don't let the site get stale. Message boards and chat rooms help spice up the site with little maintenance from the webmaster."

A Publisher's Website Checklist

By the time you read this chapter there may be lots of new features available at publishing websites. But for now, here's a checklist of the ones publishers should consider offering:

- searchable archives of past issues
- excerpts from the current issue
- subscription promotions, preferably a free sample issue offer
- links to advertisers in the print publication
- complete advertising media kit, including rates
- e-commerce options, like books or other products closely related to the magazine
- links to other sites of interest in your niche
- customer services for subscribers (like address changes), and
- message or bulletin boards so that readers can communicate with the publisher, and with each other.

People also like to see these extras:

- reader polls (plus the results)
- calculators and other computer-aided decision-making tools, like a college search program or financial aid estimators, and
- downloadable products for sale on the site, like special reports, guides, and other information products. ●

Making Strategies

Experienced publishers are always working on new strategies—for adding readers, increasing ad revenues, developing new products, and coping with competitors. The most successful publishers tend also to be very good strategic thinkers, either by nature or because they have learned how over the years. Other chapters of this book describe how to create specific strategies for key publishing issues, such as creating a winning product, selling subscriptions, ads, and ancillary products, and hiring employees and contractors. This chapter will concentrate on the process involved in making good strategic decisions. First, it examines why smart publishers spend so much time thinking about their strategic issues. Then it walks through a process that you can use to develop a new strategy or revise an old one. Finally, it offers suggestions to improve your results whenever you're developing business strategies.

Why Publishers Need Strategies

Strategy-making is the process of studying your opportunities, adding up your resources, and attempting to reconcile your current situation with your long-range goals. Whether or not you write them down, you and all other publishers are often thinking about current strategies and making new ones, if for no other reason than that the publishing business demands lots of long-range thinking. Here are just some of the conditions that all periodicals face that force their publishers to continually think about the future.

1. Healthy publications depend on subscriber and advertiser relationships that commonly take years to develop. Unless you plan for them well ahead of time, you won't get the relationships you want to achieve in the future.

2. Publishing markets change constantly as new competitors appear, audiences modify their habits or tastes, and advertisers undergo their own financial ups and downs. Lately, new technologies have

presented many unexpected publishing options like email or Web publications. Who knows, we may be publishing on wristwatches someday. Meanwhile, the best way to keep up with a changing world is to develop the habit of continually reassessing your resources and your opportunities so that you can thoughtfully respond to every new situation.

3. Making good day-to-day decisions absolutely demands long-term goals. Without them, you risk making poor short-term decisions. Let's say, for example, that your brother-in-law offers to set up a website for you. Before you can accept or reject his offer, you need to first determine what you want from your website and how it will mesh with your print publication. The answers are crucial to making a good decision, and can only be determined by taking a broad view of your overall publishing goals.

Like the person who buys a puppy on impulse or loses money on dot. com investments, many entrepreneurs leap first and ask questions later. As a result, they get lost in the throes of momentary difficulties like a short-term cash crunch or a dispute with a vendor. Decisions you make under stress can come back to haunt you later—for example, cutting prices in a hard spell can leave you stuck with a low-price strategy for a high-quality product. And firing a printer or a fulfillment company might feel good for the moment, but it can be a big mistake unless you've already located a good alternative. In short, long-range plans help publishers make smart decisions every day, and provide reliable markers to measure progress.

EXAMPLE: Linda wanted to publish a magazine for pet owners who liked to substitute organic food and medicines for traditional ones—a kind of alternative health care guide for pets. She decided to call the magazine *Whole Pets*. Although many companies were developing alternative animal-care products, few were ready to spend a lot of money on advertising because their companies were too small or their products weren't ready. In the meantime, Linda found that she could sell plenty of ad pages to established pet food and health care companies that wanted to persuade her alternative-minded readers that their slightly reformulated products were "organic enough." Linda had very little cash in reserve. In the short-term, she was persuaded to accept those ads to get the money she needed to sustain her publication until more appropriate advertisers were ready to support her. The results were deadly.

Linda's readers had a hard time buying her antichemicals and pro-organics message from a magazine full of ads that said the opposite and a website sponsored by toxic flea powders. Her single-copy sales were terrible, Web traffic was miserably low, and direct mail buyers didn't convert to long-term subscriptions. Too late, Linda realized that she had traded her editorial integrity for a short-term financial gain. Readers soundly rejected the magazine.

Linda's problem was timing and vision. Her publication couldn't hope to be profitable until a sizable organic-product advertising market developed, and she should have developed a long-term strategy to deal with the sluggish initial growth rate in her market. For example, she might have put out an issue every two or three months, and increased to a monthly schedule only when more advertisers were ready to buy ads. In addition, she could have started out with a very low-cost design, similar to a newsletter, and switched to higher production quality when she got the ad revenues to pay for it. Both steps would have let her build honest, uncompromised relationships with readers and advertisers without using up her savings too soon.

Goals and Strategies

Creating any good strategy involves answering three questions:

- What do I want?
- Are there ways to get it?
- If so, what's the best one for me?

The first question—what do I want?—forces you to deal with your overall vision: What kind of publishing business do you really want to own? There are lots of choices. You could be a wealthy magazine magnate like Malcolm Forbes, an influential publishing personality like Gloria Steinem, or a highly successful newsletter publisher—like Jack O'Dwyer (whose public relations newsletter, *Jack O'Dwyer's Newsletter*, recently celebrated 25 years in print) or Richard Benson (who founded the personal health care newsletter, *University of California at Berkeley Wellness Letter,* 15 years ago, which currently counts its subscribers in the hundreds of thousands). No matter what your key goals, one thing is sure: The better you define them, the more likely you are to achieve them.

The next question deals with a crucial issue: Is it possible to achieve the goals you have identified given your circumstances and your resources? Here the challenge is to gather necessary information and then use it to judge whether or not your ideas are practical. This is never a frivolous exercise, since honestly examining your circumstances will, in some cases, cause you to change or even abandon certain goals.

The last question—deciding your best course—deals with choosing the best strategies and tactics given what you've learned about the situation. Strategies usually take time to develop and implement, because they normally involve changes in several different parts of your business. For example, to get the most readers in your niche, you could borrow money and use it to expand your circulation among segments of the audience not served by other publishers, and at the same time add editorial material to your newsletter so that it will appeal to those new readers.

Tactics are individual steps that you take toward a specific strategy— for example, developing a direct mail campaign that approaches the new audience segments or hiring a new editorial contributor. Tactics are very immediate and linked to specific conditions. Usually, several different tactics will accomplish the same overall strategy—for example, you can't get Steve to write a column for you, but Alice will have the same appeal to readers, so you hire her instead.

A business plan usually describes a specific strategy and some of the tactics involved. But a business plan is not the same as a strategy, which involves flexibly considering future options.

Strategies Are Different From Plans

Because the world is constantly changing, so, too, must your strategies, which by definition are tied to the future. Often, your strategy deals with circumstances that are not fully developed in the present. For example, let's say you have a strategic plan to develop new products as soon as your newsletter turns a profit. Even though you are months away from having the funds you need, it makes sense to consider new product ideas and to gather information about them as soon as possible. Obviously, while you are still in the planning stage, you can change your strategic ideas several times before you actually launch any new products.

On the other hand, a business plan is a snapshot of your strategic ideas—what you're planning to do and how—at a given moment. For example, once you are ready to start working on a particular new product, you will want to write a business plan to describe the resources you'll need and the financial outcome you expect.

People use business plans to convey their strategic ideas to other people and to decide whether or not they need extra resources, such as more investment capital, new computer equipment, or a new vendor. Even though a particular plan is worked out in detail, it may never be carried out, since the strategy underlying it may change. For example, in rapidly changing markets such as the dot.com market, business plans became outdated almost as soon as someone wrote them down, because the strategic situations that supported the plans changed so rapidly.

Defining Your Vision, Goals, and Priorities

Strategy-making is a nonlinear process. It involves balancing your current situation with your expectations for the future, realizing that both variables are continually changing. Still, you have to start the process somewhere, and most planners begin by trying to define their current goals in the clearest possible terms: What are you trying to accomplish and why? Here are some tips about defining your goals.

- *Think big.* Steve Jobs and Steve Wozniak envisioned the "democratization of computers" when they founded the Apple Computer Company. Your vision can be equally grand—and equally compelling—but only if you allow yourself to dream a little.

- *Concentrate on what you want, not just on what you think is possible.* Obviously, Jobs and Wozniak by themselves could not accomplish the entire personal computer revolution, but they believed it would happen and knew they could make a significant contribution to it.

- *Be specific.* Instead of saying, "I want to grow my company," say, "I want revenues to double in the next five years so that I can hire some skilled people to help me double them again five years after that." Or "I want to hire enough good people whom I trust so that I can work only 30 hours every week and still make $80,000 or more per year."

- *Consider your values.* Recognize that since your personal philosophy —or internal guideposts—will affect your business choices no matter what you do, it makes sense to include them as part of establishing your goals. For example, if you hate to borrow money, recognize your company growth will be limited to what you can fund with your own resources.

TIP

Personal considerations are important. In creating any plan, remember that your ultimate aim is to satisfy yourself, your family, and your closest business associates. You want not only to create a viable publishing business, but to do it in a way that enhances your life.

Assessing Your Situation

As a publisher, learn as much as you can about the circumstances of your market. To succeed, this is something that you will have to do constantly. When professional planners study a business situation, they look at the company's strengths, weaknesses, opportunities, and threats (SWOT). These are exactly the elements of your competitive situation you should understand and monitor closely.

When you assess your situation, realize that while your intuition is important, it isn't enough. It's essential to test your gut feelings by collecting as much objective information as possible to see if they line up.

The next section of this chapter contains detailed information about how to gather good information. And remember, many tangible ways publishers study their SWOT have already been covered in other parts of this book:

- how to use a bull's-eye analysis of your target audience (Chapter 3)
- how to understand your competitors (Chapters 2 and 5)
- how to find growth markets and advertising prospects (Chapter 5)
- how to choose add-on or spin-off products (Chapter 6), and
- how to analyze your Internet opportunities (Chapter 11).

Creating a Strategy

Once you have a goal and a good feel for your current business situation, you are ready to develop your ideas about how to get what you want in the future. In short, you can make a specific strategic plan. There are three steps.

1. Establish priorities. Figure out what steps you need to accomplish first to reach your goal. For example, if your goal is to dominate a specific publishing niche, do you need advertiser support first, or support from readers?

2. Consider all options. It's important not to focus on a single plan before you've fairly considered all paths available to you. Usually, there are several good ways to reach the same destination. It's far better to pick the best among several than to blindly follow the first path that presents itself.

3. Choose the best tactics that fit well with your strategy. In making these choices, remember that since strategies usually involve several different parts of your business, so too must your short-term tactics. For example, a strategy to expand your readership will probably involve making tactical changes in the way you handle subscription sales, editorial development, and financing. You may also need to hire people, raise capital, and find new vendors as part of your growth strategy. The point is, don't stop working on a broad strategy until you've considered how you will accomplish all of the necessary steps in each part of the business.

A key part of creating any good strategy is to write it down. Not only does this help you remember what you've planned, but it provides an easy way to periodically review and revise your strategy. As part of creating your written strategic plan, it helps if you use the following outline.

- *Opportunity:* What's your current publishing situation?

- *Mission:* What are your goals?

- *Plan:* What specific actions will you follow to accomplish your goals?

- *Resources:* What resources will you need to carry out your plan?

- *Milestones:* How will you measure your progress toward accomplishing your goals? Your strategic plan should identify the markers you're going to aim for and when you want to reach them. For example, how many subscriptions do you need? By what date? Or, what level of profitability and by when? Or, what share of the advertising dollars being spent in your market do you want to capture, and by what time?

Planning

A good student rarely takes a test unless he or she is prepared to pass. Neither should you attempt to launch a new publication—or change or significantly expand an old one—without assuring yourself that it has a solid chance of success. A smart publisher, like a smart student, follows a few solid rules to help ensure success.

- *Use good information.* Since their success depends on having accurate and unbiased intelligence, good strategists establish as many reliable information resources as they can find, even if some seem redundant.

- *Trust your instincts.* You must make the key business decisions and bear the ultimate responsibility for their outcomes. Pay attention to your own mind, listen to your fears, weigh your thoughts, and make your own judgments.

- *Involve important people.* Although the publishing vision must be yours, you will need lots of other people to help you succeed. From the start, you should involve smart, hardworking people to test and refine your ideas.

Gathering Good Information

There are a million ways for new publishers to gather information on new opportunities and markets—from reading books, magazines, and newspapers to scanning the Internet to polling their own customers. The trick is to find the right material and to find it quickly. Since this allows you to stand on the shoulders of people who know more than you do about a particular subject, this is a very efficient way to gather information and insights. Fortunately, there are experts for every situation. They include industry leaders, research scientists, government regulators, reporters, and trade journalists. The key is to tap the knowledge and experience of a person who is well informed about what you need to know.

> **RESOURCES**
> You'll find some very helpful suggestions in a book called *Find It Fast: How to Uncover Expert Information on Any Subject Online or in Print,* by Robert Beckman (Harper & Row Perennial Library). In particular, Beckman offers tips on locating knowledgeable people who are willing to share their insights with you.

Another commonly used information-gathering method is survey research, where you poll a group of people whose opinions are likely to mirror the thinking of a larger population. For example, if you want to know whether teenagers read magazines, pick a representative group of teens and ask them about their reading habits.

There are two big problems you can run into when you are trying to gather information, either from experts or from surveys: bias and irrelevance. Biased information isn't correct, and irrelevant information isn't useful. Both of them not only waste your time, but relying on either can result in poor decisions. Fortunately, being a little skeptical can usually help you avoid both problems. Don't put all your trust in any one type or source of information. Instead, always try to corroborate information you obtain with a second source. If the information is accurate, this shouldn't be hard to do. Finally, trust your own instincts: If something seems too good to be true, dig deeper.

Overcoming Bias

Any one of the following habits will help reduce bias that may infect the information you want to use. And all of these habits together will practically guarantee that your facts are reliable.

- *Ask enough people.* The simplest way to escape bias is to pose the same question to lots of people. That way, you aren't misled by the secret motives or hidden agendas of any individual or small group. A common and acceptable practice is to survey 1,000 people or more. And most researchers reject a survey unless at least half of the participants responded. The higher the response rate, the better, but if 50% or more of the people answered most of the questions, then the overall findings are probably reliable.

- *Ask the right people.* If you want to know how all U.S. teens behave, you can't just talk to teens in New York City. They are not likely to represent kids from Kansas or California. A study only reflects the whole population if everyone in it has an equal chance to participate. That's why researchers are careful to select the right broad survey group and then to draw a random sample. For example, to learn more about the preferences of all U.S. teens, you would pick your sample at random from a group that covers the whole country.

- *Ask the right questions.* Experienced researchers ask people about behavior rather than opinions, reasoning that people's actions accurately represent their underlying attitudes. And behaviors are easier for people to describe. For example, if you ask, "Do you like magazines?" many people won't know what to tell you. But if you ask, "How many magazines have you read in the past month?" most people can give a very close estimate. Unscrupulous pollsters sometimes prejudice their results by slanting the questions. Look for fair questions that are easy to understand and to answer honestly.

Seeking Relevance

There is a huge amount of information available about any subject. You can waste a lot of time wading through details that aren't important to you. For example, our model railroading magazine publisher can doubtless find tons of details about his market, from the average price of a model train to the total linear feet of model tracks sold during the past ten years. But what information will help him publish a better magazine, or increase his profits? Which details are relevant?

The key to determining what information will make a difference to you is to decide in advance what you will do with the information once you get it. This will allow you to find the information you need efficiently. In other words, linking your research to action helps you focus your inquiries on the right details.

EXAMPLE: Tony Thomas was considering publishing 12 issues of his model railroading magazine a year instead of six. The crucial question was: Could he double his advertising pages? That question became the focus of Tony's market research. He decided to interview his top 20 advertisers, whose opinions and behaviors, after all, would go a long way toward deciding whether his publication would succeed.

The worst thing that could happen, Tony felt, would be if the advertisers said they would support his magazine and then didn't. So he needed to design a survey that would result in honest responses. He hired two students from the business school at a nearby university to help him. Together they developed a survey that asked advertisers their opinions about all of the publications in the model railroading field. Since respondents were not told who was sponsoring the survey, they would be more likely to give unbiased answers. The researchers asked each advertiser to report where they were currently placing ads, why they had made that choice, and how much they spent on advertising. They also asked each one to project its future advertising spending in each publication.

The results were discouraging. Tony learned that very few of the businesses in his industry were currently planning to buy more ads in *Tracks* or, for that matter, any of the other railroading magazines. Most of them reported that there were too many publications in the field, and they put his magazine low on their priority list. Although that was not what he wanted to hear, Tony believed the results and abandoned his plan to publish more issues, at least for the time being.

When you are building your own publishing strategy, you may find it very useful to conduct surveys. For example, if you want to know whether or not your audience plans to adopt a new technology that may impact your publishing business (like the Internet), it's always a good idea to ask. Or, you may even find that someone else has already done survey research on the same issue and, assuming they have followed reliable methods, you can learn from their results.

Whether you do your own surveys or study someone else's, don't abandon your skepticism just because so-called scientific methods were used to collect the data. You should always trust your own judgment, look for corroboration, and think about the possibly oblique motives of people who offer "scientific" proof to support their opinions. Bias can creep in everywhere.

Enlisting Help

Many publishers seem to have a blind spot about the necessity of enlisting any help. Instead, they often set out to do the whole job alone. This approach is almost always a mistake.

By contrast, wise strategists will find good helpers and consult with them and with other allies as early as possible in the strategic planning process. First, this ensures they have friends and resources on board when they need them. Second, they learn whatever good information others may have. For example, when you consult people with both Web and print publishing experiences, each brings a different vantage point and may be able to provide important information you wouldn't otherwise know. And finally, working collaboratively ensures that all key members involved with your publication understand and support your overall strategy. Even a brilliant strategic plan won't work if nobody follows it.

Sadly, publishers often avoid talking about strategic questions with their supporters and collaborators. Instead, they allow all their communications to remain on the tactical level—often centering on the next immediate problem and seldom on the big picture.

EXAMPLE: Harry's wife Alice was a successful real estate agent and a good salesperson. She spent some of her time helping out on subscription sales for Harry's software newsletter, *Programming Trends*. Harry would have been wise to ask Alice to help him study the software market and develop a new subscription sales strategy. He didn't, both because he was reluctant to ask her for more of her time, and because he didn't want to admit to her that he was afraid that *Programming Trends* would never sell enough subscriptions to make the business profitable, no matter how good the newsletter and how hard they tried to sell it. Finally, and probably most importantly to Harry, he didn't want to distract Alice from selling subscriptions for the next few weeks because they badly needed that revenue to pay the bills.

For her part, Alice had a very realistic attitude about *Programming Trends'* potential. If Harry had asked her, she would have helped him make a balanced estimate as to its prospects and a workable plan for achieving higher subscription revenues. Furthermore, because Alice was already familiar with the faults in *Programming Trends'* strategy, she would have been relieved to learn that Harry was working on a new plan. But since Harry never asked Alice, he never got the benefit of her good judgment.

Your allies probably have insights about your business that could be useful to you. You should find an appropriate time and place to talk to your vendors, employees, investors, editorial and creative contributors, and all of your informal advisors, including your family and personal supporters. Tell them your goals and your ideas. Ask for their opinions. You may receive good information then and there, or sometimes days, weeks, or even months later. Once people know more about what you are doing—and that you are open to their suggestions—many will go out of their way to bring you information they believe might be of help.

TIP

Create an advisory board. Lots of small publishers get regular advice from their most trusted advisors by putting them on an official advisory board or an informal board of directors. One publisher meets with editorial advisors while he is designing each quarterly issue of his magazine. Another invited four experienced publishers and businesspeople to serve as informal directors to her small publishing company. She brings them together once a year and calls on them individually as needed between meetings.

Developing Instincts and Judgment

Publishers who operate alone, or with very little access to expert advice and experienced counselors, tend to rely too much on their own judgment. While this isn't always fatal, it often is. Even the most skilled among us have blind spots.

TIP

Form a peer group. I helped a group of book publishers in my town form a peer group that meets regularly to exchange ideas with one another. With another consultant, I hosted their meetings for about two years, but now, the group survives on its own. The members take turns hosting meetings in their offices every couple of months. Most of them own very small companies, some with no employees at all, and were feeling isolated before the group formed. Others have employees, but felt very isolated anyway. They needed to talk with other business owners. Now, each publisher has friends to call for good advice or plain old sympathy. Few of them can afford to hire consultants except in very specific situations, and often their peer group provides the same support they would get from a consultant, but for free.

It's easy to imagine many scenarios in which a publisher can go astray by neglecting or even refusing to get necessary advice or information.

The most common manifestation of this refusal to learn is a tendency to focus on day-to-day busywork while ignoring big problems. That is, willful ignorance. (Read "Signs of Willful Ignorance," below, for a quick test to see if you might be suffering from willful ignorance yourself.) Many publishers have been forced to close down their businesses, defeated by problems that could have been avoided had the publishers looked more honestly at their business situations early on. Instead of making plans to deal with a weak market or a strong competitor, these publishers threw themselves into their daily tasks, essentially ignoring their strategic problems, and ended up burning themselves out for nothing. For example, if there aren't enough advertisers to support your monthly magazine, you have two choices: to publish fewer issues or to find alternative revenue sources. It's not helpful to retreat to your desk to spend 12 hours editing next month's feature story.

One reason willful ignorance occurs so often in publishing is that it is relatively easy to start a new publication. In other businesses, barriers to entry are so high that people with a badly flawed vision never get started. But publishing is different: All you need to do is think up a name, create a first issue, invest a few thousand dollars printing and distributing a few copies and—Voila! You are in the publishing business. As long as you can scrape together enough money to turn out another issue, you are still a publisher, even though there is virtually no chance that you will succeed in the long run.

EXAMPLE: John published *Baytown Fishing*, a locally oriented boating and fishing magazine, for four years without ever once asking himself the most important question: "Is the Baytown recreational fishing market big enough to support a profitable magazine?" He avoided that question probably because he secretly suspected that the answer would be, "No; there simply are not enough readers or advertisers to support my editorial goals." Instead of facing this question, John kept the magazine going by tightly controlling his spending. He scrimped and scrambled to put out issue after issue, doing most of the work by himself, without pay. He became an expert at what he began to call "penniless publishing."

Unfortunately, but not surprisingly, this strategy eventually fell apart. No matter how little he spent, John's magazine still could not earn enough to cover his publishing expenses. Not only did John have trouble sleeping at night, but he worked so hard his health began to suffer. And despite spending as little money as possible, he eventually used up his savings. As fast as he ran, John couldn't escape the day when the whole business finally fell apart.

John's situation, in the example above, is far from unique. Novice publishers' worst fears are often right. Whether they are willing to say it out loud or not, many publishers know exactly what's wrong with their businesses.

Signs of Willful Ignorance

If one or more of the following describes your situation, you are almost certainly practicing willful ignorance in the management of your business.

- You don't have a budget or a business plan.
- You avoid people who challenge your judgment.
- You spend most of your time fussing about the contents of your publication and very little time talking to your readers, advertisers, suppliers, and other constituents.
- You have trouble dragging yourself away from the office, no matter how tired you are.
- You have trouble sleeping at night.
- You chew on the same problems over and over again without resolving them.
- You are losing money or not making enough to pay yourself a decent salary.
- Your business doesn't make you happy.

On the flip side, often the simple act of facing your fears can be a mental breakthrough, and may stimulate some of your best problem-solving efforts. For many people, a critical step toward developing a clear vision of their market and their business is to face up to what is inside their own minds. Or, put another way, only when you directly confront your biggest doubts and fears can you access your most creative intelligence.

Going back to the example of John, the publisher of the failed little fishing magazine, rewind and consider an alternative scenario in which John takes a week off.

EXAMPLE: Nearly at the point of quitting, John decided to spend a week at his favorite fishing hole to relax and reflect. His mind clearer after just one day, he finally asked himself the right question: Could the local fishing industry support his magazine? When he faced the problem head-on, he began to see several possible solutions that he had never considered before. For instance, he could repackage his magazine as the communication vehicle of a nonprofit fishing advocacy group and seek grants or donations from local benefactors like the regional boating association. Or he could shrink its size and cost by publishing a newsletter instead of a magazine. Or he could extend its territorial reach and publish a regional fishing journal. In short, there were several reasonable and viable alternatives staring him in the face as soon as he was open to them.

Here are a few positive suggestions for stimulating your best creative thinking.

- *Give yourself time and mental space for reflection.* Take a short break from the office and put aside all of your tactical issues so you can think about the big picture.

- *Really listen.* Take the time and effort to evaluate the thoughts, feelings, and ideas that arise during your period of reflection. Often it's a good idea to write them down.

- *Talk over your ideas with someone you respect.* These should be intimate conversations, not business planning sessions. Many people choose a person with good common sense from among their friends or family to be a sounding board. Certainly one big criterion should be to select a person who will tell you the truth, which is why an employee or vendor is probably a poor choice for a confidante.

TIP

Trust yourself. Once you decide that your own intelligence is a highly valuable resource, it becomes easy to schedule time for reflective thinking. And once you have developed the habit of listening to your own intelligence (and the compassionate commentary of your intimates), you are likely to find that you will make fewer errors of judgment.

Making a Strategy: An Illustration

Consider the strategic planning efforts of two young entrepreneurs who want to launch a publication online.

Looking forward to graduating from college in a year, Leo and Anthony decide to work together on an online publication aimed at mountain climbing enthusiasts like themselves. Their dream is to help develop the sport and at the same time encourage climbers to actively protect irreplaceable wilderness areas. From the beginning, Anthony and Leo envision an Internet publication, because they know that many sports activists and environmentalists are already sophisticated Internet users, not to mention all the trees they'll save by not printing on paper.

Anthony and Leo do a lot of research about Internet publishing, looking for other climbing information resources and environmental activist organizations, and studying online publications in other fields. They also buy a couple of books about business planning and loosely follow them as they develop their own ideas. The planning books lead them to think about issues they might have overlooked on their own, like ways to legally organize their business, and options for gathering the financial resources to grow their business down the road.

The two friends enjoy talking over their plans and debating some of the details: Who will write for them? How will they find subscribers? Who will buy advertising space from them and who will help them sell it? As they work on these issues, they take notes. Eventually, they have a written plan.

When Leo and Anthony tell their parents about their postgraduation plans, both families are somewhat skeptical. They raise a whole set of concerns the pair had overlooked—for example, how would the business fit into their lives? Do they want to be publishers to make a mark in the world, to make money, or to have fun? The two friends talk these issues out with their families and with each other. These discussions add a hefty dose of reality to their business plan. In particular, they are inspired to think about the payback for their hard work and even an exit strategy if the business becomes so successful that it risks being overtaken by competitors with deep pockets.

To learn more about both these issues, they look at other publishing companies to see how they cope with these common concerns. All the while, they keep taking notes, and refining their plan.

By the time the two friends decide to look for investors and start their business, they have crafted a thoughtful, articulate strategy. Their plan is basically to use the Internet to link mountain climbers and environmentalists—people who both love wilderness and know how to enjoy it. They will sell subscriptions, advertising space, and stand-alone information products like tour books and climbing tip sheets.

As a result of their thorough research and thoughtful strategic plan, they are able to find both environmentalists and sports enthusiasts who are interested in investing in their publication. They strike a deal with two of them—a well-known environmental activist and a climbing gear manufacturing company. Even without any publishing experience, their plan convinces the investors that the two friends have a knack for business and a well-grounded understanding about the work ahead of them. Finally, the partners open their website called Mountain Vistas, and it quickly becomes a popular site.

Since they enjoyed writing it in the first place, Leo and Anthony make it a habit to keep their strategic plan updated. They talk about the future often, and they keep notes about specific goals they want their business to reach. When one of them comes up with a new idea—like organizing climbing tours themselves, or writing a book—the other asks, "Where does this fit into our plan?" Interestingly, it isn't so much the planning document that helps them over the years, but the habit of often stepping back to look at strategic issues together. ●

Troubleshooting

Every publishing business occasionally runs into trouble. This chapter shows you how you can restore things to an even keel if you run into some of the most common publishing problems.

All problems are not equally serious. In particular, a flawed strategy is much harder to fix than a short-term setback. The chapter contains a list of the common strategic problems that can ruin your publishing business, and offers some suggestions about how to distinguish between "big picture" issues and regular, run-of-the-mill publishing problems.

It's wise for most publishers to get expert help with strategic problems, and the chapter also contains tips on how to work with consultants, collaborators, and other advisors. Even with their help, it's easier to fix your problems if you understand them, so you'll also find guidance about how to analyze the situation so you can begin to figure out what's wrong.

Recognizing Trouble

You can fix most problems if you catch them early and define them correctly. Unfortunately, it's not always easy to correctly diagnose your publishing problems before they get you into deep trouble.

For example, a publisher who constantly runs out of cash may not realize he has a serious problem. He may think that cash shortages are a fact of life for publishers. To some extent he's right—healthy publications occasionally run out of cash: But cash flow problems can also signal a fatal business flaw, a strategic dilemma like subscribers who can't really afford the publication, or a dying advertising market. If the publisher tries to fix the cash crisis without addressing the strategic issues, he can dig himself deeper into trouble by borrowing more money, adding more salespeople, or trying to enrich his line of products, even though his market is slowing down.

Obviously, you can't fix a problem until you figure out what's wrong. But overworked and inexperienced publishers often attempt to do just that. They rush to fix everything without taking time to fully understand what's happening. If you feel the urge to jump into action, try taking these three steps. You can do them quickly, and they will invariably help you find the right solution.

- *Reflect on the problem.* Step back and think about the situation. When did the trouble start? What might have caused it? Who might be able to help you deal with it? Make notes if possible so that you can clearly explain the situation to other people.

- *Ask for help.* Ask employees, vendors, customers, and other trusted advisors for help if you aren't sure about the source of your troubles. Some of these people may be itching to tell you where you're going astray, and often they have good suggestions to help set things straight. Consider bringing in outside experts. Most consultants will give an initial consultation for free. (See Chapters 9 and 10 about getting people to help you.)

- *Gather information.* Explore your own ideas and your associates' recommendations by looking for additional information. In particular, study your financial situation. (See Chapter 8 on financial information and accounting.) You may also need to conduct some market research. (Covered in Chapter 3.) Some problems are easy to fix if you just learn a little more about them. For example, an unhappy employee often feels much better if you simply ask him or her what's wrong and then listen to the explanation. Another example: Your renewal responses are low, and when you investigate, you find out that someone goofed up and mailed out the renewal letters a month behind schedule. Even when a problem is not that easy to solve, gathering good information will always help.

- *Set benchmarks to measure progress.* It's easy to kid yourself into thinking that things are getting better when perhaps they aren't, so set and watch very specific benchmarks that will mark your actual progress. For example, aim to achieve a 20% increase in renewals, or a 10% lift in newsstand sales, or 500 new subscribers, or some other specific target. If you aren't making progress as measured by these benchmarks, keep working on the problem until you reach your business goals.

If you have a habit of setting specific financial goals and measuring your progress against them, it will be relatively easy to catch business problems when they first arise. The plans and scorecards described in Chapters 11 and 12 amount to a ready-made early warning system to highlight trouble early on.

Most often, you'll know what to do after you take the time to reflect, discuss the situation, and collect important information. If you still can't figure out what's wrong, then you may have a strategic problem. (See "Common Strategic Problems," below.)

If you do have a strategic problem, you probably need to stop and reconsider your entire publishing strategy, but if it's not a strategic problem, then you may find an easy solution in the suggestions provided in this chapter.

Any problem can take time to fix. You'll need time to assess the situation and develop an appropriate response. The sooner you notice a problem, and the faster you recognize its significance, the more time you will have to work out a solution.

> **TIP**
> **Always act quickly.** Obviously, it's easier to fix any problem if you catch it early. Here's a suggestion: Until you know better, assume that any problem will have long-range implications and tackle it right away. Later, if the trouble turns out to be simple, you've done no harm by fixing it quickly. And if it's a bigger problem, you'll be glad that you tackled it early on.

Experienced people can solve problems faster than beginners. For this reason, as soon as you realize your business has a significant problem, find a consultant or other publisher with lots of experience to help. Remember, too, that high-priced business consultants are not the only sources of sound advice. Throughout this book other excellent resources are mentioned, including vendors, other publishers, journalism teachers, and people who have a stake in your success. You can even try posting your questions on one of the many Internet bulletin boards for publishers. (See Chapters 11 and 14.) Publishers help each other on these message boards all the time.

Common Strategic Problems

Strategic problems doom a publication either to fail outright or to struggle on the brink of failure, never reaching any state of self-sufficiency or solvency. The following is a list of the areas in which strategic problems often crop up, and the parts of this book where you may find help with each one.

- AUDIENCE. If you choose an audience that won't sustain your publication, there is nothing you can do but find a better audience. That probably means reworking your circulation strategy and revisiting your editorial mission. (Chapter 2 discusses the qualities of a good audience, and how to make sure yours is a good one.)

- EDITORIAL EXCITEMENT. Sometimes editors and publishers lack the spirit it takes to attract and maintain an audience. If the primary creative director of a publication—the person who establishes its voice and defines its content—loses touch with your audience and fails to meet its needs, then the only remedy is to find someone who can accomplish this essential task more successfully. Hire new editors, or create an editorial advisory board.

- ADVERTISER SUPPORT. If a publication depends on advertising revenues, then there must be enough advertisers in the market that have the means and the desire to advertise. When you don't have sufficient advertiser support, then you must find alternative revenue sources such as ancillary products, or cut back your publication to a format that you can sustain without advertisers. (Chapter 5 discusses how to study your advertising prospects. Additional products are covered in Chapter 6.)

- EFFICIENCY. Publishers have to be efficient to profitably meet the regular demands of a periodic publishing schedule. That means understanding the financial workings of your business so that you can monitor and control your profits. It also means using technology to maximum advantage. (See Chapter 8.)

- LEADERSHIP. Publishing is a collaborative enterprise and every publishing company needs someone who can bring a good team together and help coordinate its work. Publishers who lack leadership skills have a serious strategic disadvantage. You can either develop the skills on your own, or bring in someone who has them. (Chapters 9 and 10 discuss finding people and working with them.)

Strategic Problems

Strategic problems usually take more time to fix than tactical problems. For example, a cash-poor publisher who has picked the wrong audience or faces a dry market may have to devote considerable time and effort reworking the publication, revising circulation and sales strategies, or reorganizing the publishing operation. All of those remedies involve a major commitment of time and effort. Obviously, the sooner action is taken, the better.

Even complex strategic problems can be resolved if you go back and reconsider your original publishing decisions. For example, if your market is slowing down and advertisers don't buy enough ads to support you, consider changing to a lower frequency or a different financial structure. Can you trim production costs by switching to a newsletter or Web-only format, and make up for the advertising revenue losses by raising subscription prices?

If you have to reconsider your overall publishing strategy, bring together your key collaborators and focus your thinking on the following issues.

- *Where do you get your profits?* Analyze all your income sources (new subscriptions, renewals, advertising, and ancillary product sales) to see which customers provide the most profits. Use break-even analysis to identify your most profitable sources of income. (See Chapter 4.) You may find that your current strategy is not geared toward your best customers—for example, that you are doing a great job selling new subscriptions, but failing to renew the most profitable ones. As you identify your most profitable customers, your new strategy should be structured to target them.

- *What's happening with your most profitable customers?* Pick a few of the most critical customers and analyze your current relationship with them. Talk to some and poll more. Ask them about how your publication is or is not meeting their needs. You may find that their situations have changed and that you need to relate to them in a different way. For instance, you may learn that an important class of advertisers is facing its own hard times and cutting back on its spending. Or, you may find that your subscribers are beginning to find a new source of information (like the Internet) that is faster or less expensive than your newsletter. It will be easier to rebuild your publishing strategy around these threats if you identify and face up to them before your competitors do.

- *What new trends are developing?* Look back over the key financial variables in your business with an eye to finding new patterns. (Chapter 8 explains key variables like newsstand sell-through rates, subscription conversion rates, and advertiser contract rates.) Use these numbers to sharpen your understanding of your market or your current publishing strategy. For instance, if renewal rates are down slightly, you'll want to know if they have been falling steadily or if there is a convincing short-term explanation. While a single disappointing month is no cause to revamp your whole publishing strategy, a year of declining renewals might be.

- *Are your systems up to date?* Take a fresh look at your employment practices, technologies, and the vendors you are using, and compare them to what the most innovative, and successful publishers are using. Maybe yours have fallen behind the best industry practices. Obviously, outmoded operating systems can drive away good employees and waste money.

> **WARNING**
>
> **Flexibility is the key.** Chances are you can fix most problems if you are willing to try a few different approaches. Once you accept the fact that there is no single solution that applies to every circumstance, it may be easier to open yourself to a broader range of potential remedies.

EXAMPLE: Lila was the publisher of *Sitting Well*, a monthly Buddhist magazine sponsored by the American Buddhist Society. She posted a questionnaire on the Internet and found that thousands of Buddhists all over the world were active on the Internet. So she decided to launch a printed newsletter for Buddhists who used the Internet called *Internet Dharma*. She charged readers $28 a year for a monthly publication which focused on people's experiences exploring the Internet and contacting Buddhists from other parts of the world. Early feedback was very positive, but Lila found that renewal rates were very low, under 30%. Why?

Lila polled her readers—including the ones who had failed to renew—about how they used the Internet and how her newsletter might help them use it more effectively. She learned something important from the survey: Her readers did not have a sustained interest in the Internet. After an initial burst of searching and navigating, many of them either signed off altogether or settled down with a few favorite sites. In either case, they didn't stay interested in exploring, and therefore found little long-term use for *Internet Dharma*.

Lila decided to make a strategic change in her newsletter business based on the fact her audience would not support the newsletter as defined. Her approach was to fashion a product that was useful to readers when they were intensely interested in Internet information. This means her pricing strategy would have to be able to capture a substantial amount of income from readers before their interest faded.

She had several different business models to explore. For example, she could create a useful but low-cost publication, heavily subsidized by advertisers, that would meet the reader's short-term information needs—like a bridal magazine. Lila knew that there weren't enough advertisers in her field to support that kind of publication, so she considered putting together a book—an in-depth and thorough product, free from advertising, but sold at a higher price. For example, she could make *Internet Dharma* into a special report and sell it for $25. She also considered targeting an entirely different audience. Instead of trying to reach the individual Buddhists, she could try to reach other businesses and organizations with Buddhist practitioners: study centers, book publishers, or meditation product vendors. This special-interest business newsletter would discuss and explain the shifting interests of Buddhists online and present strategies to reach them. She could charge $98 per year and market her newsletter to a small but highly motivated business audience.

After talking with her associates about all of the potential benefits and the probable costs involved, Lila settled on a book publishing strategy for *Internet Dharma*. She decided to transform it into a booklet that could be updated as needed and sold as a stand-alone product for a profit. She published the book both in print and electronic formats. She had only to update both editions about once per year, leaving her more time to concentrate on marketing and sales. She created a very simple Web page to promote the book, including a few excerpts. She distributed the printed version at specialty bookstores and meditation centers, and promoted the electronic version to her Web visitors. That strategy was a better match with the needs of her readers than a monthly newsletter dependent on subscriptions.

Fixing the Most Common Problems

What follows are six problems that often beset publishing companies. Some of them, like cash shortages and employee problems, are common among all kinds of small businesses. That's good news, because you can look beyond the publishing community for help. All of the remedies recommended here have been tried by other publishers, who have found them effective.

Cash Shortages

If your publication is on the right track, the time will come when your cash ceases to be a chronic problem. Within two or three years of launching a publication you should reach a stage where your publication generates enough income to cover your publishing expenses. If you have been publishing for more than three years and you still experience chronic cash shortages, then you should assume that you have a strategic problem. In that case, you need to go through the process just described for solving strategic problems. Using any of the following methods for raising cash when your strategy is flawed may simply worsen your situation, because each of these tactics involves adding debt.

On the other hand, healthy publications often run into cash shortages, even when they have successfully survived the treacherous start-up period. For example, when your market is growing rapidly, you might need extra cash for investing in new circulation, buying new equipment, bringing in new employees, or starting new products.

Fortunately, once you establish a healthy foothold in your market—meaning you've clearly reached the second stage of growth described in Chapter 7—there are several different ways you can raise cash for your business.

> ! WARNING
>
> **These tactics won't work for start-ups.** The money-raising tactics recommended here will not work for brand-new publications. They depend on your having built up value in your business that you can later tap. In addition, using these methods requires that you have worked with your subscribers and advertisers long enough to have developed a good relationship with them. So if you are still at a stage where you haven't yet established a publishing track record, review Chapter 7, which discusses how to raise start-up money.

Assuming that you have a reasonably healthy publication but are experiencing a tactical cash flow problem, here are some techniques many experienced publishers have developed to raise cash quickly.

Borrow From Subscribers

An early renewal campaign—offering all of your subscribers an incentive to renew now rather than later—can raise a lot of cash very quickly. Normally, you only promote renewals among subscribers whose subscriptions are about to expire. In an early renewal campaign, you offer a generous discount, desirable gift, or extra issues to all subscribers, regardless of their expiration date—if they renew right now.

Be careful to spend early renewal money wisely, however, since there is obviously a limit to how many times you can borrow from your subscribers in this manner. And, of course, every time you do it, you reduce your future revenues. Use some of this fast cash to increase your income down the road, adding new readers or other revenue-generating products.

Borrow Against Advertising Receivables

A common source of a publisher's cash flow troubles is the industry practice of advertisers delaying payment for their ads until 60 or 90 days after the issue hits the street. To bridge this gap, you can often find a lender who is willing to lend cash against your advertising receivables. Some of these companies advertise in *Folio:* magazine. The downside of this solution is that you may be stuck with high interest rates.

Sometimes a printer who wants your business may be willing to accept partial or delayed payment on printing bills, either charging you a lower rate of interest or, if you are persuasive about your future prospects, no interest at all. Whether you borrow money from a bank or a vendor, your advertisers—with whom you are struggling to build creditability— need never know about your cash flow difficulties.

Borrow From Your Advertisers

Like an early renewal campaign among subscribers, you can sometimes accelerate ad revenues by offering advertisers an incentive to pay earlier —like 10% off if they pay when the contract is signed. There are many ways to negotiate early payment schedules with advertisers: payment on acceptance of an insertion order, for example, or on delivery of the issue to newsstands. Just be careful not to damage your relationships with advertisers by giving them the idea that your publication is on shaky financial ground. In other words, make sure advertisers understand that you need cash because you're growing, not because you're about to go out of business.

Use Your Personal Credit

Small publishers often use their personal credit cards, home equity loans, and retirement savings to finance growth spurts. Generally, the interest on these loans is so high that it would be crazy to consider them for long-term financing. But if you desperately need cash to roll out a direct mail campaign—for example, a campaign that your tests tell you will result in significantly increased revenue—you may consider using your own personal credit. If you can recapture your mailing costs within three or four months and promptly pay off the credit card, the credit costs will be acceptable.

EXAMPLE: Anne launched her travel newsletter, *Cruises Update*, via a successful direct mail campaign in late January. Two thousand orders arrived in February and March. In the middle of her second year, Anne faced a cash flow problem. Because most of her subscriptions began in the same two months, most of her renewals would come due at the same time, so her revenues were bunched in the early part of the year. Here is a chart of Anne's subscription income during her second year.

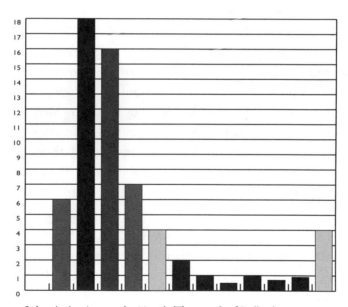

Subscription Income by Month (Thousands of Dollars)

Anne's cash flow problem was tactical, not strategic. It was not a serious long-term problem, because subscription income would spread out as the publication aged and began to successfully draw upon a mix of different subscription sources. To speed up the smoothing-out process, Anne could make some simple tactical changes. She could stagger her future direct mail campaigns and develop alternative sales channels. She could also spread out her subscription income by giving her charter subscribers an incentive to renew early—for example, as early as July, even if their subscriptions didn't expire until December. Or, she could simply adopt tight cash management procedures to be sure her money lasted through the dry spells.

A Lackluster Response

Sometimes your publication itself is your main problem. You should suspect this problem if readers who should be wild about your publication are actually lukewarm. Maybe you get a few love letters from satisfied readers, but the bulk of them simply aren't behaving like you'd hoped: They are not subscribing, renewing, or buying gift subscriptions for their friends in healthy numbers and they are not visiting your website.

Occasionally, publishers and editors will not acknowledge product problems because they are too in love with their own publications. For example, a publisher may hire consultants to fix low renewals or poor subscription sales but either explicitly or implicitly forbid them to offer a critical review of the product itself. Carried to an extreme, publishers sometimes destroy their businesses simply because they are unwilling to relinquish a cherished misconception about what their readers want or need from them.

No publishing business can survive without a viable product. If you find that your renewals are too low, that nobody buys the copies distributed on newsstands or in retail outlets, or that people pick up or order a single issue but don't subscribe, you must face the possibility that the product itself is at least part of the problem.

If you suspect that your publication is the problem, you'll need to figure out specifically what's wrong with it. You may have a minor problem, such as poor page layout, or a deeper one such as a misunderstanding of your market. To clearly define your problem, try the following approaches. These same steps will help you solve both tactical and strategic problems with your publication.

Expand Your Creative Outlook

Publishers make assumptions about what their audience needs from a publication. Your first task is to make sure your assumptions about your own audience are accurate. Often, if you look objectively at your relationship, you will think of new and better ways to meet your readers' needs.

- *Test your assumptions about the readers.* How do you know what the readers want? Look for opportunities to measure reader responses against your expectations. For example, study circulation statistics like renewal rates and newsstand sell-through rates to see if you can find any patterns to help you understand reader reactions. You can also create new opportunities for readers to respond such as faxback polls, contests, or website email contacts.

- *Review your competitors.* What are you doing for your readers that is special and compelling? How does this compare to what they get from other sources? It's possible that your publication has fallen out of step with the market. Take a fresh look at every alternative information source your audience is using and measure your publication against them all.

- *Reexamine your editorial mission.* Are you still doing what you set out to do? Can you think of a better way to accomplish the same mission? Test new ideas about the contents and design of your publication. For example, try a different story idea and then try to measure how readers respond to it—count the letters you get, or the newsstand sales for that issue.

- *Renew your personal contacts with readers.* How can you deepen your relationships with readers? Are there places you can meet them, such as trade shows or online newsgroups, and learn more about them? Some publishers don't take full advantage when they have the chance to talk in person with their readers: they talk instead of listening. See if you can find occasions to listen to readers in person, because generally that's where the best ideas are born.

> **TIP**
>
> **Keep up with the latest fashions.** Visit newsstands often and study how the popular magazines are packaged. You may spot trends in type styles, paper choices, or page designs that would give fresh energy to your magazine if you adopted them. And it's good to keep up with the overall fashions in your industry.

Do Some Audience Research

If asked, readers will often come right out and tell you how you are missing the mark. You may discover critical information about them that your competitors don't know, such as topics they want to read about or people they'd like to hear from. Listening to your readers can give you a strong competitive edge.

Survey your readers as well other people who match your target audience. You can poll readers in many ways: on the telephone, through the mail, on your website, in focus groups, or by including a fax or mail-back questionnaire in your publication. Once in a while, conduct anonymous opinion polls without revealing who you are when you ask readers to critique your publication. You may get more objective information if readers don't know they're talking to the publisher.

Ideally, you can create a regular stream of information that will keep you in touch with the changing needs of your audience. Many publishers conduct audience surveys every quarter. Others routinely poll attendees at trade shows and conferences. Every link is valuable when it helps you understand what your readers are doing and thinking.

Ask Your Team to Help

Once you've identified what your audience really needs, and you have some new ideas about how to deliver a winning product, you can begin to make some changes. It's a mistake to believe the old saw, "If it ain't broke, don't fix it." In today's fast-moving world, if a periodical is truly broken, it's usually too late to fix it. It's far better to maintain a plan of continuous improvement.

Often you can make simple adjustments—add new contributors or new topics, or cover the regular topics from a fresh angle, or toss in a few more charts and illustrations. However, if your research uncovers some serious flaws, you may decide to do a major overhaul.

An overhaul should involve all of your key contributors as well as the circulation and marketing people—everyone who works with your audience. You probably should include professional advisors, too. Take your time and carefully consider your goals.

Some well-established magazines are completely redesigned every five years or so. Others wait a bit longer, but most experienced publishers undertake editorial renovations at least every few years. And in between major overhauls, the editors are constantly looking for ways to improve their product.

> **WARNING**
>
> **Don't throw out the good with the bad.** Find out ahead of time what readers like about your publication as well as what they think is wrong with it. Then make sure you preserve their favorite features.

New Voices Often Help

When you are a solo operator, and there is no one who challenges your editorial point of view, you risk losing perspective. Even without hiring a staff of editors or consultants, you can escape the dangers of tunnel vision by bringing in some new editorial voices to complement your own. Find writers who share your editorial vision but express themselves in fresh ways. Look for people who have influence or special connections within your field and ask them for their editorial ideas and contributions. If you like what they have to say encourage them to do more, perhaps by giving them a column or department of their own. And don't forget design: Bring in new illustrators or graphic artists to keep your publication looking fresh and contemporary.

EXAMPLE: Janet didn't have any children. She had watched her close friends run themselves ragged when they became mothers, and she developed some ideas about how moms could take better care of themselves. She decided to create a monthly magazine for the new mothers in her city called *Mom's Work*. The magazine would feature articles about time management, delegating, and other business skills that Janet thought moms could apply to their child-raising problems.

Advertisers were lukewarm about *Mom's Work*. Janet managed to sell only about half as many ad pages as she needed to cover her printing and distributing costs. For the magazine to succeed, Janet needed her readers to demonstrate their enthusiasm so that she could persuade advertisers to buy more ads. She hoped that lots of readers would buy subscriptions or give them as gifts to their friends.

Janet distributed 80,000 copies of *Mom's Work*—10,000 copies each of eight monthly issues—for free at day care centers, pediatric offices, and preschools. Each copy was loaded with well-written subscription cards and promotions, but after two years, Janet had only 900 paid subscribers. In other words, for every 800 copies that Janet gave away for free, only nine people subscribed. By every measure, that was a terrible response, and certainly not impressive to Janet's prospective advertisers.

Janet called in a publishing consultant named Martha to help her make *Mom's Work* into a profitable magazine. Together, Janet and Martha reviewed all of her key strategic decisions: pricing, distribution, and marketing. They eliminated every possible explanation for her business problems except for one: Janet's product.

To find out exactly what could be wrong, Martha set up a blind survey of Janet's readers. She gathered a dozen readers in a conference room and asked them about a handful of magazines, including *Mom's Work*. The results clearly indicated that Janet had a problem with content. Readers complained that lots of Janet's recommendations were unrealistic and impossible to follow. They also said that they didn't have time to read *Mom's Work* because the articles were too long to finish in one sitting. Several readers complained that the articles sounded preachy; rather than inspiring, they were annoying.

Martha also encouraged Janet to meet with her outside editors and contributors. Once this group understood the problems Martha's research had uncovered, they had lots of ideas about how to fix them. First, they enlisted more contributions from professional writers who were also moms with young children. Next, the team encouraged Janet to hire a freelance designer to remake the magazine, changing its look entirely. And finally, they advised Janet to set up an editorial review board composed of a dozen parents who agreed to read and critique articles.

Once the changes were in place, Janet set two goals in order to monitor whether she was on the right track: increasing subscription orders from an average of 100 orders per issue to 200, and getting two-thirds of her subscribers to renew. If she could reach both of those goals within a year, Janet would know that her redesigned product was doing a better job matching the interests of her readers.

Trouble With Employees, Vendors, and Others

When your business is small or just getting started, you depend on every person who works with you. People problems are somewhat inevitable. The most troubling one is often the simplest: People sometimes just don't deliver what you need. People you need can let you down for many reasons: sometimes you misunderstand their capabilities, sometimes they deliberately mislead you, and often people simply expect that someone else will take care of an important task which never gets done. These specific problems are discussed in detail below, but remember this: No matter what goes wrong with employees, vendors, or other helpers, you can always improve the situation if you take these steps.

- *Stop and pay attention to what is going on.* Time is often a problem for overworked publishers, but you can always save time in the long run if you deal with people problems the moment you spot them. Putting them off always makes them worse.

- *Be as objective as you can.* Take advantage of any objective measures that are available to help you focus on facts, not feelings. For example, before you decide that a salesperson is not doing her job, look at her efforts: How many calls did she make? What were the results of each call? How do her results compare to everyone else's? Try to judge performance on the basis of objective, quantifiable details.

• *Make notes.* Your objectivity will improve if you document events as they are happening. Write notes to yourself about how you noticed a problem, what you did to resolve it, and the results. Writing things down will improve your discipline about being fair and impartial. You will be more likely to fulfill your agreements, for example, if you have written them down. If you wind up in a legal battle with someone years from now—the worst-case scenario—your notes will help you remember what happened, and possibly win the legal argument.

• *Obey the law.* People have rights, both as employers and as employees. If you are not certain about your own rights or someone else's, find out what laws may apply. You can do much of this research on your own, without a lawyer. (See Chapter 14 for some excellent resources.)

• *Get help quickly if you can't resolve the problem alone.* Check with mediators, consultants, lawyers, or other people who have the skill to help you resolve disputes. Helpers like these may seem expensive, but a long-standing dispute with an employee, vendor, or other collaborator can also cost a lot of money and aggravation. You may save both time and money in the long run if you bring in the right kind of skilled advisors early on.

Incompetence

Small businesses often start out with relatively untrained or unskilled people. As they expand, some of their employees will grow, and some of them won't. Vendors, consultants, and other collaborators can also fail to keep up with your growth. When employees, vendors, and other people aren't meeting your needs anymore you need to replace them, but many publishers find this difficult. Bear in mind that it's not loyal or noble to keep an employee in a position he or she can't handle, especially if you endanger your business in the process.

Deal with competence problems as soon as you realize someone isn't meeting your expectations. Face the issue head-on and discuss it openly with the person involved. Then give the person a chance to learn new skills or redefine the job responsibilities. If all else fails, help an employee or contractor find more suitable work somewhere else.

Crooks and Frauds

Everyone is vulnerable to crooks and cheaters, and when you are new to a business like publishing that has many highly specialized functions, you are especially vulnerable. For instance, a savvy fellow once snookered us at *PC World* by pretending to have much more sales and marketing experience than he really had. We spent a bundle to move him across the country and set him up in a high-level management job. We soon realized that he could not meet our expectations, but even though we acted quickly to replace him, we lost valuable time and money dealing with him. And he came close to permanently damaging several important advertiser relationships before we got rid of him.

The lesson is to be careful about trusting people you don't know. Check their references. Monitor their work. Ask questions and demand explanations if you don't fully understand everything they tell you. You can discourage many kinds of dishonesty simply by showing that you are paying attention.

As an employer, you are responsible for the actions of your agents and employees. If a freelance writer steals an article off the Internet and you reprint it without proper authorization, your publication may be held accountable. If an employee sells ads using false circulation information, your publication will bear the consequences. Again, your vigilance will discourage many kinds of fraud. Establish explicit ethical standards for your business, and then hold each contributor or collaborator accountable for meeting them. Pay attention so that you know how your agents represent you.

Boundary Issues

Sometimes even skillful and honest people are not clear about what you expect them to do for you. People who are working under pressure sometimes assume that somebody else will handle a task that lies on the boundary between two of them, so nobody completes the job. Or they take the other extreme, and improperly interfere in each other's work. There are many common examples. What should your printer do if your editors always miss their deadlines? What should the editor do if she thinks the renewal letters are poorly written? Should the ad salespeople handle production or customer service problems?

As the publisher, you must decide and spell out where individual responsibilities begin and end to avoid confusion among your collaborators. Be specific when you tell people what to do. Describe your expectations fully. And be prepared to mediate when individual boundary disputes flare up.

EXAMPLE: Tony Thomas hired a new circulation manager named Alice who had lots of publishing experience. Based on her experience, Tony gave Alice a generous profit-sharing plan, a chance to earn some stock in the company, and a very good salary—one of the highest salaries among his nine employees.

Tony began to have problems with Alice's work almost from the day she started. She didn't make decisions or take responsibility for solving problems. Instead, she waited for Tony to tell her what to do, and even then, she often ignored his instructions. She was a very pleasant person, and quickly became popular with Tony's staff. When Tony tried to confirm his judgment about Alice by checking with other employees, they were universally eager to defend her because they liked her so much. Even though other employees had serious problems because Alice didn't complete the work she was expected to do, no one except Tony seemed to be aware that Alice wasn't doing a good job as circulation manager. Nonetheless, Tony began to think hiring her was a big mistake, and he started looking for a way to resolve the problem.

He started by talking with Alice. He described specific situations where her performance disappointed him. He asked her if she thought she could do a better job and what help she might need from him to improve her performance in the future. Unfortunately, Alice took offense and refused to cooperate. She threatened to sue Tony if he tried to withhold her profit-sharing payments or the stock options he had promised to her. Getting nowhere with Alice, Tony called his business consultant, Carl, who had more publishing experience than Tony. Tony wanted Carl's independent assessment of Alice and perhaps some help teaching her to do a better job. Carl agreed to step in and give Tony his opinion about Alice.

Carl spent a few hours over several weeks working with Alice on a circulation promotion project. He accompanied her to meetings with the fulfillment company and he participated in a couple of meetings with her and the rest of Tony's staff. Carl concluded that Tony's needs were totally beyond Alice's capabilities. That left Tony with two choices: He could replace her or invest some serious time and money in training her.

Unfortunately, since Alice didn't realize how poorly she was handling her job she was not likely to cooperate, no matter what Tony chose to do. Tony decided to replace her and called his lawyer to help devise a severance package that would fulfill all of his commitments to Alice. On his lawyer's advice, and with his help, Tony reached a settlement with Alice. Later, Carl helped Tony find a more qualified circulation manager.

Outdated Systems

Sometimes your people keep up with you but your systems break down, especially if you are highly dependent on a specific technology. Technology includes everything from your telephone system to your mailing list software to your printing press. Since it usually takes both time and money to fix a technical problem, system breakdowns can mean big trouble for a small company.

Unfortunately, once your computer or your telephone system crashes, there's not much you can do except to stop everything and fix it. Your best chance to handle system problems intelligently is to choose the right ones in the first place and manage them properly. Here are some steps you can take to make sure your systems last as long as possible.

- *Outsource instead of buying.* This is especially true when technology is changing rapidly. For example, if you want to publish on the Internet, hire an Internet service provider instead of buying your own hardware and software. A chief advantage of outsourcing is that you let someone else spend the cash it takes to keep up with evolving technologies.

- *Explore all your options.* Keep investigating alternative vendors and products, even when you've already selected the ones you want to use right now. Your business needs are likely to change as you grow and you may need to switch to a new vendor in the future. Knowing your alternatives will also help you to negotiate the best deals with your current suppliers.

- *Find reputable dealers and stick with them.* Computer, telephone, and office machine manufacturers don't always support their products very well. Small-business people sometimes have to depend on retailers to help them choose the right product, use it correctly, and fix it when something goes wrong. Therefore, unless you have a compelling reason to use one product over another, you should find a retailer who gives good service and then buy whatever products that dealer is selling.

- *Establish backup procedures and use them.* Technical consultants always offer the same advice—and their clients generally ignore them: Back up anything that matters to you. That is, if you can't live without some machine or service provider, then find a backup and make sure you know how to use it if your primary systems break down.

EXAMPLE: Anne Cox published a "Cruises Hot List" that she faxed every business day to about 900 travel agent subscribers. The fax service subscriptions cost $450 per year. Unfortunately, even at that price, Anne couldn't make money with her Hot List because of the technology she used. She owned a five-year-old fax machine linked to a personal computer. Anne's "fax blaster" could send about 250 faxes per hour—not fast enough. It already took almost four hours to send all her faxes, and the more popular Anne's Hot List became, the longer it took to transmit them all. Even worse, the transmissions often didn't get through because the subscribers' phone lines were busy. Anne paid her nephew Chuck to monitor her fax machine while it was working and to make sure that all of the subscribers got their faxes on time. After paying her nephew and her long-distance phone bills, Anne couldn't make any profits from her Hot List. She asked her business consultant, Jack, to help her make the Hot List more profitable.

Anne wanted to buy a newer, more reliable fax machine, but Jack discouraged her. He suggested that she instead try to find an outside vendor to handle the transmissions. Anne discovered that several phone companies offered fax transmission services. They would guarantee on-time delivery, no matter how many subscribers Anne had, and their costs were much cheaper than Chuck's salary. Anne negotiated a good deal with one of them, and handed over all of her faxes to it. Besides saving money, the deal had other benefits. For instance, since the vendor sent all of the faxes within a few minutes, Anne could email the master copy to them in the middle of the night. As a result, she could produce the Hot List much later in the day, even after dinner if she needed the extra time. That flexibility was great.

Slow Markets

Markets change, sometimes very quickly. The toughest problems can come when your growing market suddenly slows down. Excellent publishers with great ideas and well-run operations have failed simply because their markets changed. In other words, you have the same boat and the same crew, but without any wind, you are dead in the water. New subscriptions and renewals may suddenly fall off, or ad sales can quickly dry up, despite your best efforts.

If your market suddenly crashes, you may consider simply letting your publication quietly die or selling it to someone else because you don't want to continue struggling with a business that is hunkered down and barely hanging on. If you are determined to keep publishing even in a very slow market, you really have only two options, and you probably should explore them both.

Concentrate on Growth Segments

When any market slows down, many publishers leave, but others remain. Those who stay find narrow segments of their industry that are still growing or stable, and they concentrate on those small growth areas. For example, ad revenues in upscale travel magazines took a dive after September 11, sometimes by 33% or more. But ad spending in *Arthur Frommer's Budget Travel* rose by 21% during the same period. *Business Week* lost 30% of its ad revenues because its advertisers switched to television news programs. But *Atlantic Monthly*, which publishes in-depth analysis instead of news, saw a 30% increase in ad revenues at the same time. Overall, the post-9/11 recession has been hard on business and technology advertisers and publications, but relatively good for home and family publications.

Cut Back Your Spending

Sometimes shifting focus isn't an option, or it doesn't completely solve your problems in a declining market. For instance, someone else may beat you to the punch and claim the only viable niches within your industry. Or there simply might not be a niche you can hide in, as could happen to a publication like *Texas Monthly*. That publication depends on the economic conditions in Texas and when the state goes through a severe recession, the publisher has no place else to go. In circumstances like those, you must learn to publish on a smaller scale, even if you believe that your industry will someday recover.

If you must retrench, do it quickly. The faster you move, the less you will lose. Here are some steps you can consider.

- *Drop your publishing frequency.* Even *Texas Monthly* could become simply *Texas* and put out only six issues a year during a recession if the lower frequency saves money. That strategy might keep the publication going despite falling ad and subscription revenues.

- *Cut out marginal readers and print fewer copies.* You can usually save a lot of money if you cut your circulation back, even if you also have to lower your advertising prices. The key is to trim away the readers who take the most money and effort to acquire and to renew, leaving the most loyal (and the most profitable) segments of your audience.

- *Eliminate ancillary products and services unless they are highly profitable and likely to continue generating profits even in hard times.* Set profit goals for every product and eliminate the ones that don't reach them.

- *Create a new design that is less expensive to produce.* Consider using cheaper paper, a smaller trim size, or less color.

- *Trim your overhead expenses.* This is often the least effective step you can take—unless of course, you've been wasting money on unnecessary overhead expenses all along.

> **WARNING**
>
> **Don't borrow more money to weather a shrinking market.** You can hope that your market will spring back to life someday soon, but you can't count on it. Magazine ad revenues drop off quickly in a recession and take longer to recover than other sectors of the economy. So, whatever else you do to survive a weak market, don't borrow more money simply to meet your basic publishing expenses. Borrowing under these circumstances is likely to increase your troubles down the road.

Competitors

Sometimes, your market is growing so fast that you can hardly keep up with it. The danger in a growing market, of course, is competition. You can never keep a promising niche all to yourself—somebody will always try to displace you. There are a few things you can do when a serious competitor (or two) comes barreling down on you, guns blazing.

Don't Panic

Competitors—which are inevitable among publishers—can be very good for you if you aren't too afraid of them. Chapters 2 and 5 discussed how competitors can help you to define and expand your market. You may want to review Chapter 2 if you are spooked about specific competitors. When you are worried about a competitor, your best bet is to try to understand his or her strategy—maybe you can find compatible positions within your niche.

EXAMPLE: Tony Thomas realized that model railroading was moving out of the hobby scene and into the mainstream. Sure enough, MegaBucks Publications launched *TrackWorld*, a head-on competitor to Tony's magazine, *Tracks*. MegaBucks spent a fortune growing *TrackWorld* from zero to 500,000 readers in just two years. Tony couldn't match its direct mail spending, so he concentrated on matching it at the newsstands.

Because it had clout, MegaBucks was able to win newsstand space for *TrackWorld* that Tony had been unable to get from the same distributors. Instead of calling his lawyer to sue MegaBucks or the distributors, Tony decided to see if he could profit from the situation. He hired the best newsstand consultant he could find to help negotiate better distribution for *Tracks*. To Tony's delight, MegaBucks had convinced newsstand distributors that model railroading was a growing market, and Tony's new consultant convinced them that *Tracks* would be as popular as *TrackWorld*. The distributors gave *Tracks* the same exposure they gave to *TrackWorld*.

Next, Tony concentrated on making *Tracks* appeal to newsstand buyers. He hired a designer to add sizzle to the artwork and cover designs. He discussed new feature ideas with the editors, thinking about how to reach a broader audience without alienating loyal readers. He met with his printer and chose a new paper stock for his covers and a varnishing process to make them shine.

After a couple of years, MegaBucks claimed first place in the model railroading market simply by outspending Tony nearly three-to-one. But Tony was able to secure a solid, profitable second-place position by riding on MegaBucks' coattails.

Stand Your Ground

Concentrate on your strengths as a publisher and don't let competitors redefine the game. If somebody enters your market with a new idea, don't automatically assume you have to follow along. Perhaps you should stick to your own sources of power and make the competitor deal with you on your own terms.

> **EXAMPLE:** Alicia published a popular newsletter about children's literacy called *Reading With Kids*. Each issue included many contributions from kids and parents. Suddenly, Mark jumped into the same market with his own newsletter. However, Mark's newsletter drew much more from experts—educators, physicians, psychologists, policymakers, and the like. If Alicia panicked and tried to mimic Mark's newsletter, she could damage the grassroots, homespun quality of her own publication. If she stuck to what she already did well, however, and looked for ways to develop using her own strengths, Alicia might find that there was plenty of demand for both newsletters among the same readers.

Team Up With Others in Your Market

Whether or not you are the first player in a market, you can often strengthen your hand by finding allies. These allegiances can really make a difference for small publishers trying to compete against a bigger company with more money and publishing experience. Use your expertise in your field—and your contacts—to link up with other important forces in your market, including professional organizations, manufacturers, other niche publishers, and retailers. Your competitors may eventually establish the same links, but it could take them a while. In the meantime, your publication will be stronger and harder to displace because so many people are supporting it.

EXAMPLE: When we launched *Macworld* magazine in 1984, we worked closely with the Apple computer company, which knew our work from our earlier publication, *PC World*. Apple provided prototypes of the new Macintosh computers that our editors could study and review in secret before the computer was made public. As a result, we were able to launch our first issue of *Macworld* simultaneously with the launch of the computer itself. What's more, Apple agreed to buy two issues of *Macworld* magazine for every computer buyer willing to fill out and send in the warranty card. As a result of that deal, *Macworld* magazine reached profitability during its first year, which is quite remarkable. Later, when we also launched the Macworld Expo computer show, Apple closely collaborated with us on the content and organization of the conventions, which are still popular more than 20 years later.

Resources for Publishers

> ## Check the Web to Find the Most Current Information
>
> Use search engines such as Yahoo! and Google to search for keywords. More and more publishers and publishing industry suppliers are opening shop on the Web every day. Keep looking for them.
>
> - After the Internet, magazines and newsletters are the next best choice for current information.
>
> If you are looking for vendors or employees or contractors, try to get the latest issues of related professional publications and check their ads.
>
> - Associations often have job banks, conferences, or membership directories.
>
> These can lead you to qualified employees, vendors, consultants, or freelance contractors. Their online message boards can be useful resources, too.

Associations

A number of associations cater to small publishers: the Independent Press Association, Society of National Association Publications, and American Amateur Press Association. If you are looking for a community of like-minded people willing to help each other in the rough-and-tumble publishing world, these associations should be your first stop. Bigger publishers have their own brand of help to offer too, even for nonmembers. For example, it would cost several thousand dollars per year to join the Magazine Publishers of America (MPA). Few small publishers have that kind of money, but some MPA services are available to nonmembers, such as great industry data, a terrific education program, internships, scholarships, and publications.

Alliance of Area Business Publications (AABP) and City and Regional Magazines Association (CRMA), 4929 Wilshire Boulevard, Suite 428, Los Angeles, CA 90010, 323-937-5514. These groups provide members with audience studies, a newsletter, and annual performance awards. Visit online at www.bizpubs.org or www.citymag.org.

American Amateur Press Association (AAPA). Founded in 1936, with 250 current members who are "hobby" publishers. The association has no headquarters, but it has been around for about six decades. You can visit its website at www.members.aol.com/aapa96/index.html.

American Business Media (ABM) is an association of business-to-business and specialized consumer publishing firms. There are about 215 members. Contact ABP at 675 Third Avenue, New York, NY 10017, 212-661-6360. Its annual convention is held in the spring. Regional meetings are held throughout the year. Its website is located at www.americanbusinessmedia.com.

American Copy Editors Society (ACES) was formed in 1997 and offers books, training, job listings, and other resources for copy editors. Its Web address is www.copydesk.org.

American Society of Magazine Editors (ASME), 810 Seventh Avenue, 24th Floor, New York, NY 10019, 212-872-3700. The ASME is an association of people who edit consumer magazines, business papers, and farm publications. It holds seminars as well as an annual conference, and sponsors magazine awards. Its Web address is www.magazine.org.

Direct Marketing Association (DMA), 1120 Avenue of the Americas, New York, NY 10036, 212-768-7277. The DMA offers seminars, publications, and conferences for people actively involved in direct marketing. It may be a useful lead to consultants in this field. The DMA has a website at www.the-dma.org.

Editorial Freelancers Association (EFA), 71 W. 23rd Street, Suite 1910, New York, NY 10010, 212-929-5400. This group offers classes and several other very good member benefits as well as a job board. It's a great place to find skilled editorial freelancers who are committed to developing their talents. Visit online at www.the-efa.org.

Independent Press Association (IPA), 65 Battery Street, 2d Floor, San Francisco, CA 94111, 415-445-0230. The IPA works to promote and support independent publications committed to social justice and a free press. The group provides technical assistance to its member publications and is a vigorous advocate of the independent press. (I am a member of the IPA board of directors and offer discounted consulting rates to other IPA members.) The IPA's Web address is www.indypress.org.

Interactive Advertising Bureau (IAB), 116 E. 27th Street, 7th Floor, New York, NY 10016, 212-380-4700. Founded in 1996, this association is organized to promote online advertising and publishes standards that have become generally accepted in the industry. Its site has other useful information at www.iab.net.

Internet Society (ISOC), 1775 Wiehle Avenue, Suite 102, Reston, VA 20190, 703-326-9880. A nonprofit organization formed to facilitate global cooperation on the Internet. Its useful site is at www.isoc.org.

International Regional Magazine Association (IRMA). This 40-year-old association of city and regional magazines holds an annual conference and has other member benefits. If you plan to publish a local publication such as *Vermont Life* or *Oklahoma Today*, then you should contact IRMA. The organization is online at www.regionalmagazines.org.

Magazine Publishers of America (MPA), 810 Seventh Avenue, New York, NY 10019, 212-872-3700. The MPA has about 300 members, including nearly all of the established magazine publishing companies in the U.S. The MPA hosts an annual magazine conference in the fall and training seminars throughout the year. Its courses are open to nonmembers, and are very well done, so call for a schedule. The MPA website offers factsheets and industry data that most publishers will find very useful. MPA's Web address is www.magazine.org.

National Association of Publishers' Representatives (NAPR), 54 Cove Road, Huntington, NY 11743, 631-223-2200. NAPR is an association of companies that sell advertising for publishers. Its site helps to connect sales firms with publishers and offers other useful advertising industry information. Visit online at www.naprassoc.com.

Newsletter and Electronic Publishers Association (NEPA), 1501 Wilson Boulevard, Suite 509, Arlington, VA 22209, 703-527-2333. The NEPA sponsors a host of seminars all over the country. It also publishes a bi-weekly newsletter for members called *Hotline*. Membership fees depend on the size of your company and range between $395 and $4,000 per year. NEPA's website has many good links and articles: www.newsletters.org.

Small Publishers Association of North America (SPAN), 1618 W. Colorado Avenue, Colorado Springs, CO 80904, 719-475-1726. This professional trade association includes independent presses, self-publishers, and authors. Its services are detailed at its website at www.spannet.org.

Society of National Association Publications (SNAP), 8405 Greensboro Drive, #800, McLean, VA 22102, 703-506-3285. SNAP members are publishers, editors, and executives from trade and professional society publications. The association publishes its own directory and monthly newsletter, and provides access to a network of experts in specialized fields. Its Web address is www.snaponline.org.

Society of Publication Designers (SPD), 17 E. 47th Street, 6th Floor, New York, NY 10017, 212-223-3332. Members of the SPD are art directors, designers, editors, and production managers. The society maintains a placement service for people in these disciplines and publishes a newsletter. It also sponsors annual competitions. Look at its website at www.spd.org.

Western Publications Association (WPA), 823 Rim Crest Drive, Westlake Village, CA 91361, 805-495-1863. The WPA conducts regular meetings, seminars, and trade shows for magazine publishers in Western states. It also sponsors the annual Maggie Awards. A directory of its members is available at its website: www.wpa-online.org.

Books

Many of these books are not available in bookstores because their subjects are too specialized. You can order them at my website: www. publishingbiz.com. The books published by Nolo can be ordered by calling 800-992-6656 or visiting the website at www.nolo.com. You can also get them from Amazon.com, Barnes & Noble online, or other online booksellers or directly from their publishers.

Business Management

How to Write a Business Plan, by Mike McKeever, Nolo. This book provides step-by-step instructions for preparing a first-rate business plan and loan application. I recommend it highly.

Design

Editing by Design: For Designers, Art Director and Editors, by Jan White, Allworth Press. This classic book is a favorite among magazine professionals who know that the right look is key to magazine success.

Magazine Design That Works: Secrets for Successful Magazine Design, by Stacey King, Rockport Publishers. The author focuses on 20 different magazines to profile what makes them work graphically, and how their look was conceived, designed, and executed.

Newsletter Design: A Step-By-Step Guide to Creative Publications, by Edward A. Hamilton, John Wiley & Sons. A very useful book on this subject, it includes dozens of excellent design examples and offers practical advice from a professional designer of very successful newsletters.

magCulture: New Magazine Design, by Jeremy Leslie, Collins Design. This book explores the very latest trends and creative design styles in contemporary magazines from around the world. Use it to help perk up an aging magazine or design a hip new one.

Producing a First-Class Newsletter: A Guide to Planning, Writing, Editing, Designing, Photography, Production, and Printing, by Barbara A. Fanson, Self Counsel Press. This book is a best-seller among newsletter publishers. It covers all the basics.

Publication Design Workbook: A Real-World Guide to Designing Magazines, Newspapers, and Newsletters, by Tim Samara, Rockport Publishers. Covers the whole subject with examples and very practical suggestions.

Editing and Writing

The Editor in Chief: A Practical Management Guide for Editors, by Benton Rain Patterson and Coleman E.P. Patterson, Iowa State University Press. This is a journalism text, but useful if you are new to the whole process of editing, and especially helpful if you find yourself managing an editorial staff. Few books cover editing as well as this one. It sets out the whole task of editing a magazine so that a beginning publisher or editor can do the job right.

The Layers of Magazine Editing, by Michael Robert Evans, Columbia University Press. Candid and constructive comments from contemporary editors paired with practical instructions from a seasoned professional.

The Magazine Article: How to Think It, Plan It, Write It, by Peter Jacobi, Indiana University Press. Using a hands-on approach, this book shows how to captivate readers, remain focused in content, and appeal to the needs of your audience.

Magazine Editing, by John Morrish, Routledge. An examination of the editor's job that will be helpful both to people who hire editors and those who become editors.

Mark My Words: Instruction & Practice in Proofreading, by Peggy Smith, Editorial Experts. A guide for professional proofreaders that will be useful to anyone, especially if you find that you have to do your own proofreading.

National Writers Union Freelance Writers Guide, by James Waller, National Writers Union. The book discusses how to negotiate fees and rights with freelance writers.

Words Into Type, by Marjorie Skillen and Robert Gay, Prentice Hall. This is the definitive text for questions of manuscript protocol, copy editing, and grammar. It belongs on every writer's bookshelf.

Writer's Digest Handbook of Magazine Article Writing, by Jean M. Fredette (Editor), Writer's Digest Books. Articles are the meat and potatoes of magazines, and this book will help you publish great ones, either by writing them yourself or by hiring people who know how to write them.

General Information

Career Opportunities in Magazine Publishing: The Ultimate Guide to Succeeding in the Business, by Ralph Monti, Special Interest Media. Monti is a management consultant for magazines, custom publishing, and communications businesses, and his book examines the intricacies of the magazine publishing industry. This guide will aid those who are looking for a first job, changing careers, or trying to break into the magazine business.

Find It Fast: How to Uncover Expert Information on Any Subject Online or in Print, by Robert Berkman, HarperCollins. This is a great little book that will help you study your market or your competitors. It may also help you find other useful information resources.

How to Start a Magazine, by James B. Kobak, Evans and Company. Written by a seasoned magazine publishing executive and consultant, this book gives a wonderful insider's view of the magazine business at the highest levels. It is not a step-by-step how-to book, like some of the others recommended here, but this one gives an excellent industry overview.

How to Start and Produce a Magazine or Newsletter, by Gordon Woolf, Worsley Press. This completely revised and expanded edition of Woolf's book covers editing, design, printing, and distribution in better detail than any other book. It's a useful read for publishers of every stripe, from a club newsletter to a corporate communications magazine to a newsstand consumer magazine.

Launch Your Own Magazine: A Guide for Succeeding, by Samir A. Husni, Hamblett House Inc. Husni teaches journalism and also studies magazine startups. He offers good case studies and practical tips from the publishers he has interviewed. His book is a good complement to the one you are holding in your hands.

The Magazine from Cover to Cover: Inside a Dynamic Industry, by Sammye Johnson and Patricia Prijatel, McGraw Hill. This book examines the planning and organizing of a magazine and its staff and explains editorial, design, production, legal, and ethical issues, as well as industry trends. It shows how magazines reflect and influence the world around them.

Magazine Publishing, by Sammye Johnson, Patricia Prijatel, NTC Publishing Group. This is a textbook for college journalism students. I find it a bit light on the business side of publishing, but great on the editorial and creative issues. (Look out; it costs nearly $50.)

The Magazine Publishing Industry, by Charles P. Daly, Patrick Henry, and Ellen Ryder, Allyn & Bacon. This somewhat scholarly book offers a history of the magazine industry as well as an introduction to its major players.

Publish Your Own Magazine, Guidebook, or Weekly Newspaper: How to Start, Manage, and Profit From a Home-Based Publishing Company, by Thomas A. Williams, Sentient Publications. Williams started, edited, and published city and regional magazines and a weekly newspaper in North Carolina, and dozens of other magazines. His book is a dynamic step-by-step guide to creating everything from tourism books and niche market magazines to specialty tabloids, using a home computer.

Legal Help

Dealing With Problem Employees: A Legal Guide, by Amy DelPo and Lisa Guerin, Nolo. Combines the practical and legal information employers need to head off potential conflicts and problems, investigate problems and complaints, conduct performance evaluations, terminate employment, and handle severances and references.

The Employer's Legal Handbook, by Fred Steingold, Nolo. This terrific handbook will help you avoid problems when you are hiring, firing, and equipping your employees.

Hiring Independent Contractors: The Employer's Legal Guide, by Stephen Fishman, Nolo. Most small publishers use lots of independent contractors. This book will help you do it right. It includes sample agreements and pull-out forms to make your life very simple.

How to Form a Nonprofit Corporation, by Anthony Mancuso, Nolo. If you are considering the nonprofit route to publishing, you should study this book.

Legal Guide for Starting & Running a Small Business, by Fred Steingold, Nolo. There are straightforward explanations of the laws businesspeople need to know, plus wonderful examples to help you avoid the most expensive and treacherous employment problems. This book is very good at recommending professional help when you need it.

The Small Business Start-Up Kit, by Peri Pakroo, Nolo. This book helps new business owners choose the right type of legal business organization, write effective business plans, and acquire good bookkeeping and accounting habits.

Small Time Operator, by Bernard Kamoroff, Bell Springs Press. Although not specifically geared for publishers, this book should be on every solo-operator's bookshelf.

Marketing

Low-Budget Online Marketing, by Holly Berkley, Self Counsel Press. This handy book details affordable marketing techniques.

Successful Direct Marketing Methods, by Bob Stone, McGrawHill. This is a classic text for direct marketing people: practically every professional you'll meet has studied this book at some point in their careers.

Website

The Non-Designer's Web Book: An Easy Guide to Creating, Designing, and Posting Your Own Website, by Robin Williams and John Tollett, Peachpit Press. This book is beautifully illustrated and informative. Written for people with little or no design background, it does a good job for advanced designers, too.

Webworks: e-zines: Explore On-Line Magazine Design, by Martha Gill, Rockport Publishers. The Webworks series covers all kinds of Web publishing issues, from e-commerce to advertising. This particular book focuses on design and provides a great look at some of the best magazine designs on the Web. The other books in this series are also worth a look.

Courses and Seminars

The Center for Publishing, New York University. NYU offers both a Master's and a seven-week summer program focusing either on book or magazine publishing. Both are highly regarded within the industry. Call 212-998-7200 for details. Its Web address is www.scps.nyu.edu.

Folio: Show. Like *Folio:* magazine, these programs are designed to meet the needs of working publishers. They deal with very practical problems. Call 800-927-5007 or 203-358-9900 for a complete schedule and conference programs, or see www.folioshow.com.

Master's of Science in Publishing, Pace University. Sponsored by the Dyson College of Arts and Sciences in New York City, this program includes a full range of publishing courses offered year-round. Call 212-346-1417 for more information or see www.pace.edu.

Stanford Professional Publishing Course. This is a nine-day program held in July every summer at Stanford University. It is a course for experienced publishing people who want to hone their skills, and you must apply for admission. Stanford also hosts a seminar called Publishing on the Web. Held in the fall, it lasts for three days. For more information, go to www.publishingcourses.stanford.edu.

University of California at Berkeley Extension. The Berkeley Extension program offers courses focusing on either book or magazine publishing. Each course can be taken independently of the others and they're offered year-round. Call 510-642-4111 for more information, or visit www. unex.berkeley.edu.

University of Chicago Publishing Program. There are three year-round programs: editing, design, and production. Call 773-702-1682 for a catalogue and details, or visit their website at www.grahamschool. uchicago.edu.

University of Denver Publishing Institute. There are practical workshops offered in the summer covering book publishing, but some magazine-related material is included. Call 303-871-2570 or visit www.du.edu/pi.

Periodicals

Advertising Age, published weekly by Crain Communications, 740 North Rush Street, Chicago, IL 60611, 888-288-5900. *Advertising Age* is edited for media buyers and advertising sales executives. If your publication will carry paid ads, you should read at least a few copies of *Advertising Age* to get a handle on the media-buying business. The publishers of *Advertising Age* also publish a Web newsletter called Interactive Daily that you can read free at its website, which you'll find at www.adage.com.

Adweek, published weekly by BPI Communications, 1515 Broadway, New York, NY 10036, 800-722-6658. *Adweek* is a news magazine for people who work at advertising agencies. Website: www.adweek.com.

Circulation Management is published monthly by Primedia, 212-745-0100. You can contact *Circulation Management* by mail at Primedia, 745 Fifth Ave., New York, NY 10151. Subscriptions are free if you qualify as a circulation specialist or publisher. Like most trade magazines, *CM* is useful not only for the targeted editorial material but also for its ads. You may find the perfect fulfillment or printing company through *CM*. It also publishes annual supplier surveys. Be warned, though: This is a professional trade magazine, edited for circulation specialists. *Circulation Management*'s November issue is an annual Buyer's Guide featuring more than 400 circulation resources and suppliers. Its Web address is www.circman.com.

Copy Editor is a bimonthly newsletter subtitled "Language News for the Publishing Professional." Editorial offices are at 1010 E. Missouri, Phoenix, AZ 85014. You can read a sample issue at its website at www.copyeditor.com.

Direct: The Magazine for Direct Marketing Management, published monthly by Intertec Publishing, 800-775-3777. You can contact *Direct* by mail at P.O. Box 4949, Stamford, CT 06907. This is a magazine for people involved in direct marketing of all kinds. Read it to learn what other publishers are doing. Call the publisher or visit the website for a sample issue and qualification card. Web address is www.directmag.com.

Editor & Publisher, published weekly by Editor & Publisher, 770 Broadway, New York, NY 10003, 646-654-5270. This weekly covers the newspaper industry. The publishers also put out a handful of annual directories and source books that you might find useful. At *Editor & Publisher*'s very helpful website, you can read or post job listings, search a library, or find links and other resources for editors. The address is www.editorandpublisher.com.

Folio: magazine, published by Primedia, 212-745-0100. The special *Folio: Super Book* issue is an excellent reference to suppliers. *Folio:* is the preeminent trade magazine for the magazine trade. As in other trade magazines, the editing is crafted for insiders. Web address: www.foliomag.com.

The Laughing Bear Newsletter is a monthly print newsletter for small publishers edited by Tom Peterson. Its website offers current articles, archives, and a free sample issue, as well as the chance to order a subscription. The Web address is www.laughingbear.com.

Web Marketing Today is a wonderful electronic publication that offers advice, resources, and support for website administrators. A subscription allows access to an online resources library and back issues. You can view the current issue free at www.wilsonWeb.com.

Publishing Industry Services

Audit Bureau of Circulation (ABC), 900 North Meacham Road, Schaumburg, IL 60173, 847-605-0909. The ABC is a nonprofit association of over 4,100 advertisers, agencies, and publishers. The association audits the circulation of over 3,400 periodicals including daily and weekly newspapers and consumer, business, and farm magazines for the benefit of advertisers and agencies. It publishes several reports including some excellent educational materials for publishers. The ABC is currently conducting auditing tests of websites. To learn more, contact the ABC by telephone or visit its website at www.accessabc.com.

Business Publications Audit International (BPA), 270 Madison Avenue, New York, NY 10016, 212-779-3200, plus regional offices. The BPA is a nonprofit provider of circulation audits for advertisers and agencies. It audits over 2,600 business and special interest consumer magazines. Publications include trend reports and consolidated circulation information for several industries or market groups. Website address is www.bpai.com.

MagazineLaunch.com assembled articles and tools for starting a new publication, in print or on the Web. You can find it at www. magazinelaunch.com.

MediaMark Research Inc. (MRI), 75 Ninth Avenue, 5th Floor, New York, NY 10011, 212-884-9200. In addition to the syndicated studies that make MRI so famous among publishers, the firm also offers a wide range of customized research programs. Don't assume that you can't afford to hire MRI. Some of its studies are quite reasonably priced. Its Web address is www.mediamark.com.

National Register of Publishing, 121 Chanlon Road, New Providence, NJ 07974, 800-340-3244. This company publishes two annual directories that you will need to own if you plan to sell national advertising: *The Standard Directory of Advertisers* (Advertiser Red Book) and *The Standard Directory of Advertising Agencies* (Agency Red Book). Use these directories to build your own target advertiser lists. If you can't afford to buy these directories (they're priced around $800 each), you may be able to find them in a well-stocked business or business school library. These products are a good resource about advertising. The Web address is www. redbooks.com.

Publishers Information Bureau (PIB), 191 Third Avenue, New York, NY 10022, 212-752-0055. The PIB was founded early in the last century as a private agency, but in 1948 it was taken over by a consortium of publishers. It compiles information about national advertising, measuring pages and revenues in consumer magazines. It is a good resource for information about any established magazine niche. The Web address is www.magazine.org/pib.

Simmons Market Research Bureau (SMRB), 230 Park Avenue South, 3rd floor, New York, NY 10003, 212-598-5400. SMRB offers a wide range of research for publishers. In addition to the syndicated studies for which it is best known, SMRB can also develop focus groups, trade show polls, and other specialized studies. The Web address is www.smrb.com.

Standard Rate and Data Service (SRDS), 1700 Higgins Road, Des Plaines, IL 60018, 847-375-5000. SRDS publishes a handful of widely used and extremely useful directories including: *Direct Marketing List Source, Consumer Magazine,* and *Agri-Media Source, Business Publication Advertising Source, Newspaper Advertising Source,* and *Community Publication Advertising Source.* Web address: www.srds.com. If you can't afford a subscription, you may find these directories in a business or business school library.

Specialists at Buying and Selling Publishing Businesses

Here are several investment banking and consulting firms that handle magazine mergers and acquisitions among established companies:

Berkery, Noyes & Company
50 Broad Street, New York, NY 10004
212-668-3022
Website: www.berkerynoyes.com

DeSilva & Phillips
451 Park Avenue South, 6th Floor
New York, NY 10016
212-686-9700
Website: www.mediabankers.com

The Jordan, Edmiston Group
150 E. 52nd Street, 18th Floor
New York, NY 10022
212-754-0710
Website: www.jegi.com

Magazine Consulting Group
11845 W. Olympic Boulevard
Los Angeles, CA 90064
310-477-1400
Website: www.magazineconsulting.com

Veronis, Suhler & Associates
350 Park Avenue
New York, NY 10022
212-935-4990
Website: www.veronissuhler.com

And there is a national clearinghouse for information and assistance setting up employee ownership programs:

The National Center for Employee Ownership
1736 Franklin Street, 8th Floor
Oakland, CA 94612
510-208-1300
Website: www.nceo.org

Software

The publishers of this software generally offer technical support and consulting services. The Newsletter and Electronic Publishers Association provides a list of currently available software at its website at www .newsletters.org. You can also see a list of Web advertising and website management software at the Internet Advertising Bureau site at www.iab .net. What follows is a very brief selection.

Accounting

QuickBooks, a general business accounting program from Intuit, is probably the single most popular program of its kind. You can find it in retail computer stores or mail-order catalogues.

Peachtree Accounting is a well-regarded business accounting program from Peachtree Software that is also widely available.

Publishing Business Software

Ad2d.com is for managing classified ads. *AdSystem,* from Datafest, 5961 S. Redwood Road, Salt Lake City, UT 84123, 801-261-4608. Website: www.datafest.com. This fully integrated software only runs on Windows and Windows NT systems (not the Mac).

ASQ Soft, from ASQSoft-Information Architects, 21 Locust Avenue, New Canaan, CT 06840, 203-829-3555. Website: www.asqsoft.com. Over 50 national magazines use this software, which is designed to accommodate multiple advertising salespeople (in other words, a big company setting). *ASQ Soft* is compatible with both Mac and PC systems.

Datatrax, from Datatrax Publishing Systems, 1799 Farmington Avenue, Unionville, CT 06805, 888-568-6157. Website: www.datatrax.cc. This software is modular, and you can add any mix of components to it. It runs on Windows systems and works for any size publishing company.

Fakebrains at www.fakebrains.com has a program called *AccountScout* to manage ad sales.

Quickfill is PC-based subscription management software widely used by small magazine and newsletter companies. Detailed information is available online at www.cwcsoftware.com.

Sequel Software is a Canadian company that provides publishing management solutions delivered through the Internet on a subscription basis. Instead of having to buy programs that you install on your own computers, you buy access to Sequel's Publish2Profit online software solutions. The products are geared for small and midsized publishing companies. Sequel is located at 609-14th Street NW, Suite 301, Calgary, Alberta T2N 2A1, 403-270-8913, and online at www.publish2profit.com.

Smart Publisher, from Pre One Software, P.O. Box 12188, Portland, OR 97212, 503-288-7500. Website: www.pre1.com. This company also makes accounting software that you can integrate with your advertising sales programs. All of Pre One's software runs both on Mac and PC systems.

Websites, Electronic Mailing Lists, Newsgroups, and Online Bulletin Boards

The ClickZ Network offers the latest market research about Internet users and their online activities. There are also links to other research providers. This is a good place to start if you're trying to pin down statistics for a business plan. The Web address is www.clickz.com/stats.

The Electronic Frontier Foundation (EFF) is a nonprofit organization devoted to keeping information as free as possible on the Internet. Its site offers useful information about copyrights and pending legislation. Its address is www.eff.org.

Marketing Sherpa is a commercial site for marketing professionals that offers useful information. Most of the content is available for free. There are also some high-quality handbooks that you can download in PDF files—for example, the "Google Adwords Handbook" and the "Buyers' Guide to Email Broadcast Services for Marketers & Publishers: How to Pick a List Host." The Web address is: www.marketingsherpa.com.

NewsDirectory.com provides an excellent list of websites and publications that you can search by name or view by category. The site is very well put together. The address is www.ecola.com.

Online Advertising is a discussion group that you can read or join by visiting its site at www.o-a.com.

Index

A

C

V

W

Y

Get the Latest in the Law

(1) **Nolo's Legal Updater**
We'll send you an email whenever a new edition of your book is published!
Sign up at **www.nolo.com/legalupdater**.

(2) **Updates at Nolo.com**
Check **www.nolo.com/update** to find recent changes in the law that
affect the current edition of your book.

(3) **Nolo Customer Service**
To make sure that this edition of the book is the most recent one, call us at
800-728-3555 and ask one of our friendly customer service representatives
(7:00 am to 6:00 pm PST, weekdays only). Or find out at **www.nolo.com**.

(4) **Complete the Registration & Comment Card ...**
... and we'll do the work for you! Just indicate your preferences below:

Registration & Comment Card

NAME _____ DATE _____

ADDRESS _____

CITY _____ STATE _____ ZIP _____

PHONE _____ EMAIL _____

COMMENTS _____

WAS THIS BOOK EASY TO USE?   (VERY EASY) 5 4 3 2 1 (VERY DIFFICULT)

☐ Yes, you can quote me in future Nolo promotional materials. *Please include phone number above.*

☐ Yes, send me **Nolo's Legal Updater** via email when a new edition of this book is available.

Yes, I want to sign up for the following email newsletters:

   ☐ **NoloBriefs** (monthly)
   ☐ **Nolo's Special Offer** (monthly)
   ☐ **Nolo's BizBriefs** (monthly)
   ☐ **Every Landlord's Quarterly** (four times a year)

☐ Yes, you can give my contact info to carefully selected
partners whose products may be of interest to me.

NOLO

MAG 5.0

Nolo
950 Parker Street
Berkeley, CA 94710-9867
www.nolo.com

YOUR LEGAL COMPANION

NOLO